Vol. 5
Pure Soul

Story and Art by
Daisuke
Higuchi

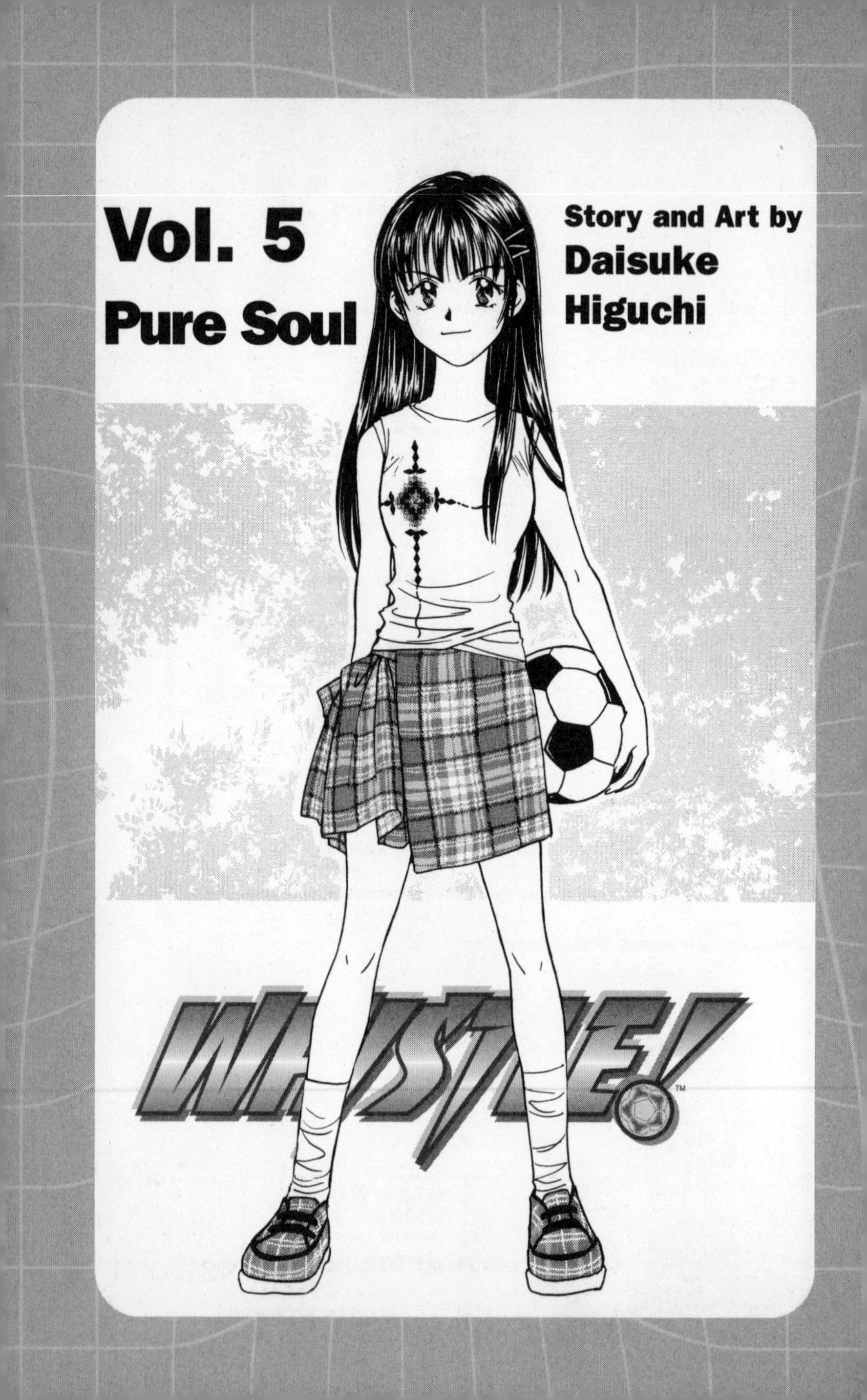
WHISTLE!™

CHARACTERS

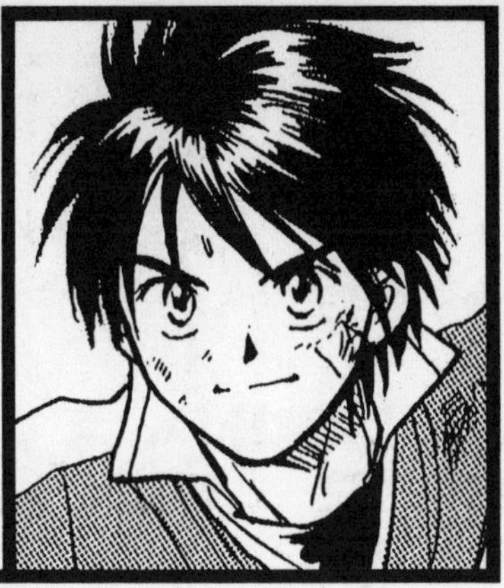

SHŌ
KAZAMATSURI

- JOSUI JUNIOR HIGH SOCCER TEAM FORWARD

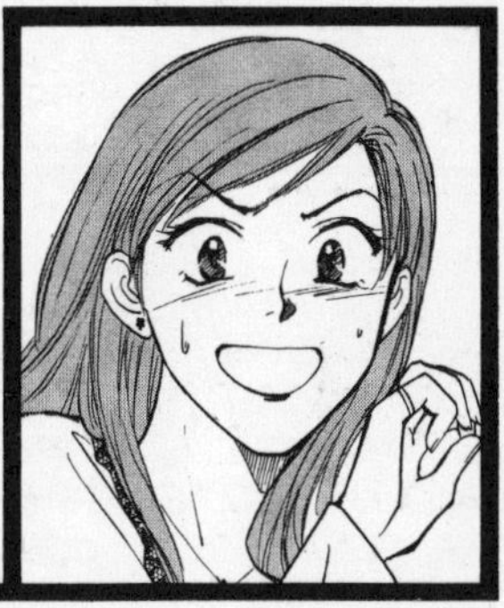

KŌ
KAZAMATSURI

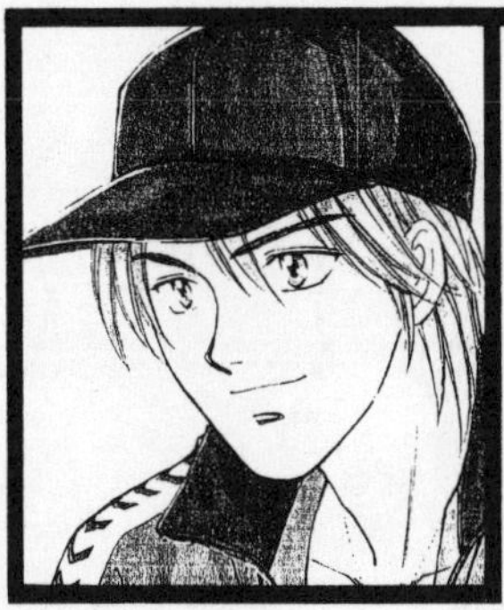

YŪKO
KATORI

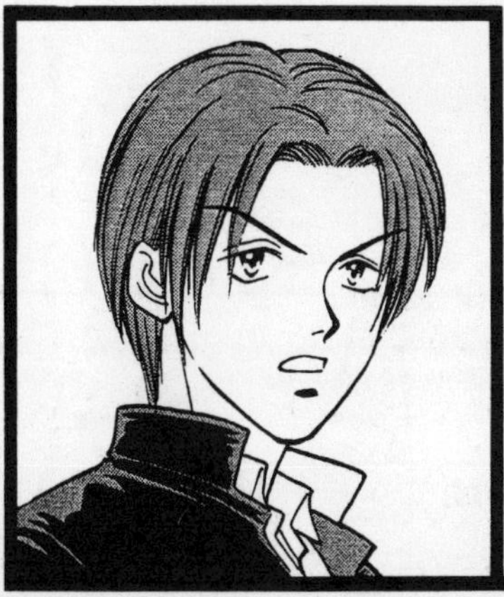

TATSUYA
MIZUNO

- JOSUI JUNIOR HIGH SOCCER TEAM MIDDLE FIELDER

SOUJŪ MATSUSHITA

FORMER JAPAN LEAGUE PLAYER

JOSUI JUNIOR HIGH COACH

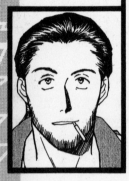

SHIGEKI SATŌ

JOSUI JUNIOR HIGH SOCCER TEAM

FORWARD

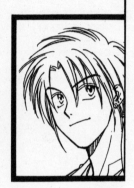

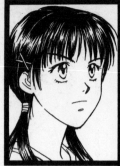

YUKI KOJIMA

JOSUI JUNIOR HIGH SOCCER TEAM

MANAGER

NOT WANTING TO GIVE UP HIS DREAM OF PLAYING SOCCER, SHŌ KAZAMATSURI, A SUBSTITUTE PLAYER AT MUSASHINOMORI, A SCHOOL KNOWN FOR ITS EXCELLENT SOCCER TEAM, TRANSFERS TO JOSUI JUNIOR HIGH.

HAVING RESOLVED THE TEAM'S BAD FEELINGS TOWARDS THEIR BEST PLAYER, TATSUYA, THE TEAM'S BOND IS DEEPENED AS JOSUI ENDEAVORS TO MAKE IT TO THE TOKYO CHAMPIONSHIP.

JOSUI LOSES THE FIRST MATCH IN THE CHAMPIONSHIP AGAINST MUSASHINOMORI. BUT IMMEDIATELY AFTERWARDS, SHŌ AND HIS TEAMMATES START THEIR POWER RETREAT TO PREPARE FOR THE SUMMER CHAMPIONSHIP. WITH SOUJŪ MATSUSHITA, A FORMER JAPAN LEAGUE PLAYER, AS THEIR NEW COACH, THE REMADE JOSUI JUNIOR HIGH SOCCER TEAM PREPARES FOR THE COMPETITION.

S T O R Y

WHISTLE!

**Vol. 5
PURE SOUL**

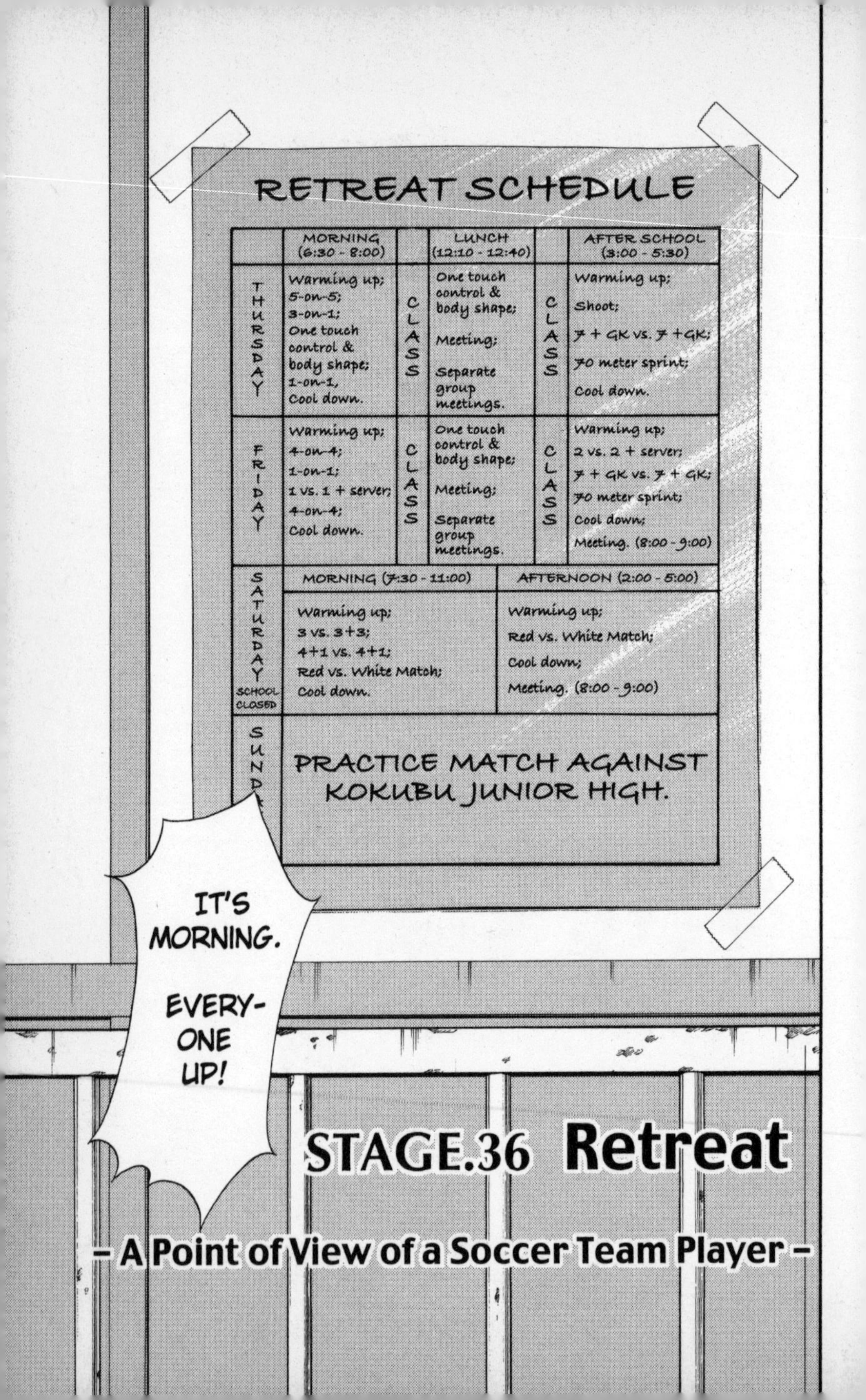
RETREAT SCHEDULE
MORNING (6:30 - 8:00)
LUNCH (12:10 - 12:40)
AFTER SCHOOL (3:00 - 5:30)
THURSDAY
Warming up; 5-on-5; 3-on-1; One touch control & body shape; 1-on-1, Cool down.
CLASS
One touch control & body shape; Meeting; Separate group meetings.
CLASS
Warming up; Shoot; 7 + GK vs. 7 + GK; 70 meter sprint; Cool down.
FRIDAY
Warming up; 4-on-4; 1-on-1; 1 vs. 1 + server; 4-on-4; Cool down.
CLASS
One touch control & body shape; Meeting; Separate group meetings.
CLASS
Warming up; 2 vs. 2 + server; 7 + GK vs. 7 + GK; 70 meter sprint; Cool down; Meeting. (8:00 - 9:00)
SATURDAY SCHOOL CLOSED
MORNING (7:30 - 11:00)
Warming up; 3 vs. 3+3; 4+1 vs. 4+1; Red vs. White Match; Cool down.
AFTERNOON (2:00 - 5:00)
Warming up; Red vs. White Match; Cool down; Meeting. (8:00 - 9:00)
SUND
PRACTICE MATCH AGAINST KOKUBU JUNIOR HIGH.
IT'S MORNING. EVERY-ONE UP!
STAGE.36 Retreat
- A Point of View of a Soccer Team Player -

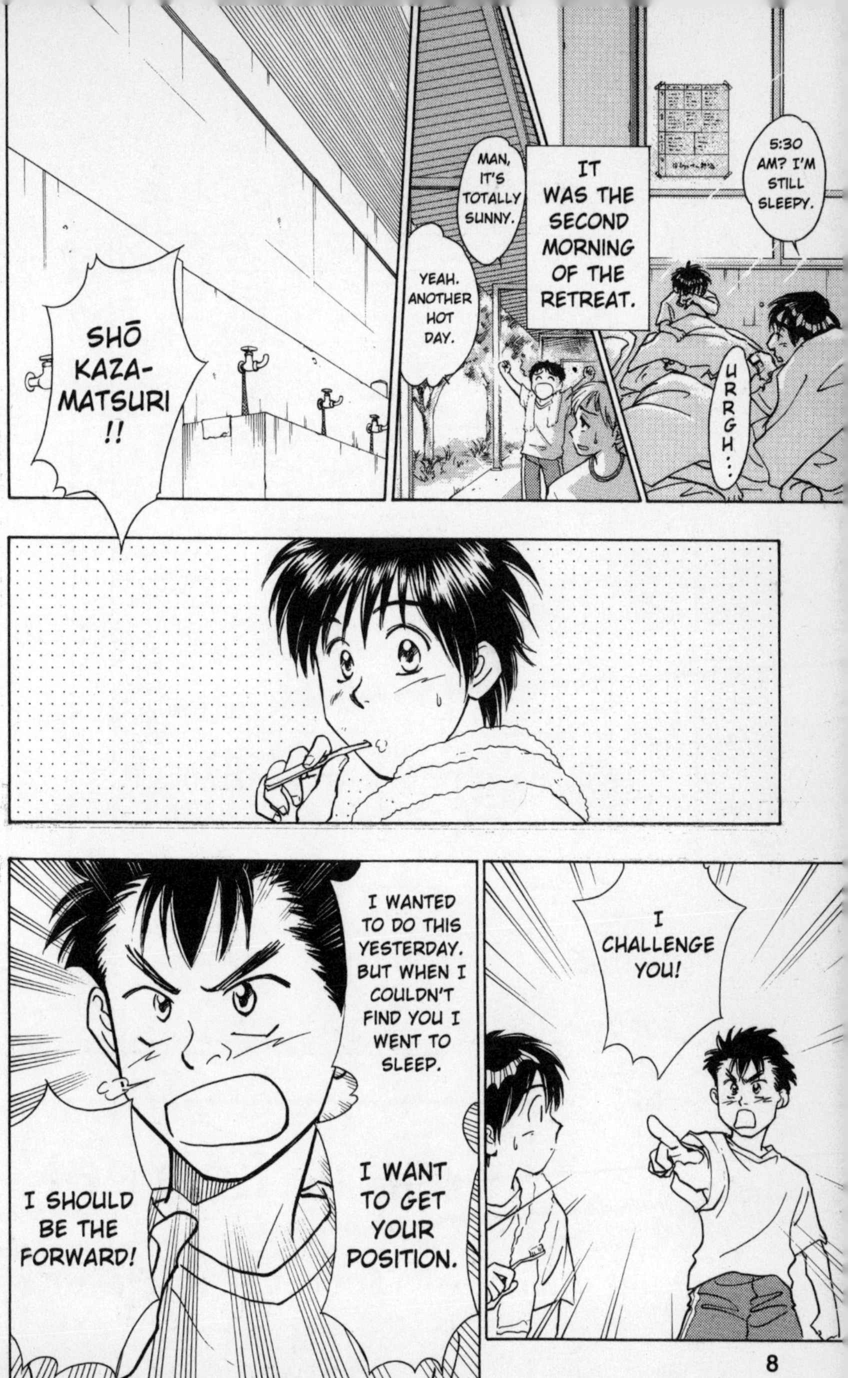
5:30 AM? I'M STILL SLEEPY.
URRGH...
IT WAS THE SECOND MORNING OF THE RETREAT.
MAN, IT'S TOTALLY SUNNY.
YEAH. ANOTHER HOT DAY.
SHŌ KAZA-MATSURI !!
I CHALLENGE YOU!
I WANTED TO DO THIS YESTERDAY. BUT WHEN I COULDN'T FIND YOU I WENT TO SLEEP.
I WANT TO GET YOUR POSITION.
I SHOULD BE THE FORWARD!

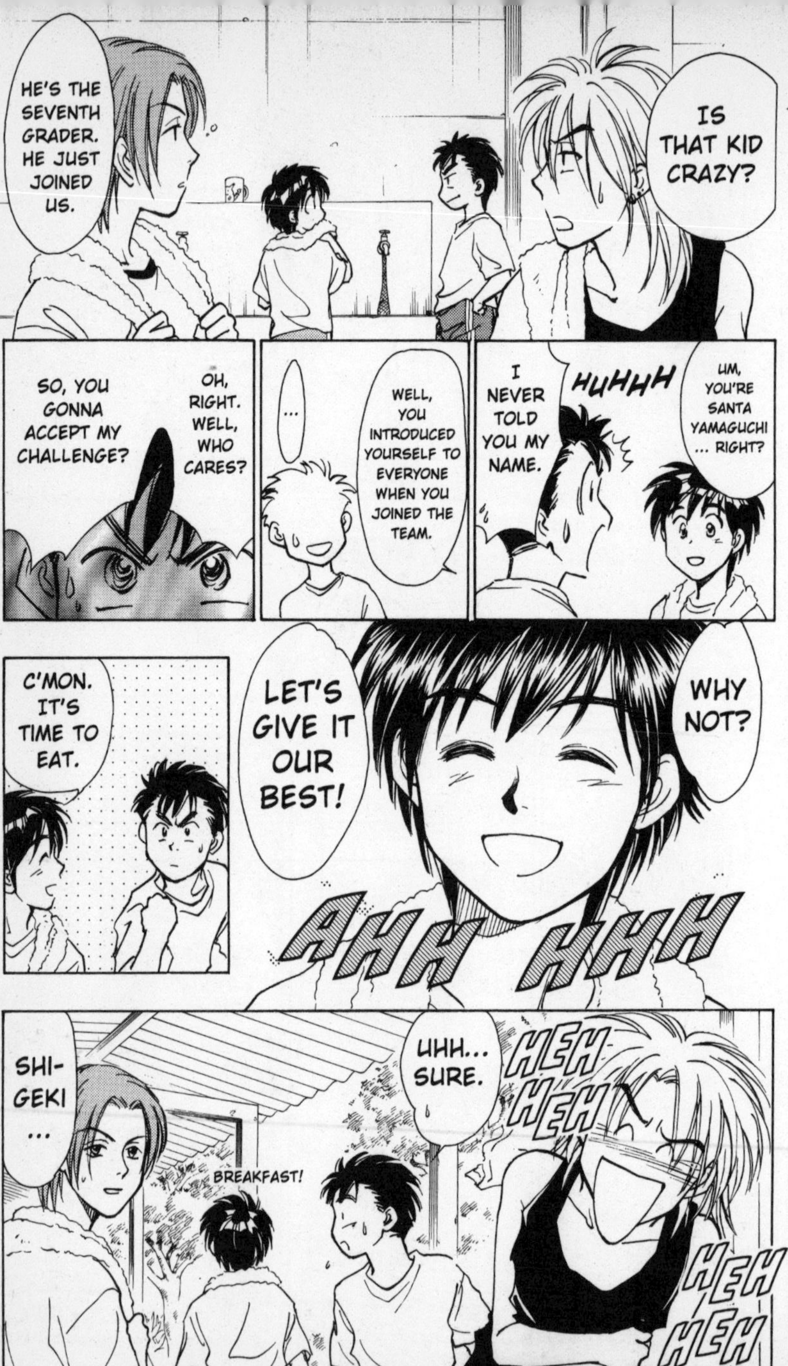
IS THAT KID CRAZY?
HE'S THE SEVENTH GRADER. HE JUST JOINED US.
UM, YOU'RE SANTA YAMAGUCHI ... RIGHT?
HUHHH
I NEVER TOLD YOU MY NAME.
WELL, YOU INTRODUCED YOURSELF TO EVERYONE WHEN YOU JOINED THE TEAM.
...
OH, RIGHT. WELL, WHO CARES?
SO, YOU GONNA ACCEPT MY CHALLENGE?
WHY NOT?
LET'S GIVE IT OUR BEST!
AHH HHH
C'MON. IT'S TIME TO EAT.
HEH HEH
HEH HEH
UHH... SURE.
BREAKFAST!
SHI-GEKI ...

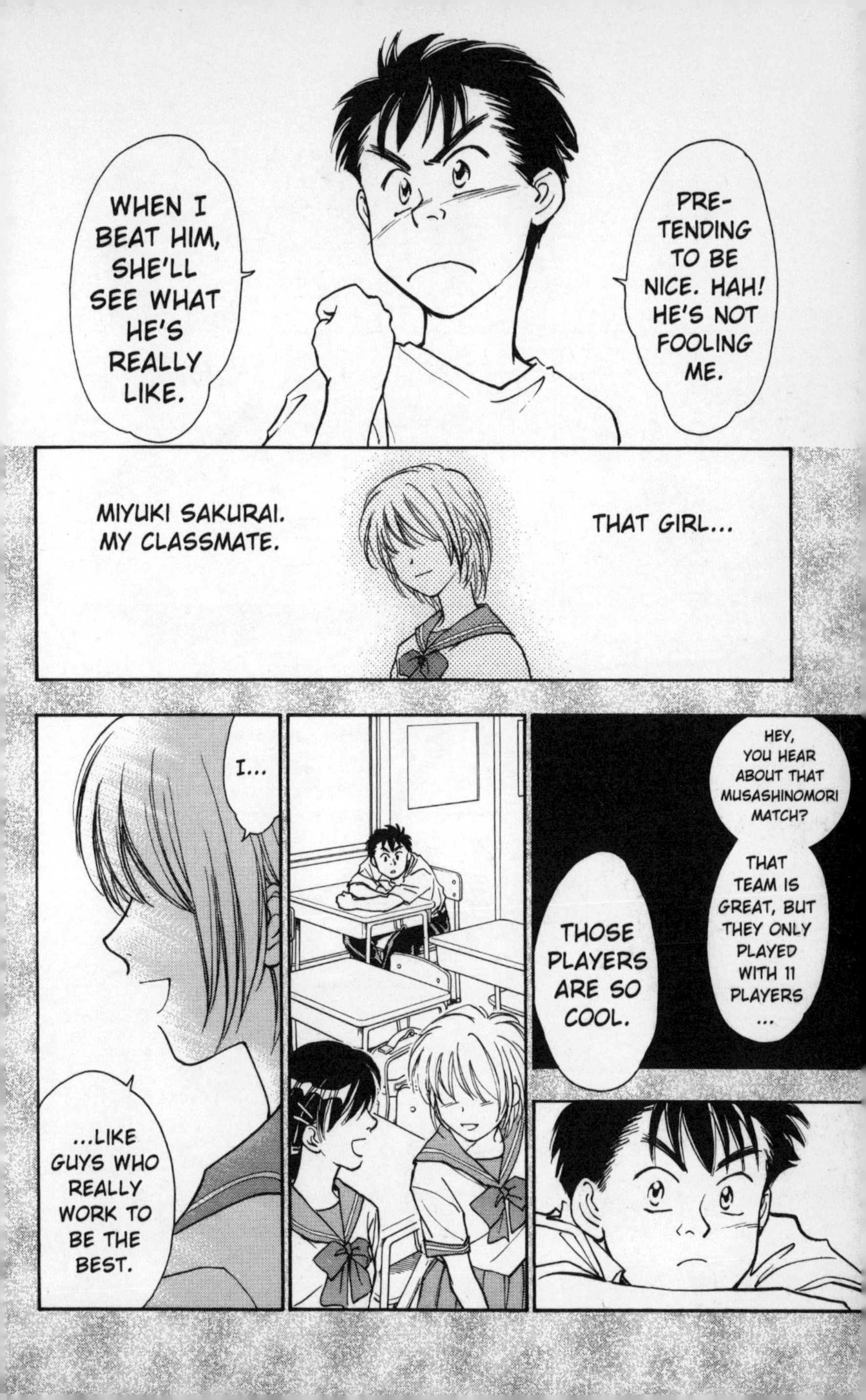
PRE-TENDING TO BE NICE. HAH! HE'S NOT FOOLING ME.
WHEN I BEAT HIM, SHE'LL SEE WHAT HE'S REALLY LIKE.
THAT GIRL...
MIYUKI SAKURAI. MY CLASSMATE.
HEY, YOU HEAR ABOUT THAT MUSASHINOMORI MATCH?
THAT TEAM IS GREAT, BUT THEY ONLY PLAYED WITH 11 PLAYERS ...
THOSE PLAYERS ARE SO COOL.
I...
...LIKE GUYS WHO REALLY WORK TO BE THE BEST.

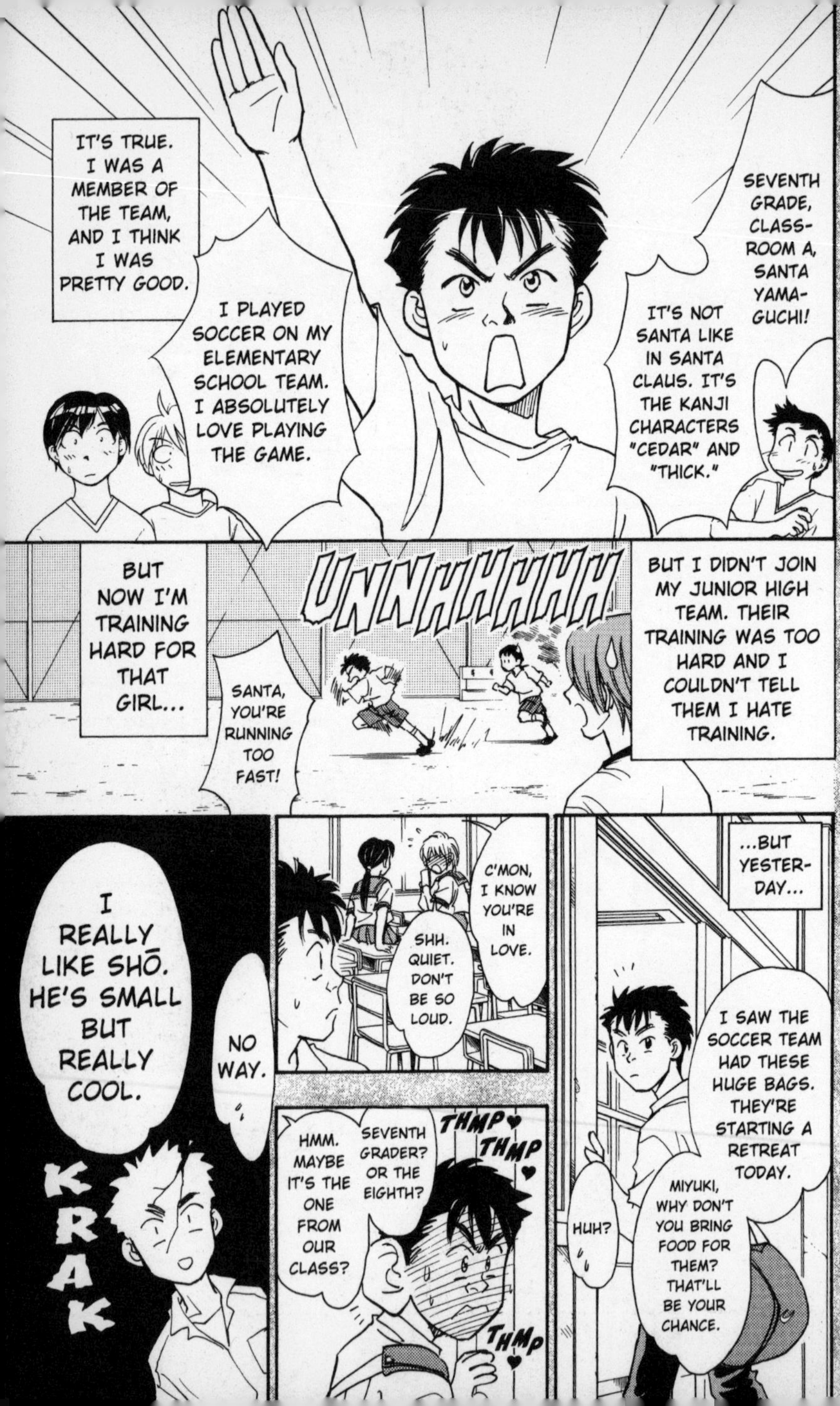
SEVENTH GRADE, CLASSROOM A, SANTA YAMAGUCHI!
IT'S NOT SANTA LIKE IN SANTA CLAUS. IT'S THE KANJI CHARACTERS "CEDAR" AND "THICK."
I PLAYED SOCCER ON MY ELEMENTARY SCHOOL TEAM. I ABSOLUTELY LOVE PLAYING THE GAME.
IT'S TRUE. I WAS A MEMBER OF THE TEAM, AND I THINK I WAS PRETTY GOOD.
BUT I DIDN'T JOIN MY JUNIOR HIGH TEAM. THEIR TRAINING WAS TOO HARD AND I COULDN'T TELL THEM I HATE TRAINING.
UNNHHHHHH
SANTA, YOU'RE RUNNING TOO FAST!
BUT NOW I'M TRAINING HARD FOR THAT GIRL...
...BUT YESTERDAY...
I SAW THE SOCCER TEAM HAD THESE HUGE BAGS. THEY'RE STARTING A RETREAT TODAY.
MIYUKI, WHY DON'T YOU BRING FOOD FOR THEM? THAT'LL BE YOUR CHANCE.
HUH?
C'MON, I KNOW YOU'RE IN LOVE.
SHH. QUIET. DON'T BE SO LOUD.
SEVENTH GRADER? OR THE EIGHTH?
HMM. MAYBE IT'S THE ONE FROM OUR CLASS?
THMP♥ THMP♥
THMP♥
I REALLY LIKE SHŌ. HE'S SMALL BUT REALLY COOL.
NO WAY.
KRAK

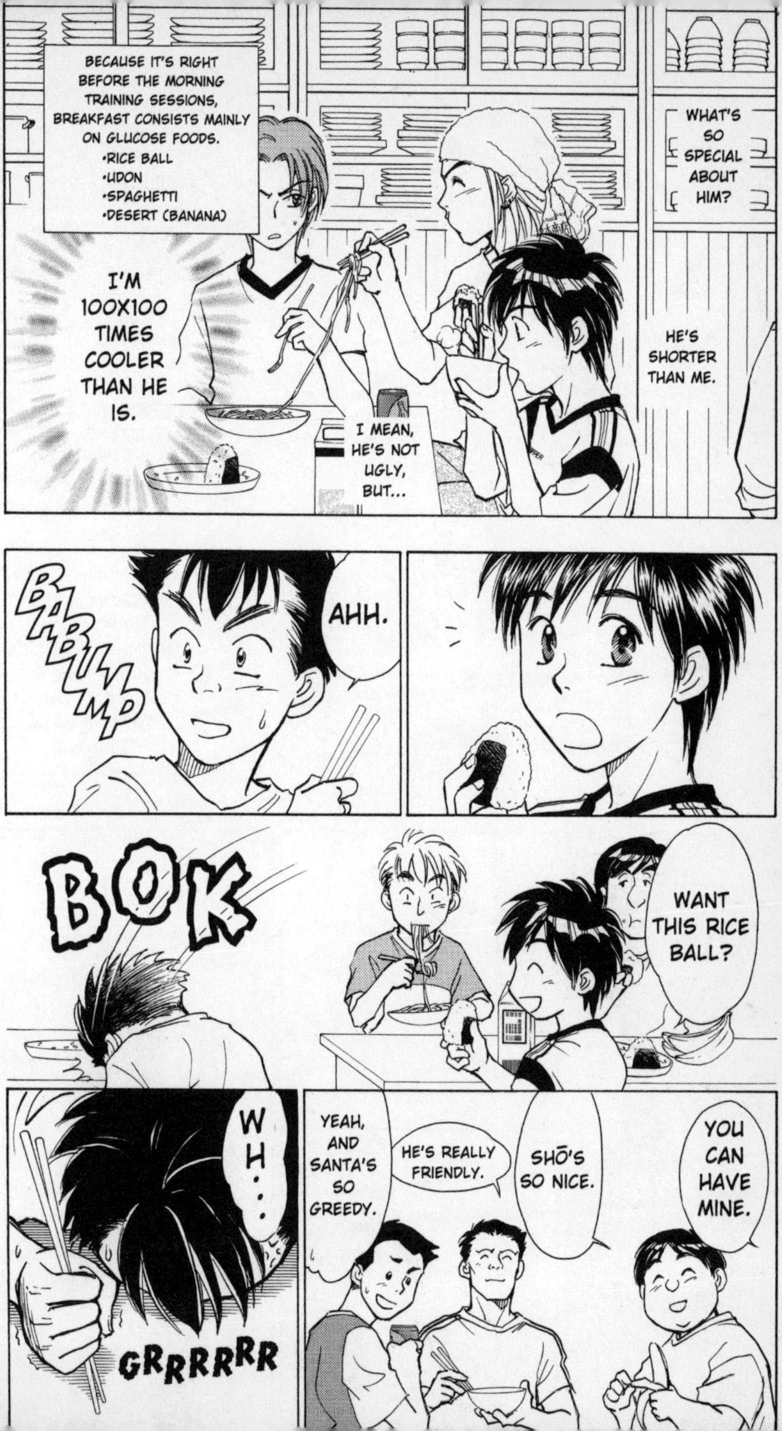
WHAT'S SO SPECIAL ABOUT HIM?
HE'S SHORTER THAN ME.
I MEAN, HE'S NOT UGLY, BUT...
BECAUSE IT'S RIGHT BEFORE THE MORNING TRAINING SESSIONS, BREAKFAST CONSISTS MAINLY ON GLUCOSE FOODS.
•RICE BALL
•UDON
•SPAGHETTI
•DESERT (BANANA)
I'M 100X100 TIMES COOLER THAN HE IS.
AHH.
BABUMP
WANT THIS RICE BALL?
BOK
YOU CAN HAVE MINE.
SHŌ'S SO NICE.
HE'S REALLY FRIENDLY.
YEAH, AND SANTA'S SO GREEDY.
WH...
GRRRRRR

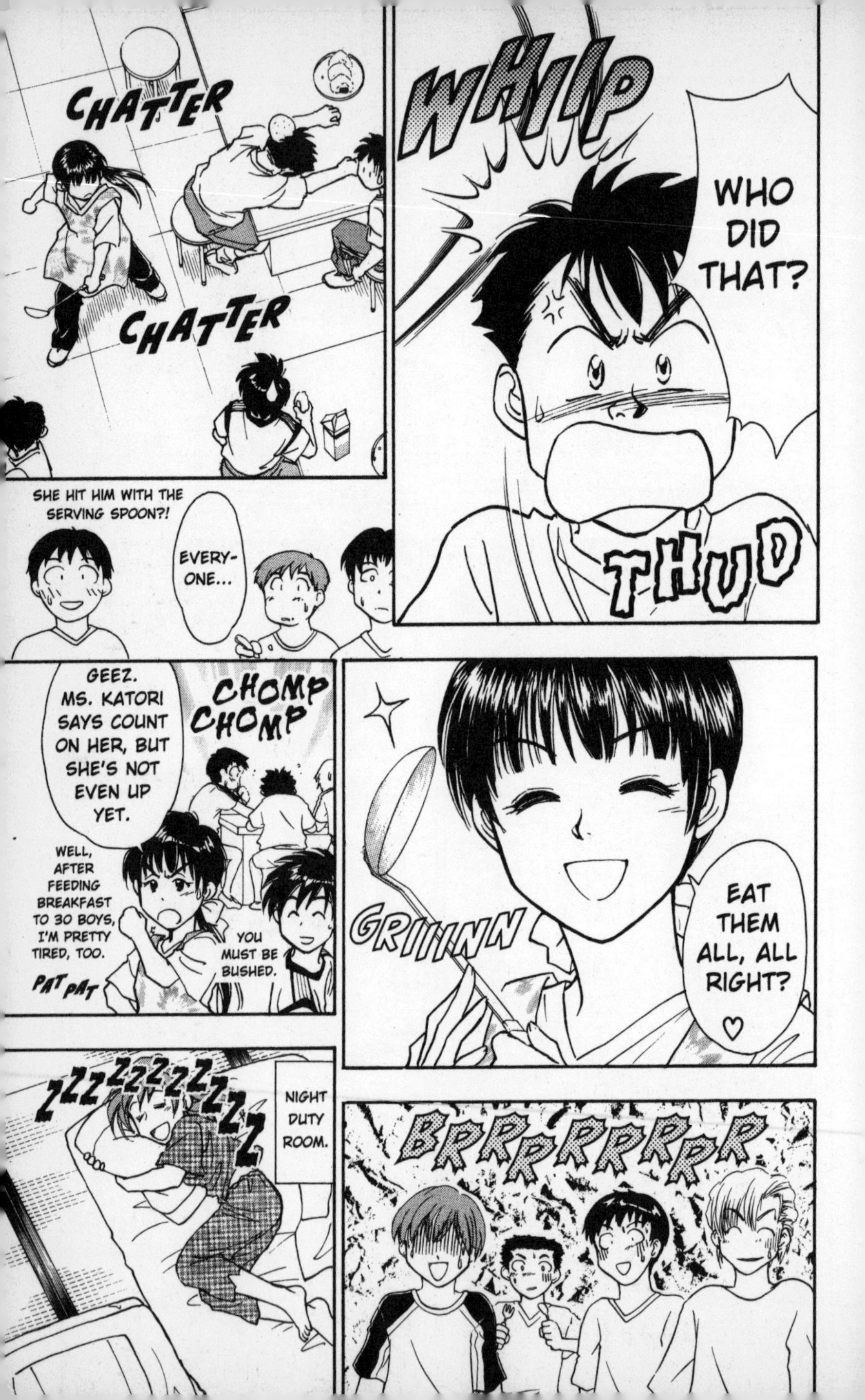
WHIP
WHO DID THAT?
THUD
CHATTER
CHATTER
SHE HIT HIM WITH THE SERVING SPOON?!
EVERY-ONE...
EAT THEM ALL, ALL RIGHT? ♡
GRIIINN
CHOMP CHOMP
GEEZ. MS. KATORI SAYS COUNT ON HER, BUT SHE'S NOT EVEN UP YET.
WELL, AFTER FEEDING BREAKFAST TO 30 BOYS, I'M PRETTY TIRED, TOO.
YOU MUST BE BUSHED.
PAT PAT
BRRRRRRRR
NIGHT DUTY ROOM.
ZZZZZZZZZZZ

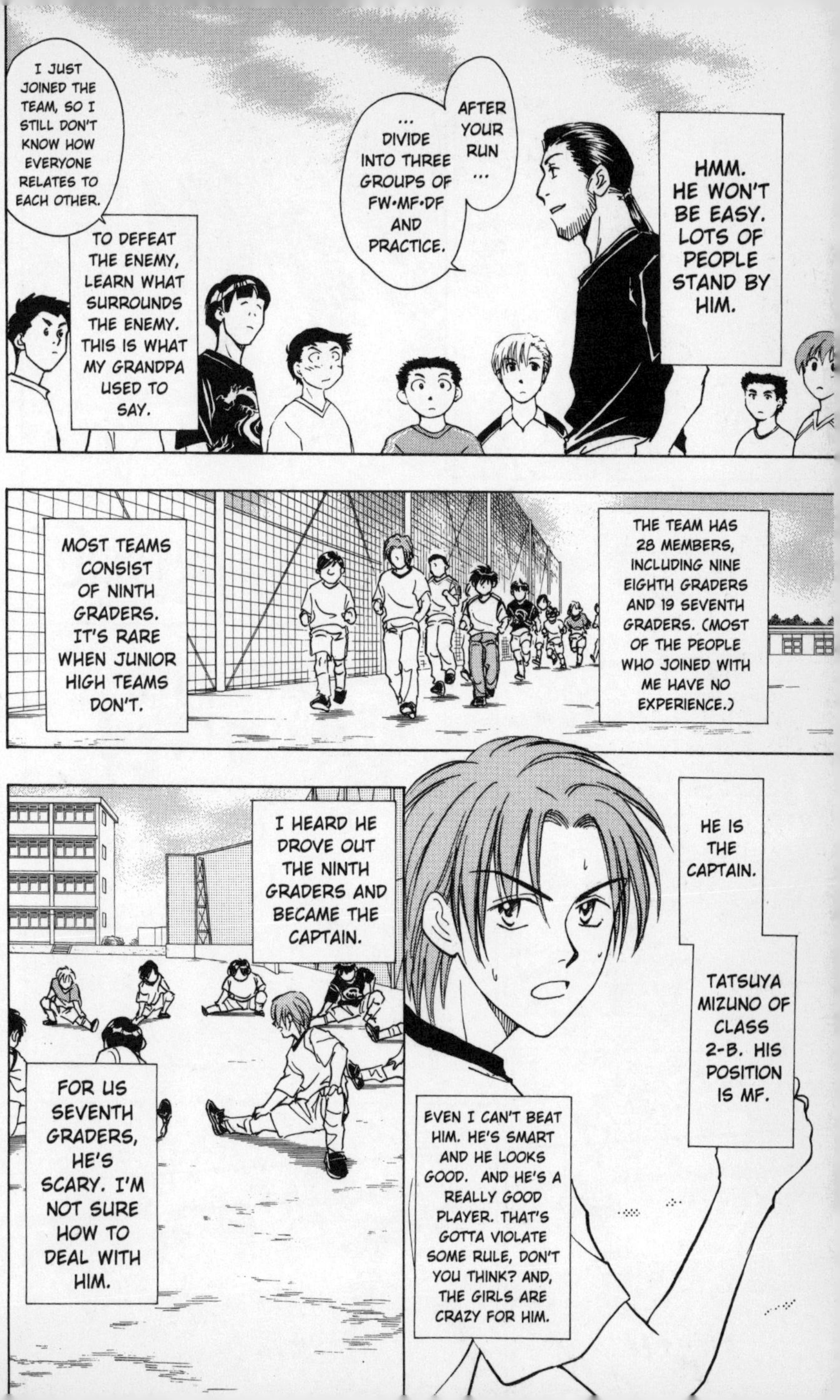
HMM. HE WON'T BE EASY. LOTS OF PEOPLE STAND BY HIM.
AFTER YOUR RUN ...
... DIVIDE INTO THREE GROUPS OF FW•MF•DF AND PRACTICE.
I JUST JOINED THE TEAM, SO I STILL DON'T KNOW HOW EVERYONE RELATES TO EACH OTHER.
TO DEFEAT THE ENEMY, LEARN WHAT SURROUNDS THE ENEMY. THIS IS WHAT MY GRANDPA USED TO SAY.
THE TEAM HAS 28 MEMBERS, INCLUDING NINE EIGHTH GRADERS AND 19 SEVENTH GRADERS. (MOST OF THE PEOPLE WHO JOINED WITH ME HAVE NO EXPERIENCE.)
MOST TEAMS CONSIST OF NINTH GRADERS. IT'S RARE WHEN JUNIOR HIGH TEAMS DON'T.
HE IS THE CAPTAIN.
TATSUYA MIZUNO OF CLASS 2-B. HIS POSITION IS MF.
EVEN I CAN'T BEAT HIM. HE'S SMART AND HE LOOKS GOOD. AND HE'S A REALLY GOOD PLAYER. THAT'S GOTTA VIOLATE SOME RULE, DON'T YOU THINK? AND, THE GIRLS ARE CRAZY FOR HIM.
I HEARD HE DROVE OUT THE NINTH GRADERS AND BECAME THE CAPTAIN.
FOR US SEVENTH GRADERS, HE'S SCARY. I'M NOT SURE HOW TO DEAL WITH HIM.

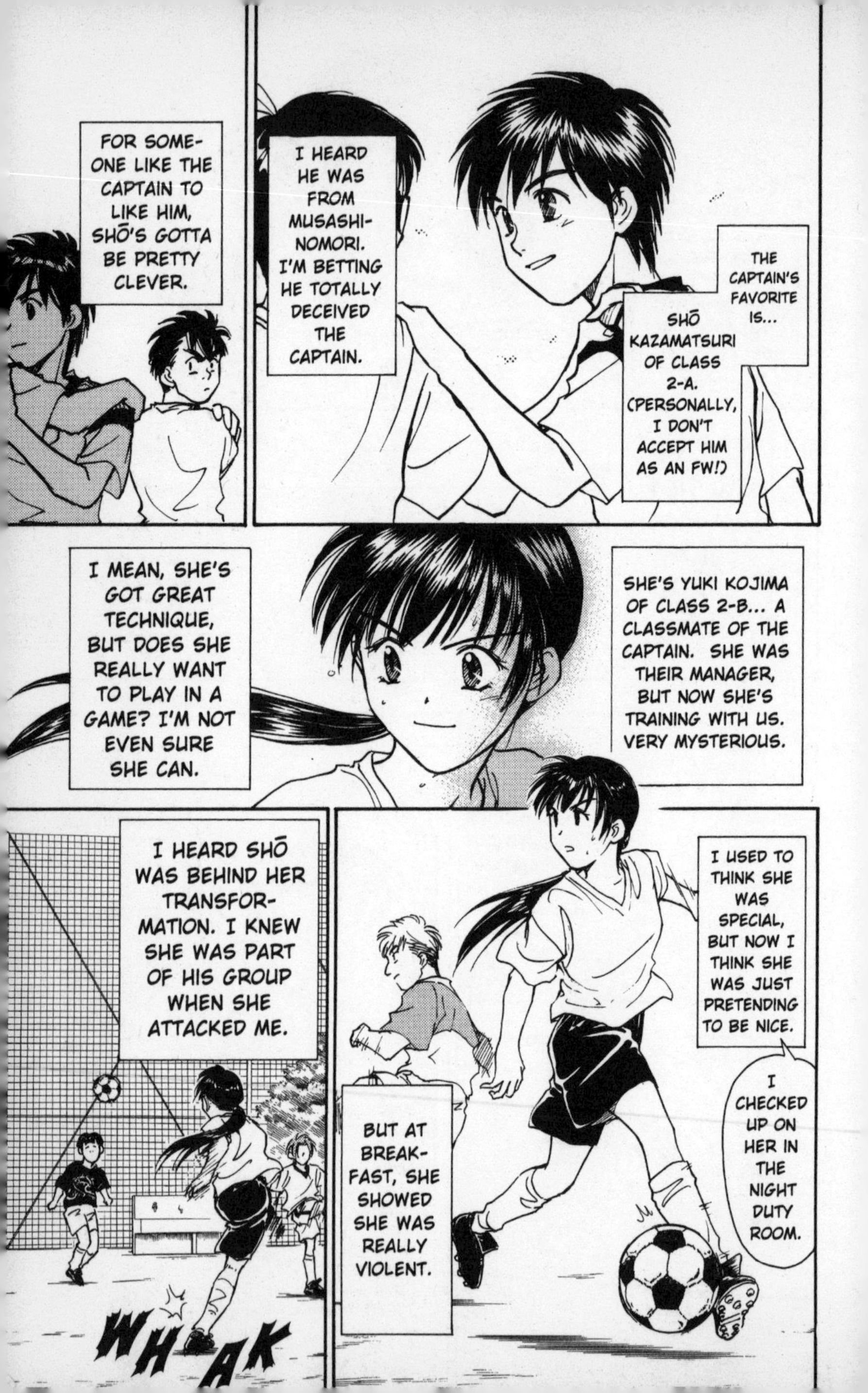
THE CAPTAIN'S FAVORITE IS...
SHŌ KAZAMATSURI OF CLASS 2-A. (PERSONALLY, I DON'T ACCEPT HIM AS AN FW!)
I HEARD HE WAS FROM MUSASHI-NOMORI. I'M BETTING HE TOTALLY DECEIVED THE CAPTAIN.
FOR SOME-ONE LIKE THE CAPTAIN TO LIKE HIM, SHŌ'S GOTTA BE PRETTY CLEVER.
SHE'S YUKI KOJIMA OF CLASS 2-B... A CLASSMATE OF THE CAPTAIN. SHE WAS THEIR MANAGER, BUT NOW SHE'S TRAINING WITH US. VERY MYSTERIOUS.
I MEAN, SHE'S GOT GREAT TECHNIQUE, BUT DOES SHE REALLY WANT TO PLAY IN A GAME? I'M NOT EVEN SURE SHE CAN.
I USED TO THINK SHE WAS SPECIAL, BUT NOW I THINK SHE WAS JUST PRETENDING TO BE NICE.
I CHECKED UP ON HER IN THE NIGHT DUTY ROOM.
BUT AT BREAK-FAST, SHE SHOWED SHE WAS REALLY VIOLENT.
I HEARD SHŌ WAS BEHIND HER TRANSFOR-MATION. I KNEW SHE WAS PART OF HIS GROUP WHEN SHE ATTACKED ME.
WHAK

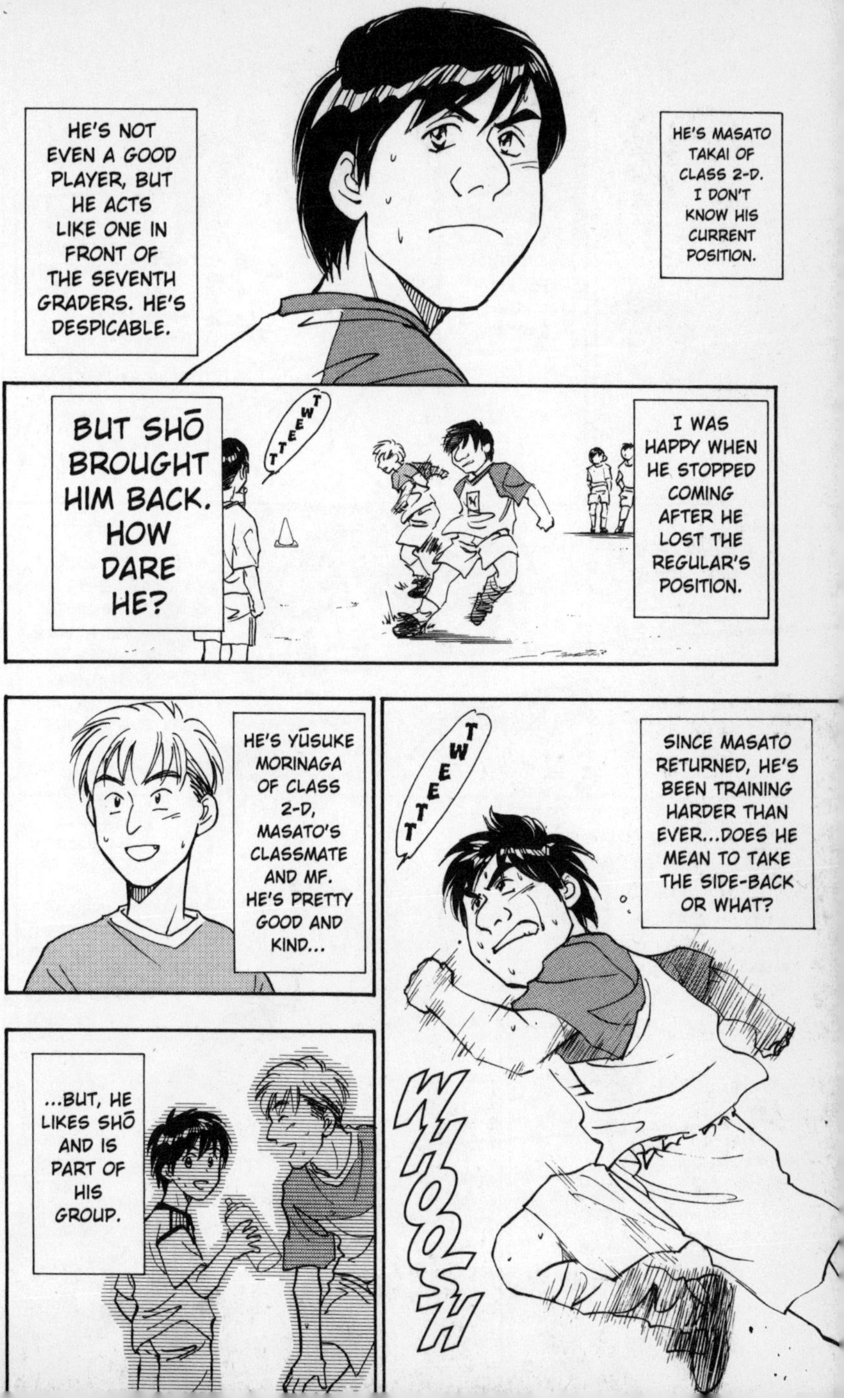
HE'S MASATO TAKAI OF CLASS 2-D. I DON'T KNOW HIS CURRENT POSITION.
HE'S NOT EVEN A GOOD PLAYER, BUT HE ACTS LIKE ONE IN FRONT OF THE SEVENTH GRADERS. HE'S DESPICABLE.
I WAS HAPPY WHEN HE STOPPED COMING AFTER HE LOST THE REGULAR'S POSITION.
TTEEWT
BUT SHŌ BROUGHT HIM BACK. HOW DARE HE?
SINCE MASATO RETURNED, HE'S BEEN TRAINING HARDER THAN EVER...DOES HE MEAN TO TAKE THE SIDE-BACK OR WHAT?
TTEEWT
WHOOOSH
HE'S YŪSUKE MORINAGA OF CLASS 2-D, MASATO'S CLASSMATE AND MF. HE'S PRETTY GOOD AND KIND...
...BUT, HE LIKES SHŌ AND IS PART OF HIS GROUP.

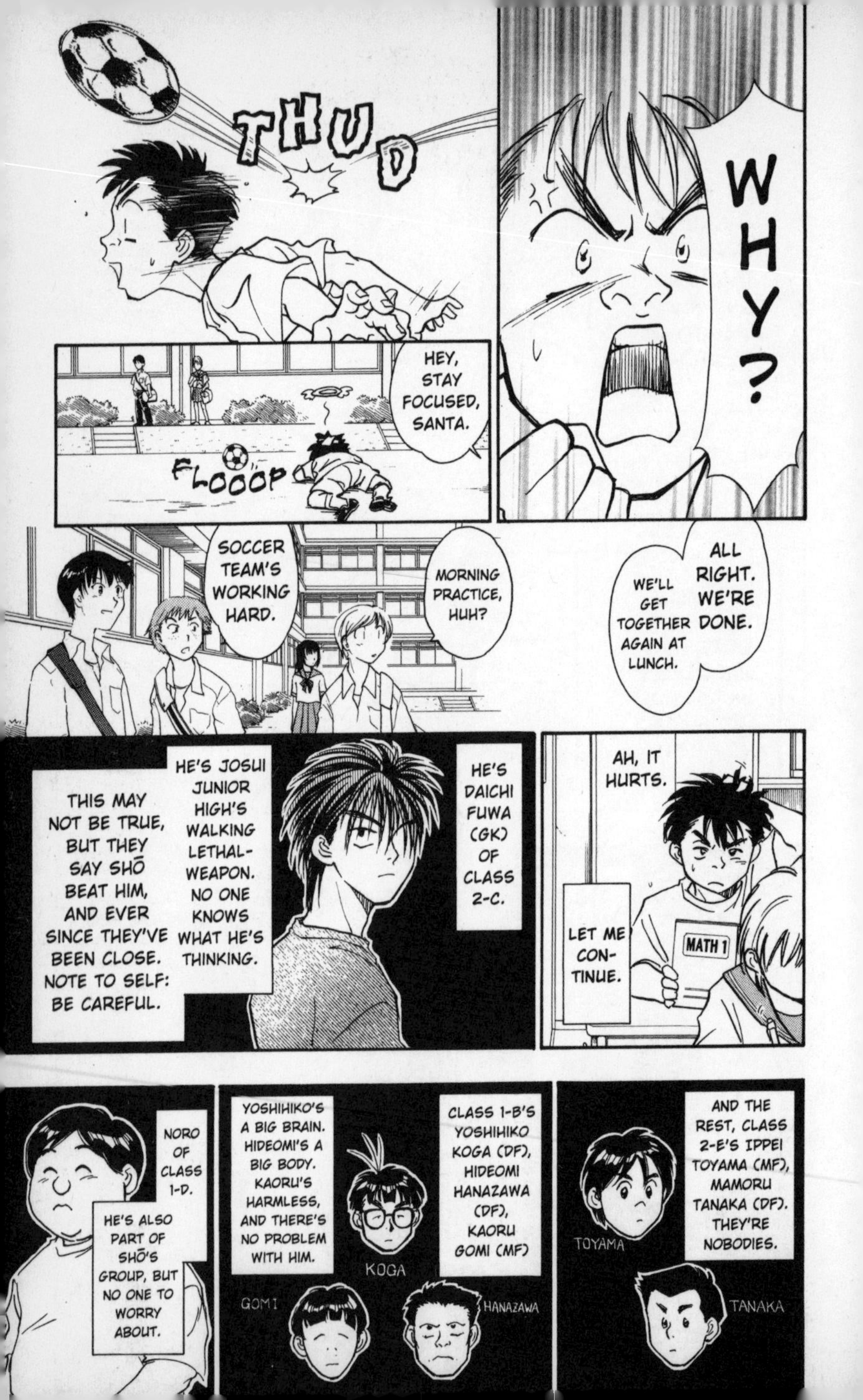

WHY?
THUD
HEY, STAY FOCUSED, SANTA.
FLOOOP
ALL RIGHT. WE'RE DONE.
WE'LL GET TOGETHER AGAIN AT LUNCH.
MORNING PRACTICE, HUH?
SOCCER TEAM'S WORKING HARD.
AH, IT HURTS.
LET ME CONTINUE.
MATH 1
HE'S DAICHI FUWA (GK) OF CLASS 2-C.
HE'S JOSUI JUNIOR HIGH'S WALKING LETHAL-WEAPON. NO ONE KNOWS WHAT HE'S THINKING.
THIS MAY NOT BE TRUE, BUT THEY SAY SHŌ BEAT HIM, AND EVER SINCE THEY'VE BEEN CLOSE. NOTE TO SELF: BE CAREFUL.
AND THE REST, CLASS 2-E'S IPPEI TOYAMA (MF), MAMORU TANAKA (DF). THEY'RE NOBODIES.
TOYAMA
TANAKA
CLASS 1-B'S YOSHIHIKO KOGA (DF), HIDEOMI HANAZAWA (DF), KAORU GOMI (MF)
YOSHIHIKO'S A BIG BRAIN. HIDEOMI'S A BIG BODY. KAORU'S HARMLESS, AND THERE'S NO PROBLEM WITH HIM.
KOGA
HANAZAWA
GOMI
NORO OF CLASS 1-D.
HE'S ALSO PART OF SHŌ'S GROUP, BUT NO ONE TO WORRY ABOUT.

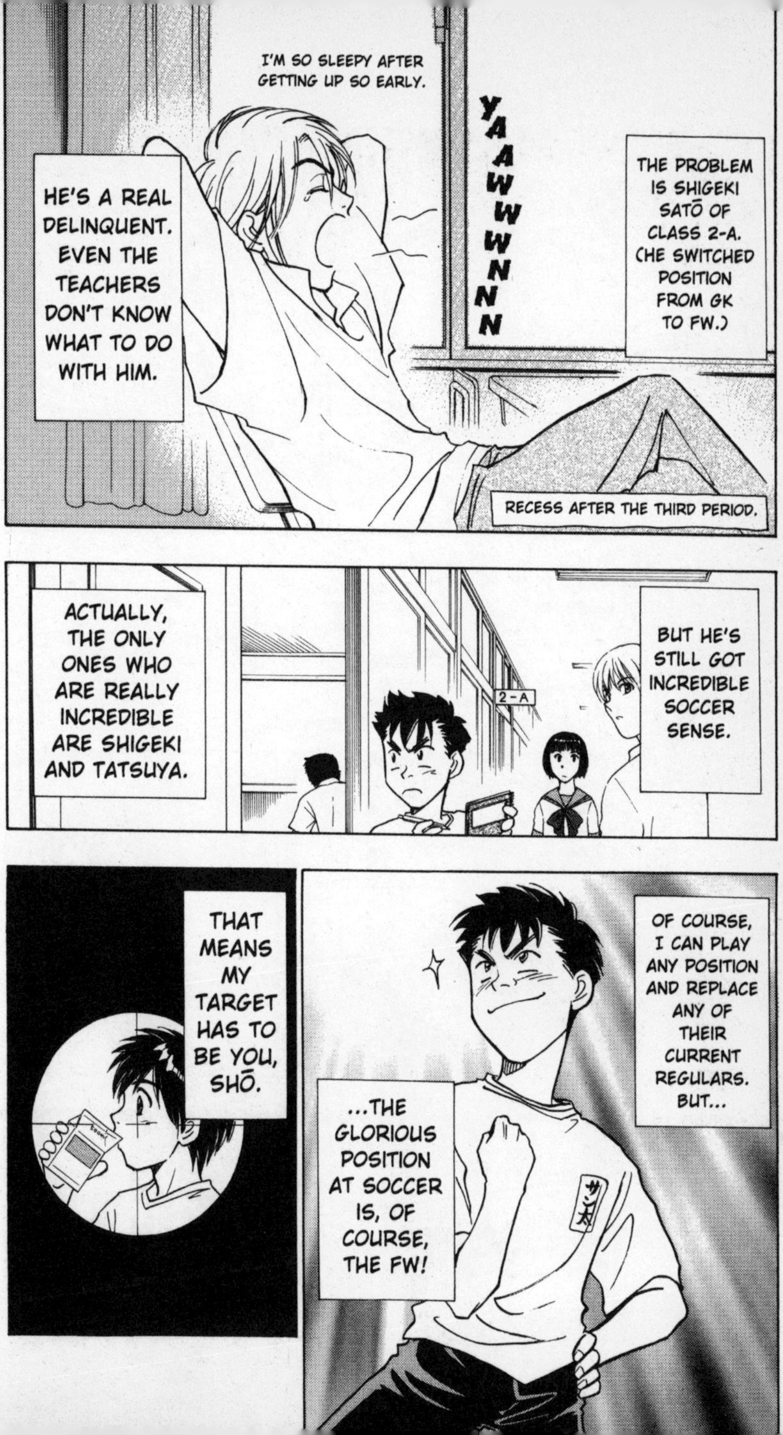
THE PROBLEM IS SHIGEKI SATŌ OF CLASS 2-A. (HE SWITCHED POSITION FROM GK TO FW.)
YAAWWWNNN
I'M SO SLEEPY AFTER GETTING UP SO EARLY.
HE'S A REAL DELINQUENT. EVEN THE TEACHERS DON'T KNOW WHAT TO DO WITH HIM.
RECESS AFTER THE THIRD PERIOD.
BUT HE'S STILL GOT INCREDIBLE SOCCER SENSE.
2-A
ACTUALLY, THE ONLY ONES WHO ARE REALLY INCREDIBLE ARE SHIGEKI AND TATSUYA.
OF COURSE, I CAN PLAY ANY POSITION AND REPLACE ANY OF THEIR CURRENT REGULARS. BUT...
...THE GLORIOUS POSITION AT SOCCER IS, OF COURSE, THE FW!
THAT MEANS MY TARGET HAS TO BE YOU, SHŌ.

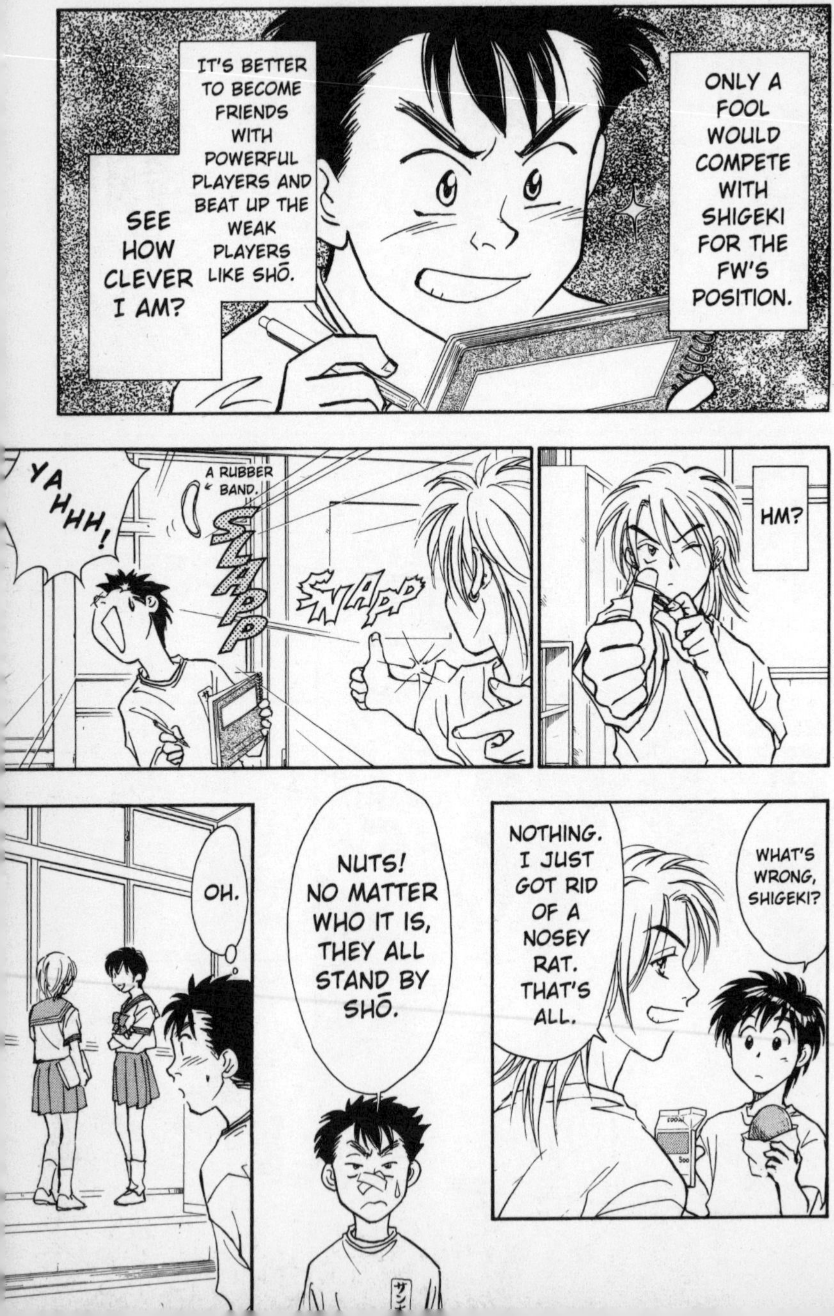
ONLY A FOOL WOULD COMPETE WITH SHIGEKI FOR THE FW'S POSITION.
IT'S BETTER TO BECOME FRIENDS WITH POWERFUL PLAYERS AND BEAT UP THE WEAK PLAYERS LIKE SHŌ.
SEE HOW CLEVER I AM?
HM?
SNAPP
SNAPP
A RUBBER BAND.
YAHHH!
WHAT'S WRONG, SHIGEKI?
NOTHING. I JUST GOT RID OF A NOSEY RAT. THAT'S ALL.
NUTS! NO MATTER WHO IT IS, THEY ALL STAND BY SHŌ.
OH.

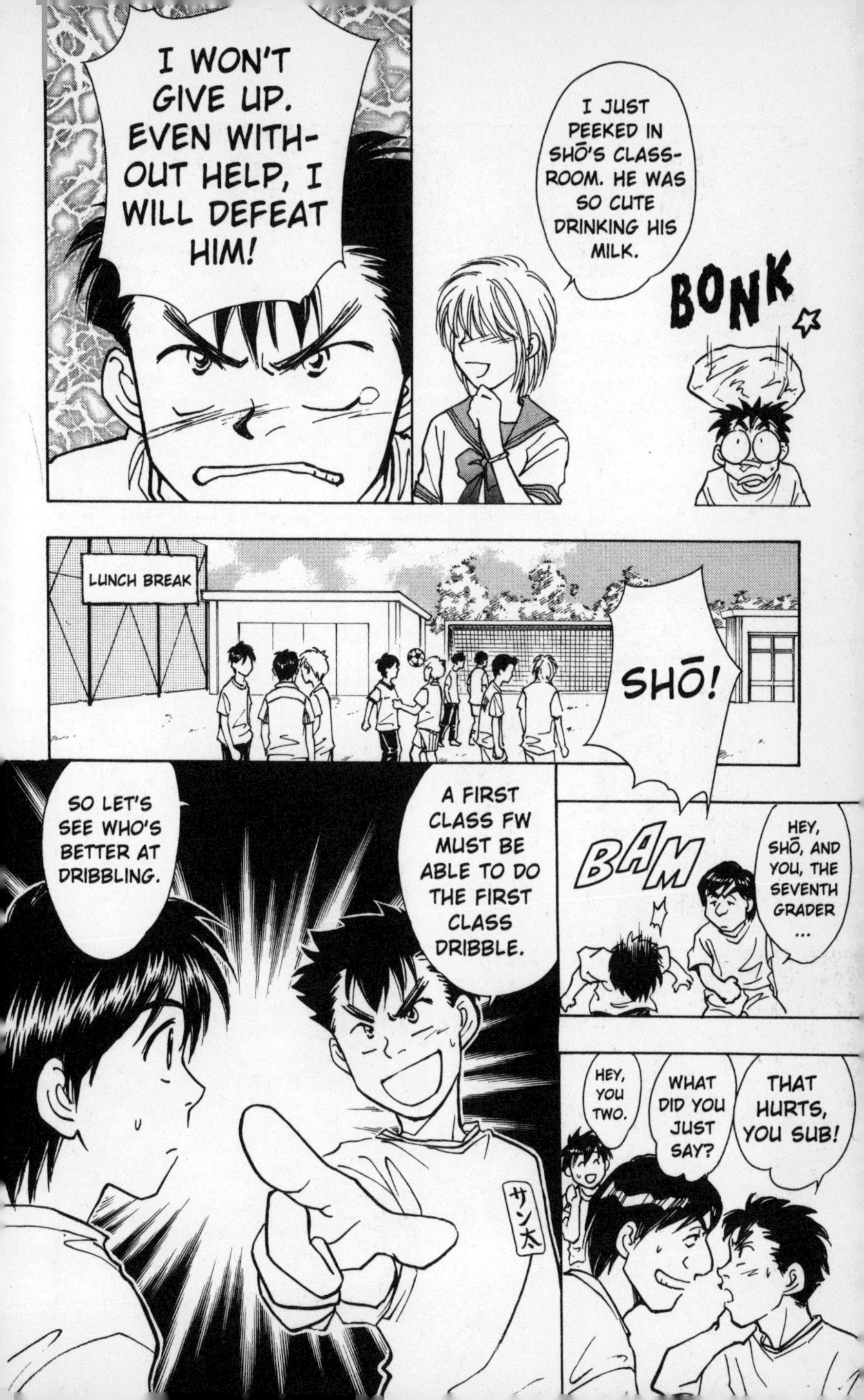
I JUST PEEKED IN SHŌ'S CLASS-ROOM. HE WAS SO CUTE DRINKING HIS MILK.
BONK
I WON'T GIVE UP. EVEN WITH-OUT HELP, I WILL DEFEAT HIM!
LUNCH BREAK
SHŌ!
BAM
HEY, SHŌ, AND YOU, THE SEVENTH GRADER ...
THAT HURTS, YOU SUB!
WHAT DID YOU JUST SAY?
HEY, YOU TWO.
A FIRST CLASS FW MUST BE ABLE TO DO THE FIRST CLASS DRIBBLE.
サン太
SO LET'S SEE WHO'S BETTER AT DRIBBLING.

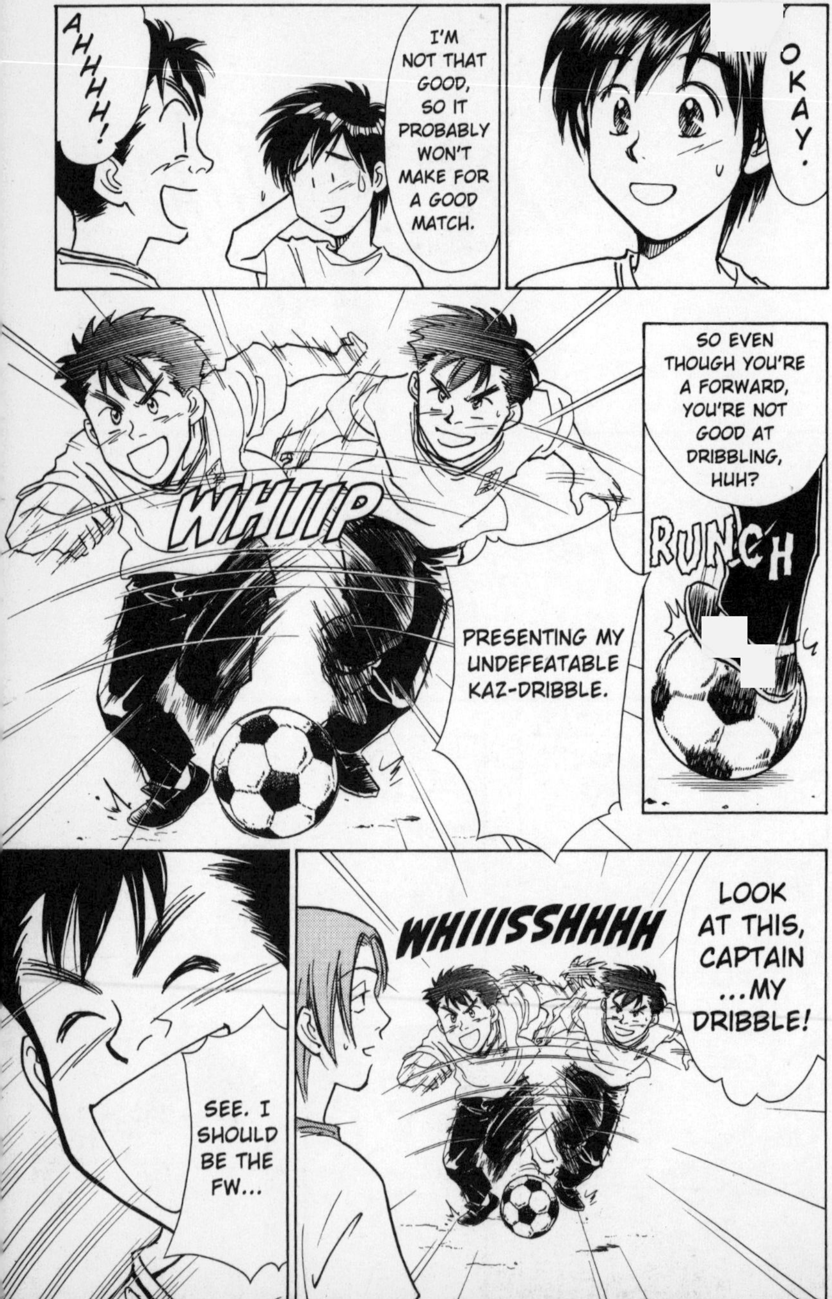
OKAY.
I'M NOT THAT GOOD, SO IT PROBABLY WON'T MAKE FOR A GOOD MATCH.
AHHHH!
SO EVEN THOUGH YOU'RE A FORWARD, YOU'RE NOT GOOD AT DRIBBLING, HUH?
RUNCH
WHIIP
PRESENTING MY UNDEFEATABLE KAZ-DRIBBLE.
LOOK AT THIS, CAPTAIN ...MY DRIBBLE!
WHIIISSHHHH
SEE. I SHOULD BE THE FW...

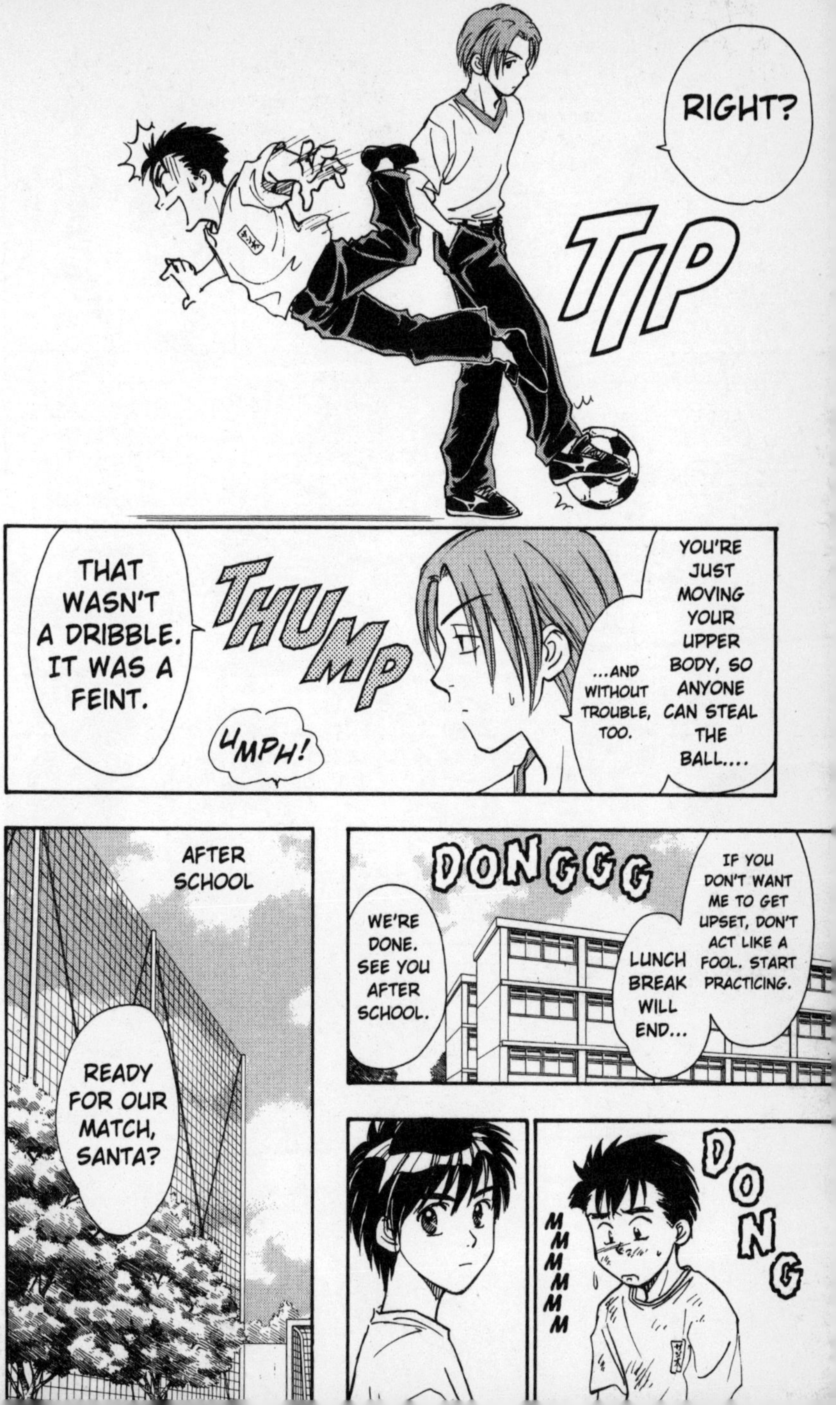
RIGHT?
TIP
YOU'RE JUST MOVING YOUR UPPER BODY, SO ANYONE CAN STEAL THE BALL....
...AND WITHOUT TROUBLE, TOO.
THUMP
UMPH!
THAT WASN'T A DRIBBLE. IT WAS A FEINT.
IF YOU DON'T WANT ME TO GET UPSET, DON'T ACT LIKE A FOOL. START PRACTICING.
LUNCH BREAK WILL END...
WE'RE DONE. SEE YOU AFTER SCHOOL.
DONGGG
DONG
MMMMMM
AFTER SCHOOL
READY FOR OUR MATCH, SANTA?

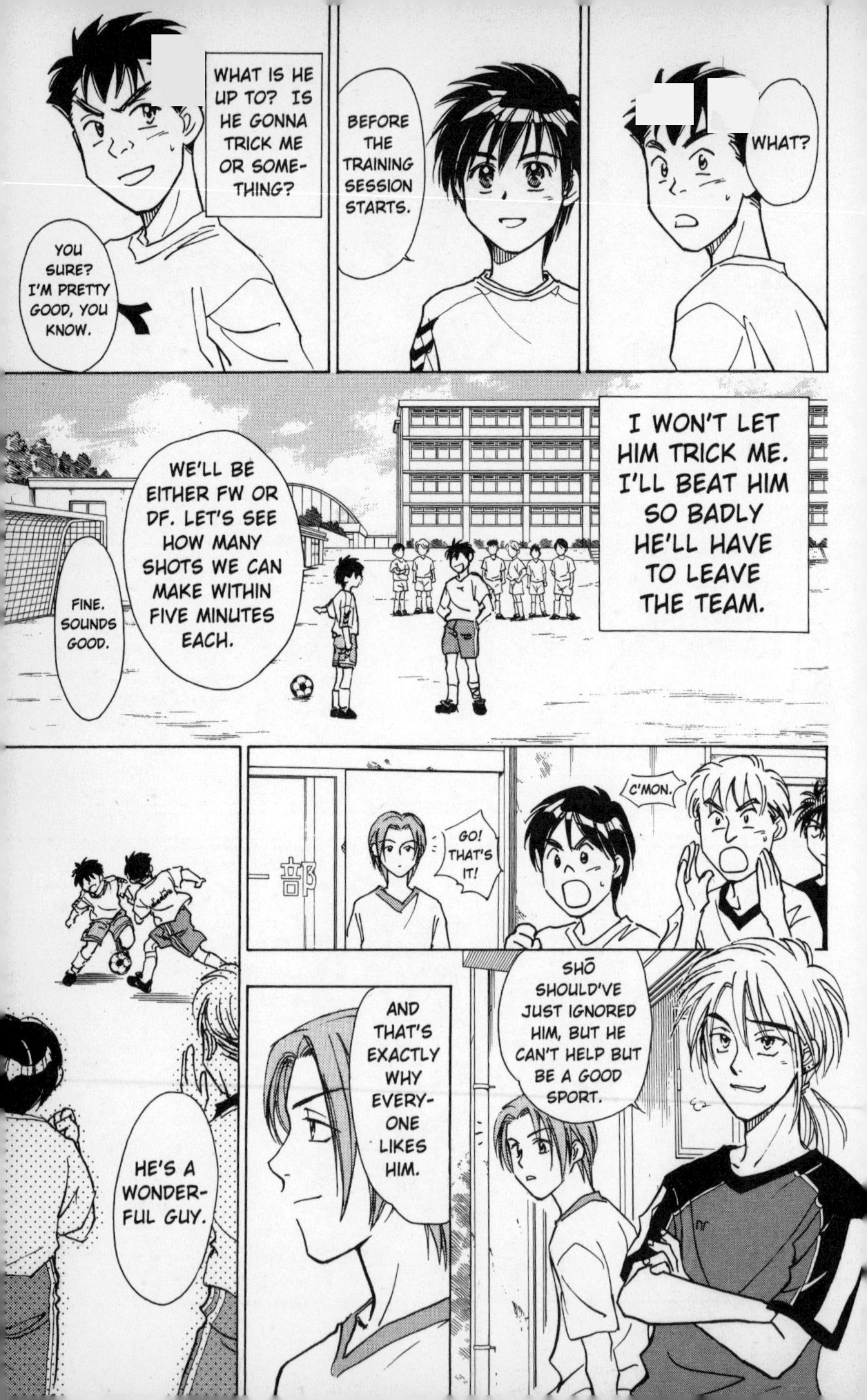
WHAT?
BEFORE THE TRAINING SESSION STARTS.
WHAT IS HE UP TO? IS HE GONNA TRICK ME OR SOME-THING?
YOU SURE? I'M PRETTY GOOD, YOU KNOW.
I WON'T LET HIM TRICK ME. I'LL BEAT HIM SO BADLY HE'LL HAVE TO LEAVE THE TEAM.
WE'LL BE EITHER FW OR DF. LET'S SEE HOW MANY SHOTS WE CAN MAKE WITHIN FIVE MINUTES EACH.
FINE. SOUNDS GOOD.
C'MON.
GO! THAT'S IT!
部
SHŌ SHOULD'VE JUST IGNORED HIM, BUT HE CAN'T HELP BUT BE A GOOD SPORT.
AND THAT'S EXACTLY WHY EVERY-ONE LIKES HIM.
HE'S A WONDER-FUL GUY.

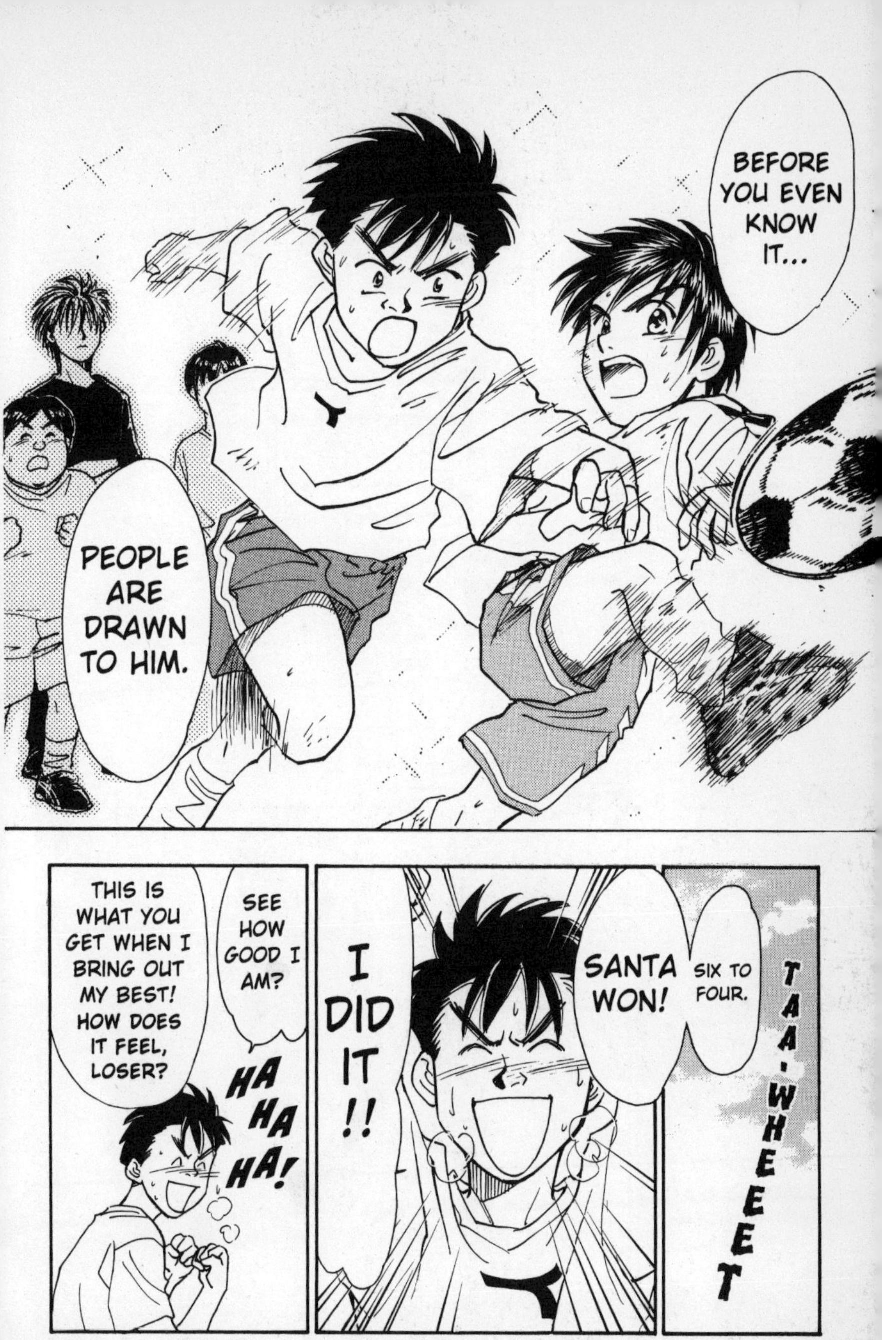
BEFORE YOU EVEN KNOW IT...
PEOPLE ARE DRAWN TO HIM.
TAA-WHEEEET
SIX TO FOUR.
SANTA WON!
I DID IT!!
SEE HOW GOOD I AM?
THIS IS WHAT YOU GET WHEN I BRING OUT MY BEST! HOW DOES IT FEEL, LOSER?
HA HA HA!

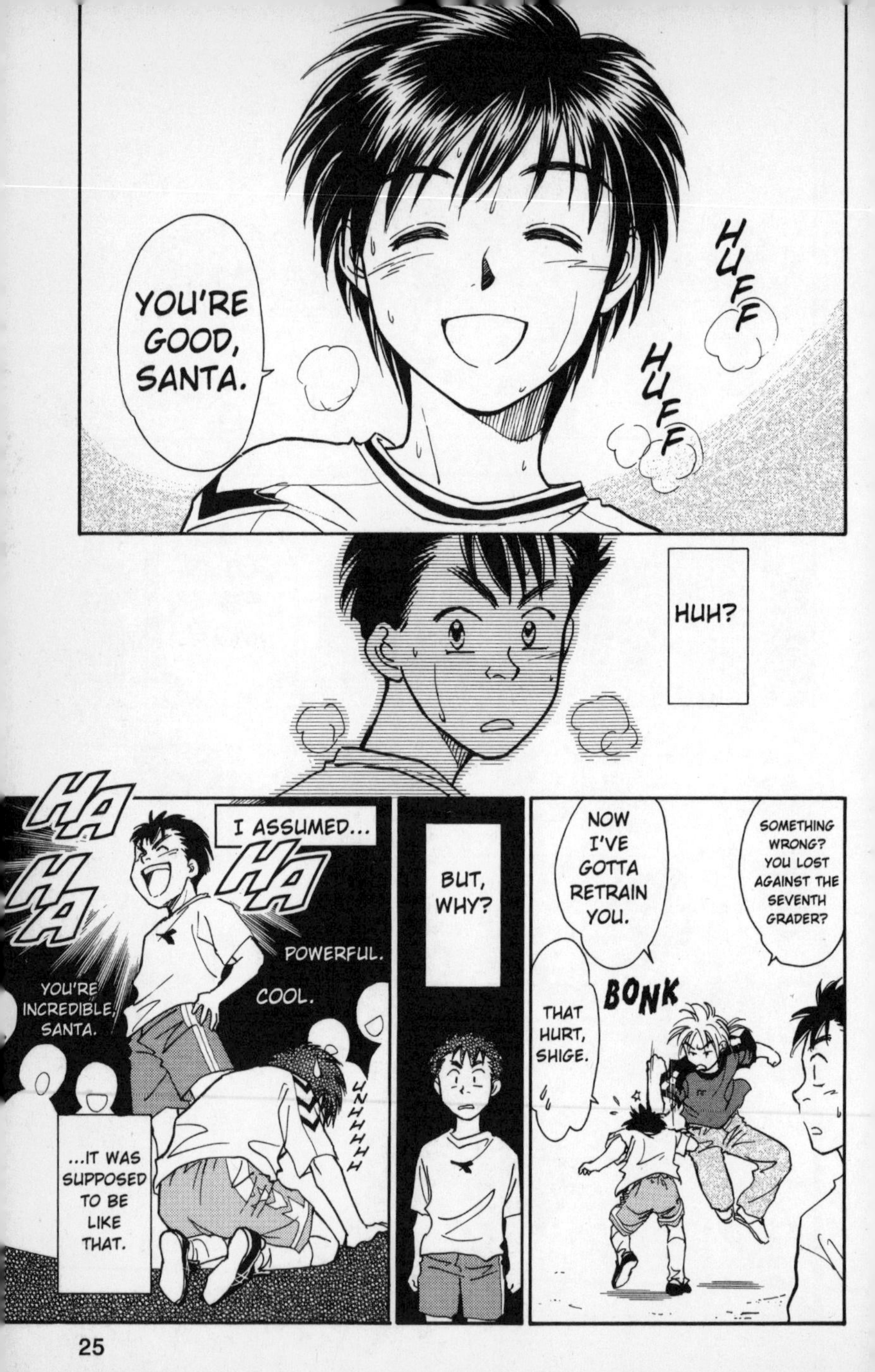
YOU'RE GOOD, SANTA.
HUFF
HUFF
HUH?
SOMETHING WRONG? YOU LOST AGAINST THE SEVENTH GRADER?
NOW I'VE GOTTA RETRAIN YOU.
BONK
THAT HURT, SHIGE.
BUT, WHY?
I ASSUMED...
HA
HA
HA
HA
POWERFUL.
COOL.
YOU'RE INCREDIBLE, SANTA.
UNHHHHH
...IT WAS SUPPOSED TO BE LIKE THAT.

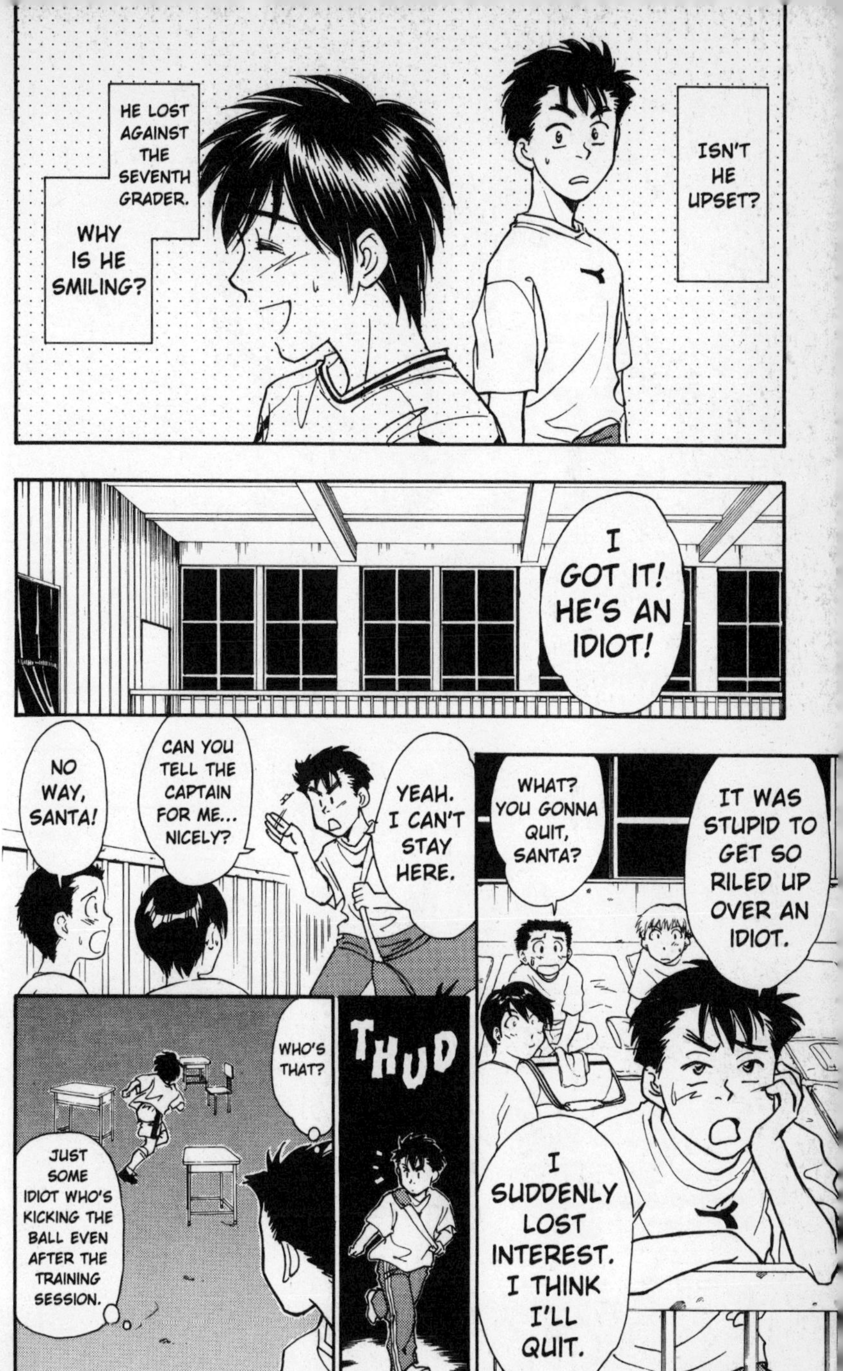
ISN'T HE UPSET?
HE LOST AGAINST THE SEVENTH GRADER.
WHY IS HE SMILING?
I GOT IT! HE'S AN IDIOT!
IT WAS STUPID TO GET SO RILED UP OVER AN IDIOT.
WHAT? YOU GONNA QUIT, SANTA?
I SUDDENLY LOST INTEREST. I THINK I'LL QUIT.
YEAH. I CAN'T STAY HERE.
CAN YOU TELL THE CAPTAIN FOR ME... NICELY?
NO WAY, SANTA!
THUD
WHO'S THAT?
JUST SOME IDIOT WHO'S KICKING THE BALL EVEN AFTER THE TRAINING SESSION.

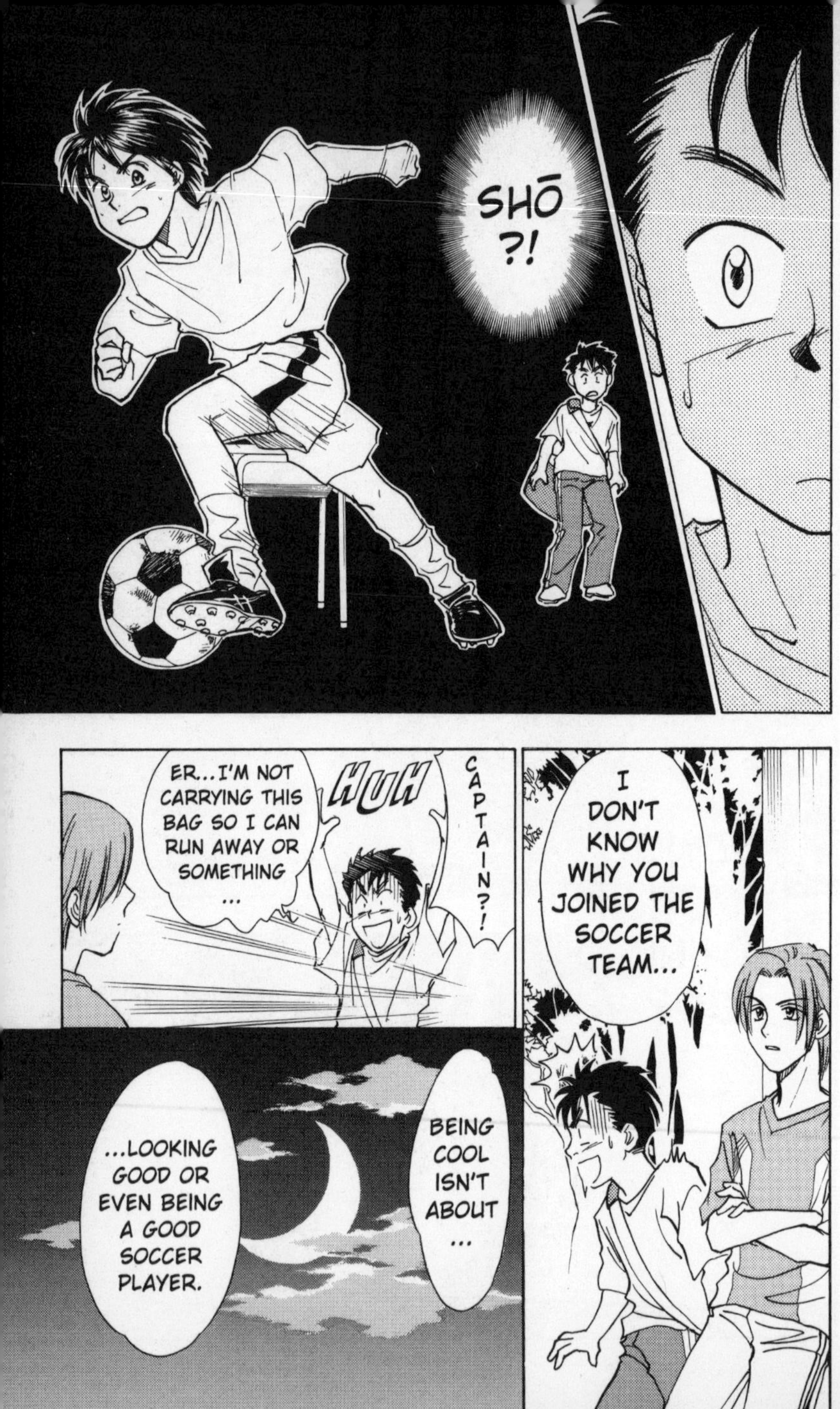
SHŌ ?!
I DON'T KNOW WHY YOU JOINED THE SOCCER TEAM...
CAPTAIN?!
HUH
ER...I'M NOT CARRYING THIS BAG SO I CAN RUN AWAY OR SOMETHING ...
BEING COOL ISN'T ABOUT ...
...LOOKING GOOD OR EVEN BEING A GOOD SOCCER PLAYER.

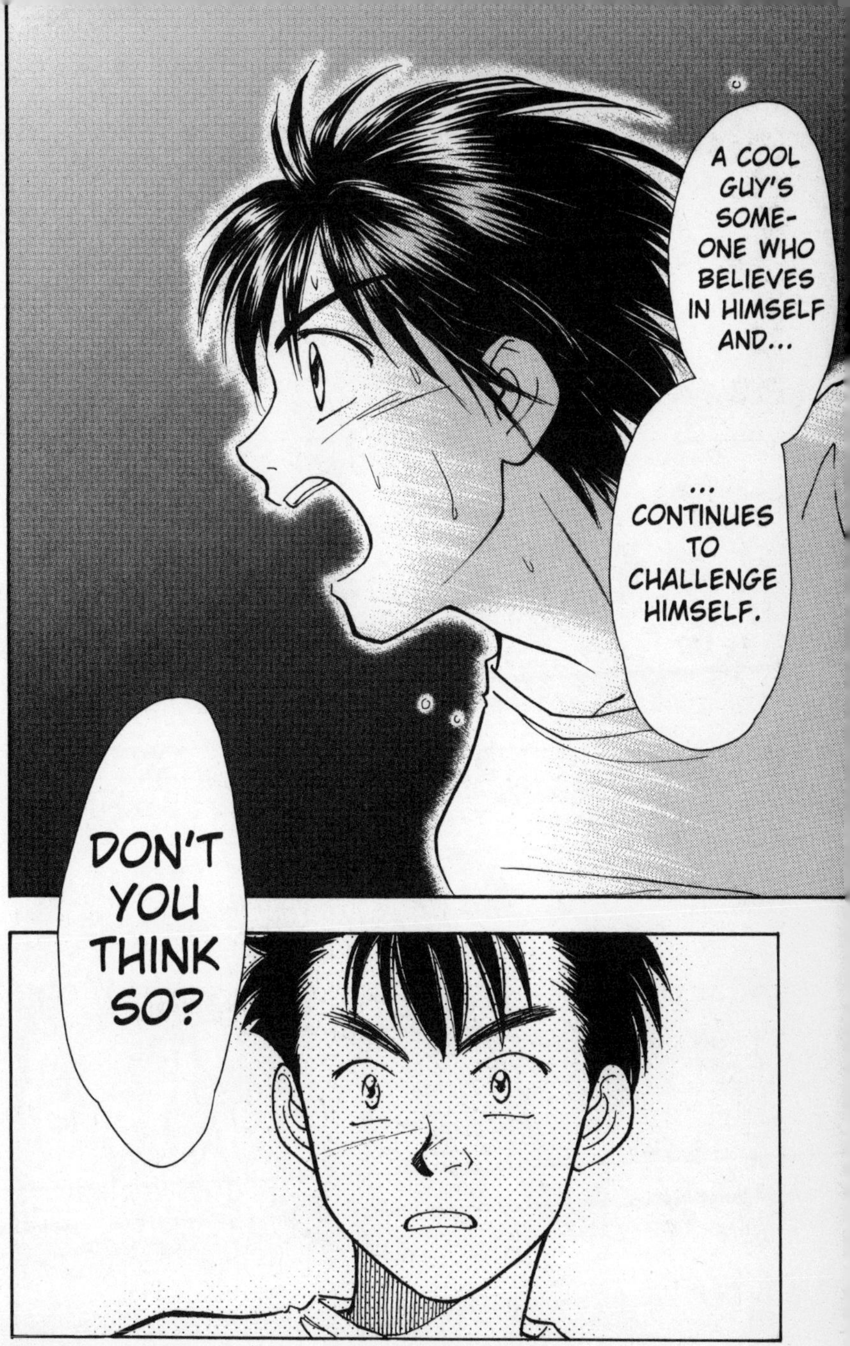
A COOL GUY'S SOME-ONE WHO BELIEVES IN HIMSELF AND...
... CONTINUES TO CHALLENGE HIMSELF.
DON'T YOU THINK SO?

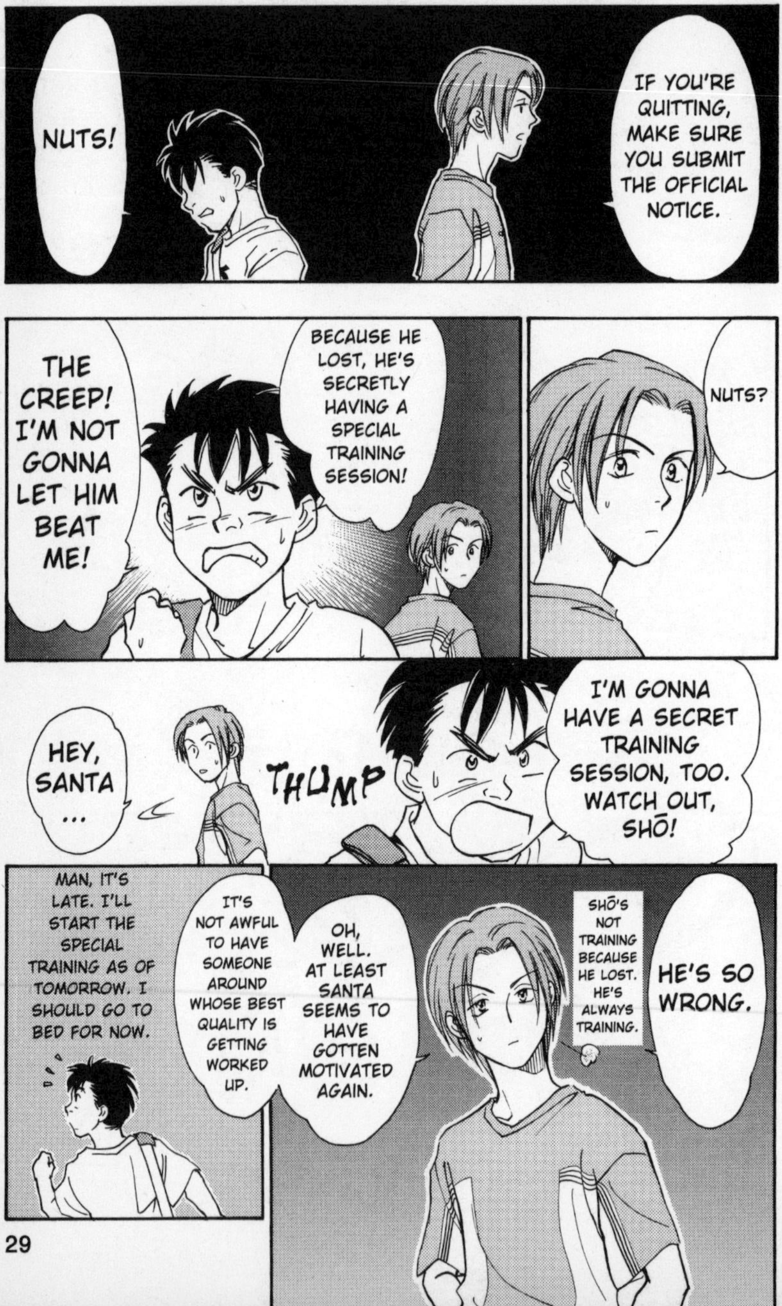
IF YOU'RE QUITTING, MAKE SURE YOU SUBMIT THE OFFICIAL NOTICE.
NUTS!
NUTS?
BECAUSE HE LOST, HE'S SECRETLY HAVING A SPECIAL TRAINING SESSION!
THE CREEP! I'M NOT GONNA LET HIM BEAT ME!
I'M GONNA HAVE A SECRET TRAINING SESSION, TOO. WATCH OUT, SHŌ!
THUMP
HEY, SANTA ...
HE'S SO WRONG.
SHŌ'S NOT TRAINING BECAUSE HE LOST. HE'S ALWAYS TRAINING.
OH, WELL. AT LEAST SANTA SEEMS TO HAVE GOTTEN MOTIVATED AGAIN.
IT'S NOT AWFUL TO HAVE SOMEONE AROUND WHOSE BEST QUALITY IS GETTING WORKED UP.
MAN, IT'S LATE. I'LL START THE SPECIAL TRAINING AS OF TOMORROW. I SHOULD GO TO BED FOR NOW.

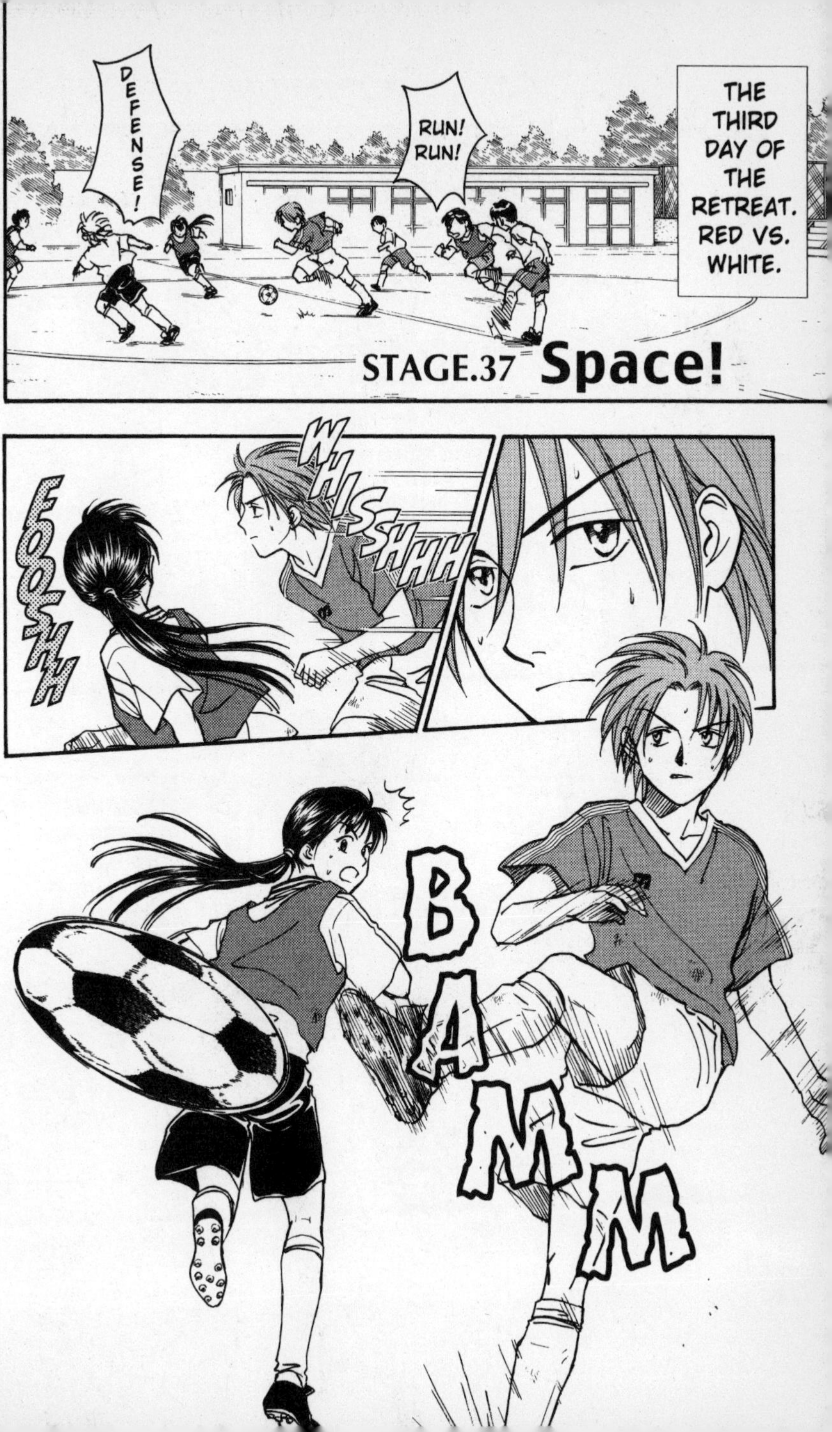
THE THIRD DAY OF THE RETREAT. RED VS. WHITE.
RUN! RUN!
DEFENSE!
STAGE.37 Space!
WHISSHHH
FOOSHHH
BAMM

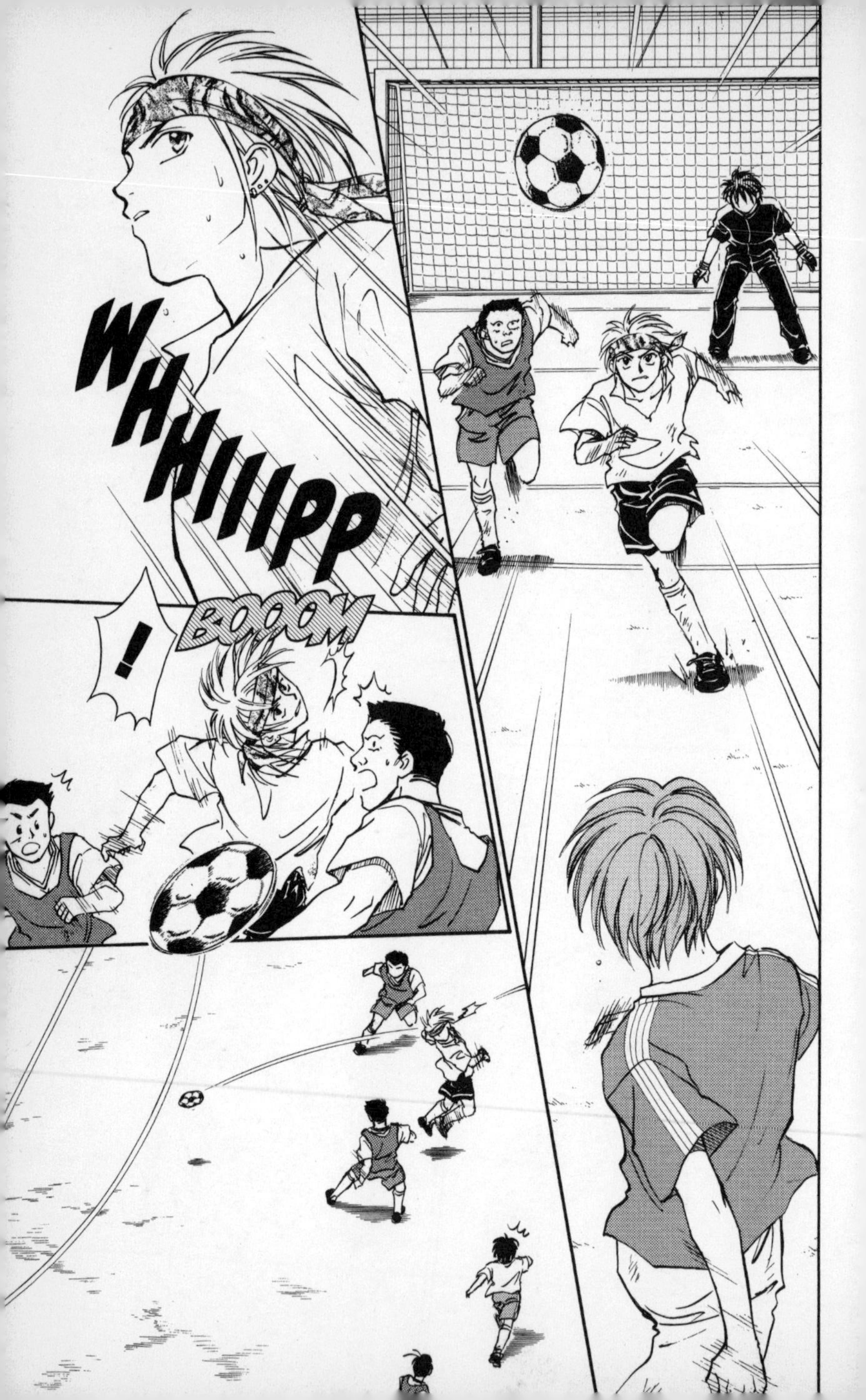
WHHIIIPP
!
BOOOM

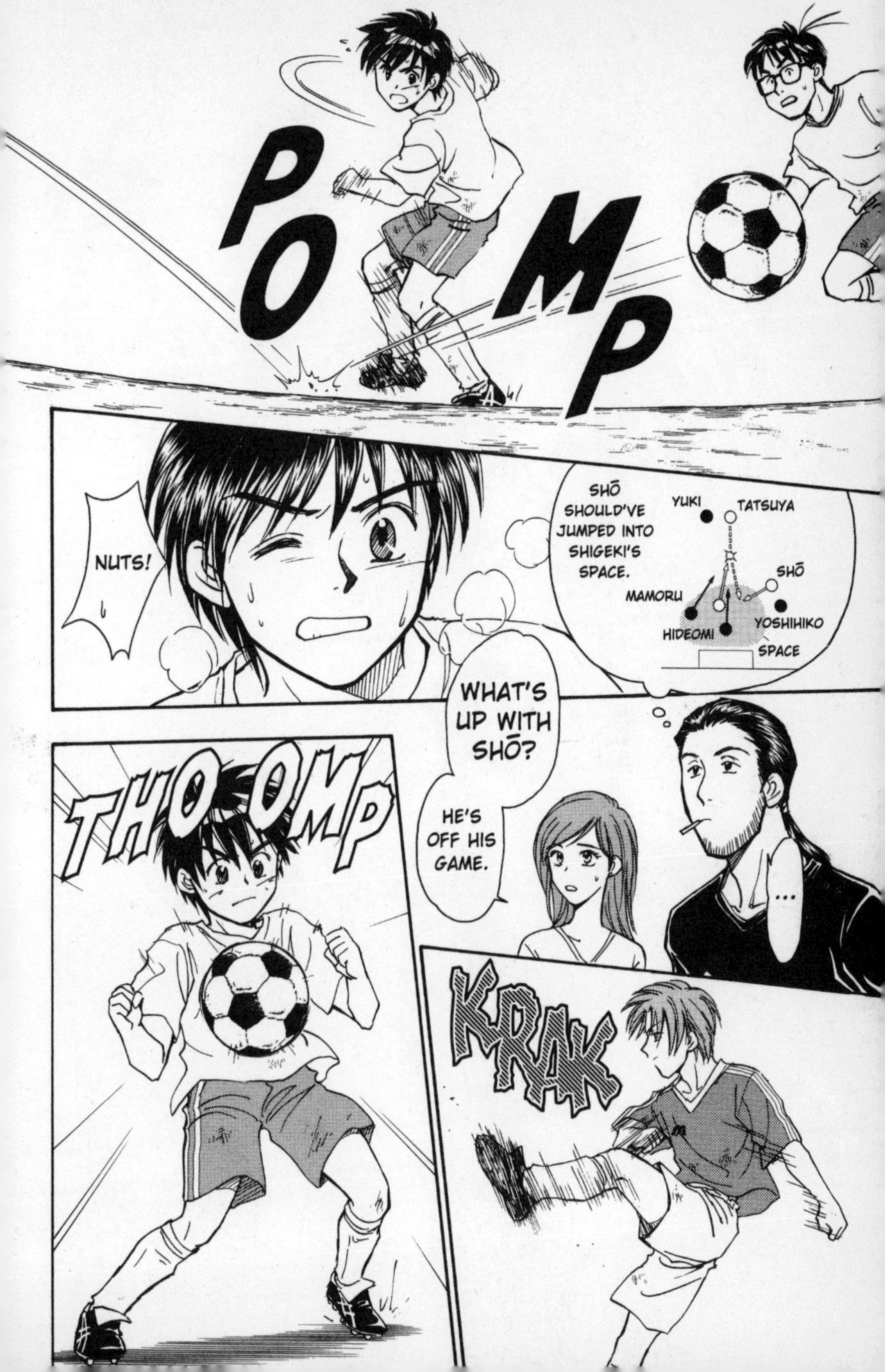
POMP
SHŌ SHOULD'VE JUMPED INTO SHIGEKI'S SPACE.
YUKI
TATSUYA
SHŌ
MAMORU
YOSHIHIKO
HIDEOMI
SPACE
NUTS!
WHAT'S UP WITH SHŌ?
HE'S OFF HIS GAME.
...
KRAK
THO-OMP

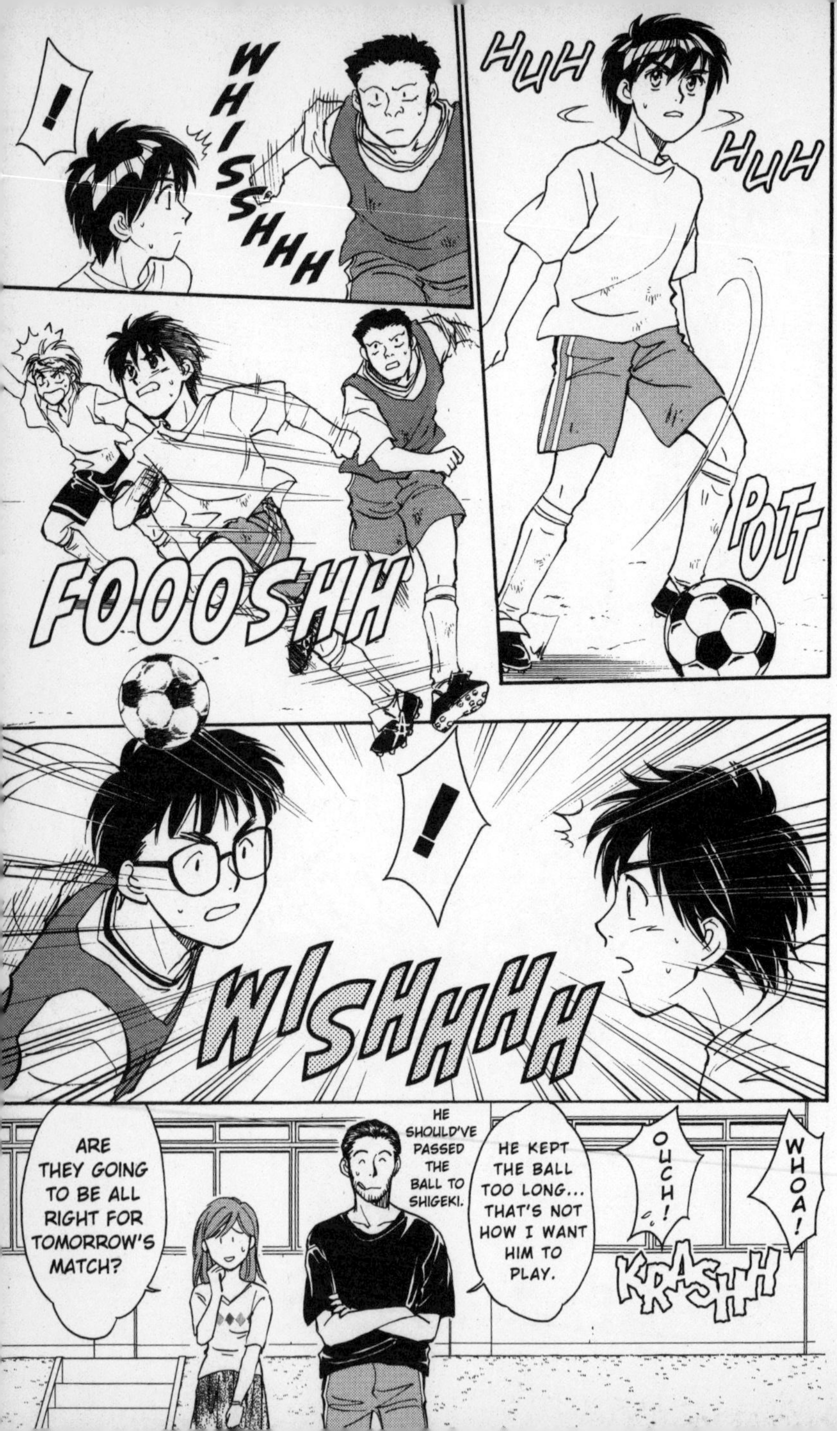

HUH
HUH
POTT
!
WHISSHHH
FOOOSHH
!
WISHHHH
WHOA!
OUCH!
KRASHH
HE KEPT THE BALL TOO LONG... THAT'S NOT HOW I WANT HIM TO PLAY.
HE SHOULD'VE PASSED THE BALL TO SHIGEKI.
ARE THEY GOING TO BE ALL RIGHT FOR TOMORROW'S MATCH?

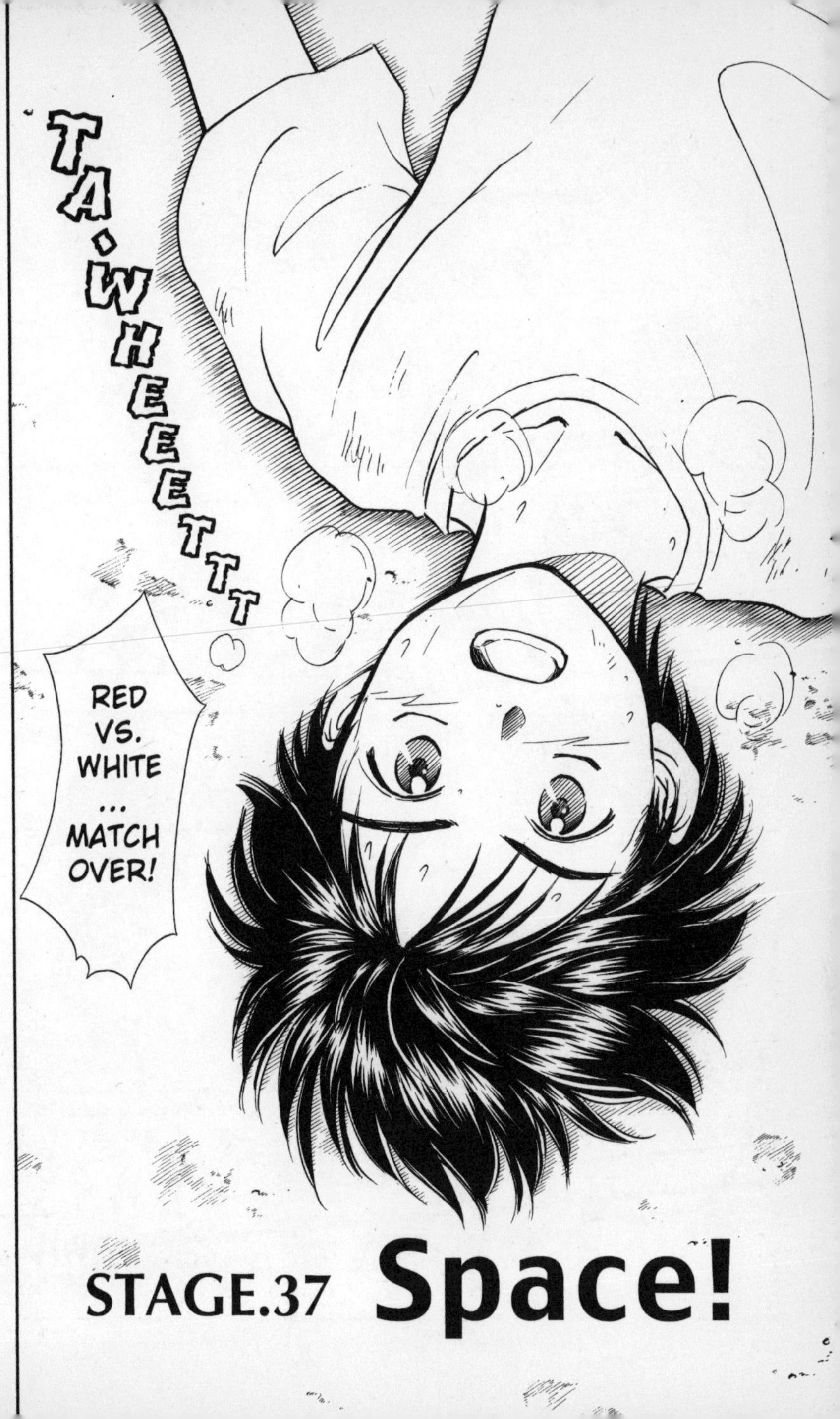
TA-WHEEETTT
RED VS. WHITE ... MATCH OVER!

STAGE.37 Space!

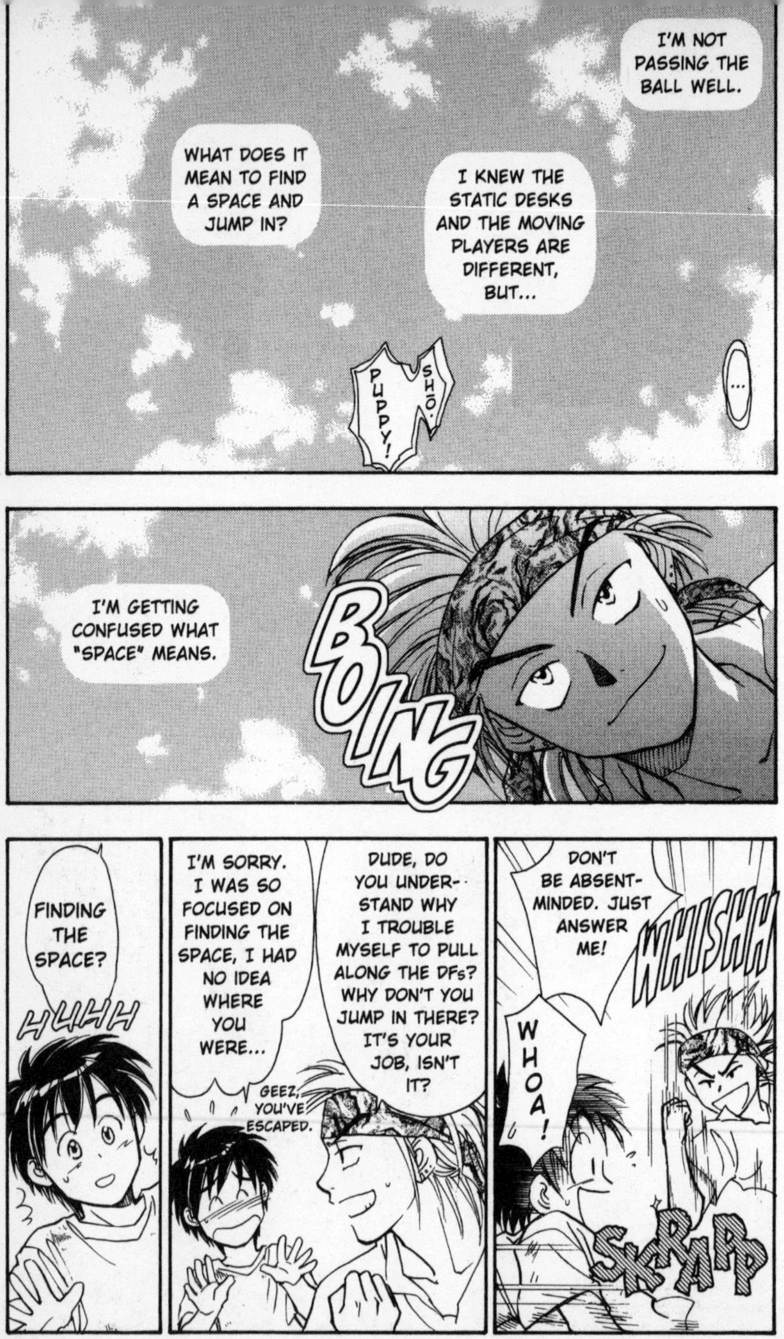
I'M NOT PASSING THE BALL WELL.
I KNEW THE STATIC DESKS AND THE MOVING PLAYERS ARE DIFFERENT, BUT...
WHAT DOES IT MEAN TO FIND A SPACE AND JUMP IN?
...
SHŌ. PUPPY!
BOING
I'M GETTING CONFUSED WHAT "SPACE" MEANS.
DON'T BE ABSENT-MINDED. JUST ANSWER ME!
WHISHH
WHOA!
SKRAPP
DUDE, DO YOU UNDER-STAND WHY I TROUBLE MYSELF TO PULL ALONG THE DFs? WHY DON'T YOU JUMP IN THERE? IT'S YOUR JOB, ISN'T IT?
I'M SORRY. I WAS SO FOCUSED ON FINDING THE SPACE, I HAD NO IDEA WHERE YOU WERE...
GEEZ, YOU'VE ESCAPED.
FINDING THE SPACE?
HUHH

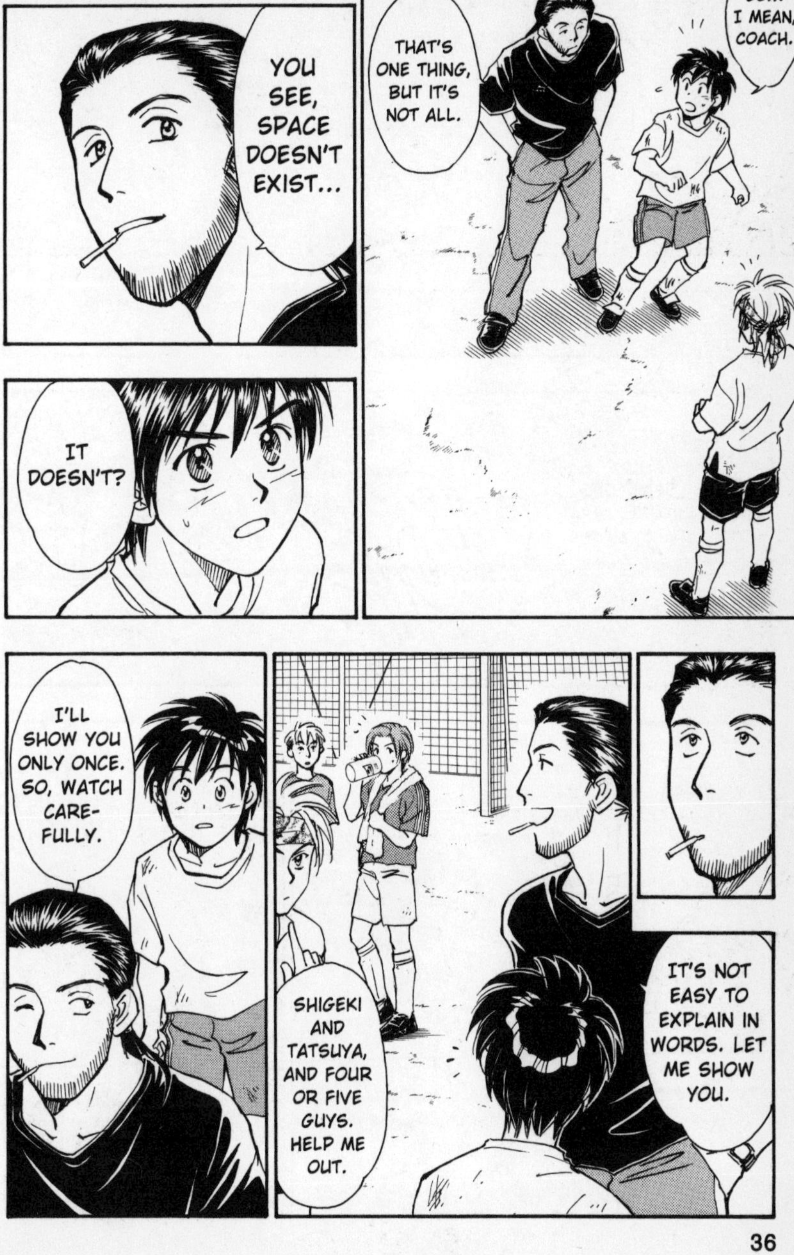
SŌ... I MEAN, COACH.
THAT'S ONE THING, BUT IT'S NOT ALL.
YOU SEE, SPACE DOESN'T EXIST...
IT DOESN'T?
IT'S NOT EASY TO EXPLAIN IN WORDS. LET ME SHOW YOU.
SHIGEKI AND TATSUYA, AND FOUR OR FIVE GUYS. HELP ME OUT.
I'LL SHOW YOU ONLY ONCE. SO, WATCH CARE-FULLY.

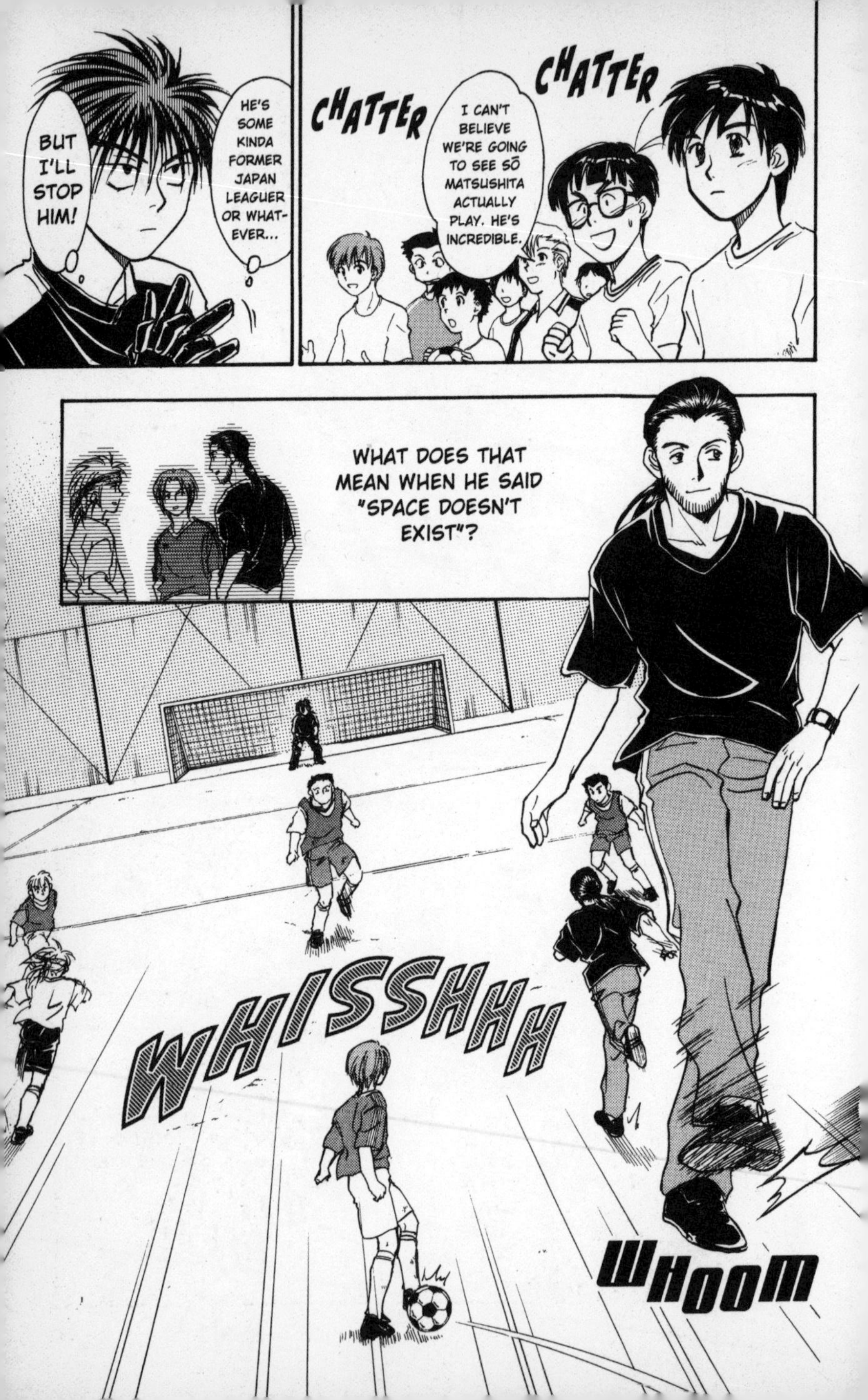
CHATTER
I CAN'T BELIEVE WE'RE GOING TO SEE SŌ MATSUSHITA ACTUALLY PLAY. HE'S INCREDIBLE.
CHATTER
HE'S SOME KINDA FORMER JAPAN LEAGUER OR WHAT-EVER...
BUT I'LL STOP HIM!
WHAT DOES THAT MEAN WHEN HE SAID "SPACE DOESN'T EXIST"?
WHOOM
WHISSHHH

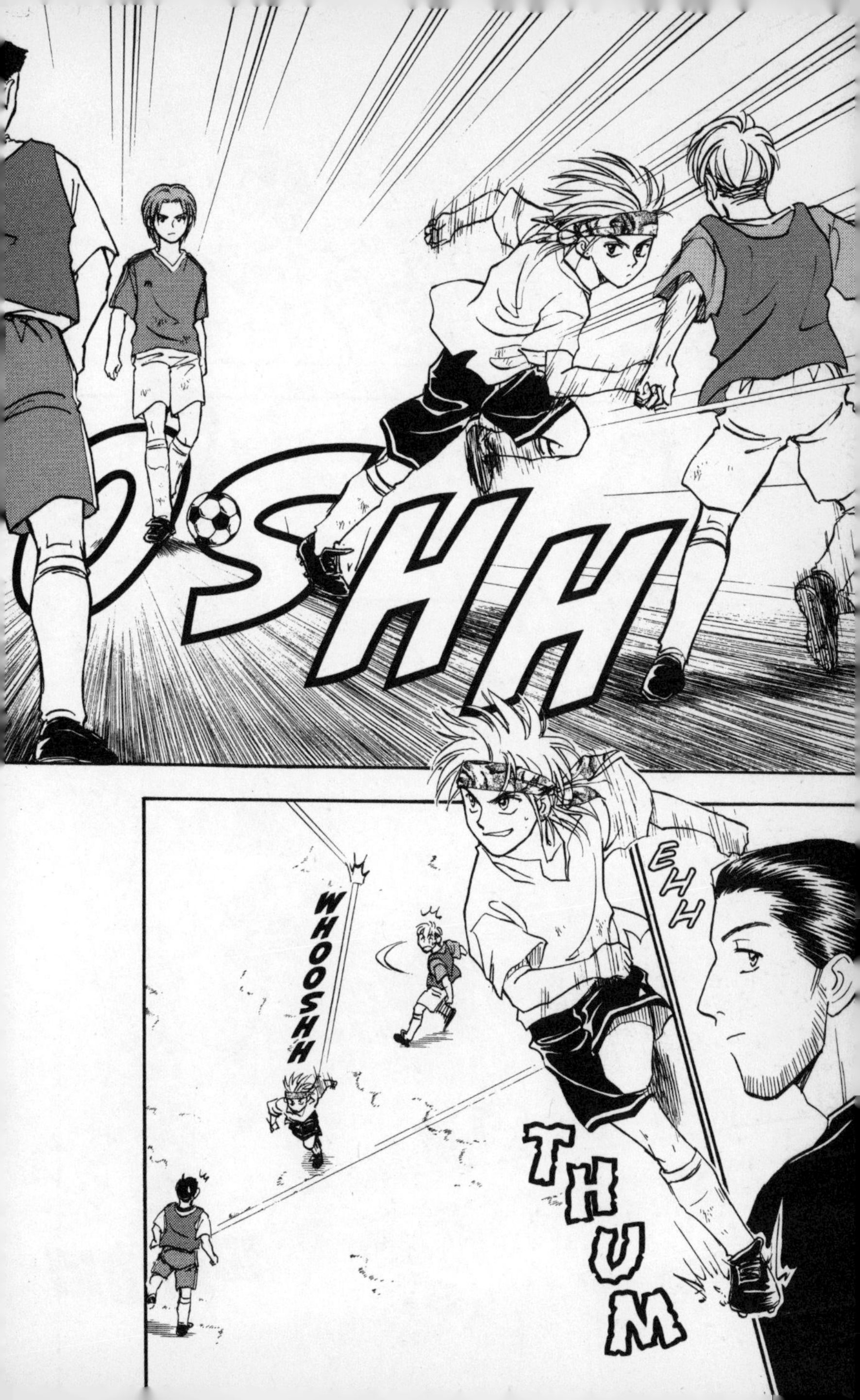
SHH
EHH
WHOOOSHH
THUM

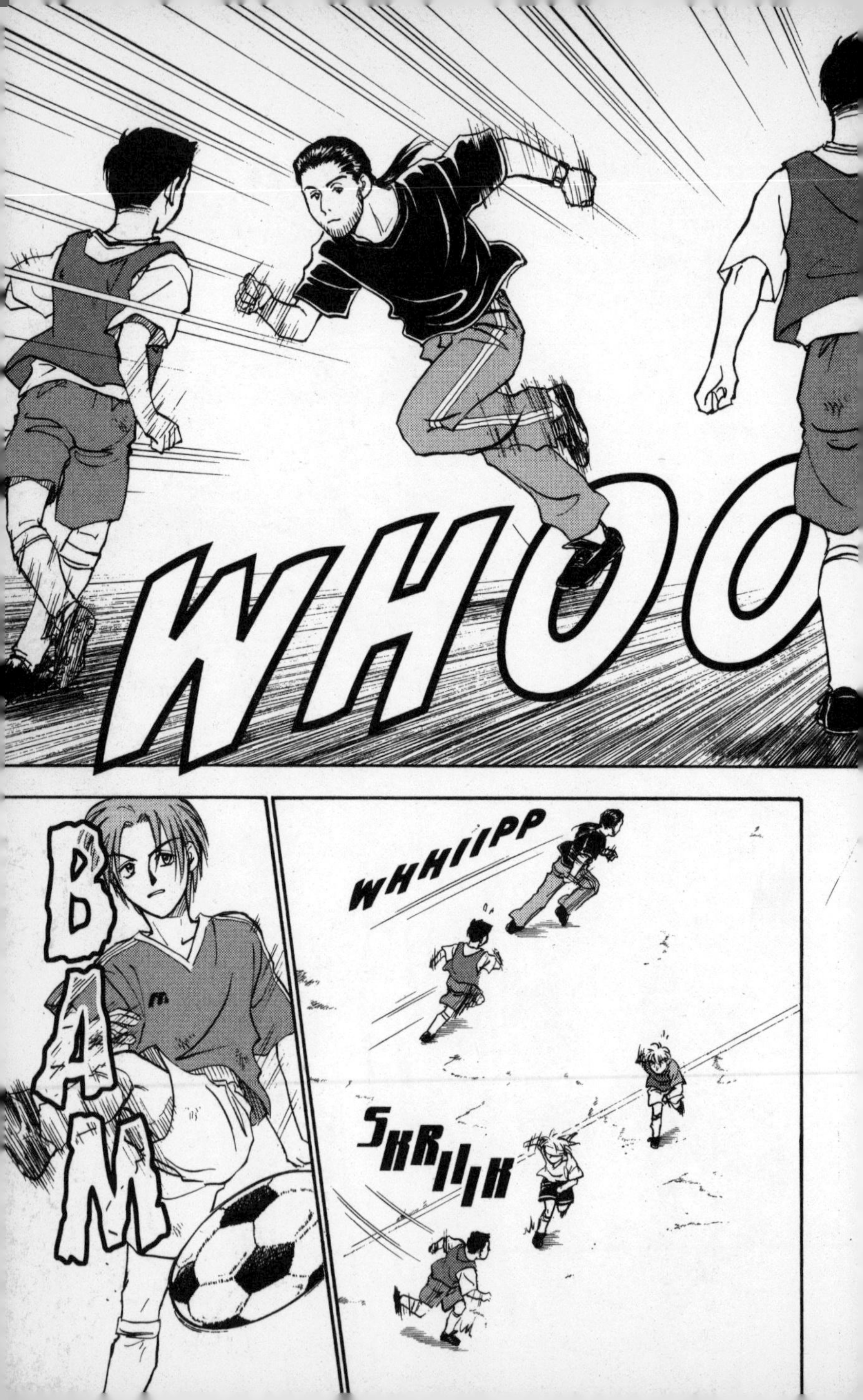
WHOO
WHHIIPP
SKRIIIK
BAM

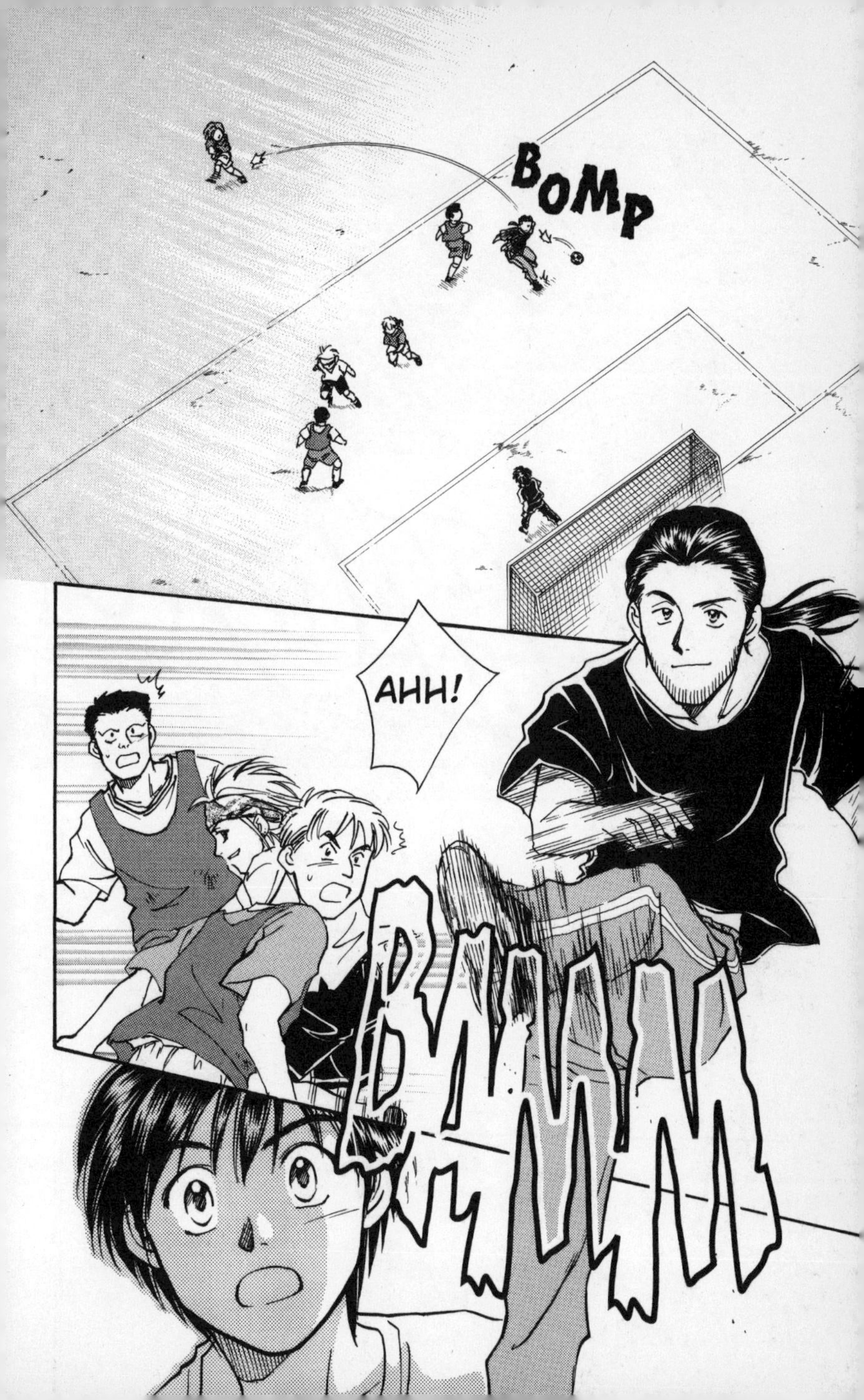
BOMP
AHH!

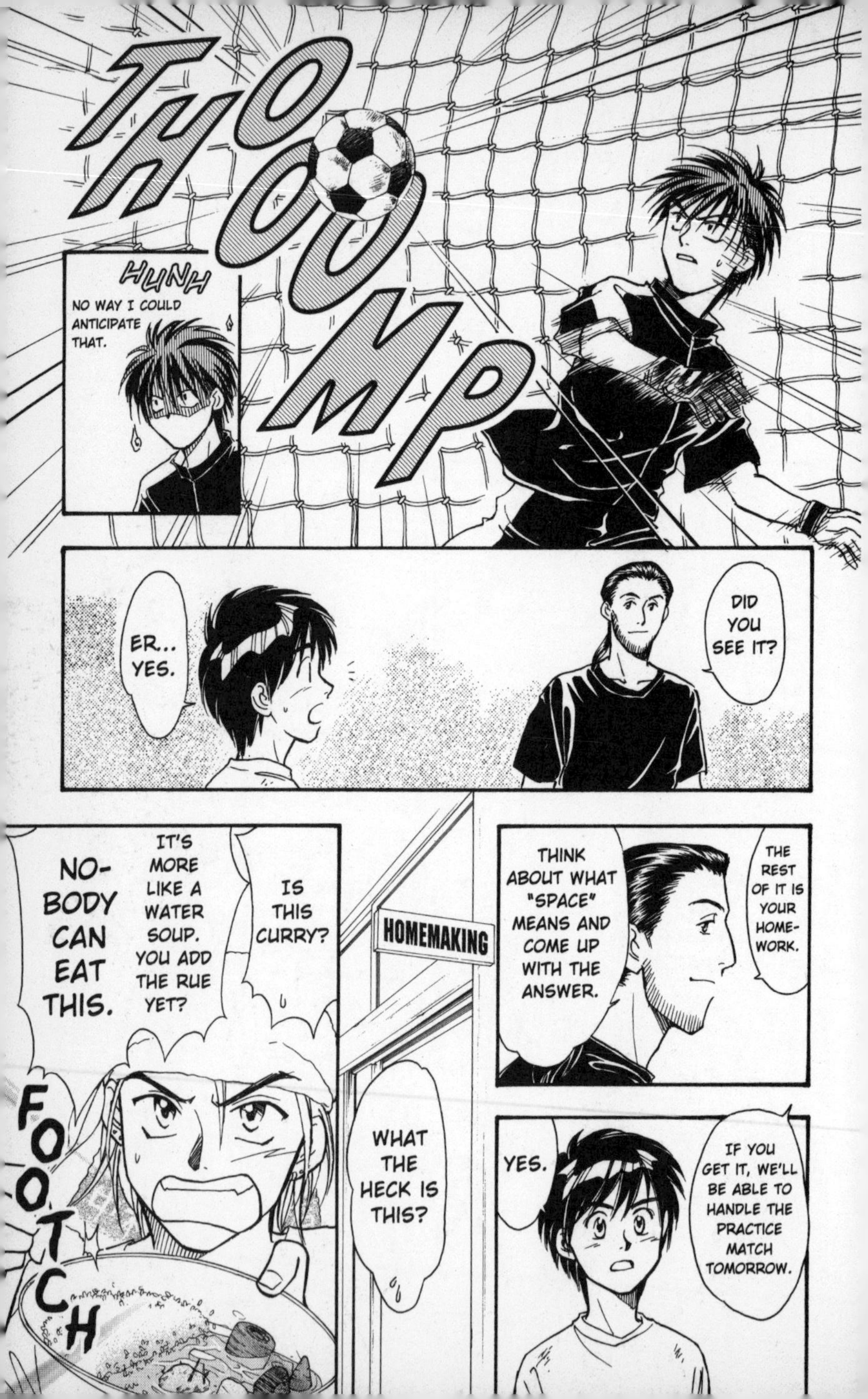
THOOOMP
HUNH
NO WAY I COULD ANTICIPATE THAT.
DID YOU SEE IT?
ER... YES.
THE REST OF IT IS YOUR HOME-WORK.
THINK ABOUT WHAT "SPACE" MEANS AND COME UP WITH THE ANSWER.
IF YOU GET IT, WE'LL BE ABLE TO HANDLE THE PRACTICE MATCH TOMORROW.
YES.
HOMEMAKING
IS THIS CURRY?
IT'S MORE LIKE A WATER SOUP. YOU ADD THE RUE YET?
NO-BODY CAN EAT THIS.
WHAT THE HECK IS THIS?
FOOTCH

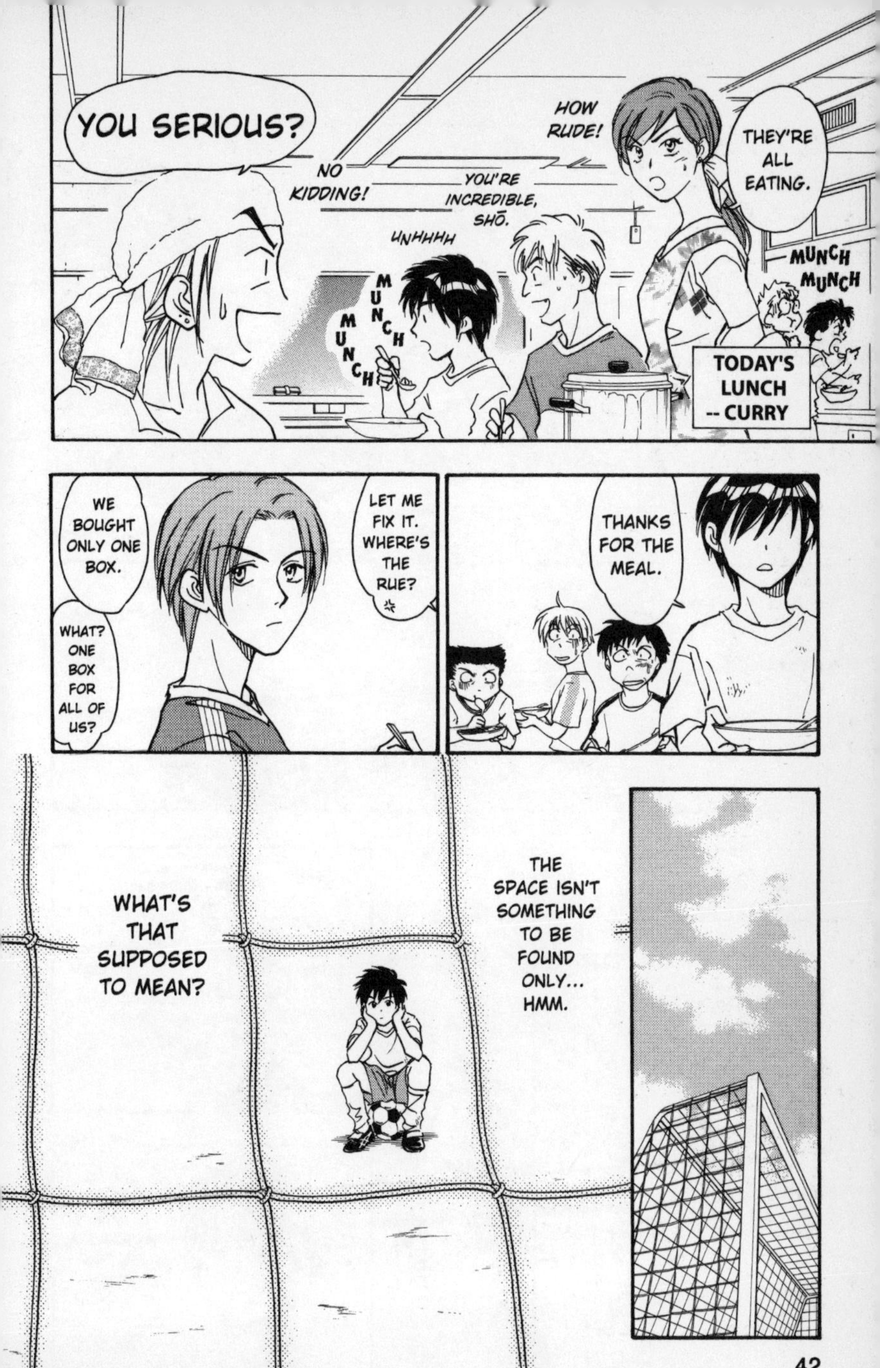

THEY'RE ALL EATING.
MUNCH MUNCH
TODAY'S LUNCH -- CURRY
HOW RUDE!
YOU'RE INCREDIBLE, SHŌ.
UNHHHH
MUNCH MUNCH
NO KIDDING!
YOU SERIOUS?
THANKS FOR THE MEAL.
LET ME FIX IT. WHERE'S THE RUE?
WE BOUGHT ONLY ONE BOX.
WHAT? ONE BOX FOR ALL OF US?
THE SPACE ISN'T SOMETHING TO BE FOUND ONLY... HMM.
WHAT'S THAT SUPPOSED TO MEAN?

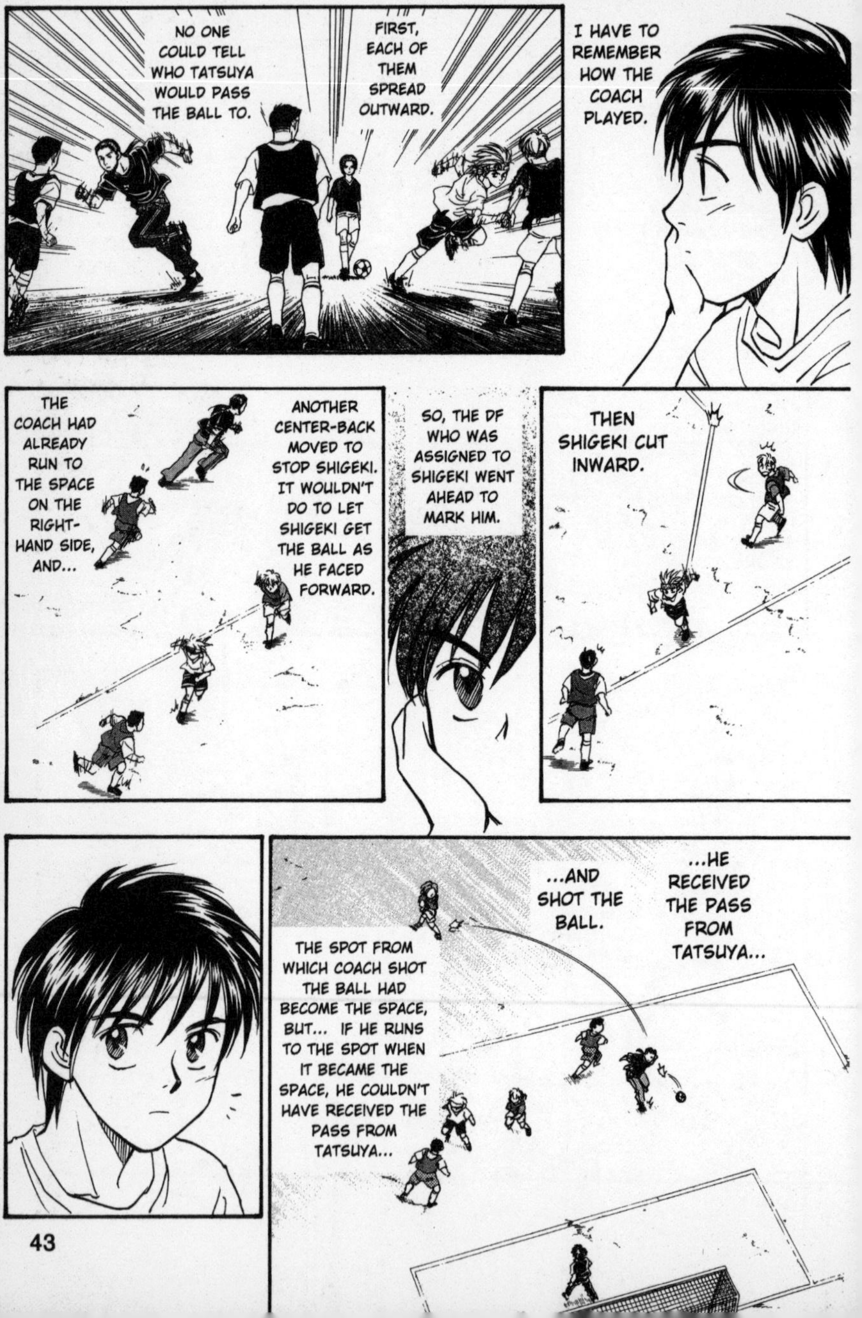
I HAVE TO REMEMBER HOW THE COACH PLAYED.
FIRST, EACH OF THEM SPREAD OUTWARD.
NO ONE COULD TELL WHO TATSUYA WOULD PASS THE BALL TO.
THEN SHIGEKI CUT INWARD.
SO, THE DF WHO WAS ASSIGNED TO SHIGEKI WENT AHEAD TO MARK HIM.
ANOTHER CENTER-BACK MOVED TO STOP SHIGEKI. IT WOULDN'T DO TO LET SHIGEKI GET THE BALL AS HE FACED FORWARD.
THE COACH HAD ALREADY RUN TO THE SPACE ON THE RIGHT-HAND SIDE, AND...
...HE RECEIVED THE PASS FROM TATSUYA...
...AND SHOT THE BALL.
THE SPOT FROM WHICH COACH SHOT THE BALL HAD BECOME THE SPACE, BUT... IF HE RUNS TO THE SPOT WHEN IT BECAME THE SPACE, HE COULDN'T HAVE RECEIVED THE PASS FROM TATSUYA...

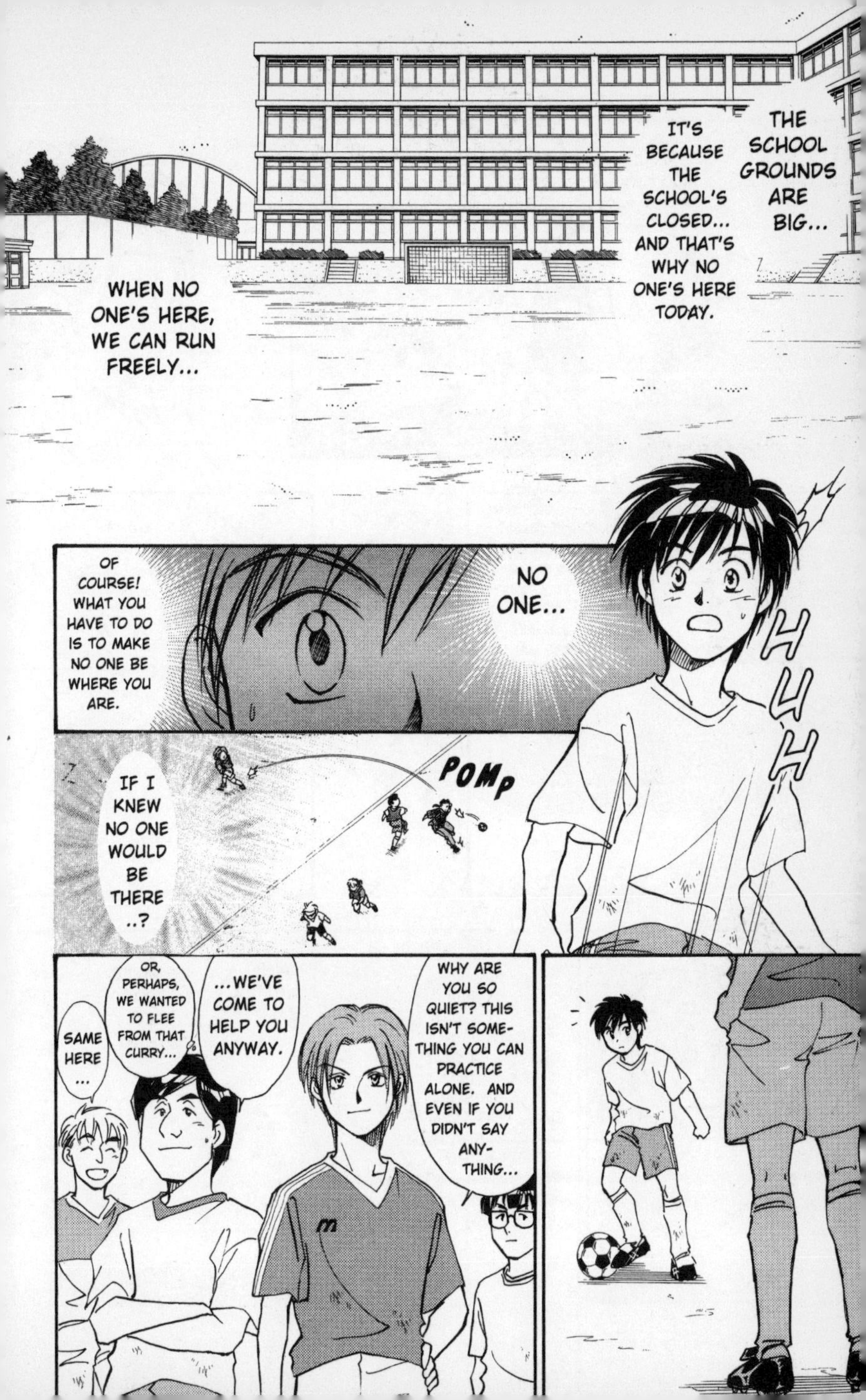
THE SCHOOL GROUNDS ARE BIG...
IT'S BECAUSE THE SCHOOL'S CLOSED... AND THAT'S WHY NO ONE'S HERE TODAY.
WHEN NO ONE'S HERE, WE CAN RUN FREELY...
HUH
NO ONE...
OF COURSE! WHAT YOU HAVE TO DO IS TO MAKE NO ONE BE WHERE YOU ARE.
POMP
IF I KNEW NO ONE WOULD BE THERE ..?
WHY ARE YOU SO QUIET? THIS ISN'T SOMETHING YOU CAN PRACTICE ALONE. AND EVEN IF YOU DIDN'T SAY ANYTHING...
...WE'VE COME TO HELP YOU ANYWAY.
OR, PERHAPS, WE WANTED TO FLEE FROM THAT CURRY...
SAME HERE ...

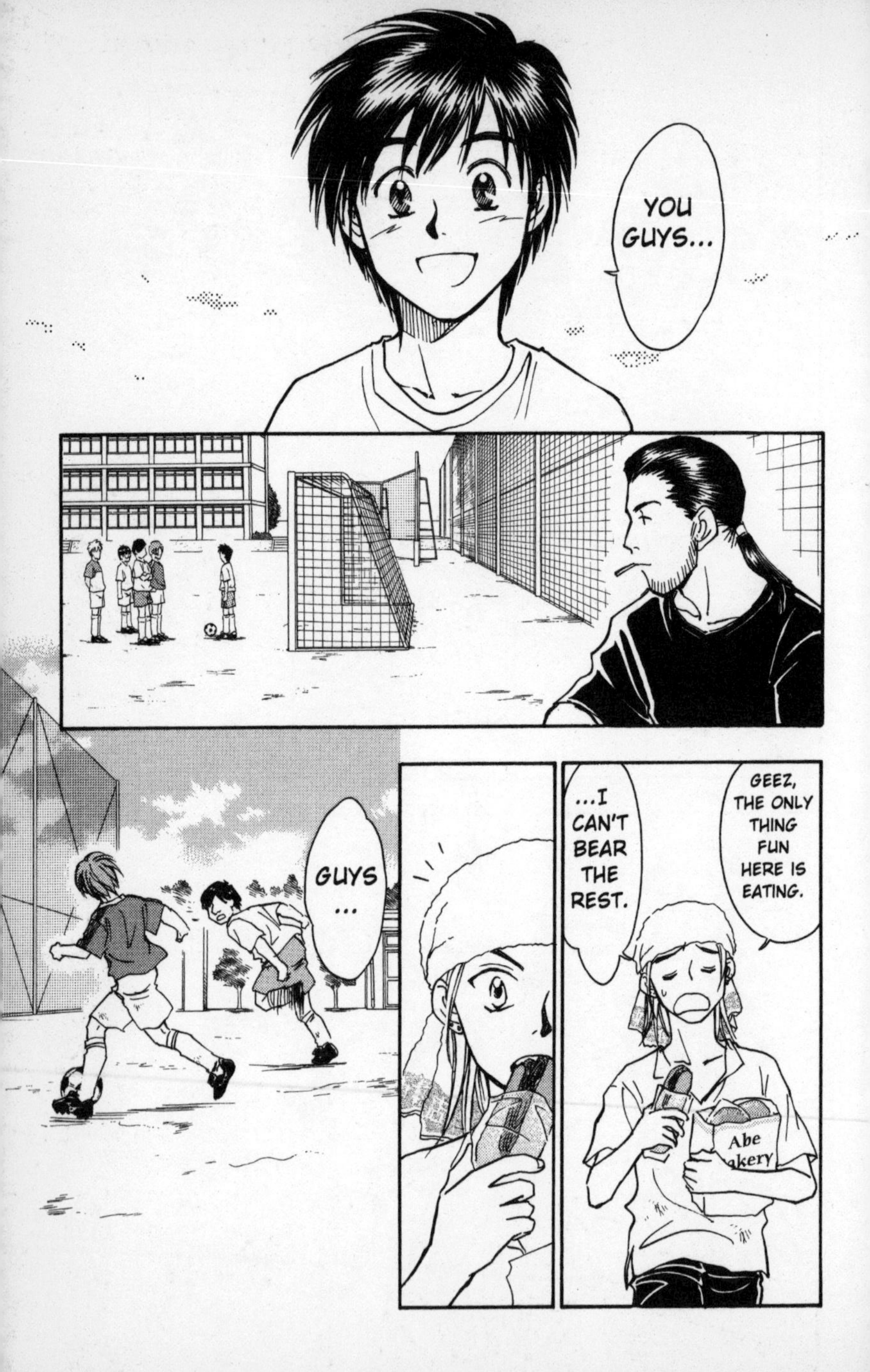
YOU GUYS...
GEEZ, THE ONLY THING FUN HERE IS EATING.
...I CAN'T BEAR THE REST.
Abe
GUYS ...

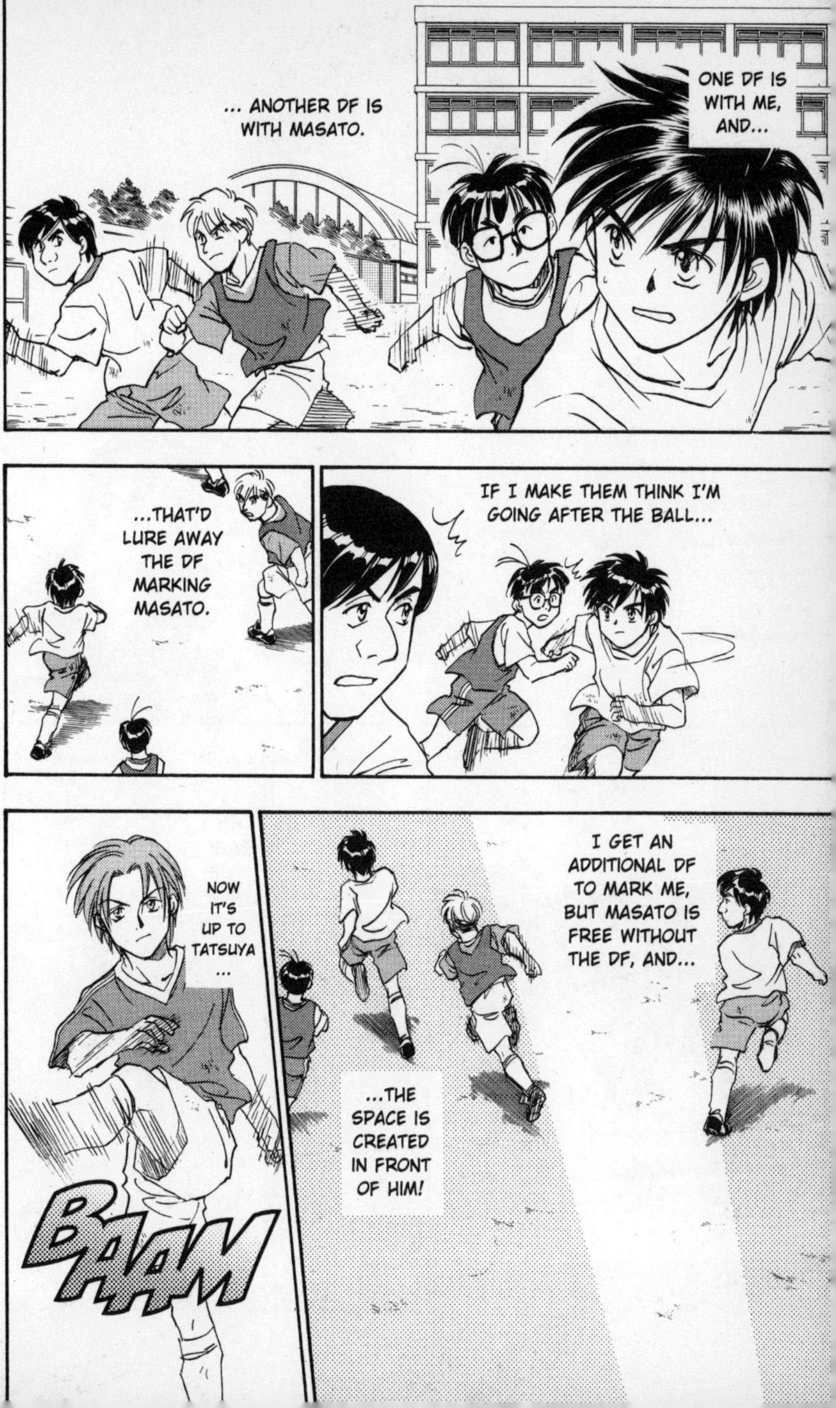
ONE DF IS WITH ME, AND...
... ANOTHER DF IS WITH MASATO.
IF I MAKE THEM THINK I'M GOING AFTER THE BALL...
...THAT'D LURE AWAY THE DF MARKING MASATO.
I GET AN ADDITIONAL DF TO MARK ME, BUT MASATO IS FREE WITHOUT THE DF, AND...
...THE SPACE IS CREATED IN FRONT OF HIM!
NOW IT'S UP TO TATSUYA ...
BAAM

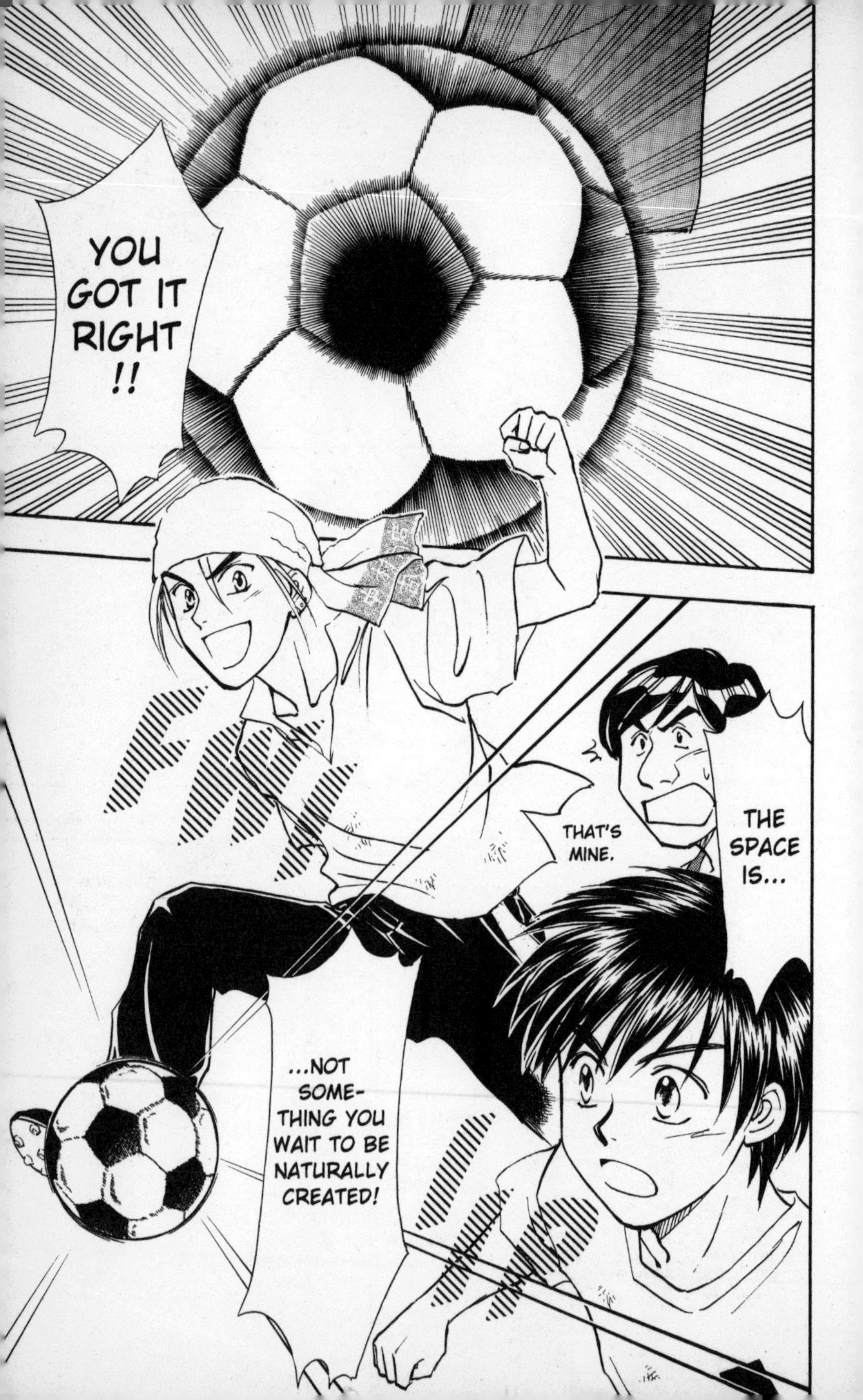
YOU GOT IT RIGHT !!
THE SPACE IS...
THAT'S MINE.
...NOT SOME-THING YOU WAIT TO BE NATURALLY CREATED!

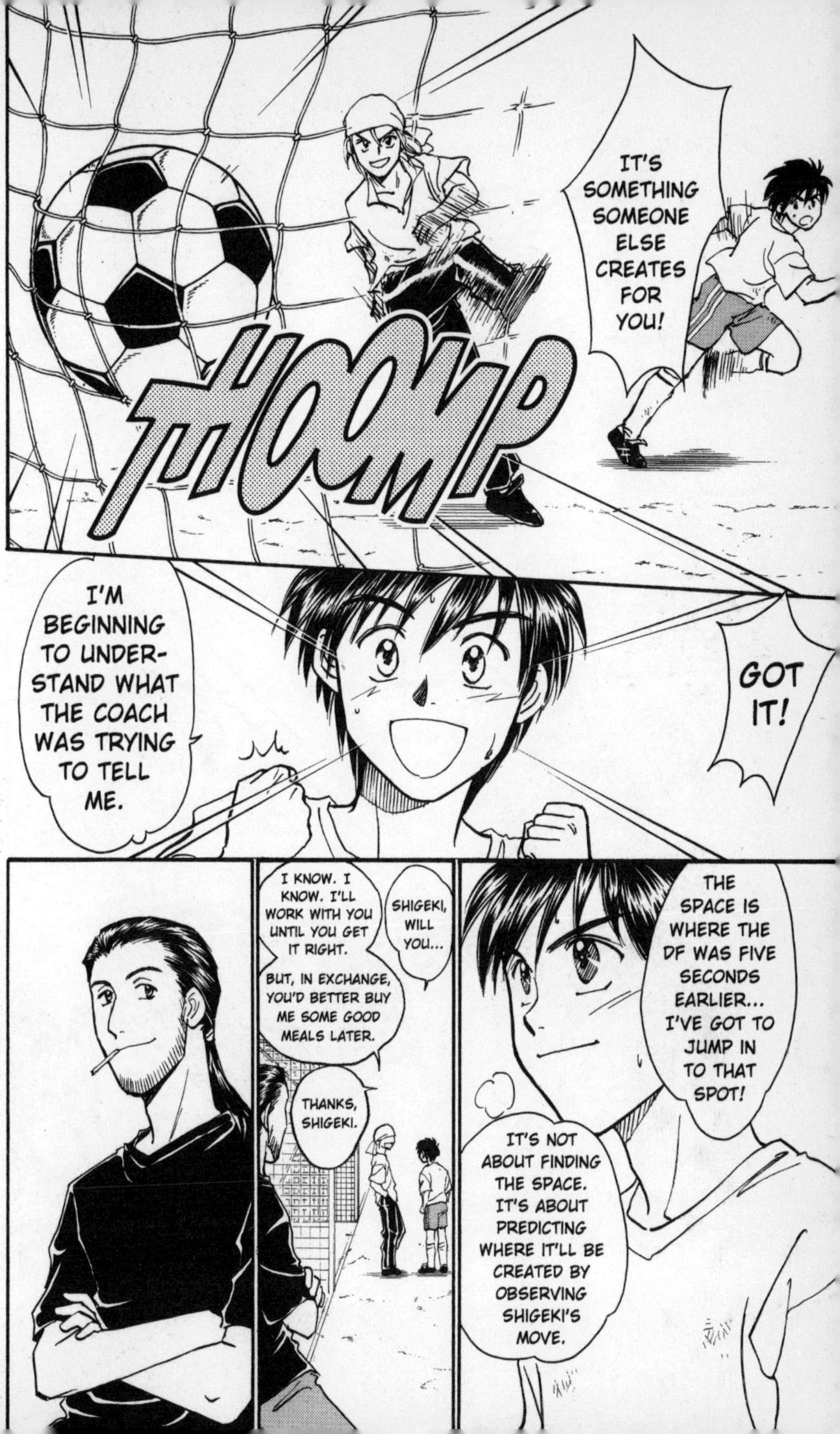
IT'S SOMETHING SOMEONE ELSE CREATES FOR YOU!
THOOMP
GOT IT!
I'M BEGINNING TO UNDER-STAND WHAT THE COACH WAS TRYING TO TELL ME.
THE SPACE IS WHERE THE DF WAS FIVE SECONDS EARLIER... I'VE GOT TO JUMP IN TO THAT SPOT!
IT'S NOT ABOUT FINDING THE SPACE. IT'S ABOUT PREDICTING WHERE IT'LL BE CREATED BY OBSERVING SHIGEKI'S MOVE.
SHIGEKI, WILL YOU...
I KNOW. I KNOW. I'LL WORK WITH YOU UNTIL YOU GET IT RIGHT.
BUT, IN EXCHANGE, YOU'D BETTER BUY ME SOME GOOD MEALS LATER.
THANKS, SHIGEKI.

STAGE.38

We're Teammates, Aren't We?

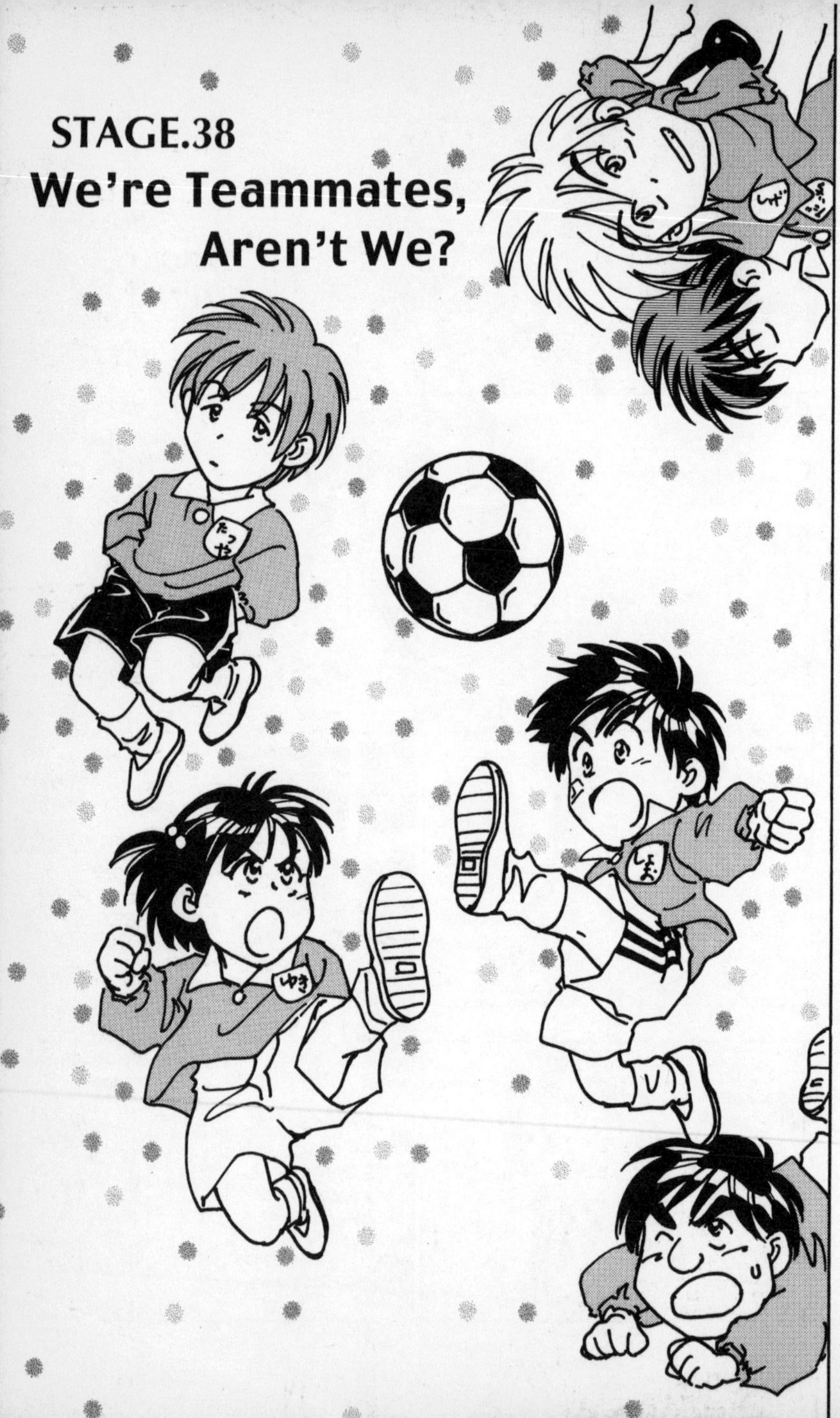

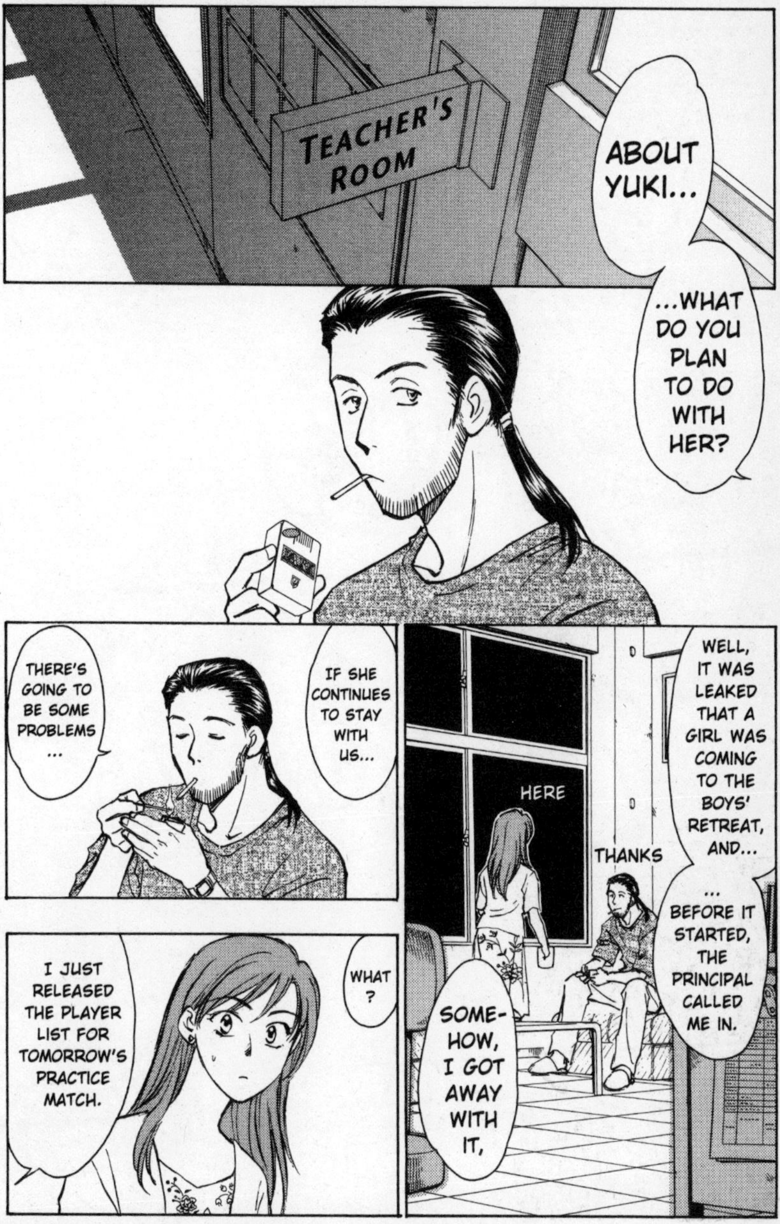
TEACHER'S ROOM
ABOUT YUKI...
...WHAT DO YOU PLAN TO DO WITH HER?
WELL, IT WAS LEAKED THAT A GIRL WAS COMING TO THE BOYS' RETREAT, AND...
HERE
THANKS
... BEFORE IT STARTED, THE PRINCIPAL CALLED ME IN.
SOME-HOW, I GOT AWAY WITH IT,
IF SHE CONTINUES TO STAY WITH US...
THERE'S GOING TO BE SOME PROBLEMS ...
WHAT ?
I JUST RELEASED THE PLAYER LIST FOR TOMORROW'S PRACTICE MATCH.

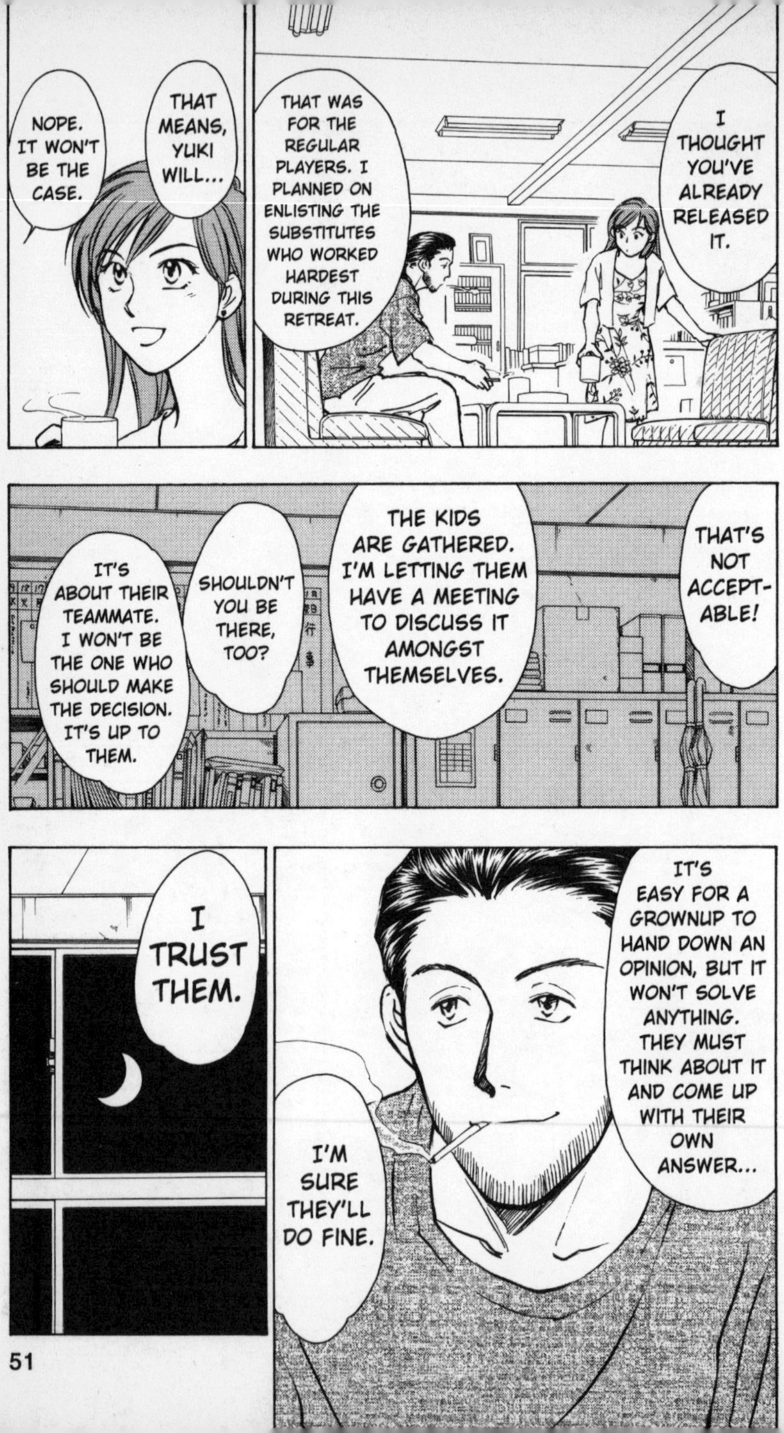
I THOUGHT YOU'VE ALREADY RELEASED IT.
THAT WAS FOR THE REGULAR PLAYERS. I PLANNED ON ENLISTING THE SUBSTITUTES WHO WORKED HARDEST DURING THIS RETREAT.
THAT MEANS, YUKI WILL...
NOPE. IT WON'T BE THE CASE.
THAT'S NOT ACCEPT-ABLE!
THE KIDS ARE GATHERED. I'M LETTING THEM HAVE A MEETING TO DISCUSS IT AMONGST THEMSELVES.
SHOULDN'T YOU BE THERE, TOO?
IT'S ABOUT THEIR TEAMMATE. I WON'T BE THE ONE WHO SHOULD MAKE THE DECISION. IT'S UP TO THEM.
IT'S EASY FOR A GROWNUP TO HAND DOWN AN OPINION, BUT IT WON'T SOLVE ANYTHING. THEY MUST THINK ABOUT IT AND COME UP WITH THEIR OWN ANSWER...
I'M SURE THEY'LL DO FINE.
I TRUST THEM.

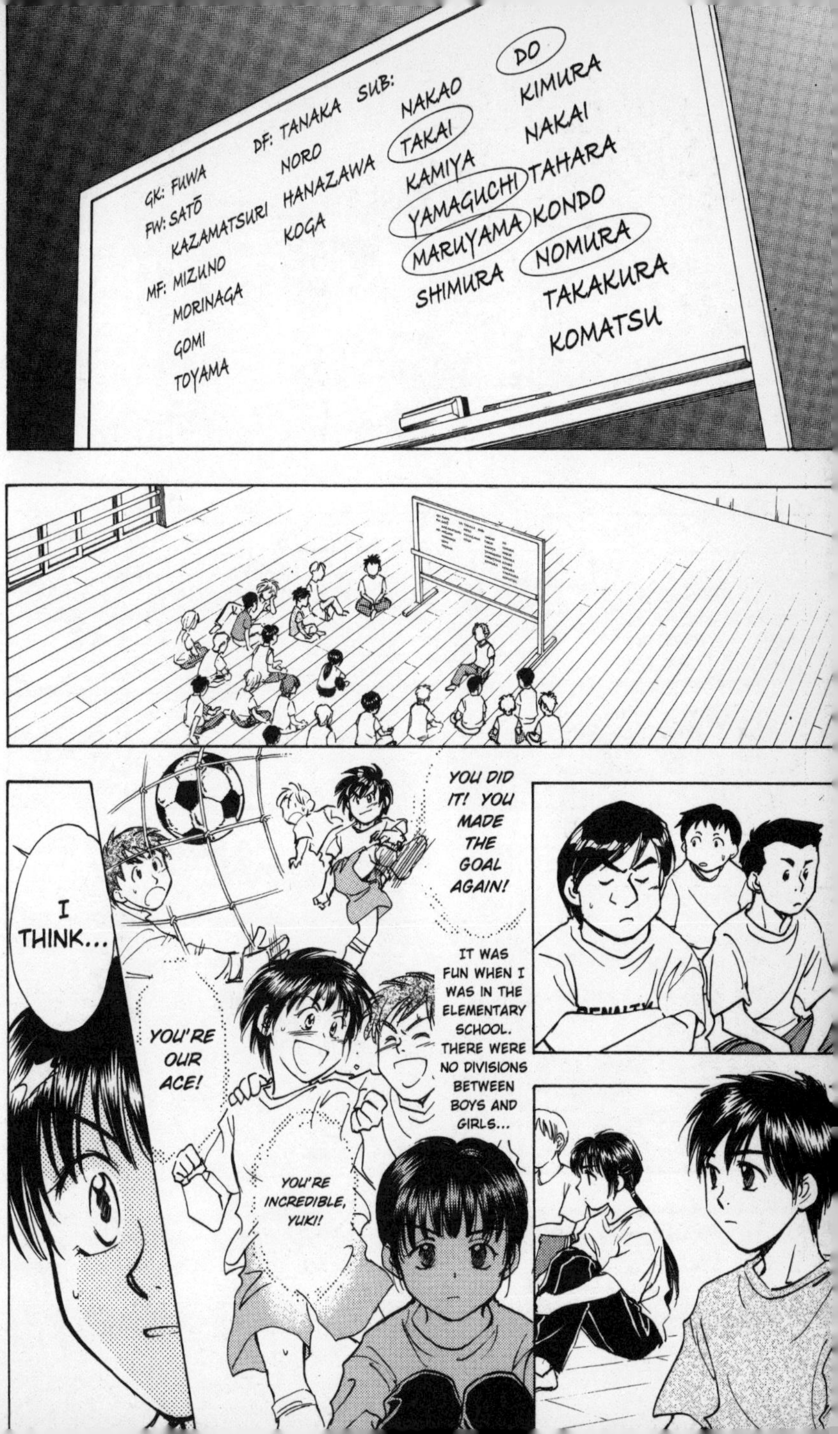
GK: FUWA
FW: SATŌ
KAZAMATSURI
MF: MIZUNO
MORINAGA
GOMI
TOYAMA
DF: TANAKA
NORO
HANAZAWA
KOGA
SUB:
NAKAO
TAKAI
KAMIYA
YAMAGUCHI
MARUYAMA
SHIMURA
DO
KIMURA
NAKAI
TAHARA
KONDO
NOMURA
TAKAKURA
KOMATSU
YOU DID IT! YOU MADE THE GOAL AGAIN!
I THINK...
IT WAS FUN WHEN I WAS IN THE ELEMENTARY SCHOOL. THERE WERE NO DIVISIONS BETWEEN BOYS AND GIRLS...
YOU'RE OUR ACE!
YOU'RE INCREDIBLE, YUKI!

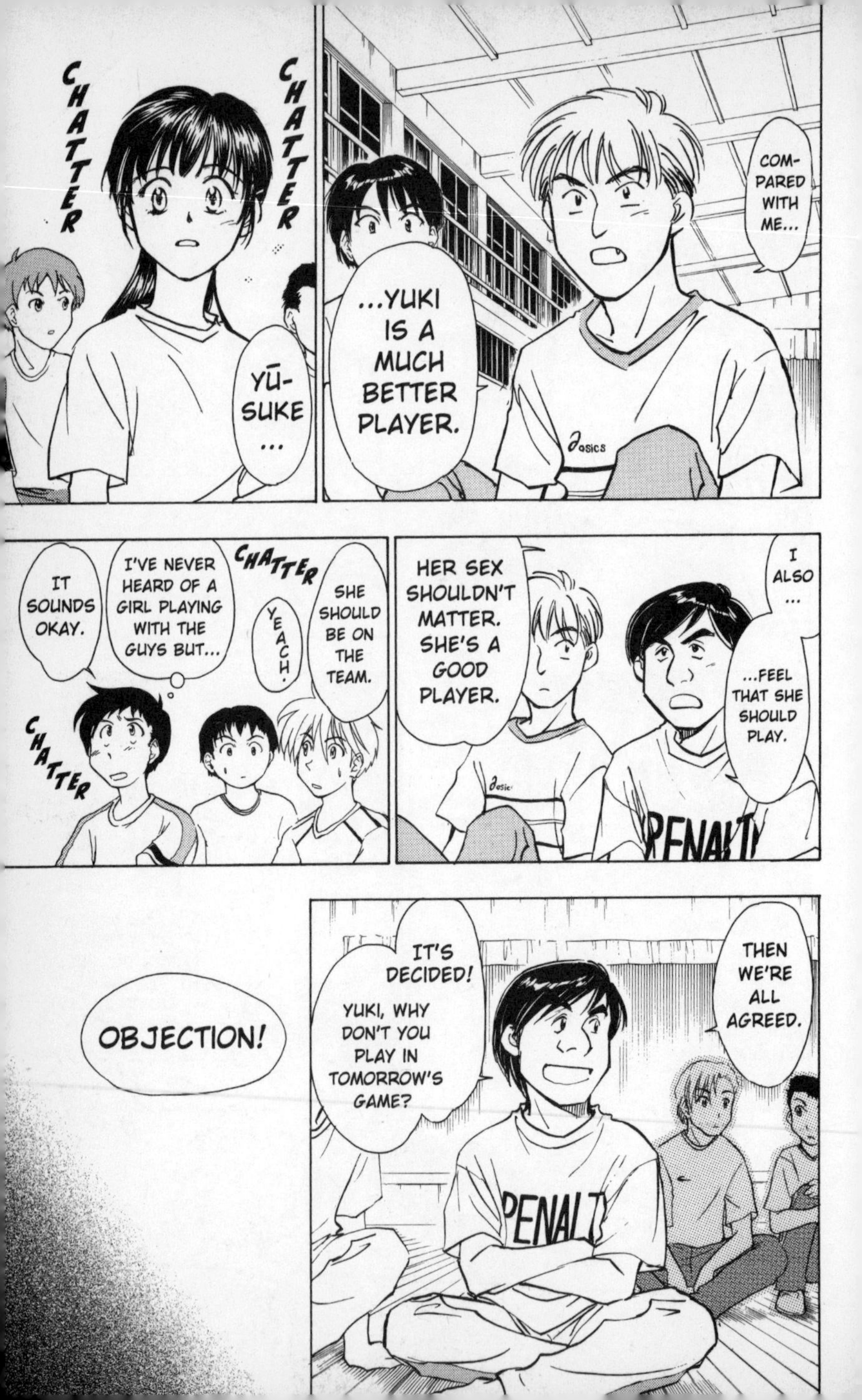
COMPARED WITH ME...
...YUKI IS A MUCH BETTER PLAYER.
CHATTER
YŪSUKE...
CHATTER
I ALSO...
...FEEL THAT SHE SHOULD PLAY.
HER SEX SHOULDN'T MATTER. SHE'S A GOOD PLAYER.
SHE SHOULD BE ON THE TEAM.
CHATTER
YEACH.
I'VE NEVER HEARD OF A GIRL PLAYING WITH THE GUYS BUT...
IT SOUNDS OKAY.
CHATTER
THEN WE'RE ALL AGREED.
IT'S DECIDED!
YUKI, WHY DON'T YOU PLAY IN TOMORROW'S GAME?
OBJECTION!

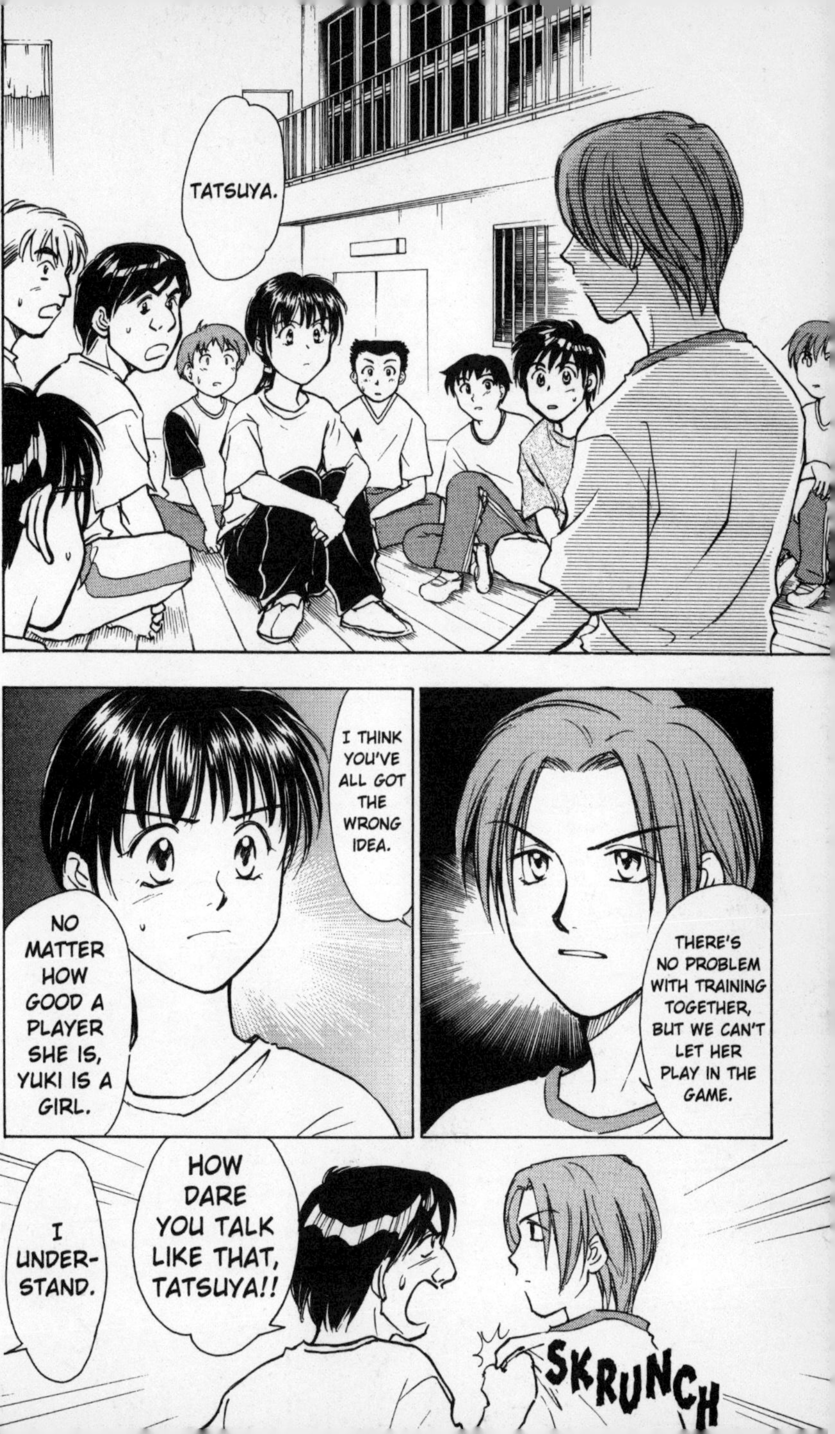
TATSUYA.
THERE'S NO PROBLEM WITH TRAINING TOGETHER, BUT WE CAN'T LET HER PLAY IN THE GAME.
I THINK YOU'VE ALL GOT THE WRONG IDEA.
NO MATTER HOW GOOD A PLAYER SHE IS, YUKI IS A GIRL.
HOW DARE YOU TALK LIKE THAT, TATSUYA!!
SKRUNCH
I UNDER-STAND.

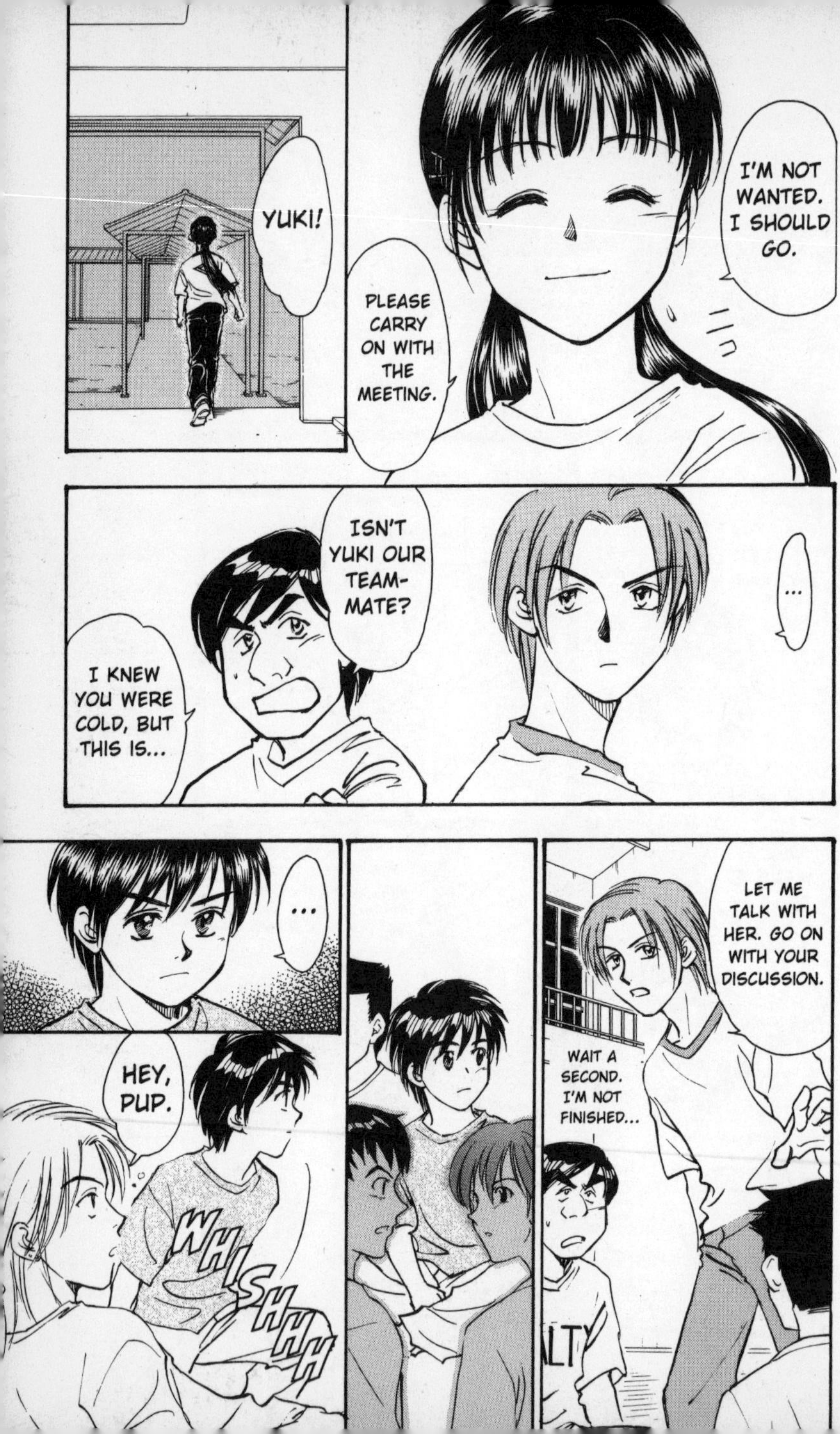
I'M NOT WANTED. I SHOULD GO.
PLEASE CARRY ON WITH THE MEETING.
YUKI!
...
ISN'T YUKI OUR TEAM-MATE?
I KNEW YOU WERE COLD, BUT THIS IS...
LET ME TALK WITH HER. GO ON WITH YOUR DISCUSSION.
WAIT A SECOND. I'M NOT FINISHED...
...
HEY, PUP.
WHISHHH

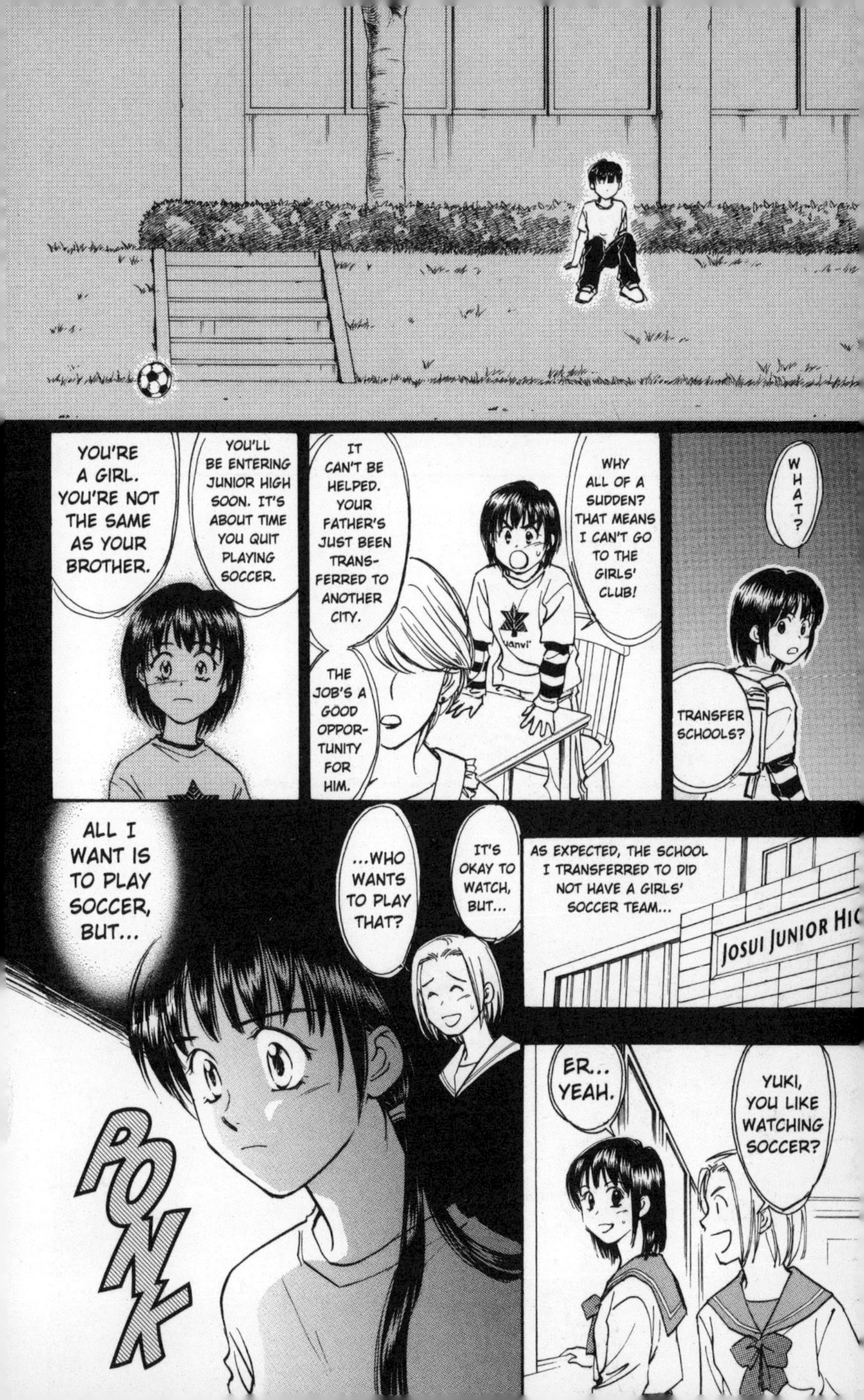
WHAT?
TRANSFER SCHOOLS?
WHY ALL OF A SUDDEN? THAT MEANS I CAN'T GO TO THE GIRLS' CLUB!
IT CAN'T BE HELPED. YOUR FATHER'S JUST BEEN TRANSFERRED TO ANOTHER CITY.
THE JOB'S A GOOD OPPORTUNITY FOR HIM.
YOU'LL BE ENTERING JUNIOR HIGH SOON. IT'S ABOUT TIME YOU QUIT PLAYING SOCCER.
YOU'RE A GIRL. YOU'RE NOT THE SAME AS YOUR BROTHER.
AS EXPECTED, THE SCHOOL I TRANSFERRED TO DID NOT HAVE A GIRLS' SOCCER TEAM...
JOSUI JUNIOR HIG
YUKI, YOU LIKE WATCHING SOCCER?
ER... YEAH.
IT'S OKAY TO WATCH, BUT...
...WHO WANTS TO PLAY THAT?
ALL I WANT IS TO PLAY SOCCER, BUT...
PONK

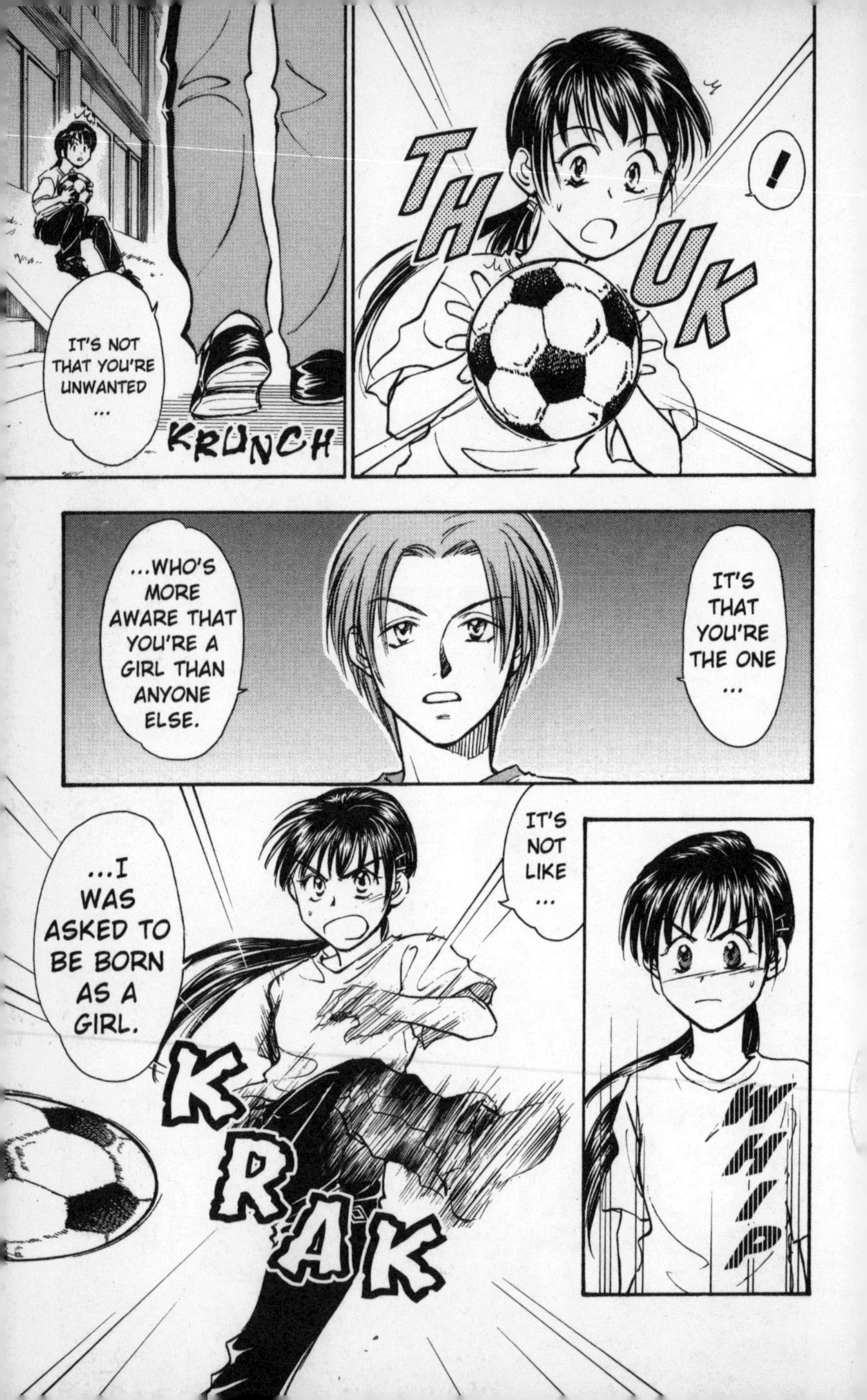

THUK
!
IT'S NOT THAT YOU'RE UNWANTED ...
KRUNCH
IT'S THAT YOU'RE THE ONE ...
...WHO'S MORE AWARE THAT YOU'RE A GIRL THAN ANYONE ELSE.
IT'S NOT LIKE ...
...I WAS ASKED TO BE BORN AS A GIRL.
KRAK

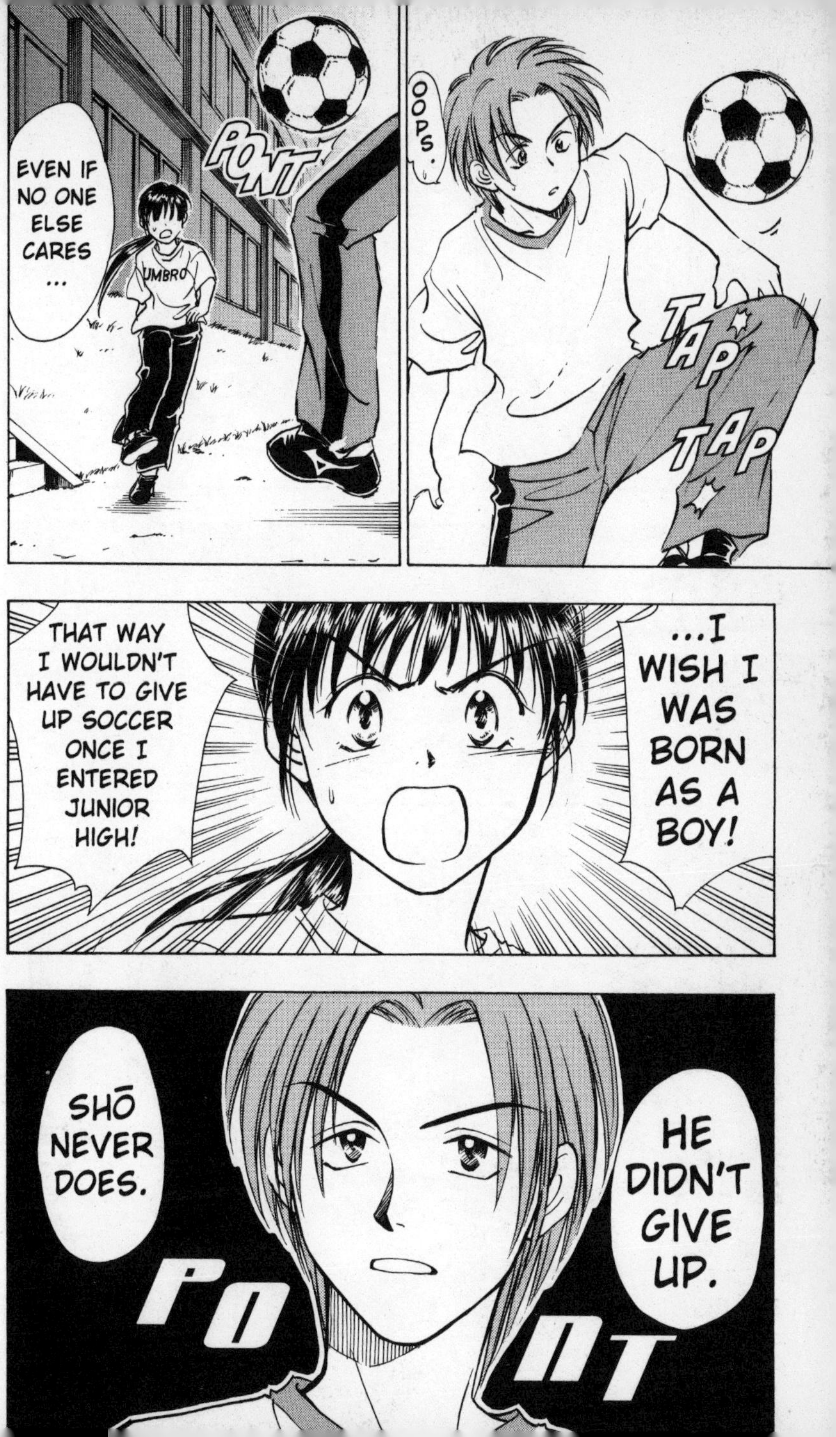
OOPS.
TAP TAP
PONT
EVEN IF NO ONE ELSE CARES ...
UMBRO
...I WISH I WAS BORN AS A BOY!
THAT WAY I WOULDN'T HAVE TO GIVE UP SOCCER ONCE I ENTERED JUNIOR HIGH!
HE DIDN'T GIVE UP.
SHŌ NEVER DOES.
PONT

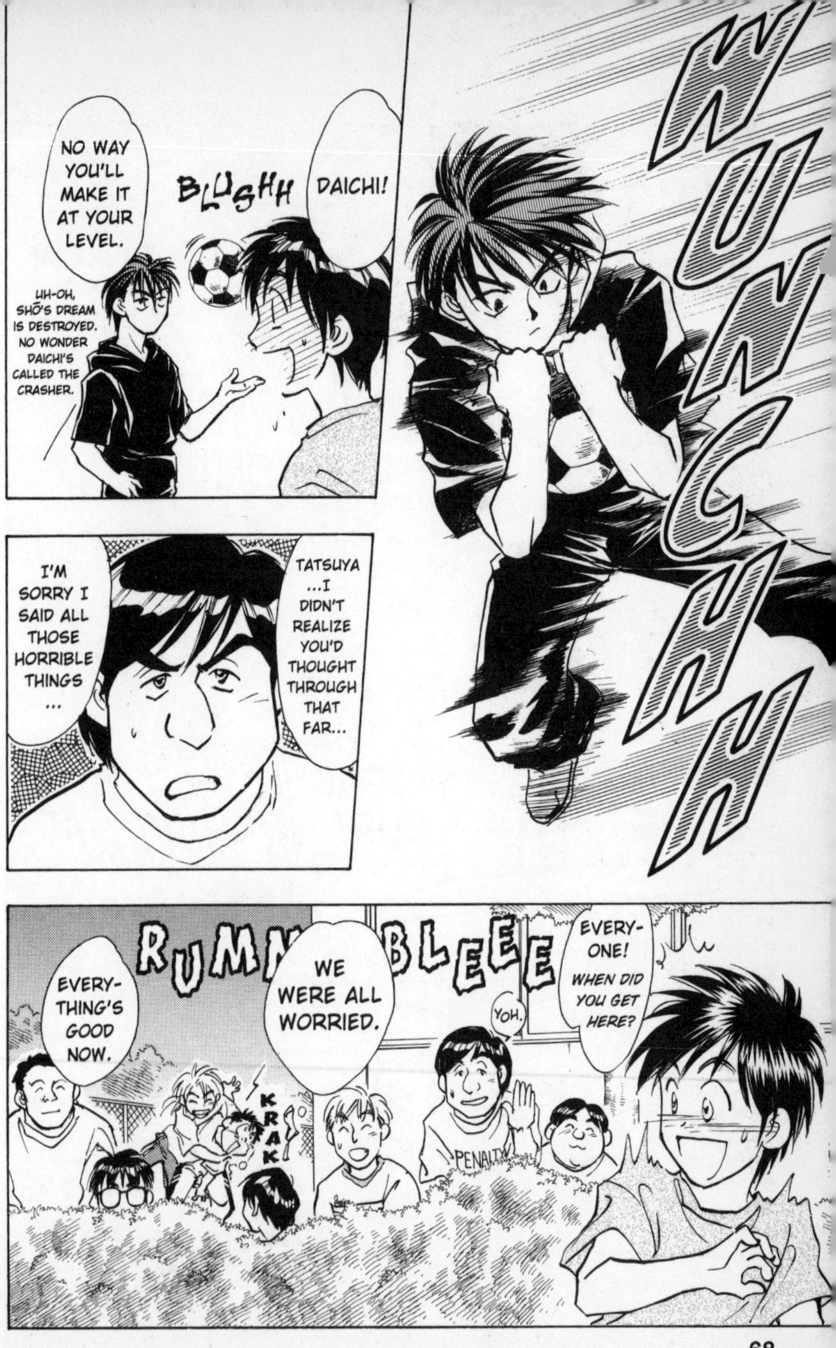
WHUNCHHH
DAICHI!
BLUSHH
NO WAY YOU'LL MAKE IT AT YOUR LEVEL.
UH-OH, SHŌ'S DREAM IS DESTROYED. NO WONDER DAICHI'S CALLED THE CRASHER.
TATSUYA ...I DIDN'T REALIZE YOU'D THOUGHT THROUGH THAT FAR...
I'M SORRY I SAID ALL THOSE HORRIBLE THINGS ...
EVERY-ONE! WHEN DID YOU GET HERE?
YOH.
RUMM BLEEE
WE WERE ALL WORRIED.
KRAK
EVERY-THING'S GOOD NOW.

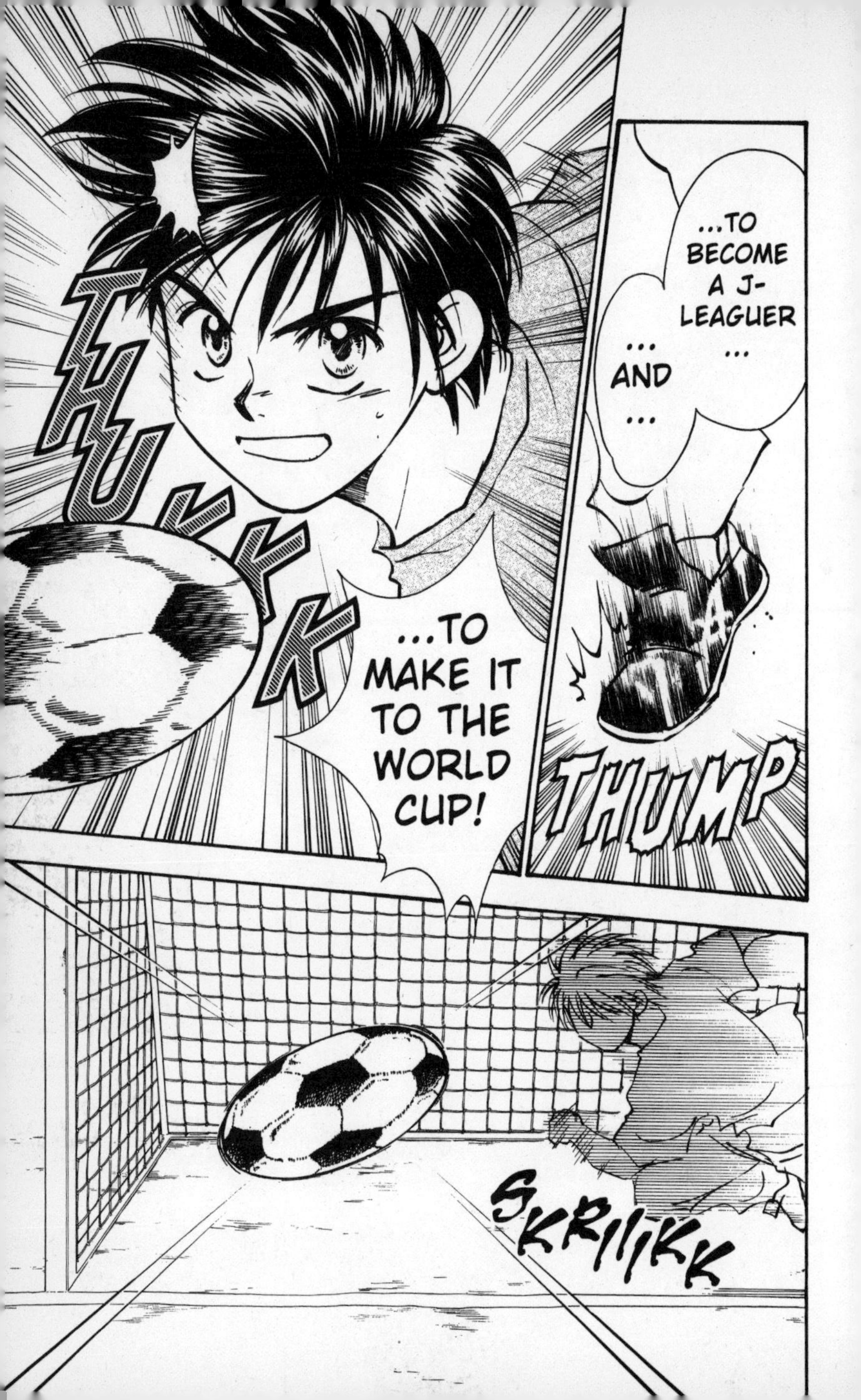
...TO BECOME A J-LEAGUER ... ... AND ...
THUMP
HUNK
...TO MAKE IT TO THE WORLD CUP!
SKRIIIKK

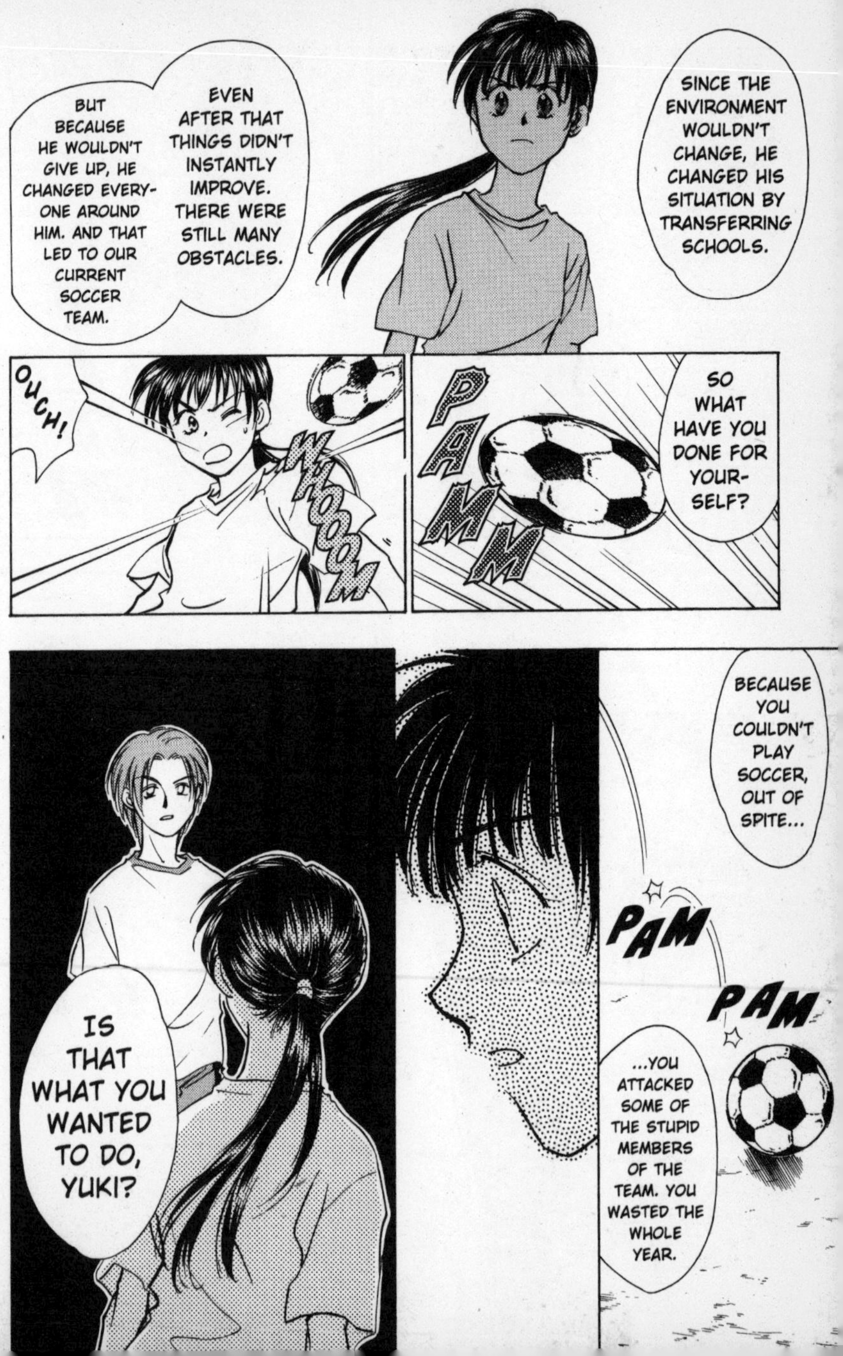
SINCE THE ENVIRONMENT WOULDN'T CHANGE, HE CHANGED HIS SITUATION BY TRANSFERRING SCHOOLS.
EVEN AFTER THAT THINGS DIDN'T INSTANTLY IMPROVE. THERE WERE STILL MANY OBSTACLES.
BUT BECAUSE HE WOULDN'T GIVE UP, HE CHANGED EVERY-ONE AROUND HIM. AND THAT LED TO OUR CURRENT SOCCER TEAM.
PAMMM
SO WHAT HAVE YOU DONE FOR YOUR-SELF?
WHOOOM
OUCH!
BECAUSE YOU COULDN'T PLAY SOCCER, OUT OF SPITE...
PAM
PAM
...YOU ATTACKED SOME OF THE STUPID MEMBERS OF THE TEAM. YOU WASTED THE WHOLE YEAR.
IS THAT WHAT YOU WANTED TO DO, YUKI?

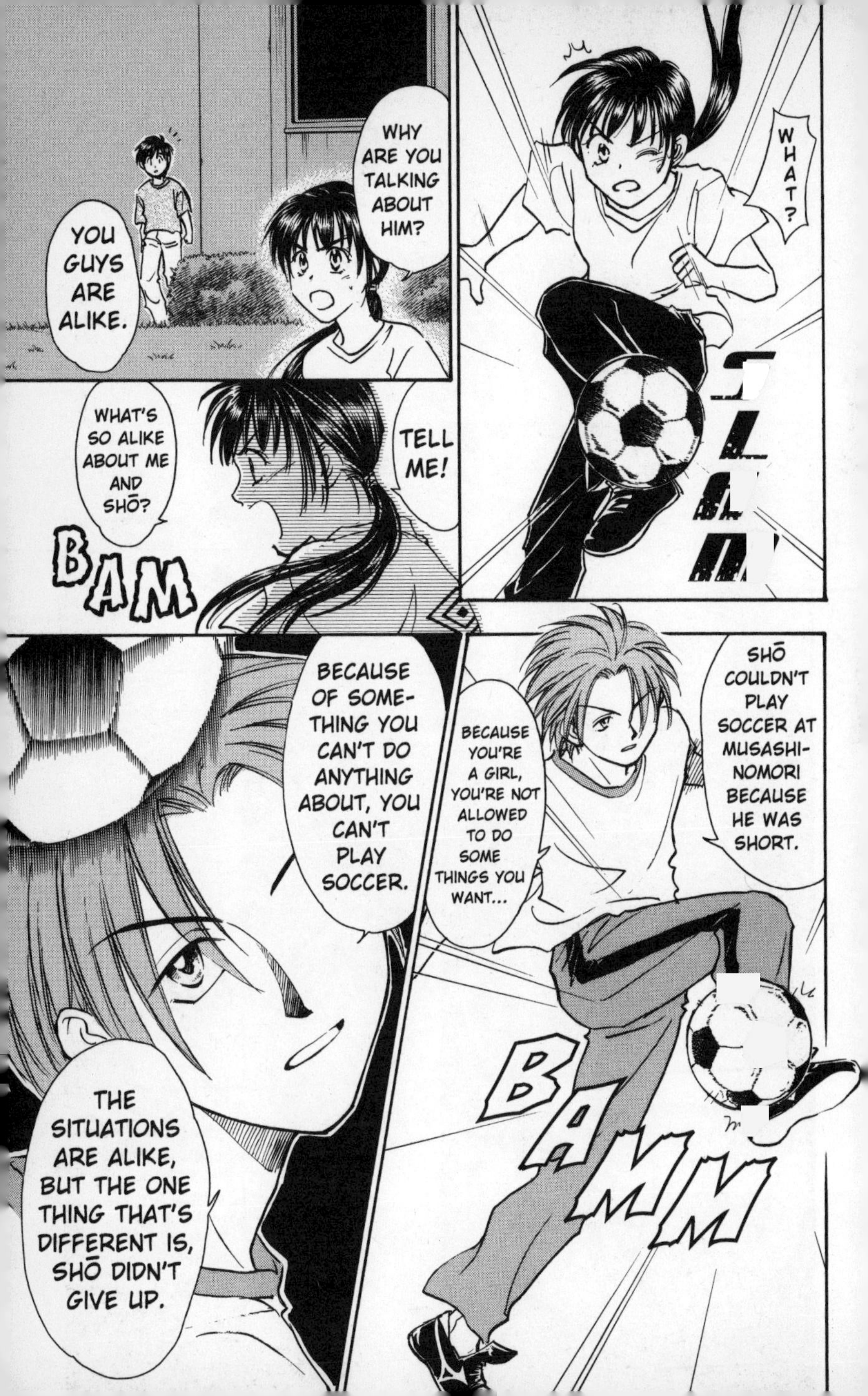
WHAT?
WHY ARE YOU TALKING ABOUT HIM?
YOU GUYS ARE ALIKE.
TELL ME!
WHAT'S SO ALIKE ABOUT ME AND SHŌ?
BAM
SHŌ COULDN'T PLAY SOCCER AT MUSASHINOMORI BECAUSE HE WAS SHORT.
BECAUSE YOU'RE A GIRL, YOU'RE NOT ALLOWED TO DO SOME THINGS YOU WANT...
BAMM
BECAUSE OF SOMETHING YOU CAN'T DO ANYTHING ABOUT, YOU CAN'T PLAY SOCCER.
THE SITUATIONS ARE ALIKE, BUT THE ONE THING THAT'S DIFFERENT IS, SHŌ DIDN'T GIVE UP.

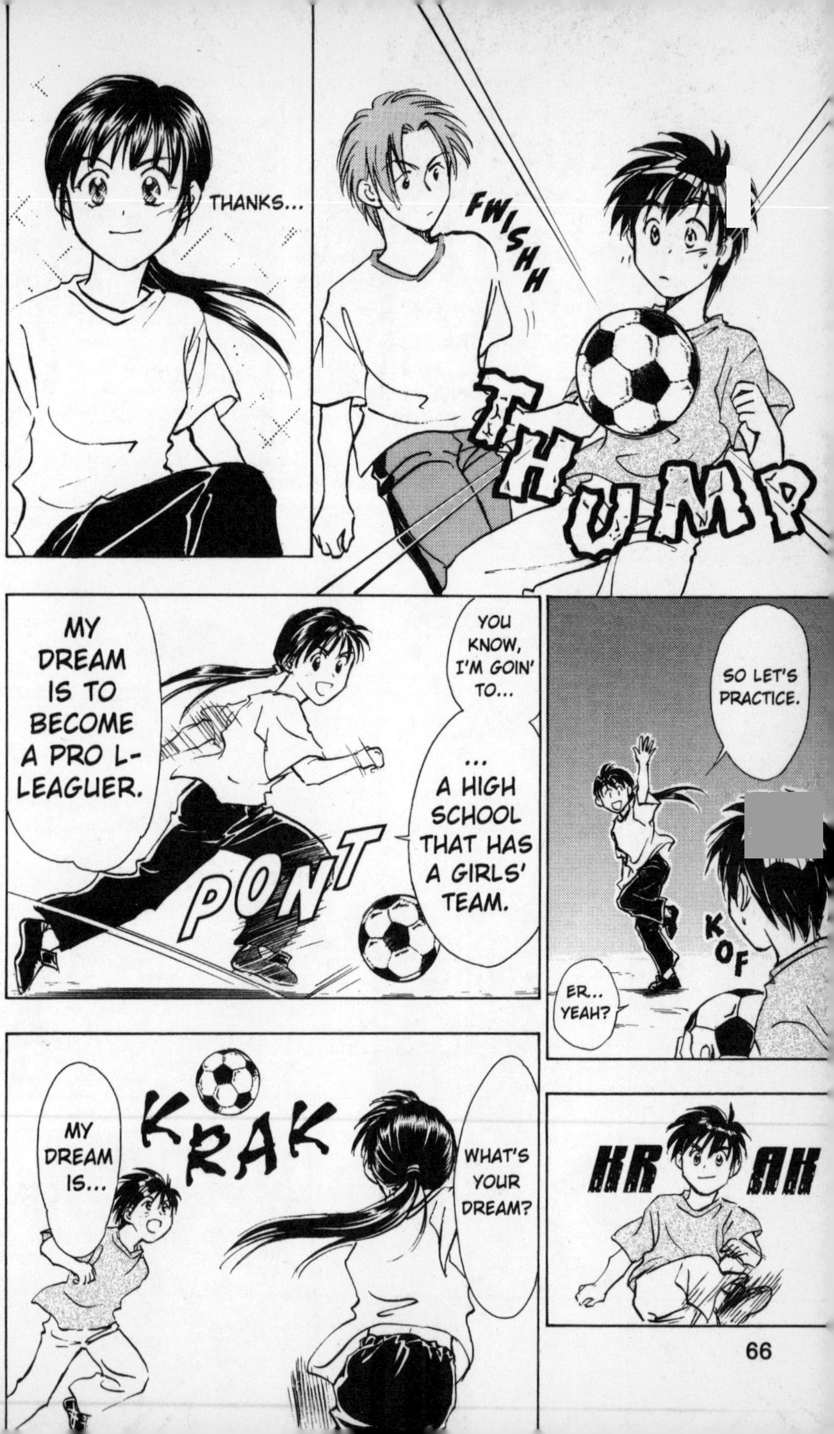
FWISHH
THUMP
THANKS...
SO LET'S PRACTICE.
KOF
ER... YEAH?
YOU KNOW, I'M GOIN' TO...
... A HIGH SCHOOL THAT HAS A GIRLS' TEAM.
PONT
MY DREAM IS TO BECOME A PRO L-LEAGUER.
KRAK
WHAT'S YOUR DREAM?
KRAK
MY DREAM IS...

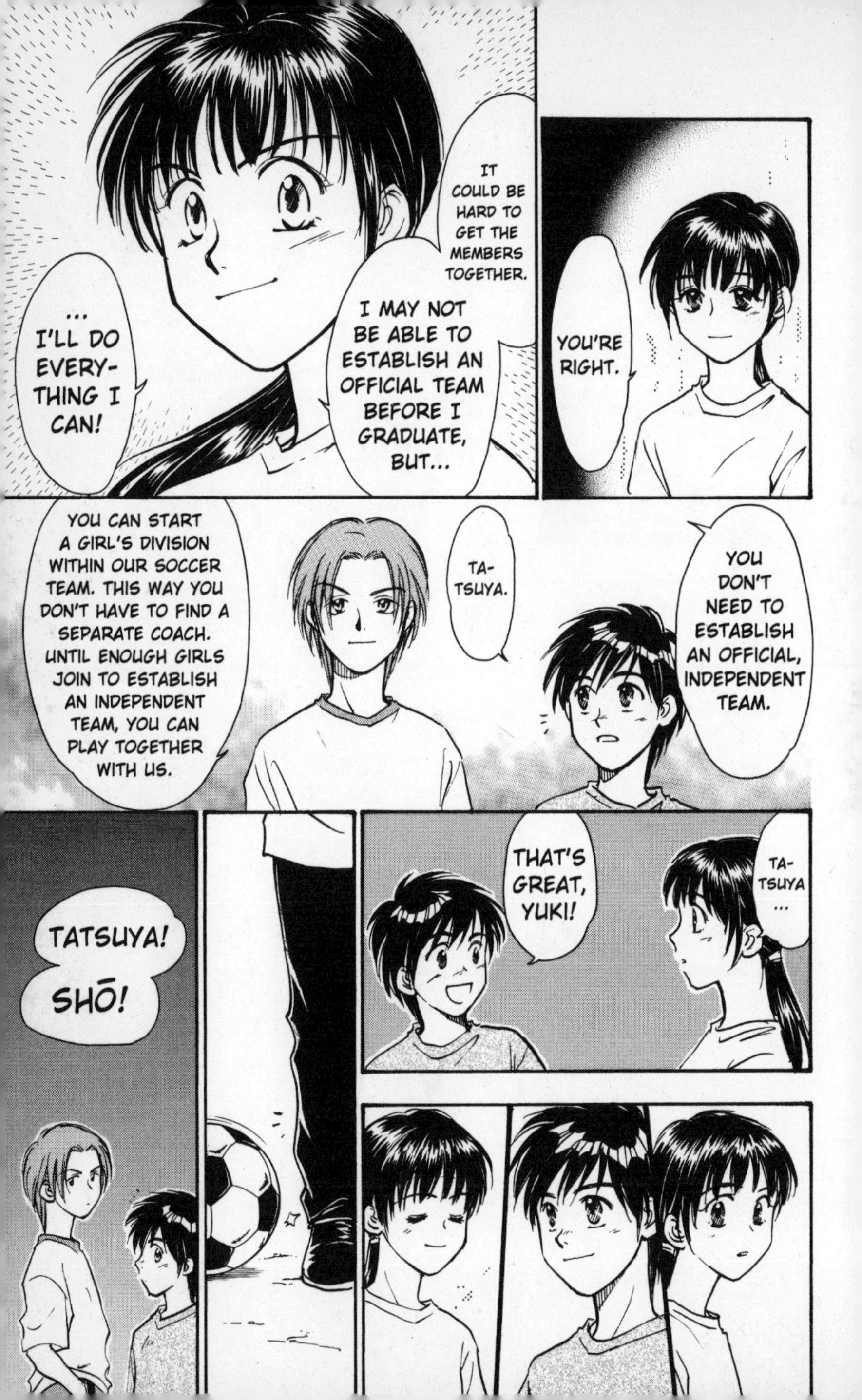
YOU'RE RIGHT.
IT COULD BE HARD TO GET THE MEMBERS TOGETHER.
I MAY NOT BE ABLE TO ESTABLISH AN OFFICIAL TEAM BEFORE I GRADUATE, BUT...
... I'LL DO EVERY-THING I CAN!
YOU DON'T NEED TO ESTABLISH AN OFFICIAL, INDEPENDENT TEAM.
TA-TSUYA.
YOU CAN START A GIRL'S DIVISION WITHIN OUR SOCCER TEAM. THIS WAY YOU DON'T HAVE TO FIND A SEPARATE COACH. UNTIL ENOUGH GIRLS JOIN TO ESTABLISH AN INDEPENDENT TEAM, YOU CAN PLAY TOGETHER WITH US.
TA-TSUYA...
THAT'S GREAT, YUKI!
TATSUYA!
SHŌ!

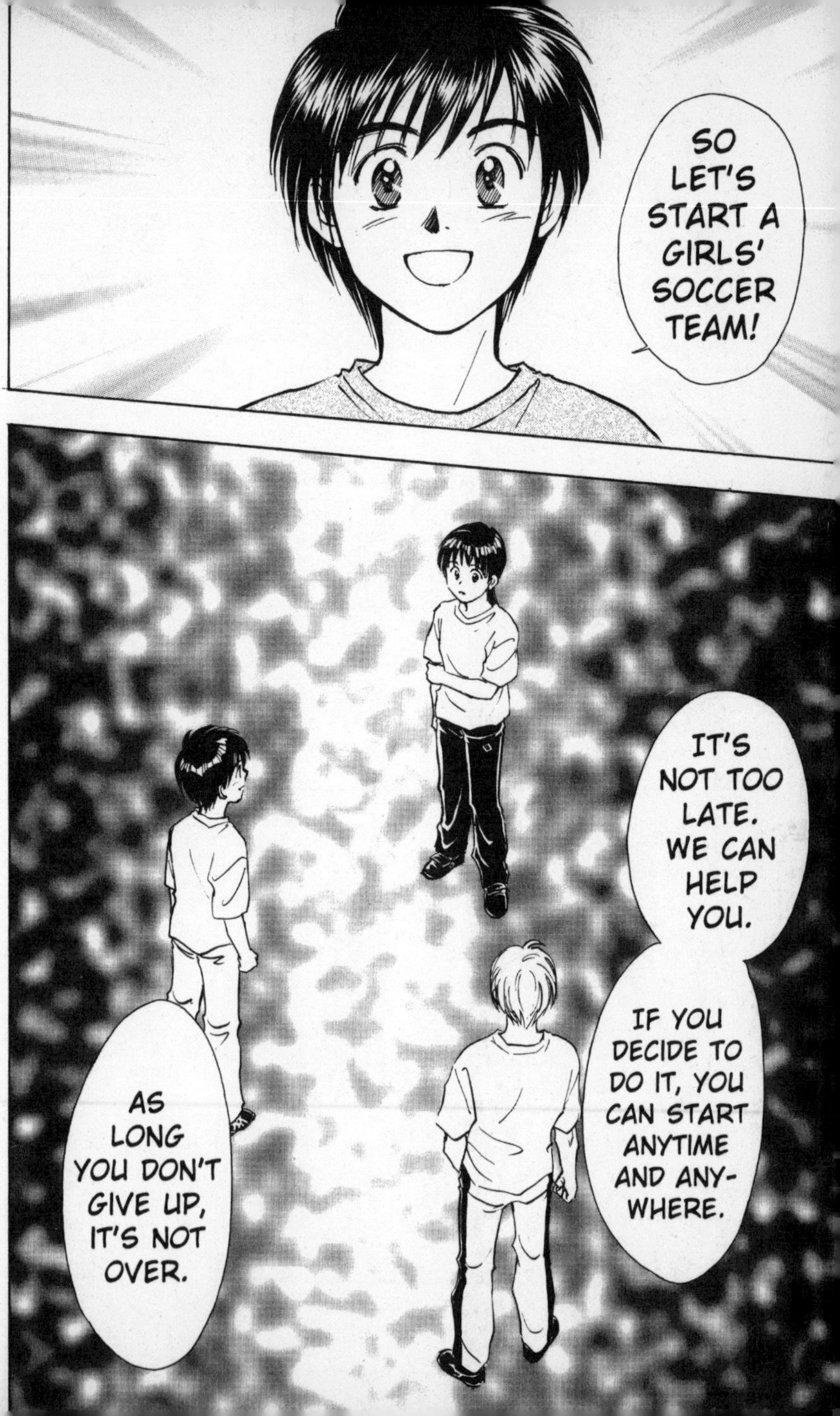
SO LET'S START A GIRLS' SOCCER TEAM!
IT'S NOT TOO LATE. WE CAN HELP YOU.
IF YOU DECIDE TO DO IT, YOU CAN START ANYTIME AND ANY-WHERE.
AS LONG YOU DON'T GIVE UP, IT'S NOT OVER.

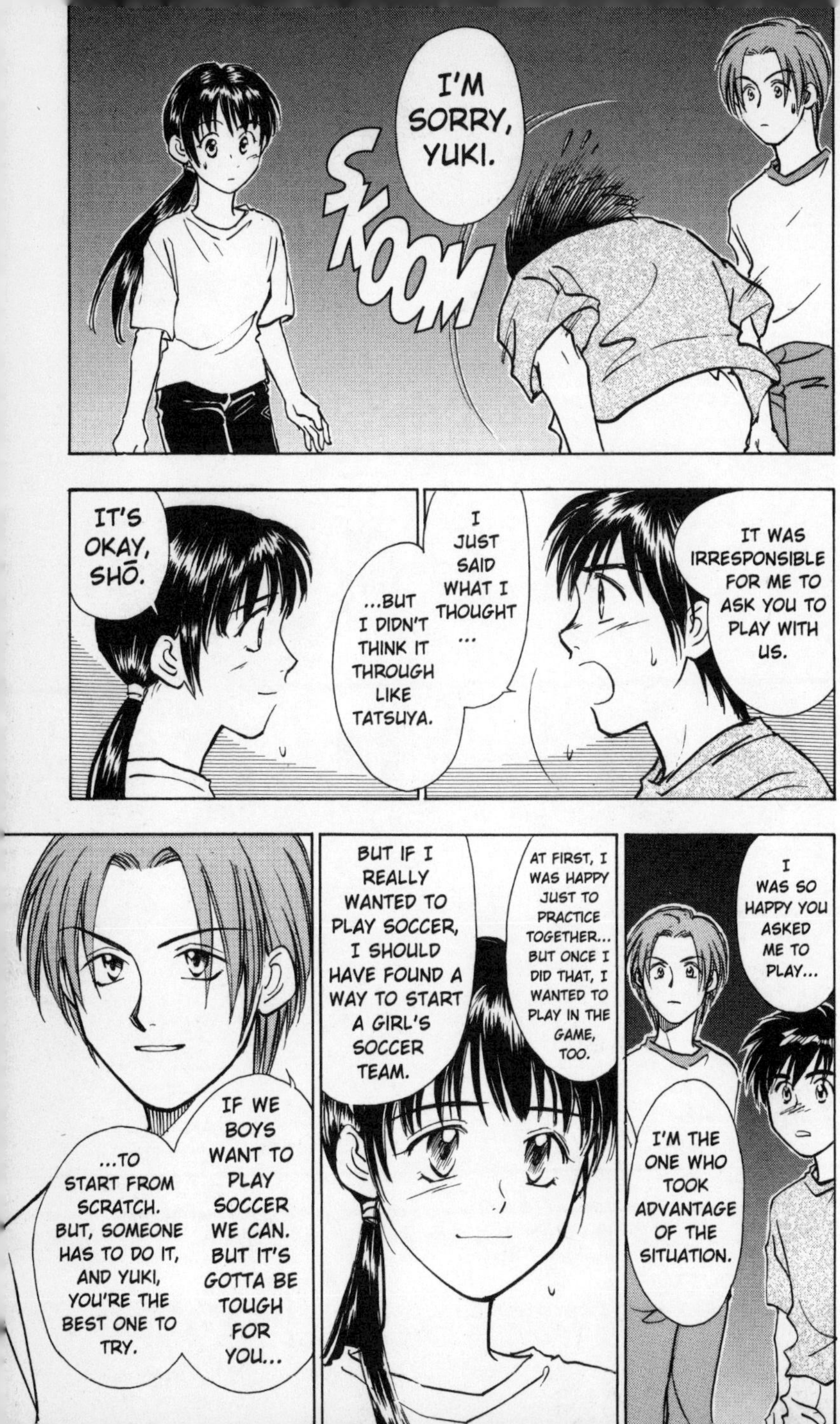
I'M SORRY, YUKI.
SKOOM
IT WAS IRRESPONSIBLE FOR ME TO ASK YOU TO PLAY WITH US.
I JUST SAID WHAT I THOUGHT ...
...BUT I DIDN'T THINK IT THROUGH LIKE TATSUYA.
IT'S OKAY, SHŌ.
I WAS SO HAPPY YOU ASKED ME TO PLAY...
I'M THE ONE WHO TOOK ADVANTAGE OF THE SITUATION.
AT FIRST, I WAS HAPPY JUST TO PRACTICE TOGETHER... BUT ONCE I DID THAT, I WANTED TO PLAY IN THE GAME, TOO.
BUT IF I REALLY WANTED TO PLAY SOCCER, I SHOULD HAVE FOUND A WAY TO START A GIRL'S SOCCER TEAM.
IF WE BOYS WANT TO PLAY SOCCER WE CAN. BUT IT'S GOTTA BE TOUGH FOR YOU...
...TO START FROM SCRATCH. BUT, SOMEONE HAS TO DO IT, AND YUKI, YOU'RE THE BEST ONE TO TRY.

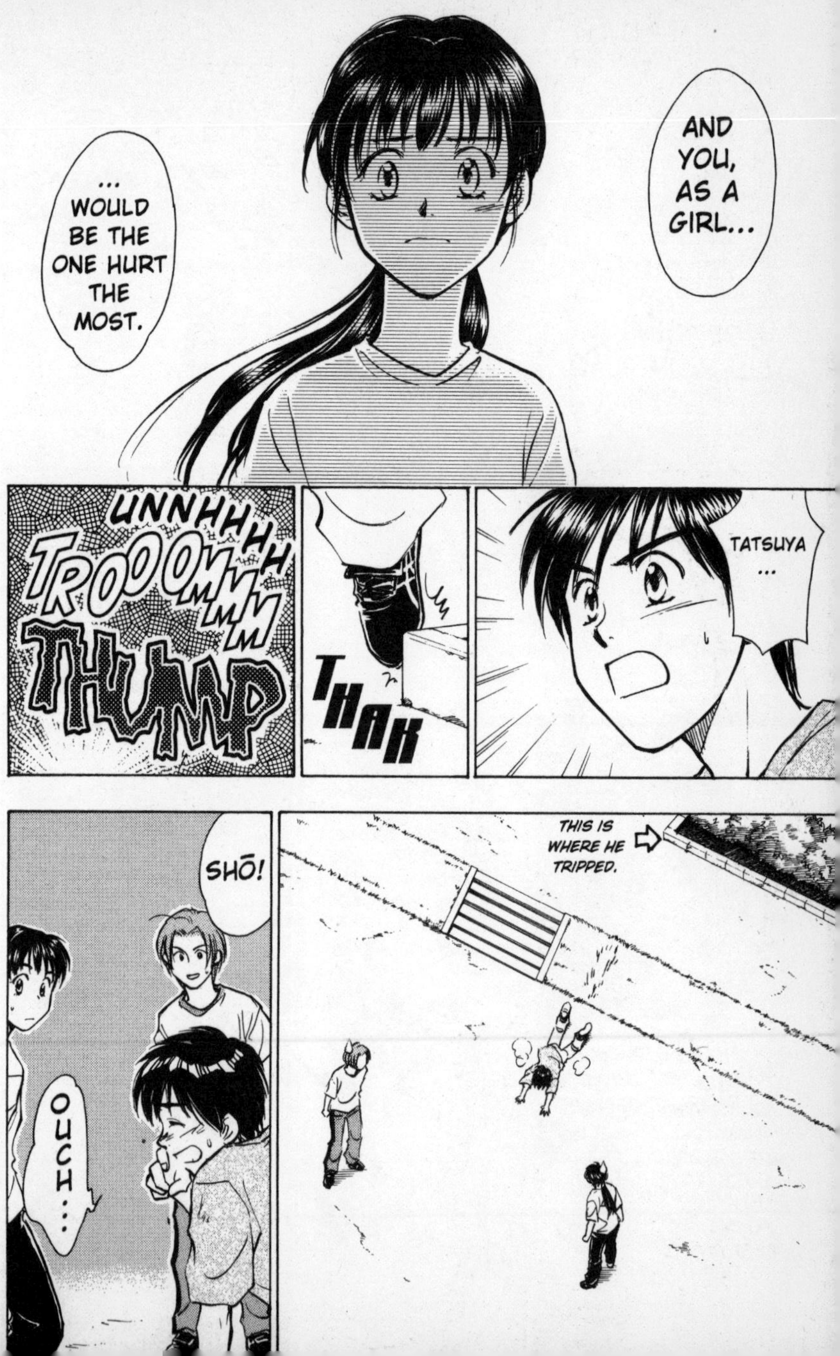
AND YOU, AS A GIRL...
... WOULD BE THE ONE HURT THE MOST.
TATSUYA ...
THAK
UNNHHHHH
TROOOMMMMMMM
THUMP
THIS IS WHERE HE TRIPPED.
SHŌ!
OUCH...

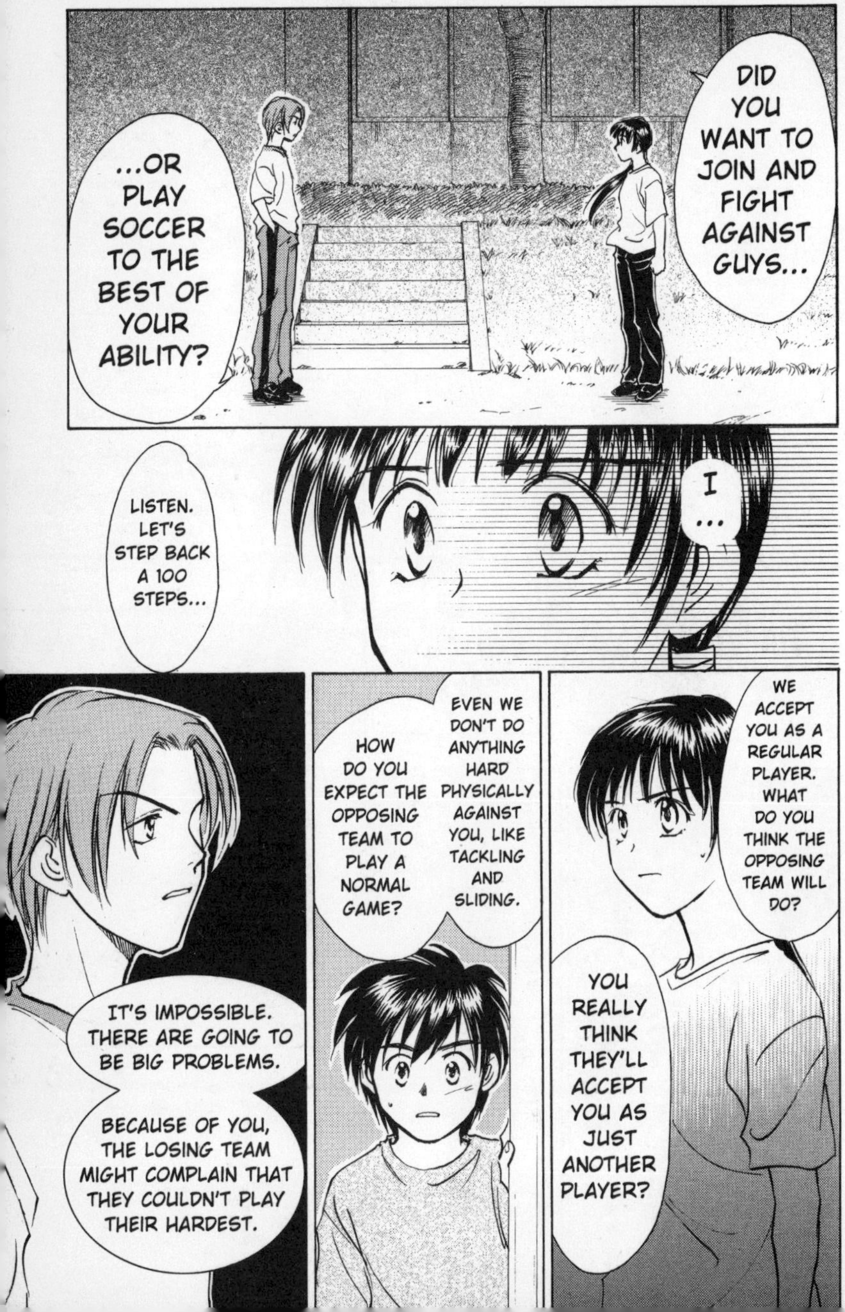
DID YOU WANT TO JOIN AND FIGHT AGAINST GUYS...
...OR PLAY SOCCER TO THE BEST OF YOUR ABILITY?
I ...
LISTEN. LET'S STEP BACK A 100 STEPS...
WE ACCEPT YOU AS A REGULAR PLAYER. WHAT DO YOU THINK THE OPPOSING TEAM WILL DO?
YOU REALLY THINK THEY'LL ACCEPT YOU AS JUST ANOTHER PLAYER?
EVEN WE DON'T DO ANYTHING HARD PHYSICALLY AGAINST YOU, LIKE TACKLING AND SLIDING.
HOW DO YOU EXPECT THE OPPOSING TEAM TO PLAY A NORMAL GAME?
IT'S IMPOSSIBLE. THERE ARE GOING TO BE BIG PROBLEMS.
BECAUSE OF YOU, THE LOSING TEAM MIGHT COMPLAIN THAT THEY COULDN'T PLAY THEIR HARDEST.

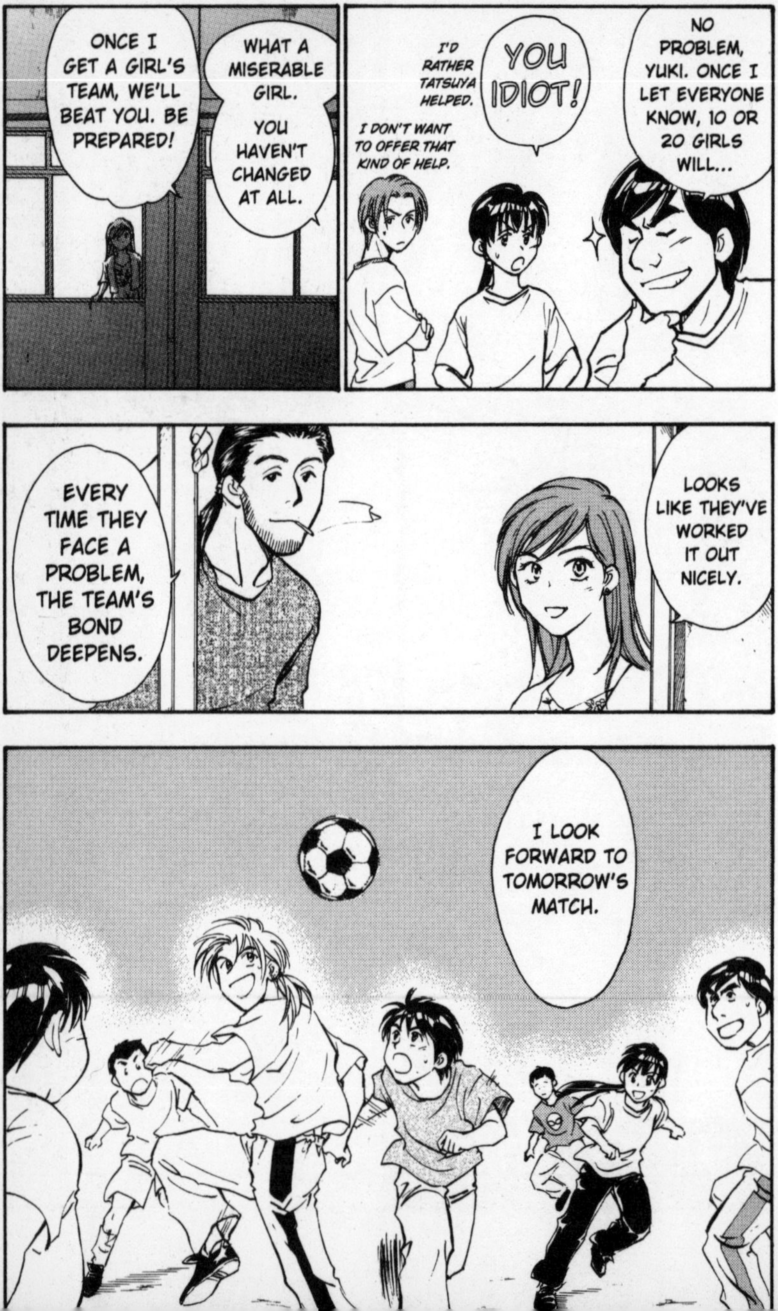
NO PROBLEM, YUKI. ONCE I LET EVERYONE KNOW, 10 OR 20 GIRLS WILL...
YOU IDIOT!
I'D RATHER TATSUYA HELPED.
I DON'T WANT TO OFFER THAT KIND OF HELP.
WHAT A MISERABLE GIRL.
YOU HAVEN'T CHANGED AT ALL.
ONCE I GET A GIRL'S TEAM, WE'LL BEAT YOU. BE PREPARED!
LOOKS LIKE THEY'VE WORKED IT OUT NICELY.
EVERY TIME THEY FACE A PROBLEM, THE TEAM'S BOND DEEPENS.
I LOOK FORWARD TO TOMORROW'S MATCH.

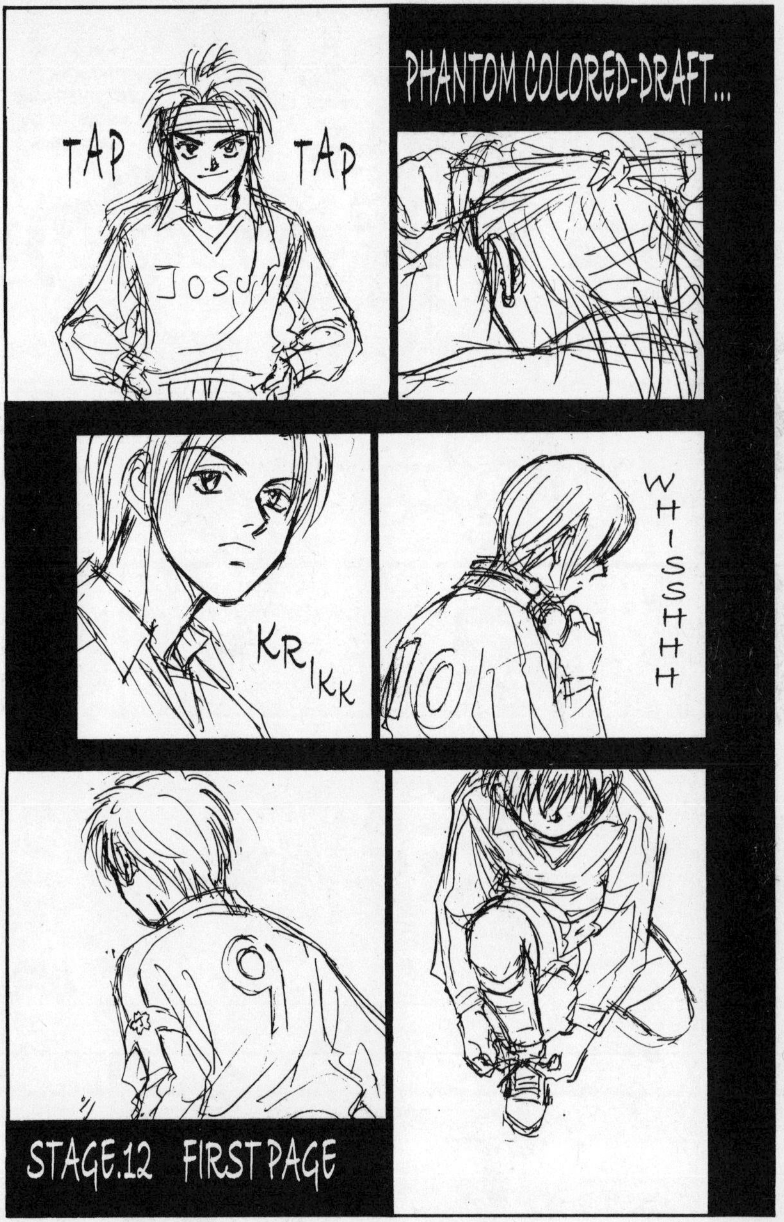
PHANTOM COLORED-DRAFT...
TAP TAP
WHISSHHH
KRIKK
STAGE.12 FIRST PAGE

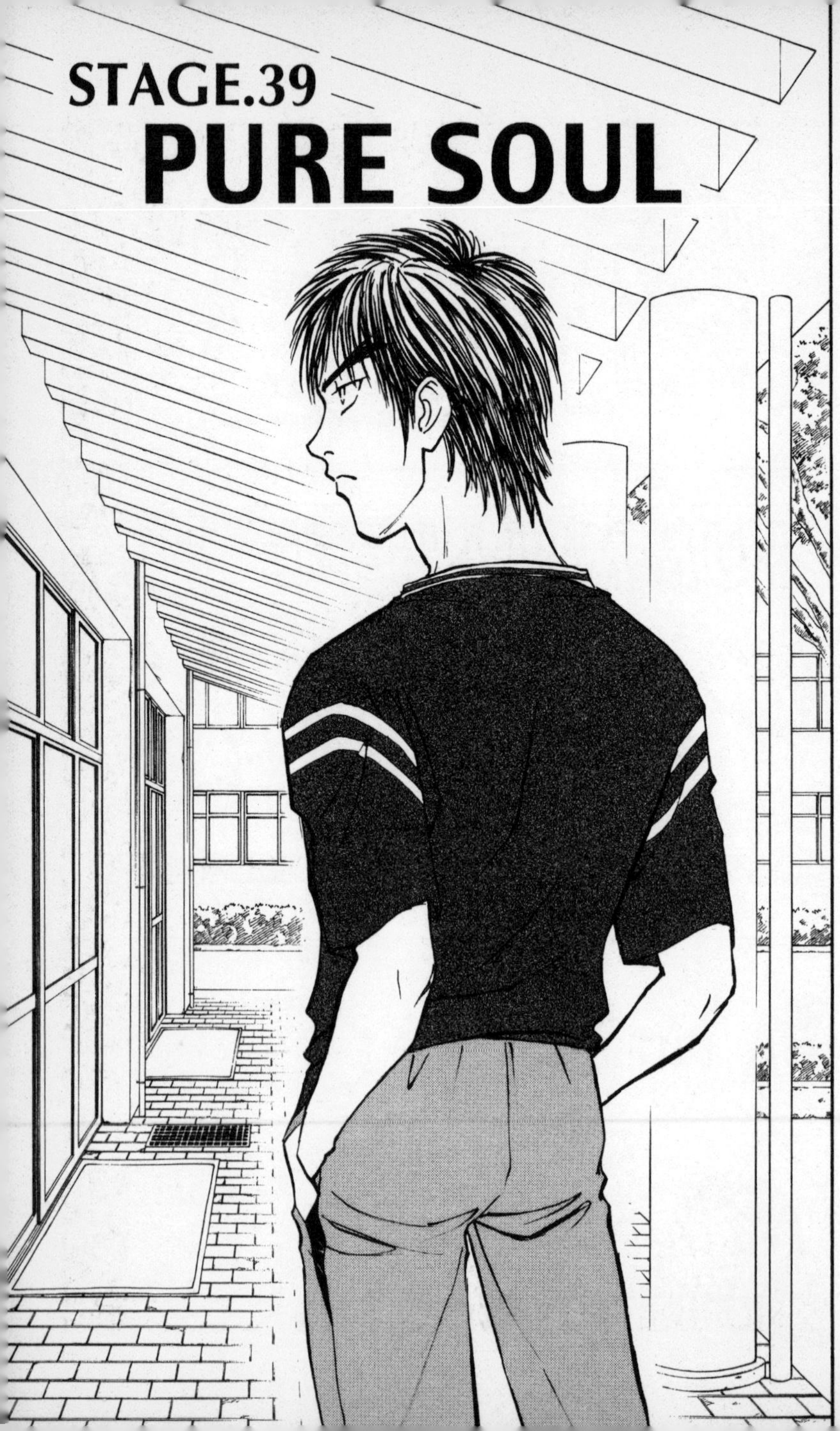
STAGE.39
PURE SOUL

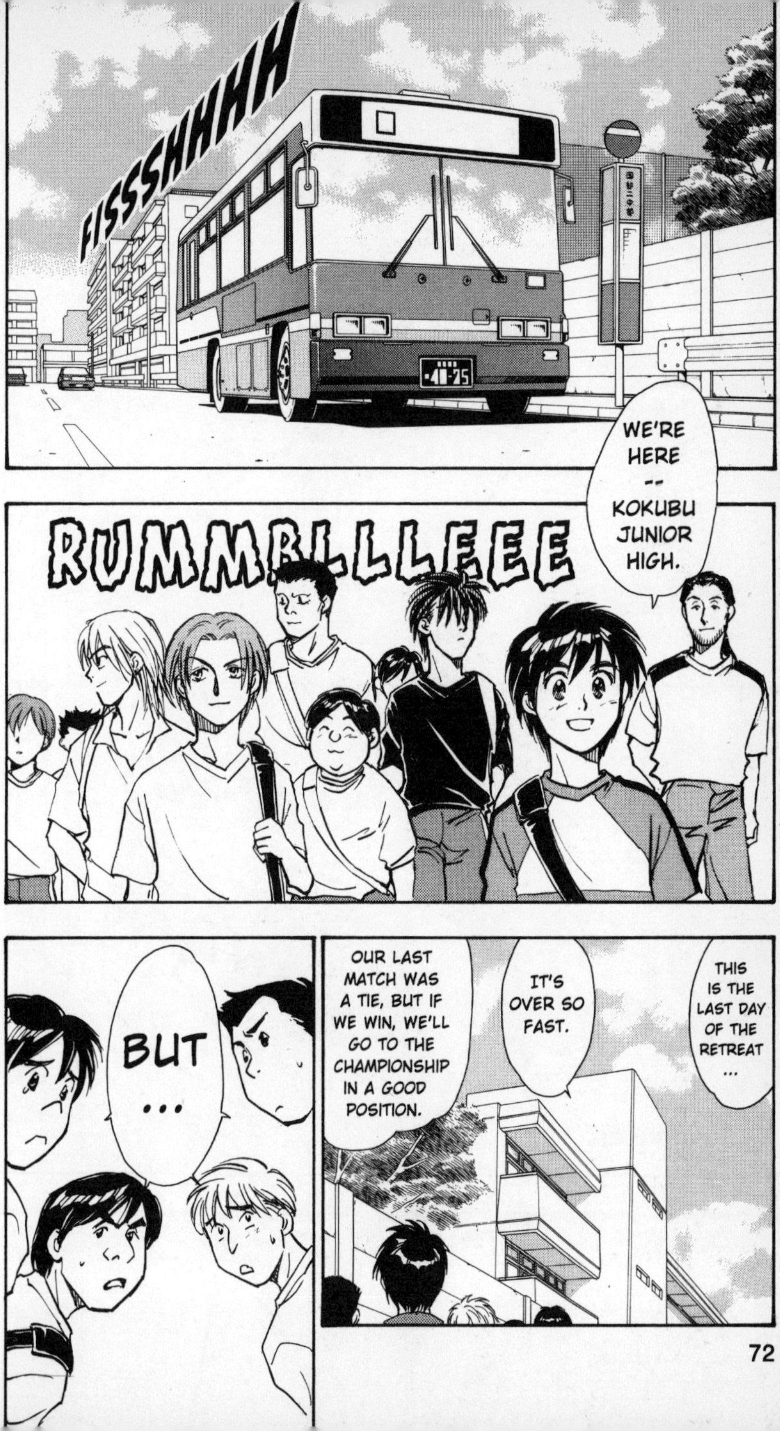
FISSSHHHH
WE'RE HERE -- KOKUBU JUNIOR HIGH.
RUMMBLLLEEE
THIS IS THE LAST DAY OF THE RETREAT ...
IT'S OVER SO FAST.
OUR LAST MATCH WAS A TIE, BUT IF WE WIN, WE'LL GO TO THE CHAMPIONSHIP IN A GOOD POSITION.
BUT ...

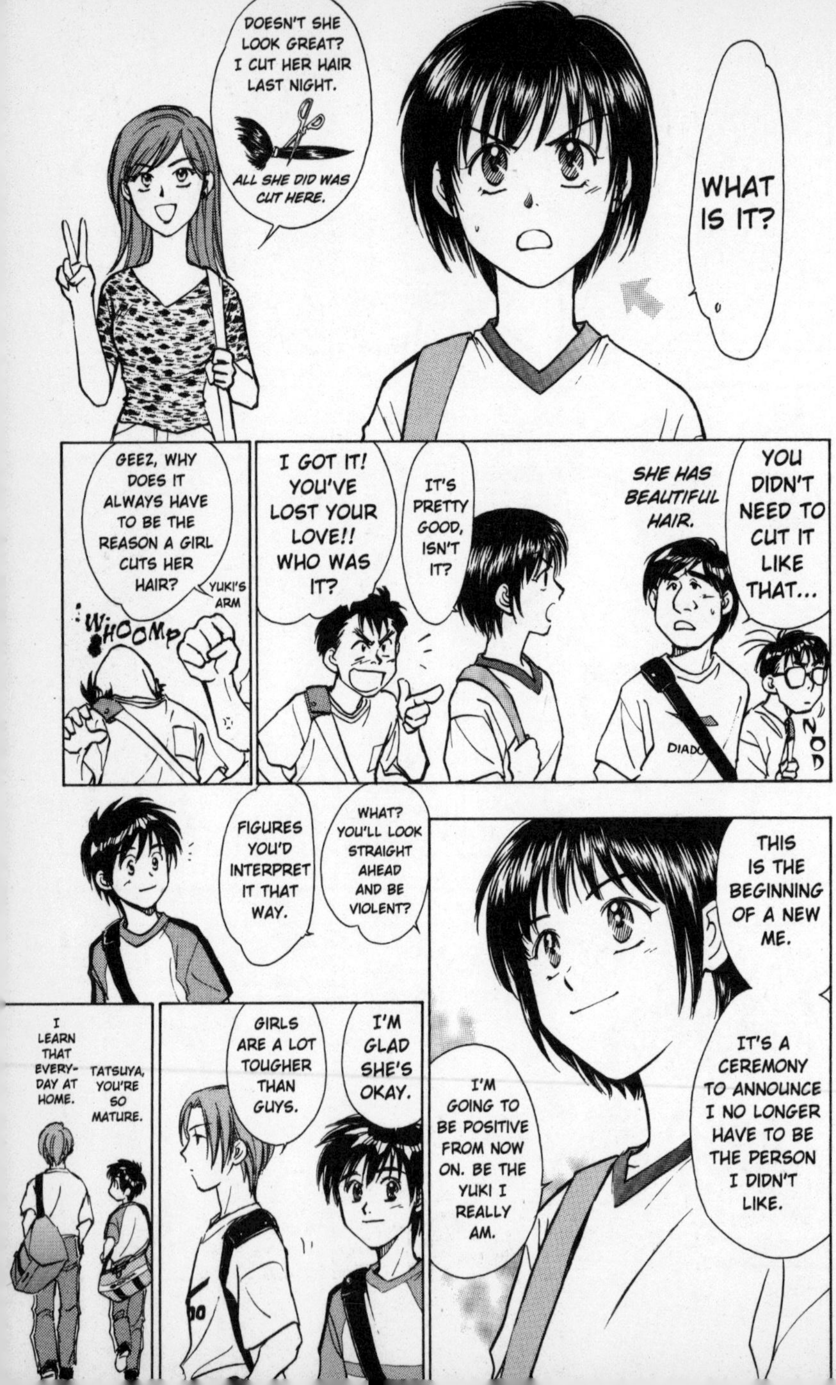
WHAT IS IT?
DOESN'T SHE LOOK GREAT? I CUT HER HAIR LAST NIGHT.
ALL SHE DID WAS CUT HERE.
YOU DIDN'T NEED TO CUT IT LIKE THAT...
SHE HAS BEAUTIFUL HAIR.
NOD
IT'S PRETTY GOOD, ISN'T IT?
I GOT IT! YOU'VE LOST YOUR LOVE!! WHO WAS IT?
GEEZ, WHY DOES IT ALWAYS HAVE TO BE THE REASON A GIRL CUTS HER HAIR?
YUKI'S ARM
WHOOMP
THIS IS THE BEGINNING OF A NEW ME.
IT'S A CEREMONY TO ANNOUNCE I NO LONGER HAVE TO BE THE PERSON I DIDN'T LIKE.
I'M GOING TO BE POSITIVE FROM NOW ON. BE THE YUKI I REALLY AM.
WHAT? YOU'LL LOOK STRAIGHT AHEAD AND BE VIOLENT?
FIGURES YOU'D INTERPRET IT THAT WAY.
I'M GLAD SHE'S OKAY.
GIRLS ARE A LOT TOUGHER THAN GUYS.
TATSUYA, YOU'RE SO MATURE.
I LEARN THAT EVERY-DAY AT HOME.

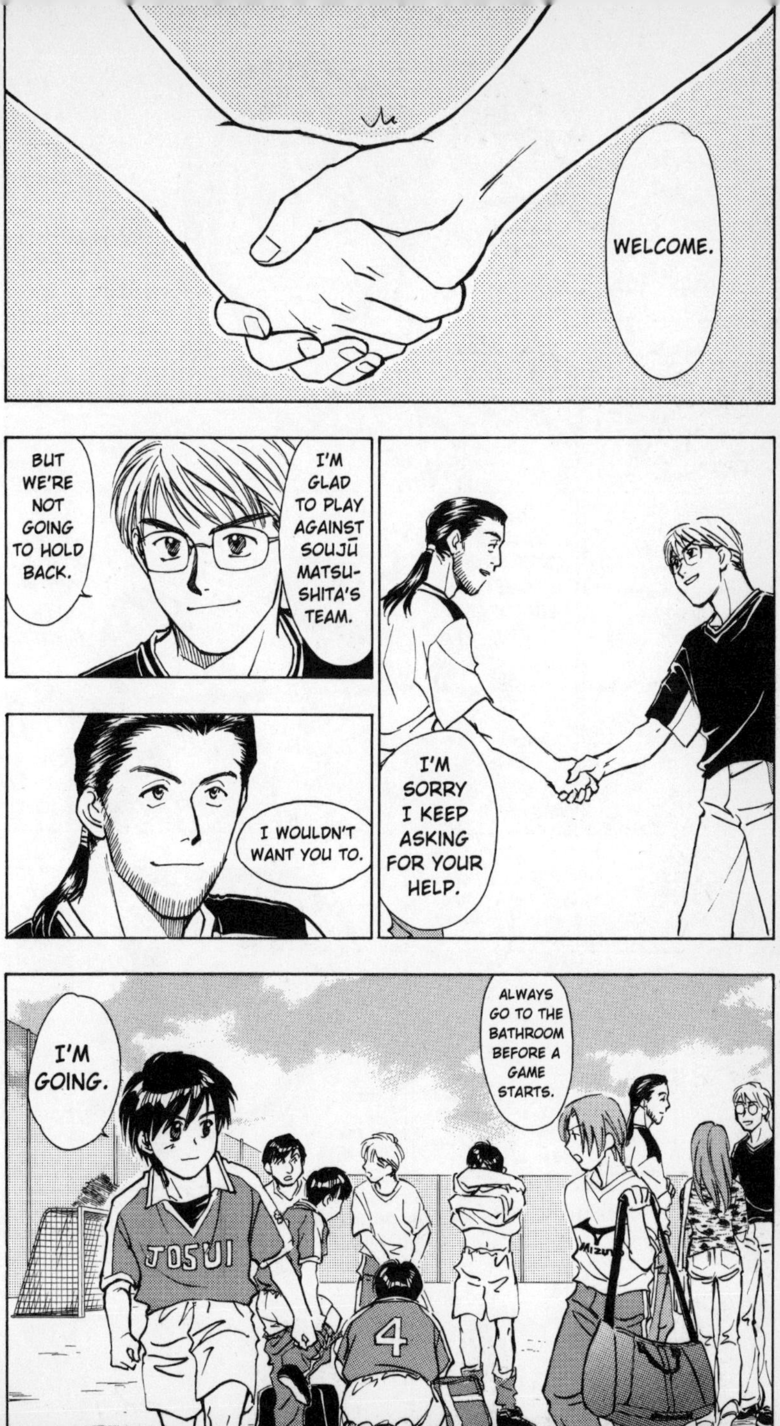
WELCOME.
I'M SORRY I KEEP ASKING FOR YOUR HELP.
I'M GLAD TO PLAY AGAINST SOUJŪ MATSUSHITA'S TEAM.
BUT WE'RE NOT GOING TO HOLD BACK.
I WOULDN'T WANT YOU TO.
ALWAYS GO TO THE BATHROOM BEFORE A GAME STARTS.
I'M GOING.
JOSUI

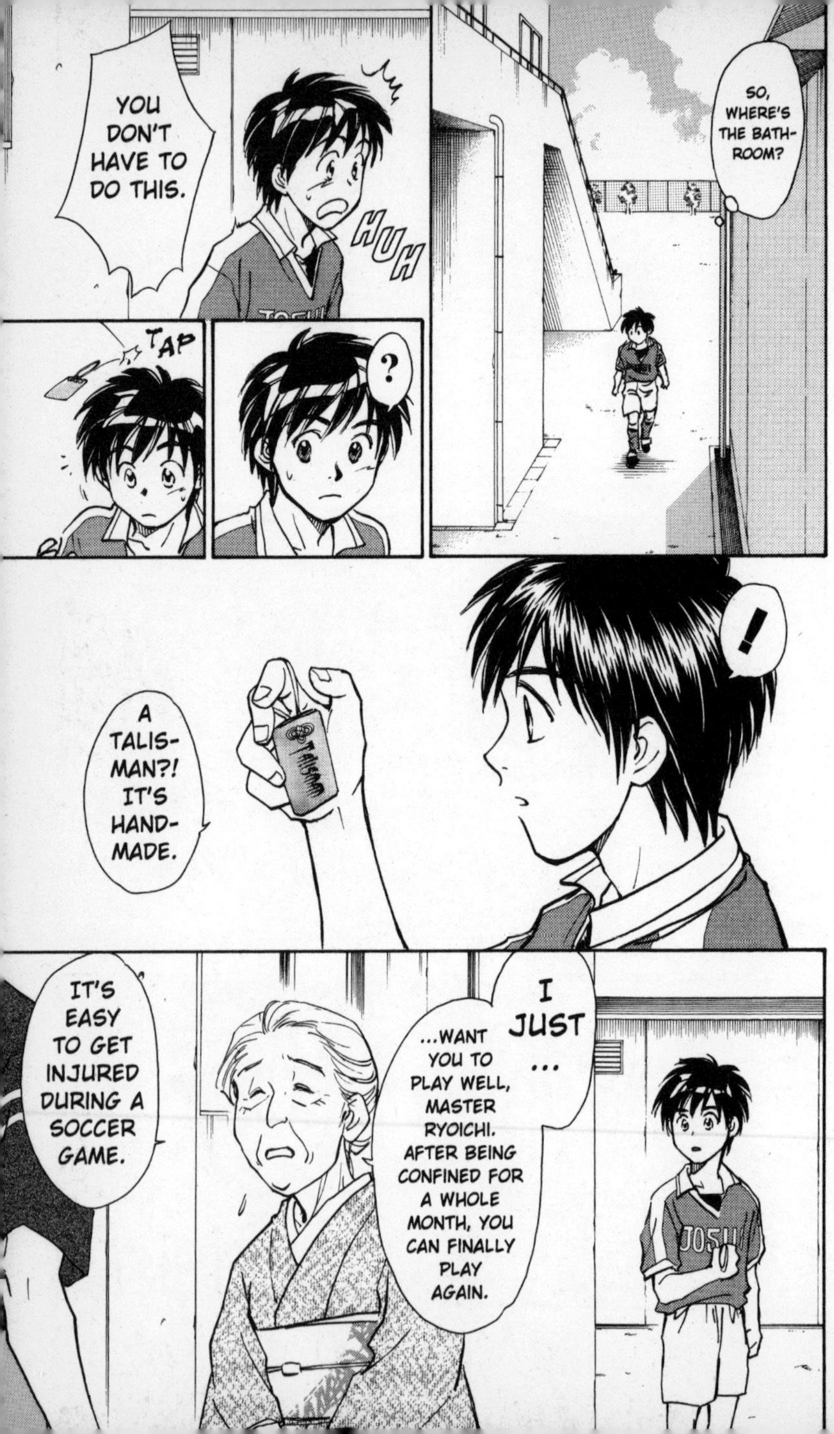
SO, WHERE'S THE BATH-ROOM?
YOU DON'T HAVE TO DO THIS.
HUH
?
TAP
!
A TALIS-MAN?! IT'S HAND-MADE.
I JUST ...
...WANT YOU TO PLAY WELL, MASTER RYOICHI. AFTER BEING CONFINED FOR A WHOLE MONTH, YOU CAN FINALLY PLAY AGAIN.
IT'S EASY TO GET INJURED DURING A SOCCER GAME.

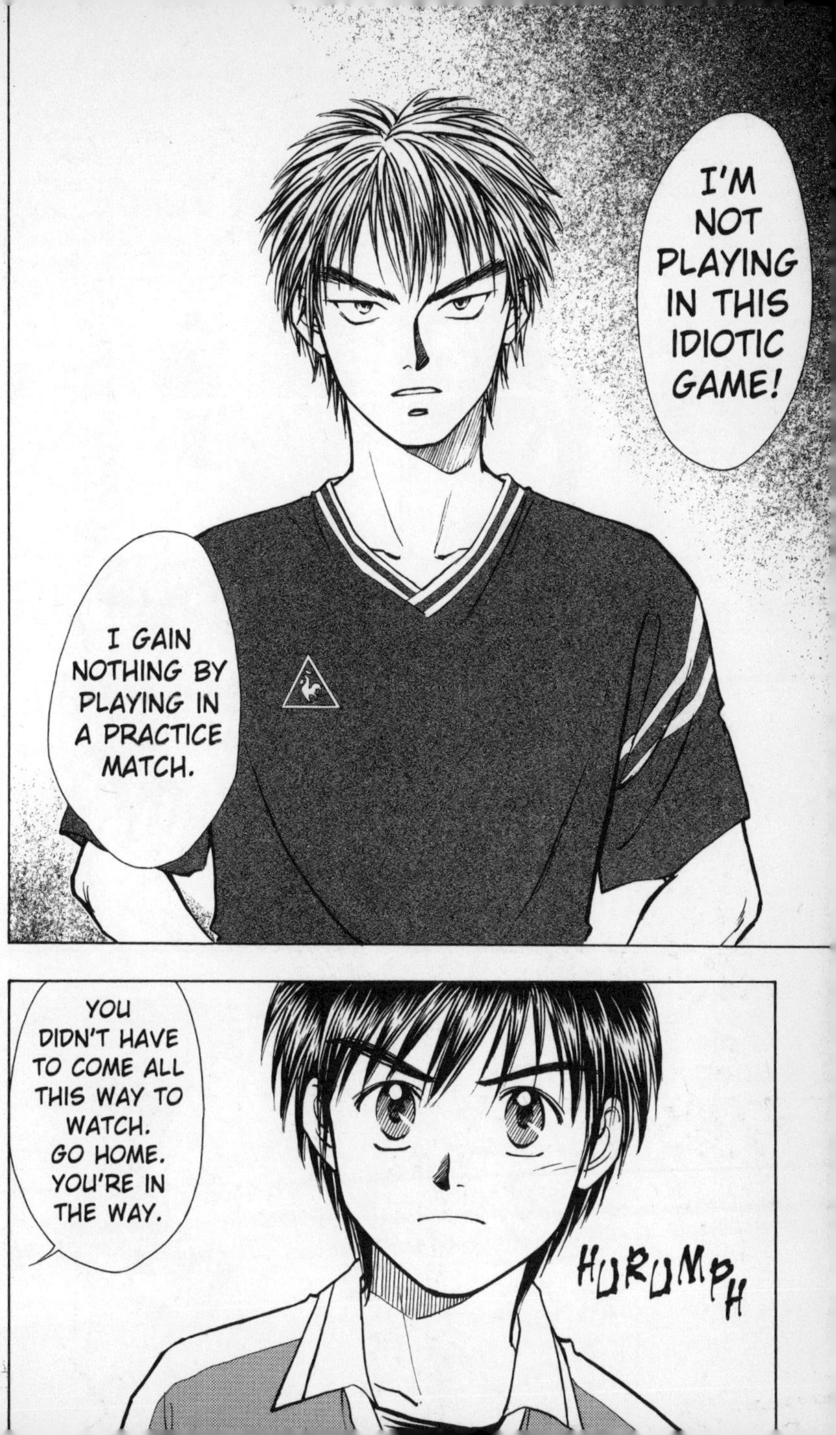
I'M NOT PLAYING IN THIS IDIOTIC GAME!
I GAIN NOTHING BY PLAYING IN A PRACTICE MATCH.
YOU DIDN'T HAVE TO COME ALL THIS WAY TO WATCH. GO HOME. YOU'RE IN THE WAY.
HURUMPH

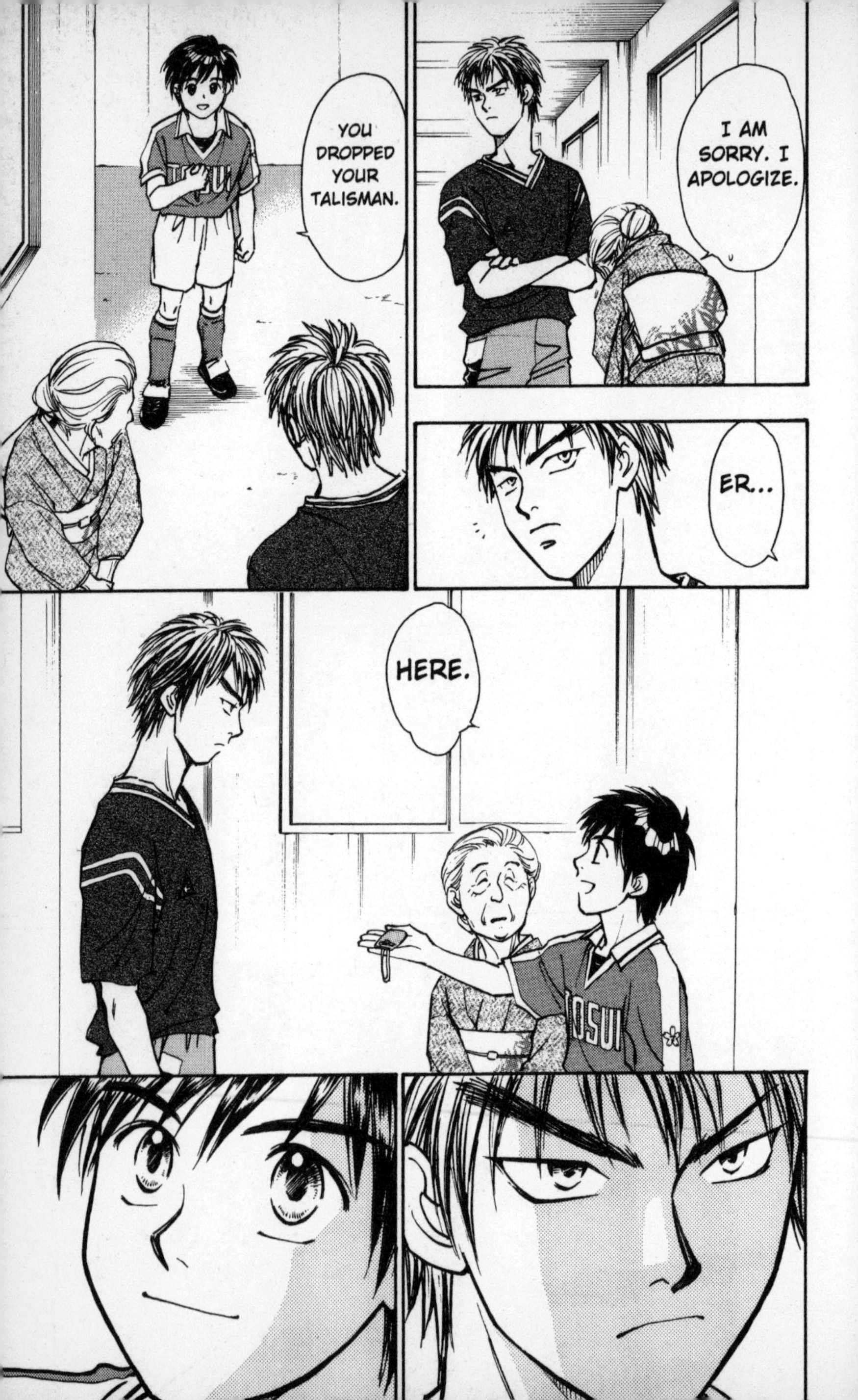
I AM SORRY. I APOLOGIZE.
ER...
YOU DROPPED YOUR TALISMAN.
HERE.

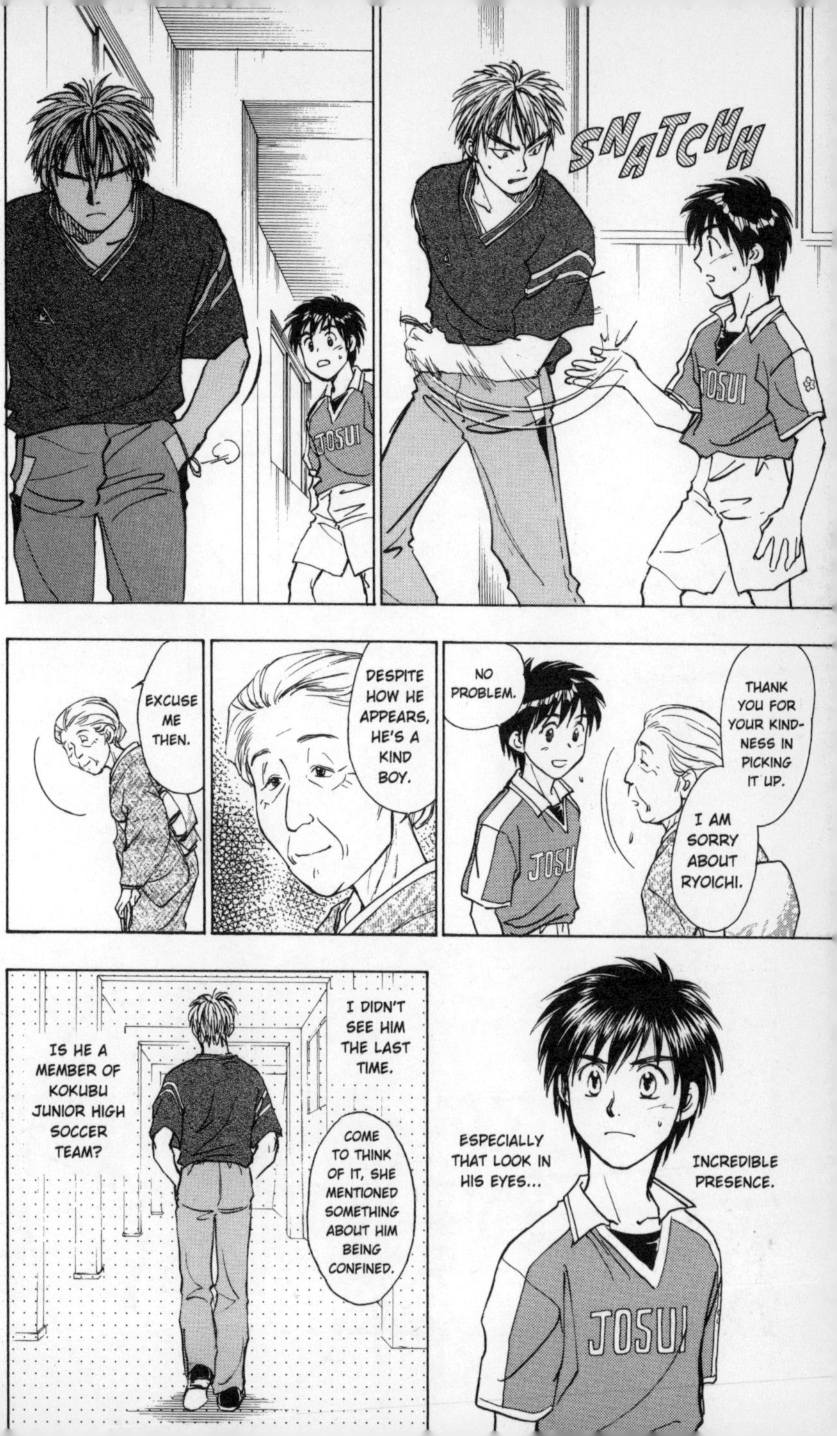
SNATCHH
THANK YOU FOR YOUR KINDNESS IN PICKING IT UP.
I AM SORRY ABOUT RYOICHI.
NO PROBLEM.
DESPITE HOW HE APPEARS, HE'S A KIND BOY.
EXCUSE ME THEN.
INCREDIBLE PRESENCE.
ESPECIALLY THAT LOOK IN HIS EYES...
I DIDN'T SEE HIM THE LAST TIME.
COME TO THINK OF IT, SHE MENTIONED SOMETHING ABOUT HIM BEING CONFINED.
IS HE A MEMBER OF KOKUBU JUNIOR HIGH SOCCER TEAM?

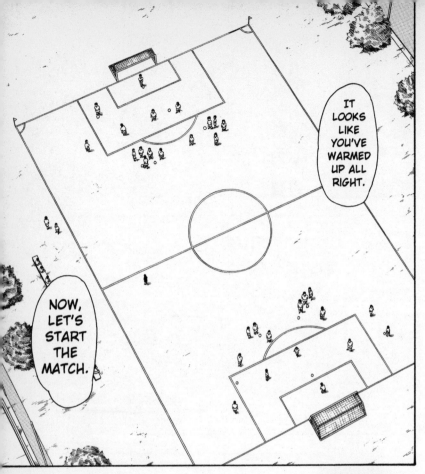

IT LOOKS LIKE YOU'VE WARMED UP ALL RIGHT.

NOW, LET'S START THE MATCH.

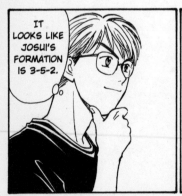

IT LOOKS LIKE JOSUI'S FORMATION IS 3-5-2.

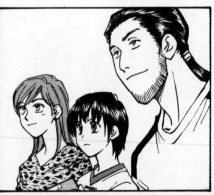

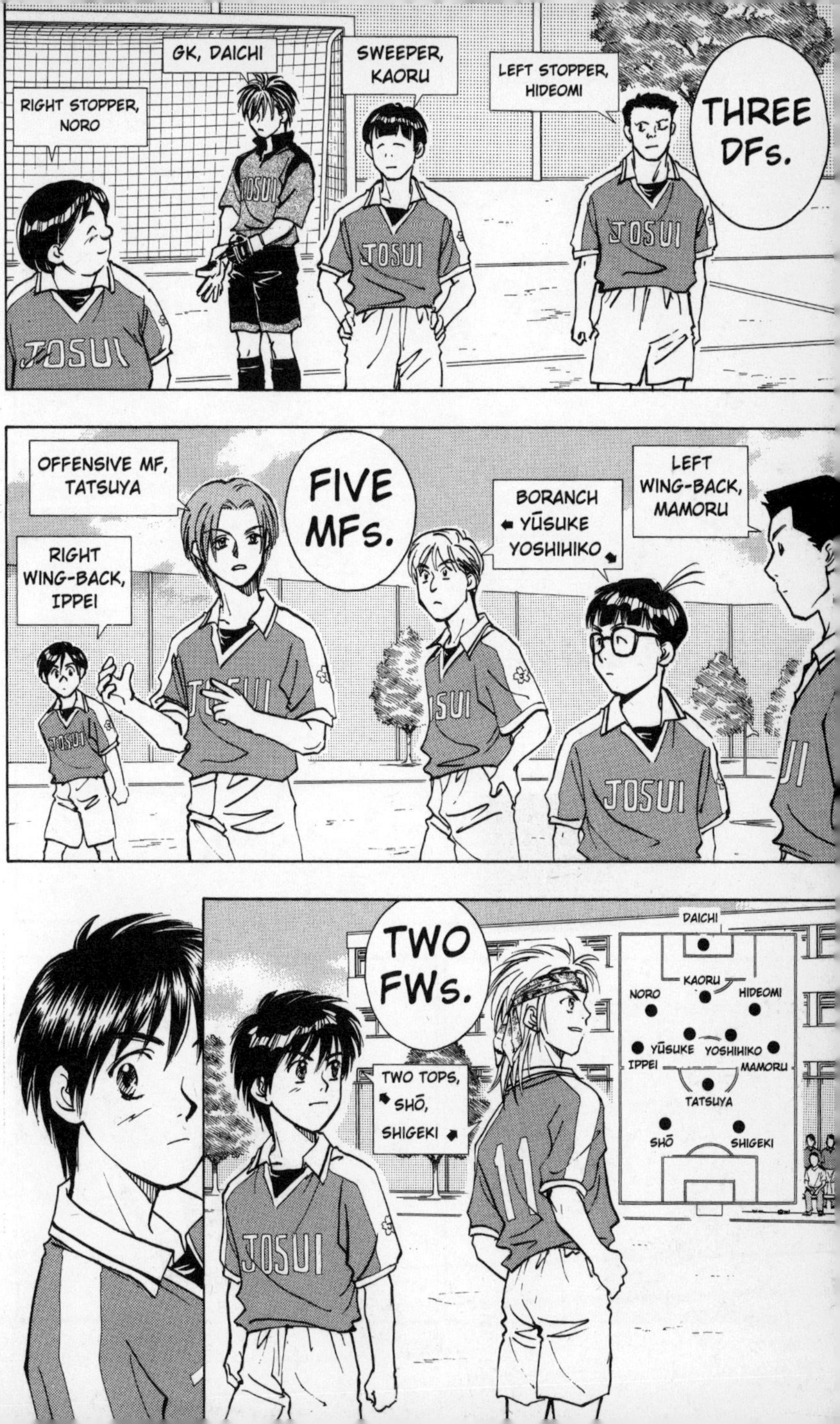
THREE DFs.
LEFT STOPPER, HIDEOMI
SWEEPER, KAORU
GK, DAICHI
RIGHT STOPPER, NORO
LEFT WING-BACK, MAMORU
BORANCH YŪSUKE YOSHIHIKO
FIVE MFs.
OFFENSIVE MF, TATSUYA
RIGHT WING-BACK, IPPEI
DAICHI
KAORU
NORO
HIDEOMI
YŪSUKE
YOSHIHIKO
IPPEI
MAMORU
TATSUYA
SHŌ
SHIGEKI
TWO FWs.
TWO TOPS, SHŌ, SHIGEKI

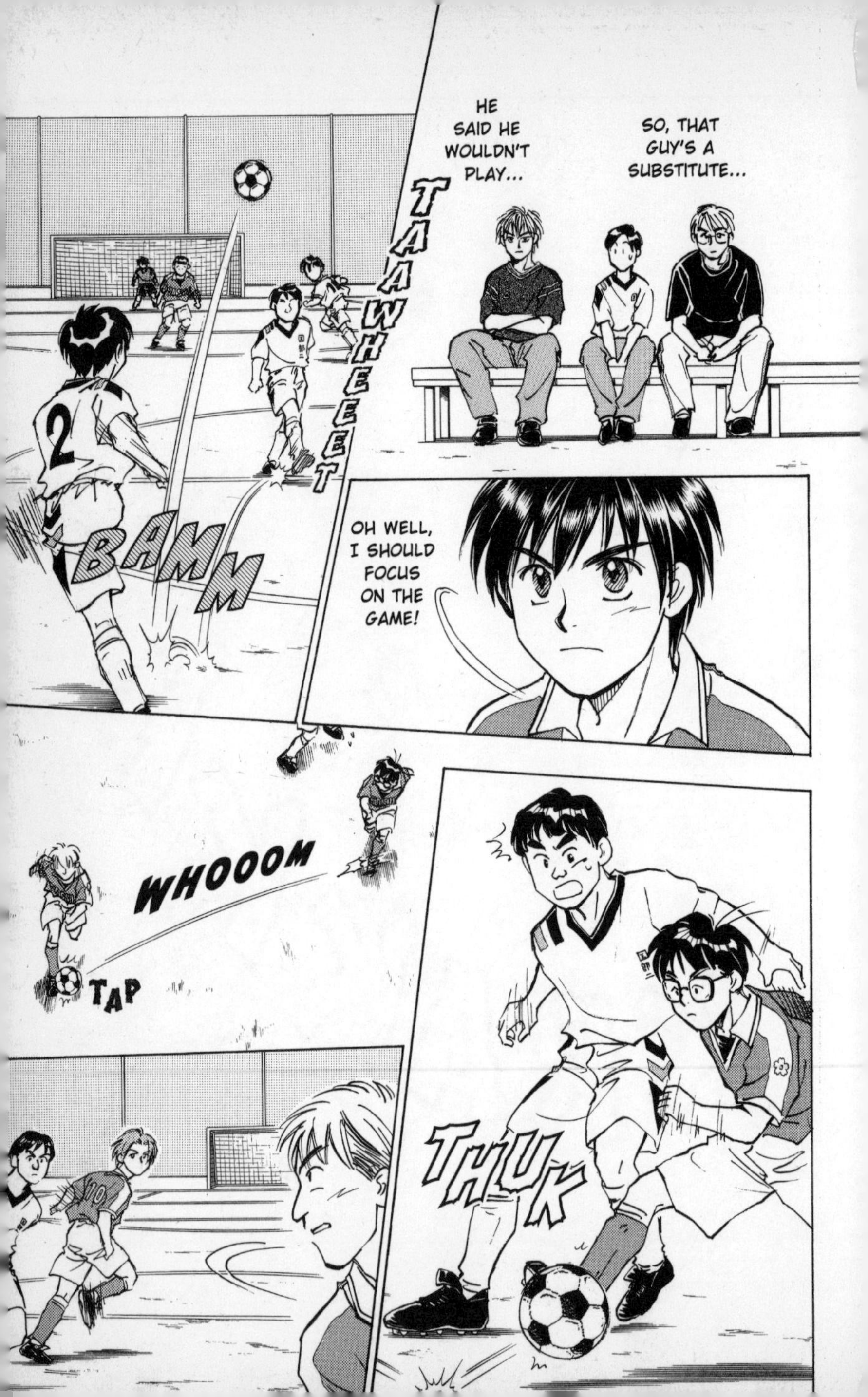
SO, THAT GUY'S A SUBSTITUTE...
HE SAID HE WOULDN'T PLAY...
OH WELL, I SHOULD FOCUS ON THE GAME!
TAAWHEEEET
BAMMM
THUK
WHOOOM
TAP

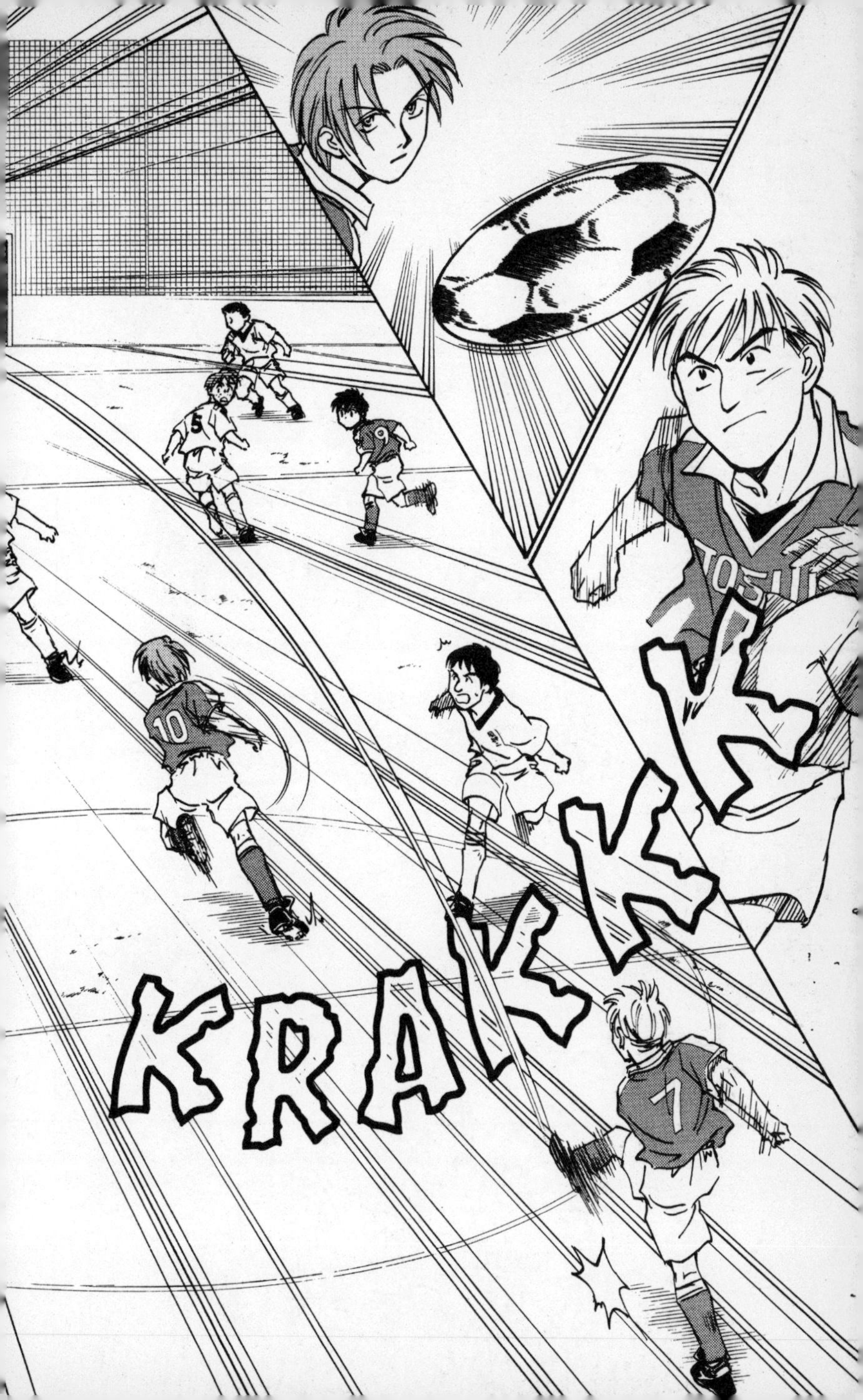
KRAKK

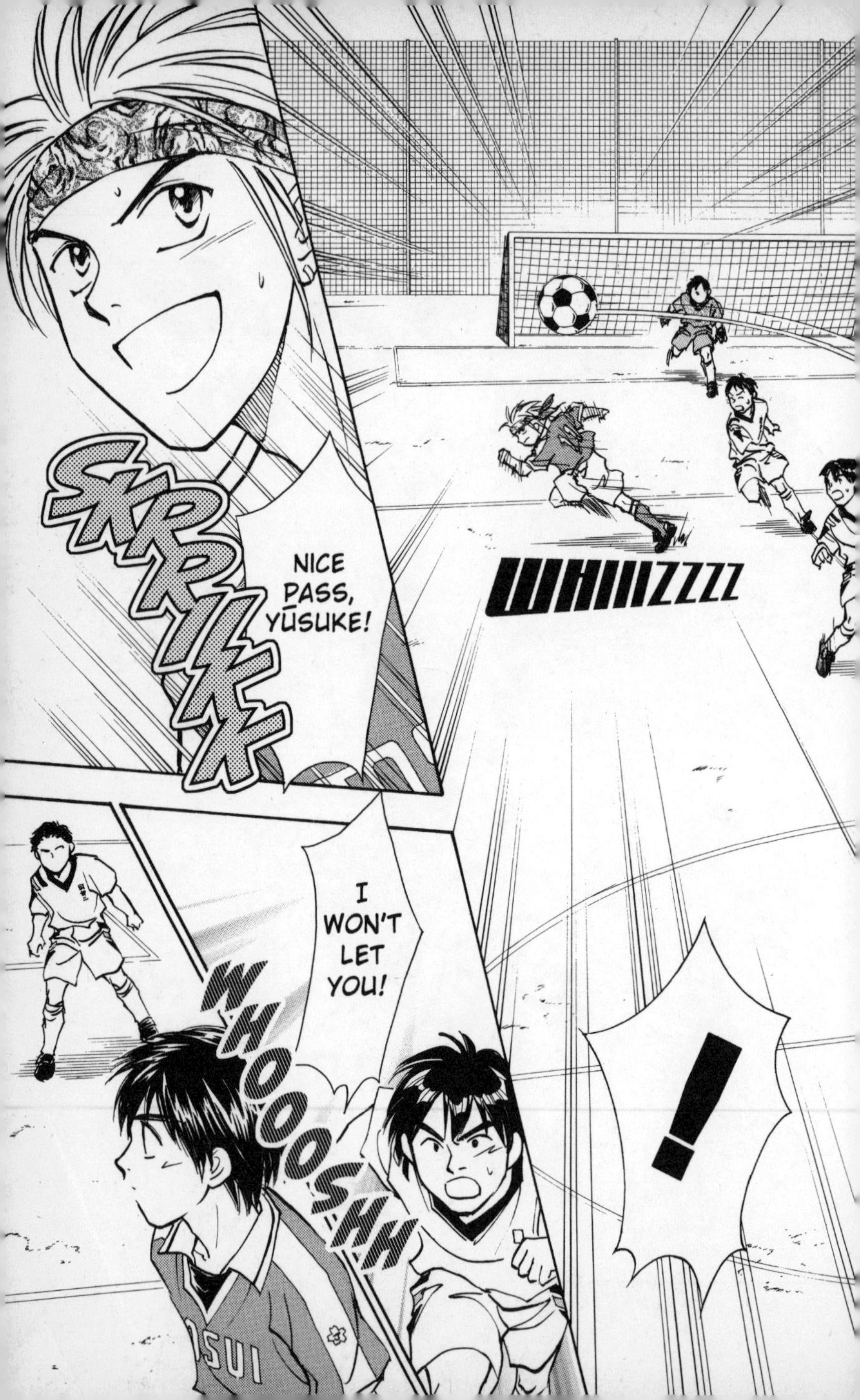
WHIIZZZZ
SKRIKK
NICE PASS, YŪSUKE!
I WON'T LET YOU!
WHOOOSHH
!

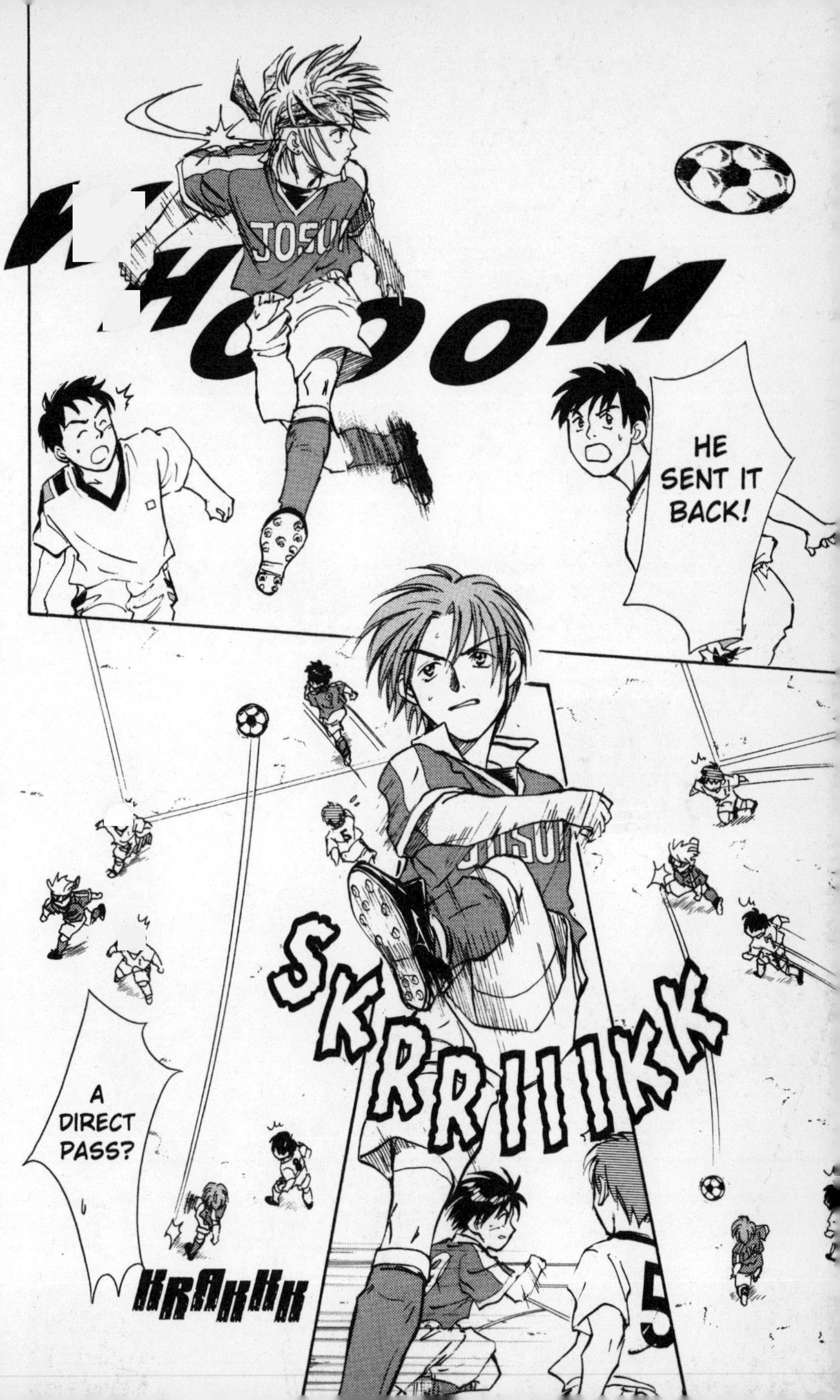
WHOOOM
HE SENT IT BACK!
SKRRIIIKK
A DIRECT PASS?
KRAKKKK

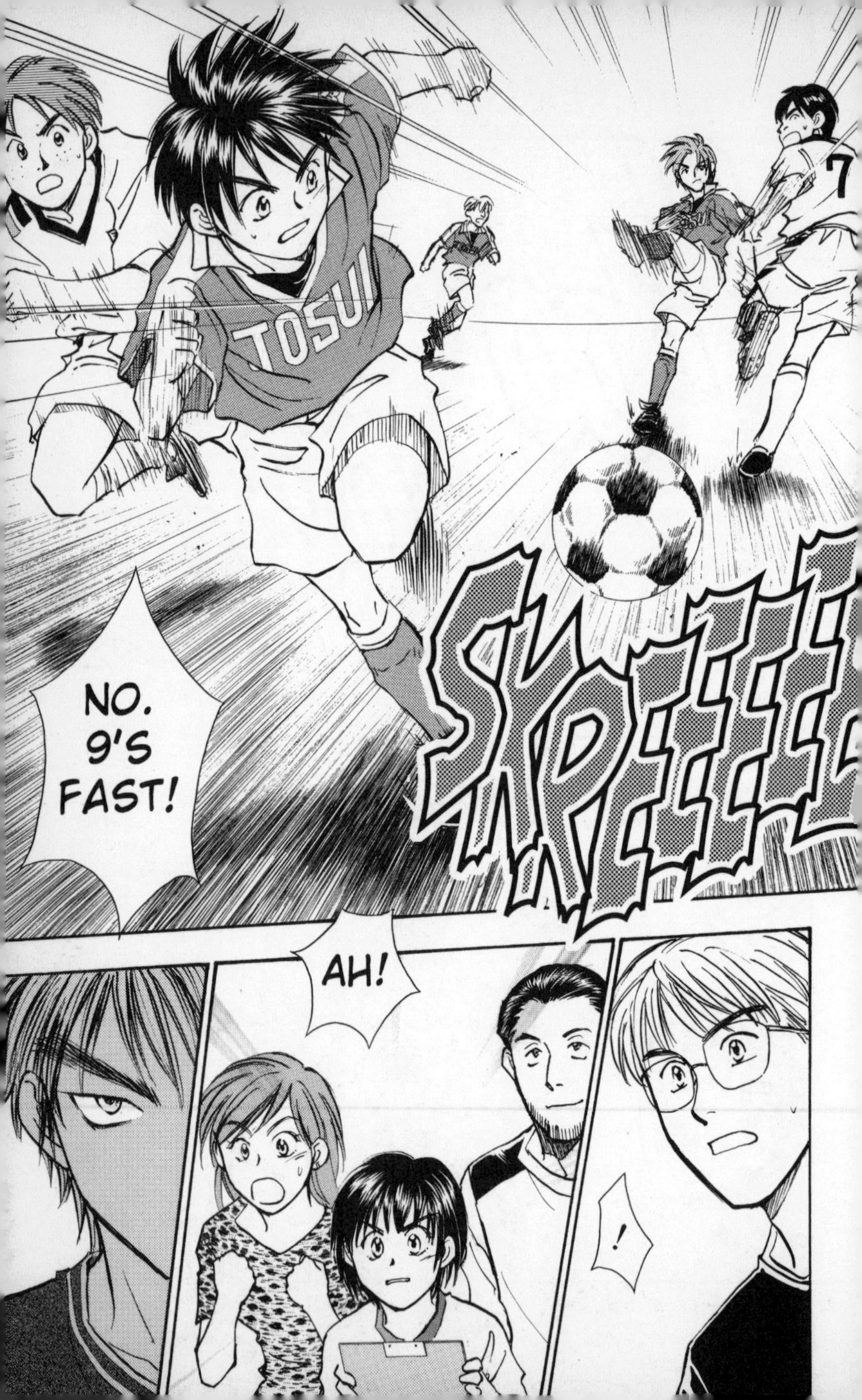
NO. 9'S FAST!
!
AH!

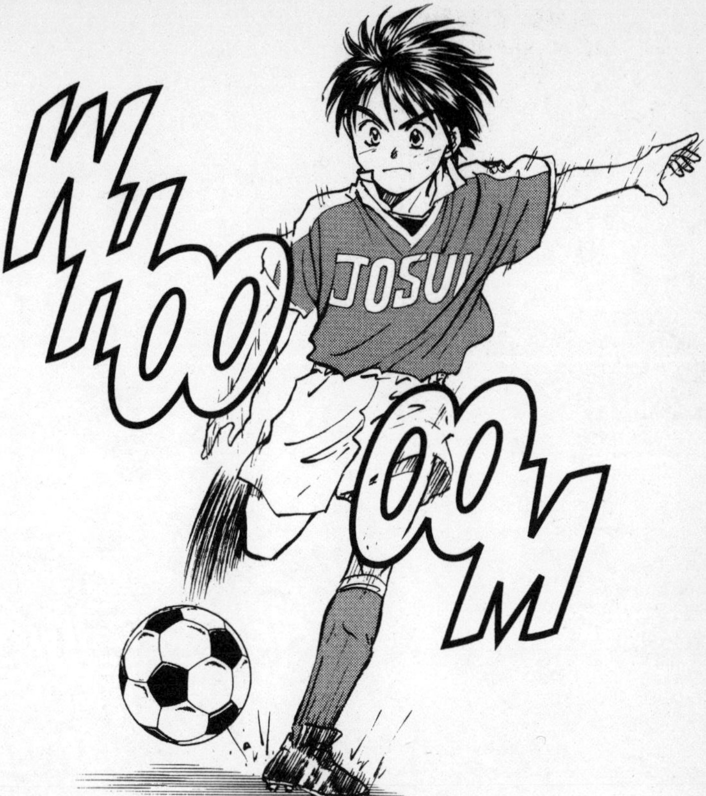
WHOOOOM
JOSUI
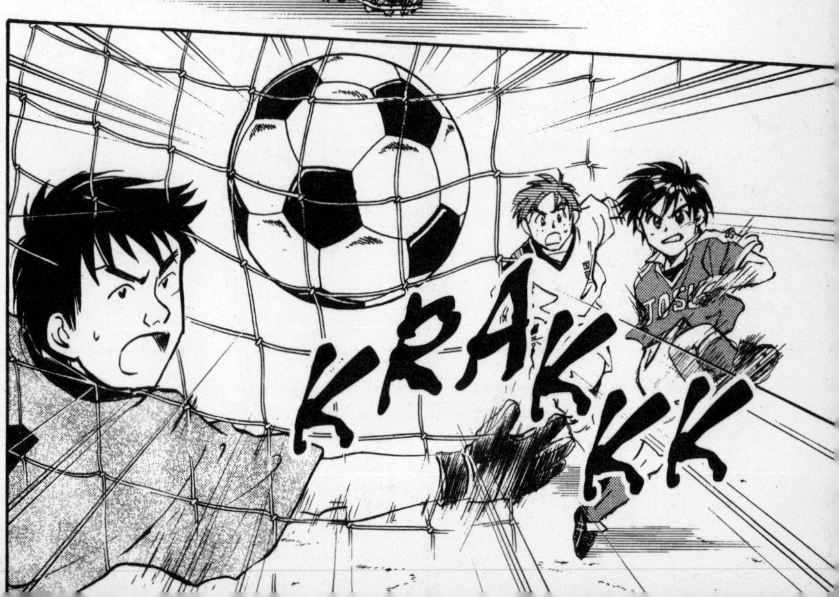
KRAKKK

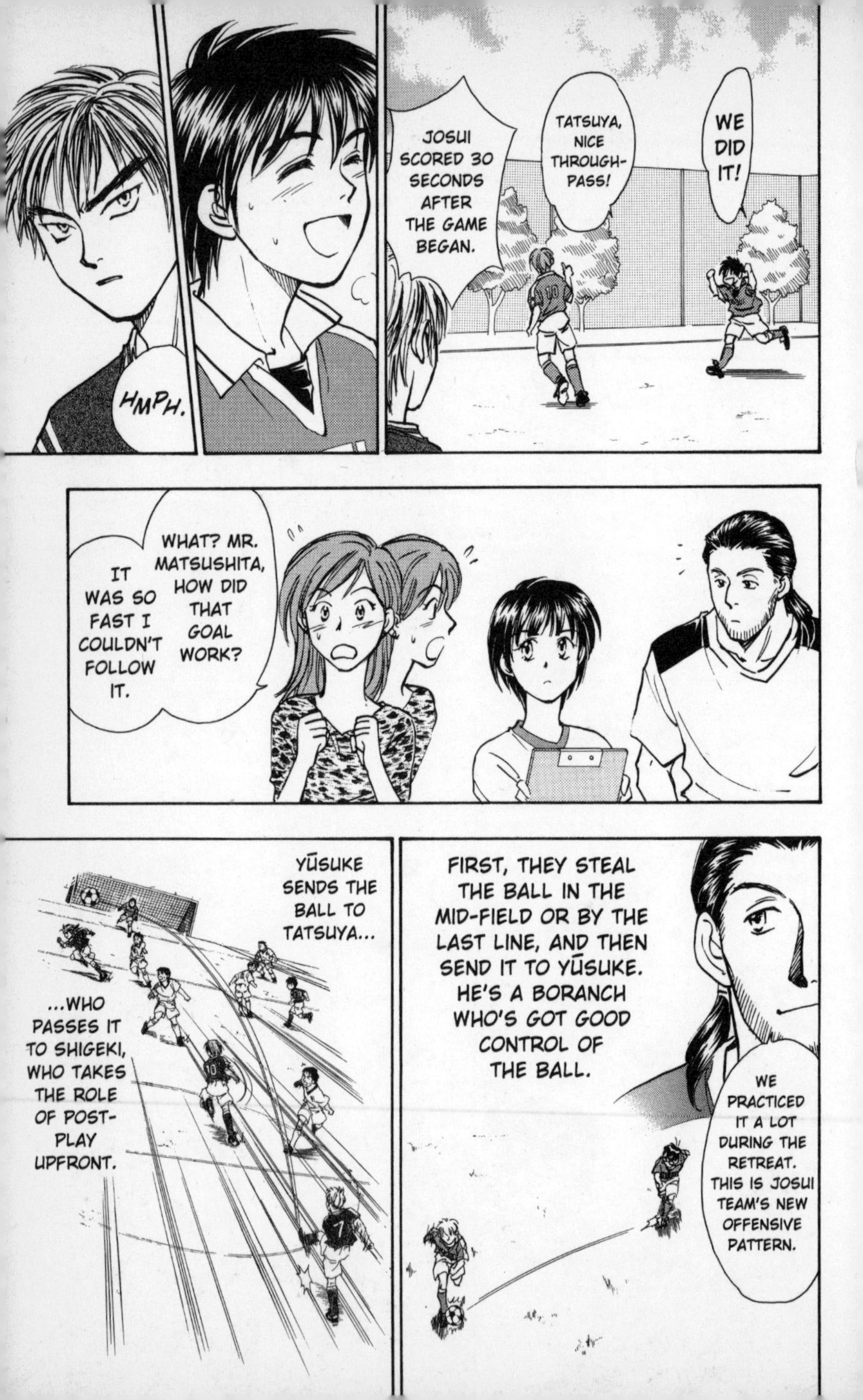
WE DID IT!
TATSUYA, NICE THROUGH-PASS!
JOSUI SCORED 30 SECONDS AFTER THE GAME BEGAN.
HMPH.
WHAT? MR. MATSUSHITA, HOW DID THAT GOAL WORK?
IT WAS SO FAST I COULDN'T FOLLOW IT.
FIRST, THEY STEAL THE BALL IN THE MID-FIELD OR BY THE LAST LINE, AND THEN SEND IT TO YŪSUKE. HE'S A BORANCH WHO'S GOT GOOD CONTROL OF THE BALL.
WE PRACTICED IT A LOT DURING THE RETREAT. THIS IS JOSUI TEAM'S NEW OFFENSIVE PATTERN.
YŪSUKE SENDS THE BALL TO TATSUYA...
...WHO PASSES IT TO SHIGEKI, WHO TAKES THE ROLE OF POST-PLAY UPFRONT.

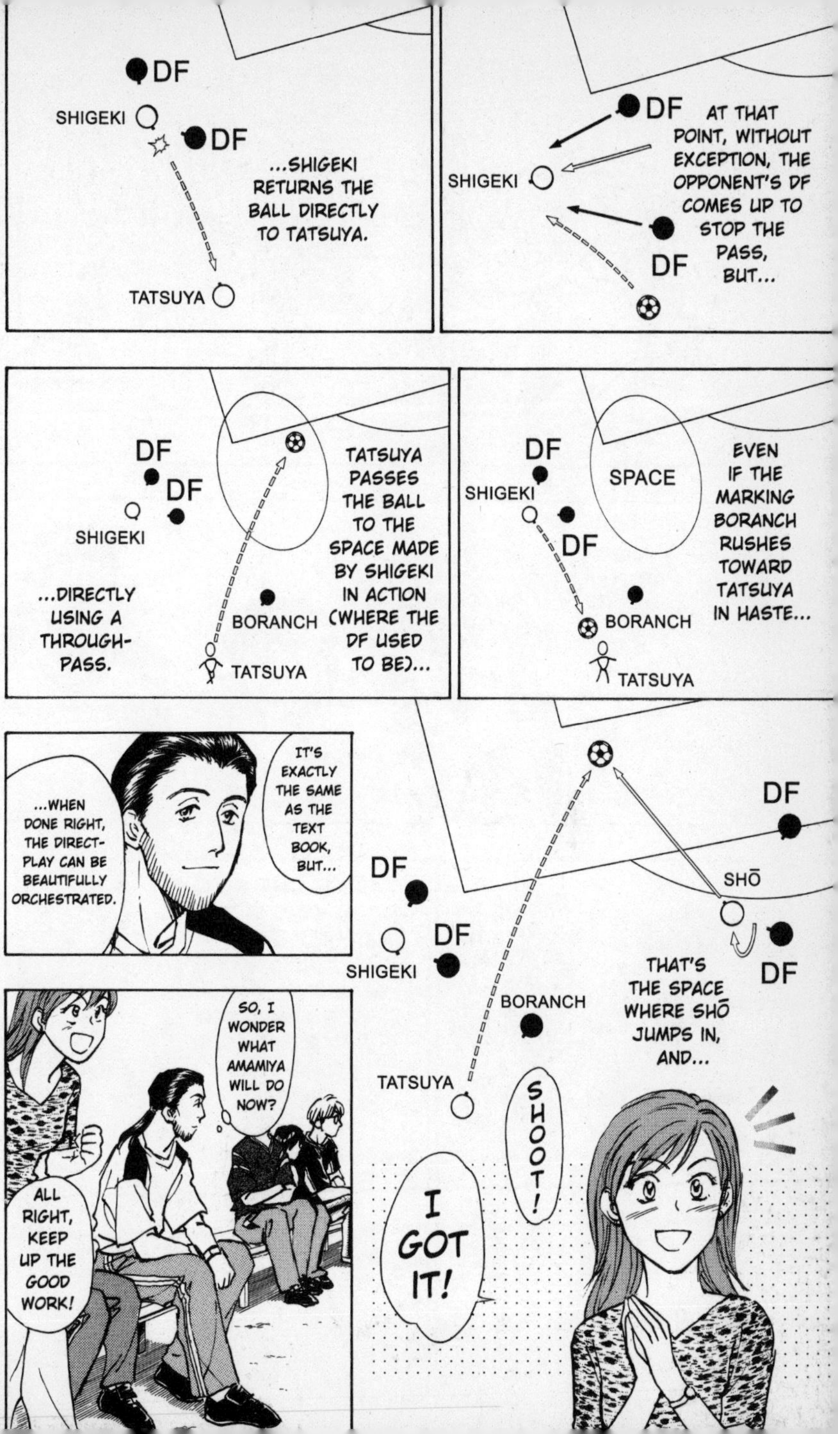
DF
DF
SHIGEKI
DF
AT THAT POINT, WITHOUT EXCEPTION, THE OPPONENT'S DF COMES UP TO STOP THE PASS, BUT...
DF
SHIGEKI
DF
...SHIGEKI RETURNS THE BALL DIRECTLY TO TATSUYA.
TATSUYA
DF
SHIGEKI
SPACE
EVEN IF THE MARKING BORANCH RUSHES TOWARD TATSUYA IN HASTE...
DF
BORANCH
TATSUYA
DF
DF
SHIGEKI
TATSUYA PASSES THE BALL TO THE SPACE MADE BY SHIGEKI IN ACTION (WHERE THE DF USED TO BE)...
...DIRECTLY USING A THROUGH-PASS.
BORANCH
TATSUYA
DF
SHŌ
DF
DF
DF
SHIGEKI
BORANCH
THAT'S THE SPACE WHERE SHŌ JUMPS IN, AND...
TATSUYA
SHOOT!
I GOT IT!
IT'S EXACTLY THE SAME AS THE TEXT BOOK, BUT...
...WHEN DONE RIGHT, THE DIRECT-PLAY CAN BE BEAUTIFULLY ORCHESTRATED.
SO, I WONDER WHAT AMAMIYA WILL DO NOW?
ALL RIGHT, KEEP UP THE GOOD WORK!

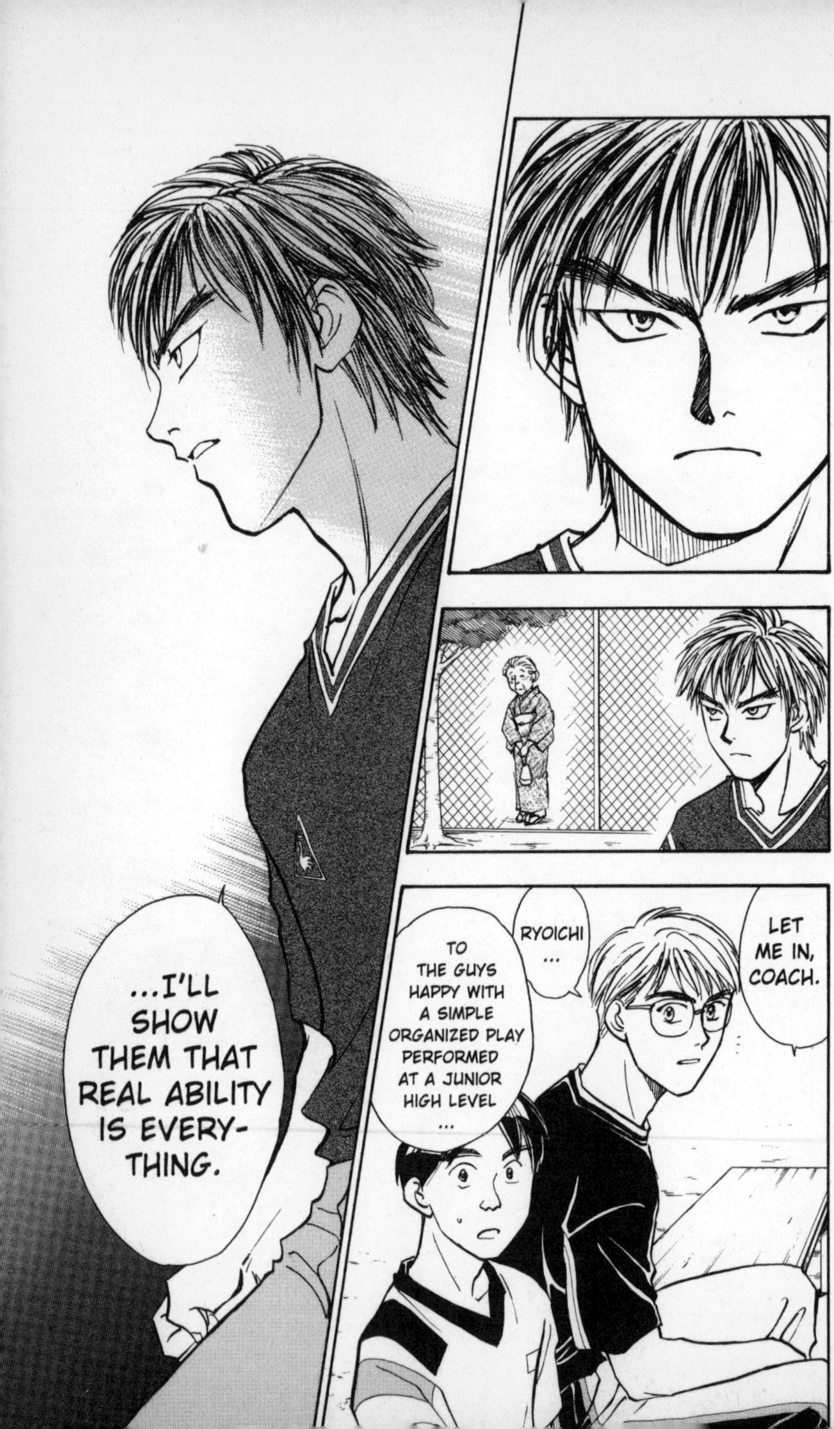
LET ME IN, COACH.
RYOICHI ...
TO THE GUYS HAPPY WITH A SIMPLE ORGANIZED PLAY PERFORMED AT A JUNIOR HIGH LEVEL ...
...I'LL SHOW THEM THAT REAL ABILITY IS EVERY-THING.

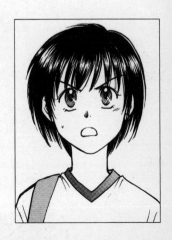

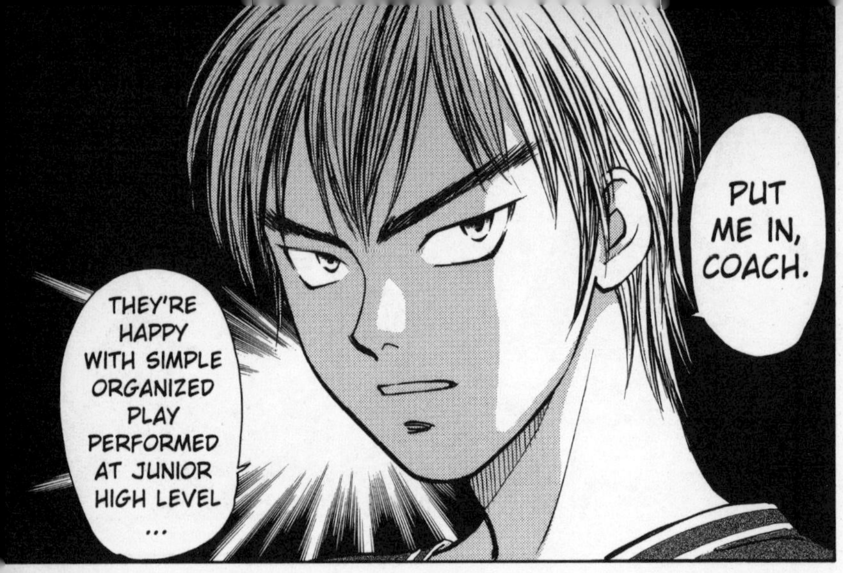
PUT ME IN, COACH.
THEY'RE HAPPY WITH SIMPLE ORGANIZED PLAY PERFORMED AT JUNIOR HIGH LEVEL ...

STAGE.40 My Position

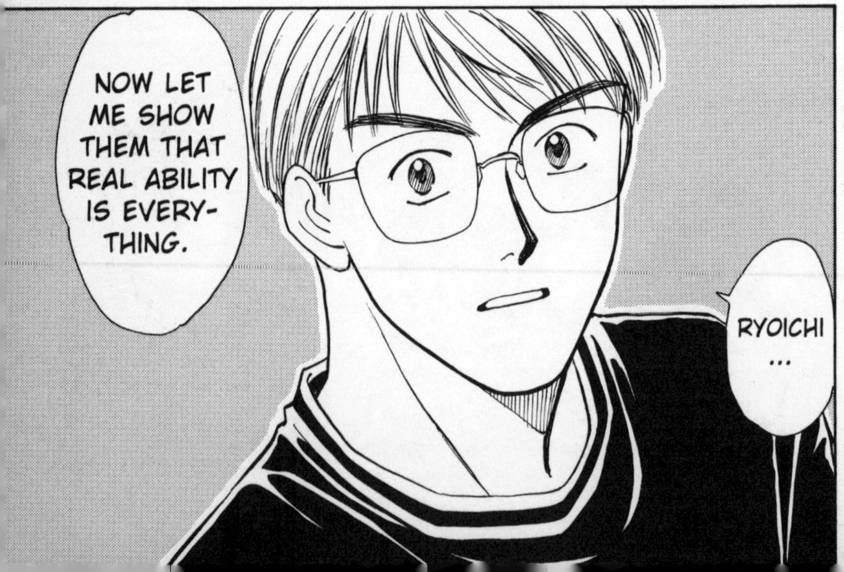
NOW LET ME SHOW THEM THAT REAL ABILITY IS EVERY-THING.
RYOICHI ...

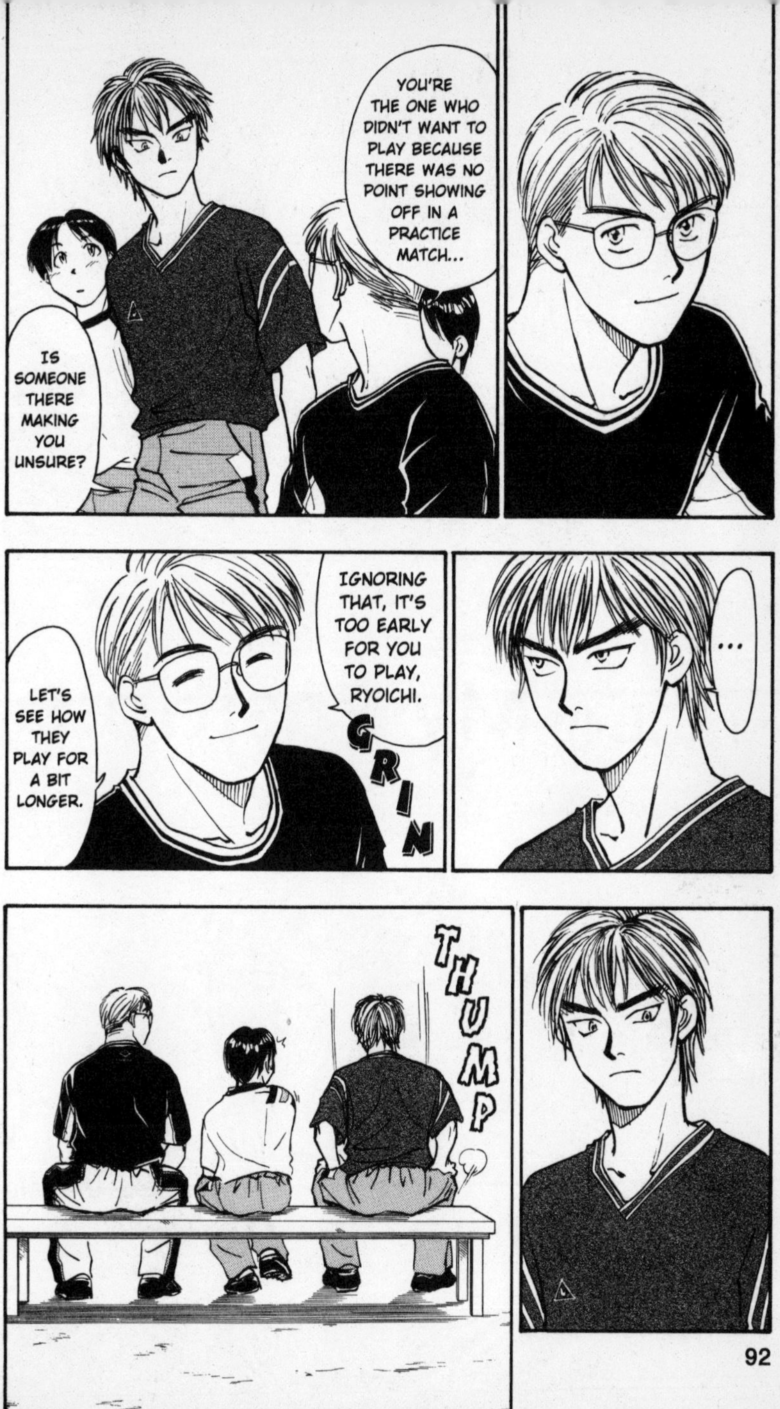

YOU'RE THE ONE WHO DIDN'T WANT TO PLAY BECAUSE THERE WAS NO POINT SHOWING OFF IN A PRACTICE MATCH...
IS SOMEONE THERE MAKING YOU UNSURE?
...
IGNORING THAT, IT'S TOO EARLY FOR YOU TO PLAY, RYOICHI.
GRIN
LET'S SEE HOW THEY PLAY FOR A BIT LONGER.
THUMP

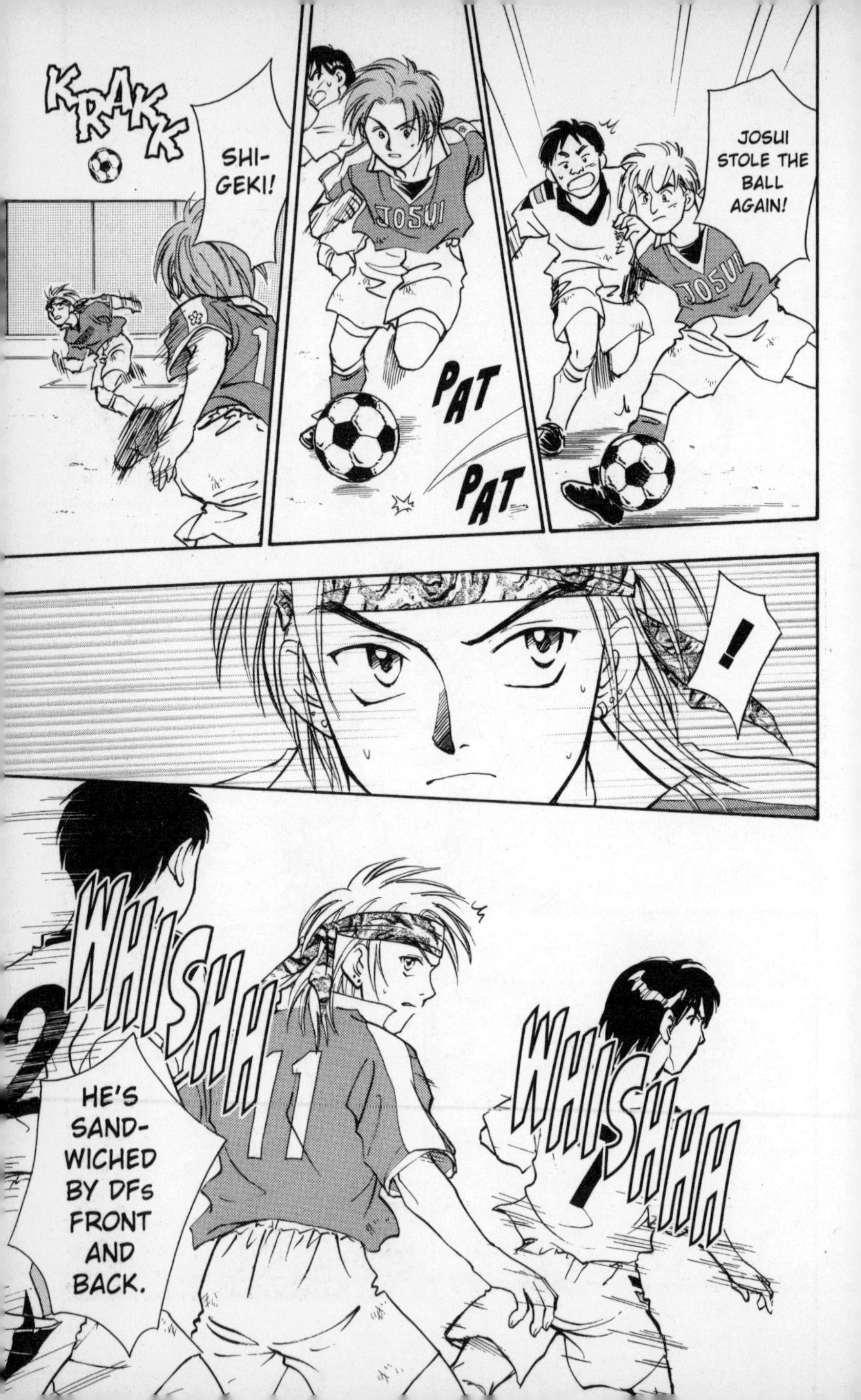
JOSUI STOLE THE BALL AGAIN!
PAT
PAT
KRAKK
SHI-GEKI!
!
WHISHHH
WHISHH
HE'S SANDWICHED BY DFs FRONT AND BACK.

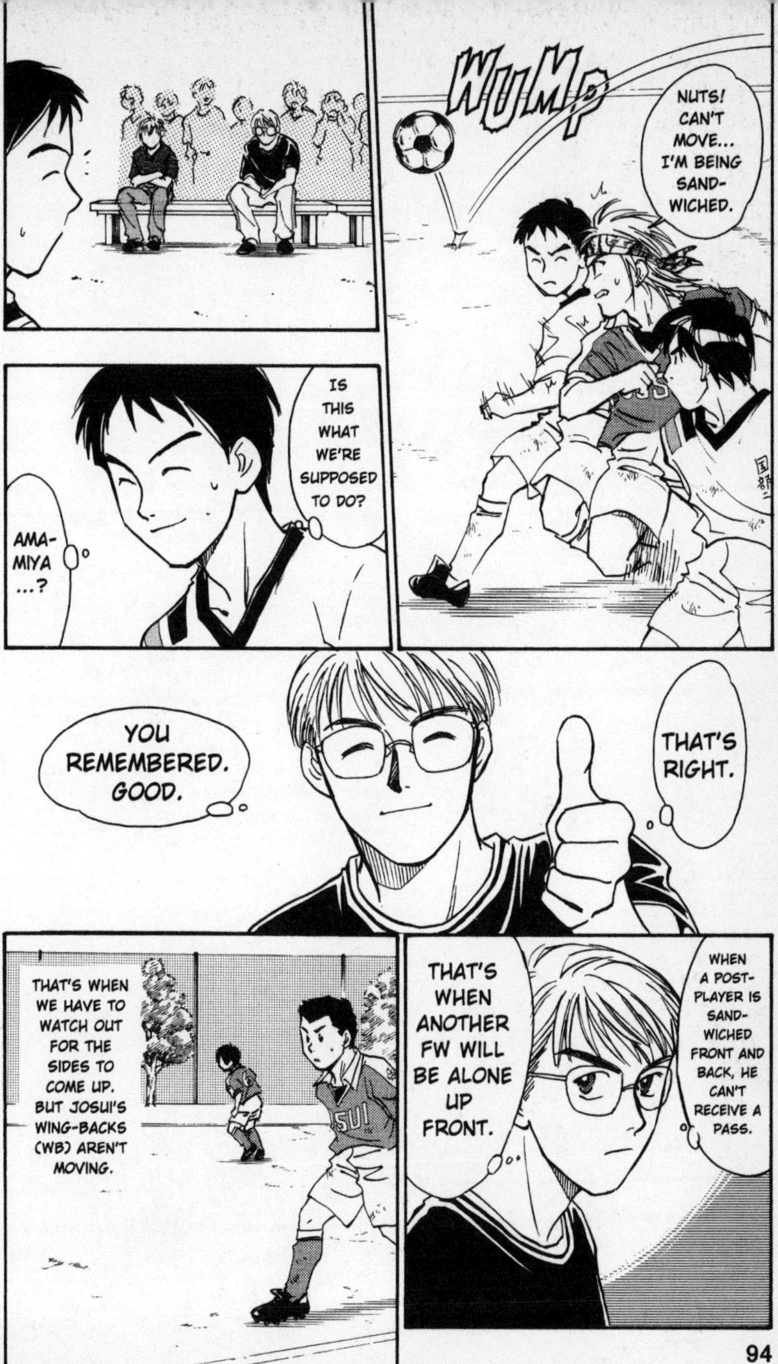
WUMP
NUTS! CAN'T MOVE... I'M BEING SAND-WICHED.
IS THIS WHAT WE'RE SUPPOSED TO DO?
AMA-MIYA ...?
THAT'S RIGHT.
YOU REMEMBERED. GOOD.
WHEN A POST-PLAYER IS SAND-WICHED FRONT AND BACK, HE CAN'T RECEIVE A PASS.
THAT'S WHEN ANOTHER FW WILL BE ALONE UP FRONT.
THAT'S WHEN WE HAVE TO WATCH OUT FOR THE SIDES TO COME UP. BUT JOSUI'S WING-BACKS (WB) AREN'T MOVING.

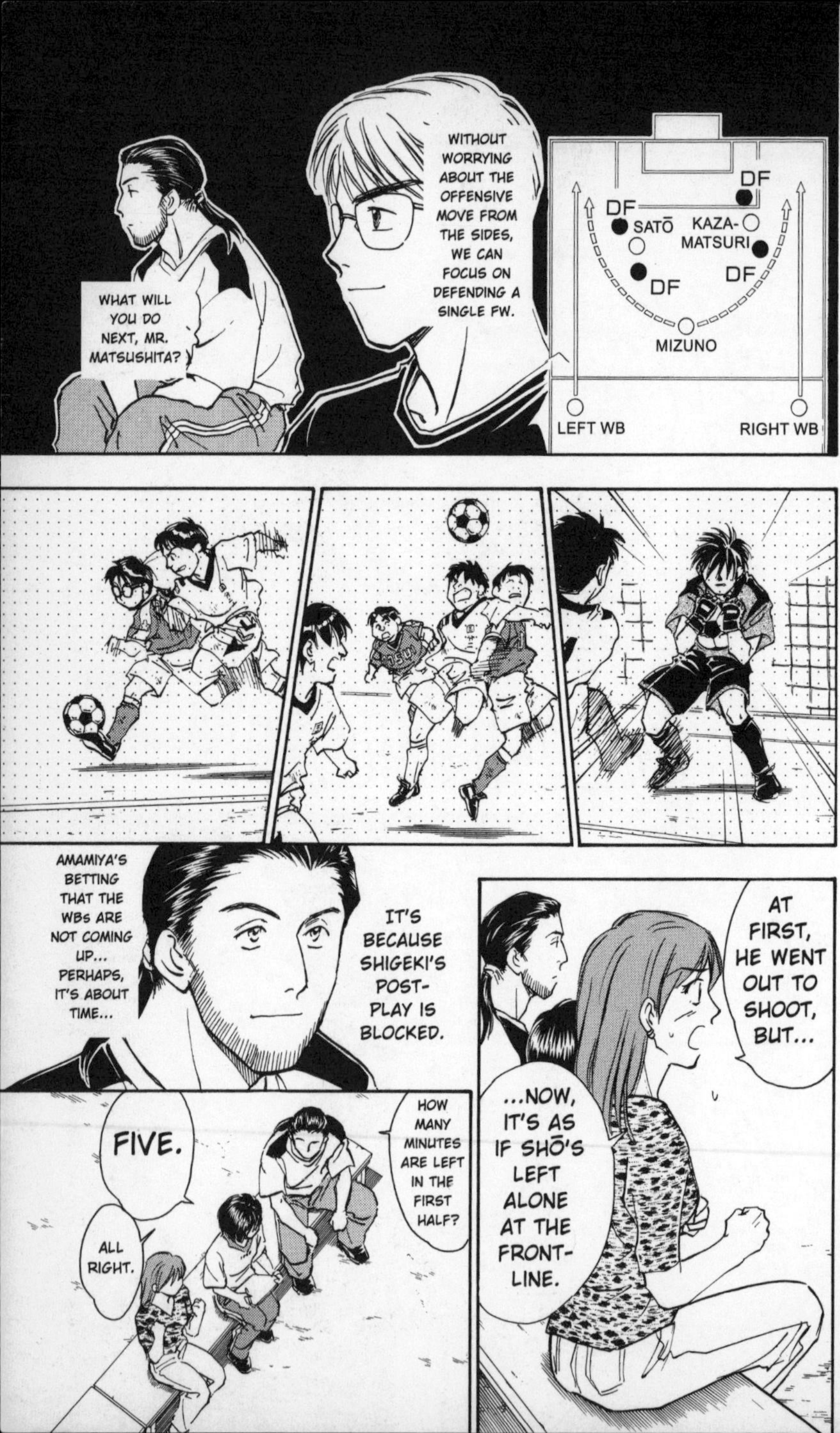
DF
DF
SATŌ
KAZA-MATSURI
DF
DF
MIZUNO
LEFT WB
RIGHT WB
WITHOUT WORRYING ABOUT THE OFFENSIVE MOVE FROM THE SIDES, WE CAN FOCUS ON DEFENDING A SINGLE FW.
WHAT WILL YOU DO NEXT, MR. MATSUSHITA?
AT FIRST, HE WENT OUT TO SHOOT, BUT...
...NOW, IT'S AS IF SHŌ'S LEFT ALONE AT THE FRONT-LINE.
IT'S BECAUSE SHIGEKI'S POST-PLAY IS BLOCKED.
AMAMIYA'S BETTING THAT THE WBs ARE NOT COMING UP... PERHAPS, IT'S ABOUT TIME...
HOW MANY MINUTES ARE LEFT IN THE FIRST HALF?
FIVE.
ALL RIGHT.

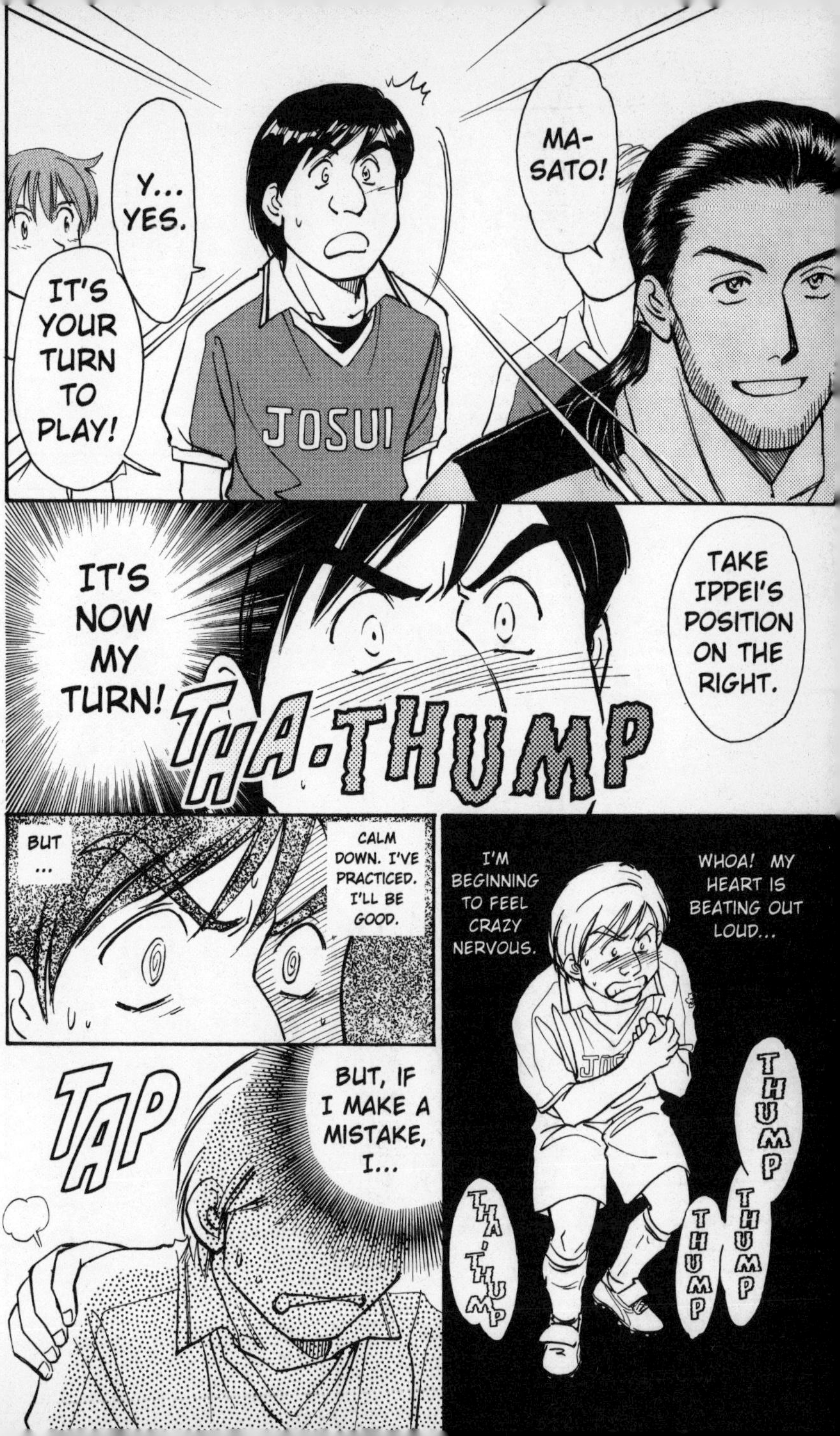
MA-SATO!
Y... YES.
IT'S YOUR TURN TO PLAY!
TAKE IPPEI'S POSITION ON THE RIGHT.
IT'S NOW MY TURN!
THA-THUMP
WHOA! MY HEART IS BEATING OUT LOUD...
I'M BEGINNING TO FEEL CRAZY NERVOUS.
THUMP
THUMP
THUMP
THA-THUMP
CALM DOWN. I'VE PRACTICED. I'LL BE GOOD.
BUT ...
BUT, IF I MAKE A MISTAKE, I...
TAP

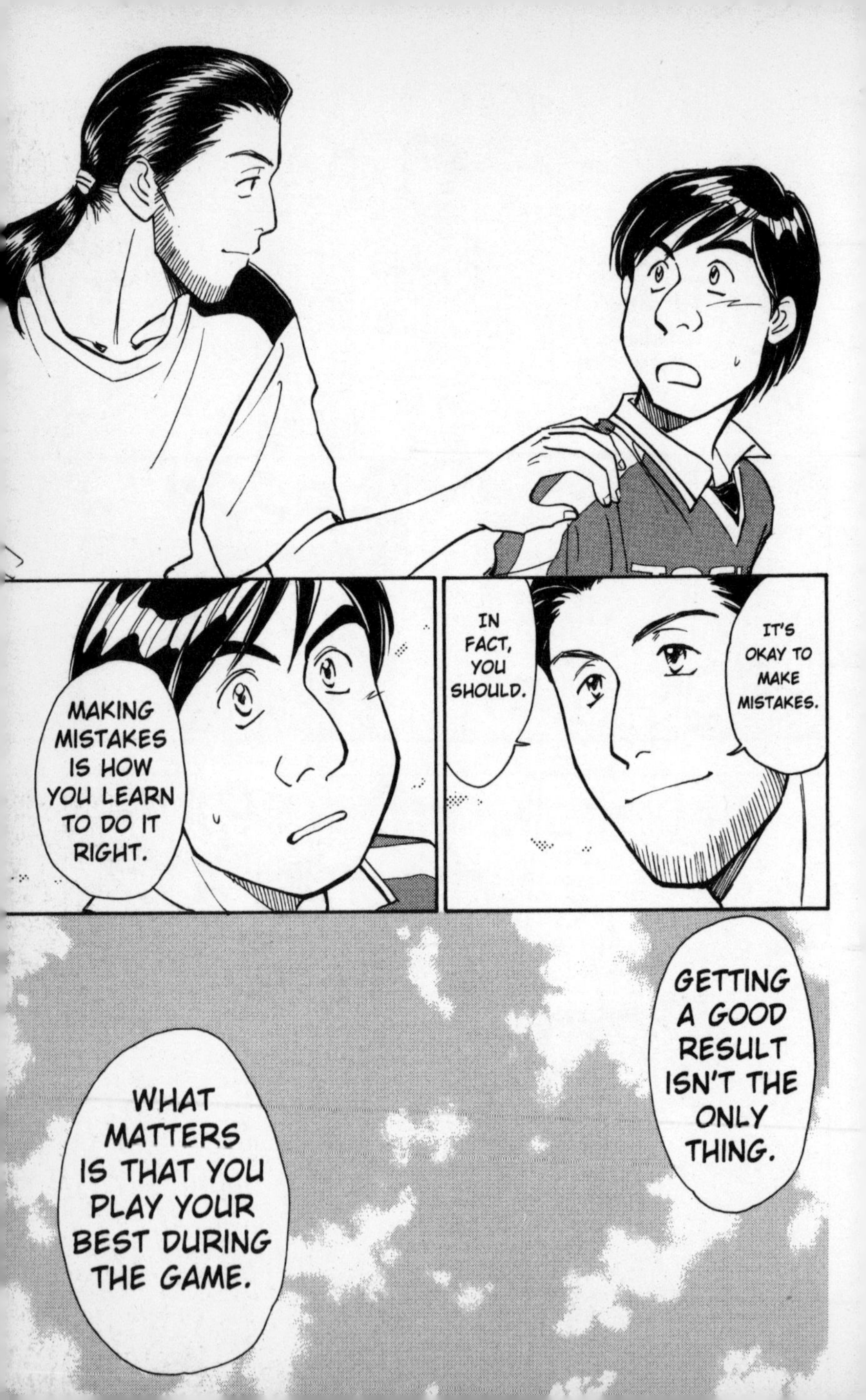
IT'S OKAY TO MAKE MISTAKES.
IN FACT, YOU SHOULD.
MAKING MISTAKES IS HOW YOU LEARN TO DO IT RIGHT.
GETTING A GOOD RESULT ISN'T THE ONLY THING.
WHAT MATTERS IS THAT YOU PLAY YOUR BEST DURING THE GAME.

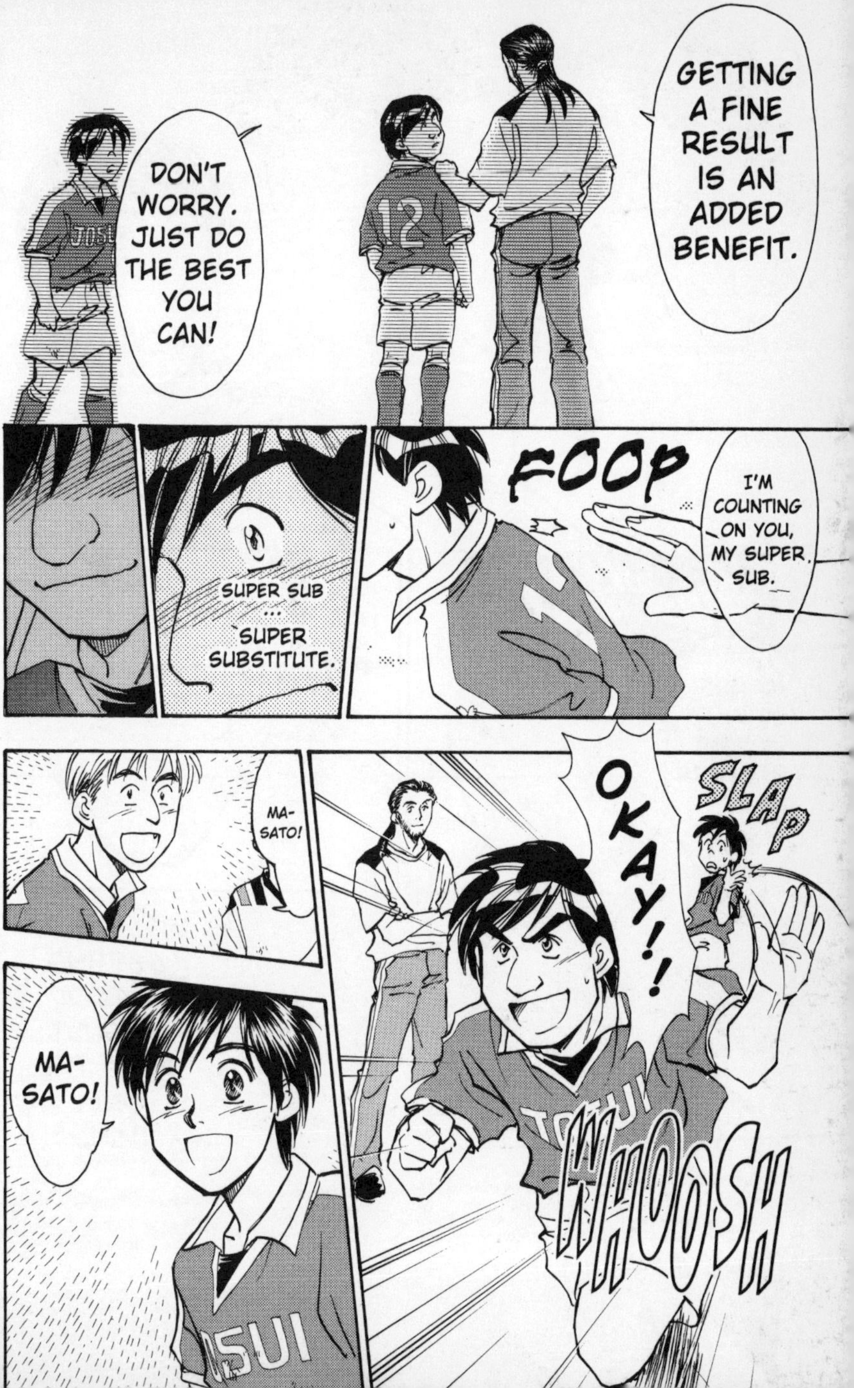

GETTING A FINE RESULT IS AN ADDED BENEFIT.
DON'T WORRY. JUST DO THE BEST YOU CAN!
FOOP
I'M COUNTING ON YOU, MY SUPER SUB.
SUPER SUB ... SUPER SUBSTITUTE.
SLAP
OKAY!!
WHOOSH
MA-SATO!
MA-SATO!

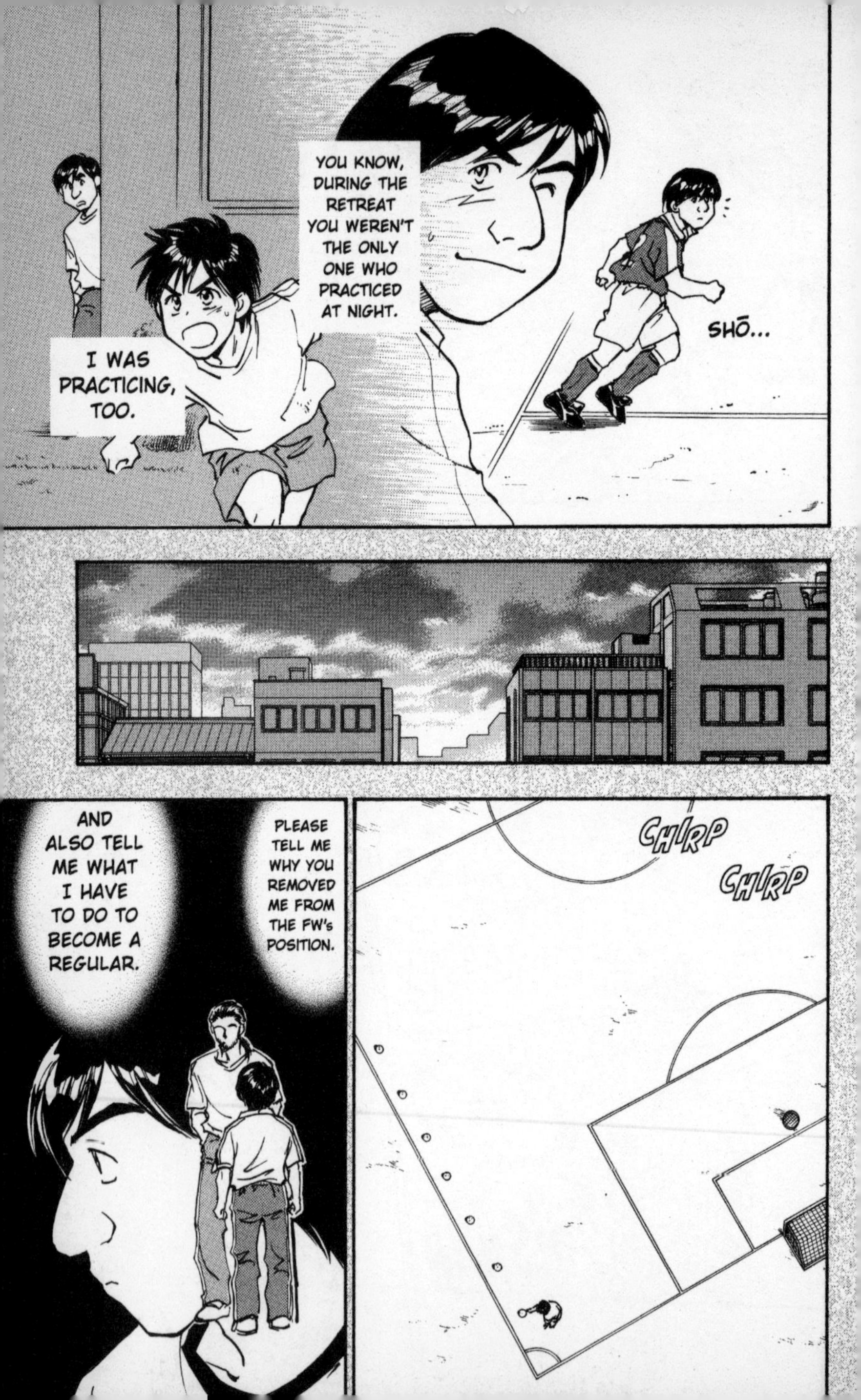
SHŌ...
YOU KNOW, DURING THE RETREAT YOU WEREN'T THE ONLY ONE WHO PRACTICED AT NIGHT.
I WAS PRACTICING, TOO.
CHIRP
CHIRP
PLEASE TELL ME WHY YOU REMOVED ME FROM THE FW's POSITION.
AND ALSO TELL ME WHAT I HAVE TO DO TO BECOME A REGULAR.

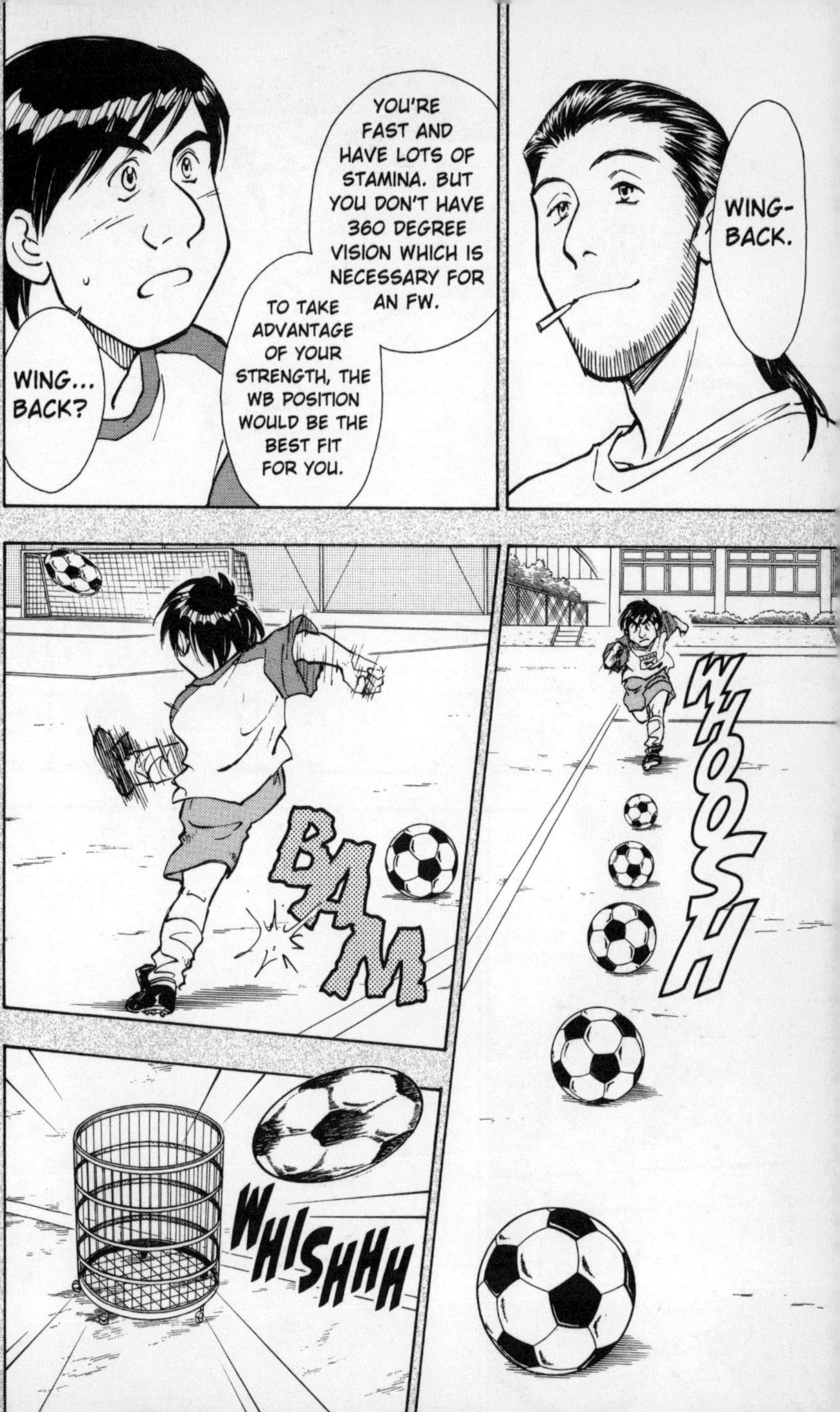
WING-BACK.
YOU'RE FAST AND HAVE LOTS OF STAMINA. BUT YOU DON'T HAVE 360 DEGREE VISION WHICH IS NECESSARY FOR AN FW.
TO TAKE ADVANTAGE OF YOUR STRENGTH, THE WB POSITION WOULD BE THE BEST FIT FOR YOU.
WING... BACK?
WHOOSH
BAM
WHISHHH

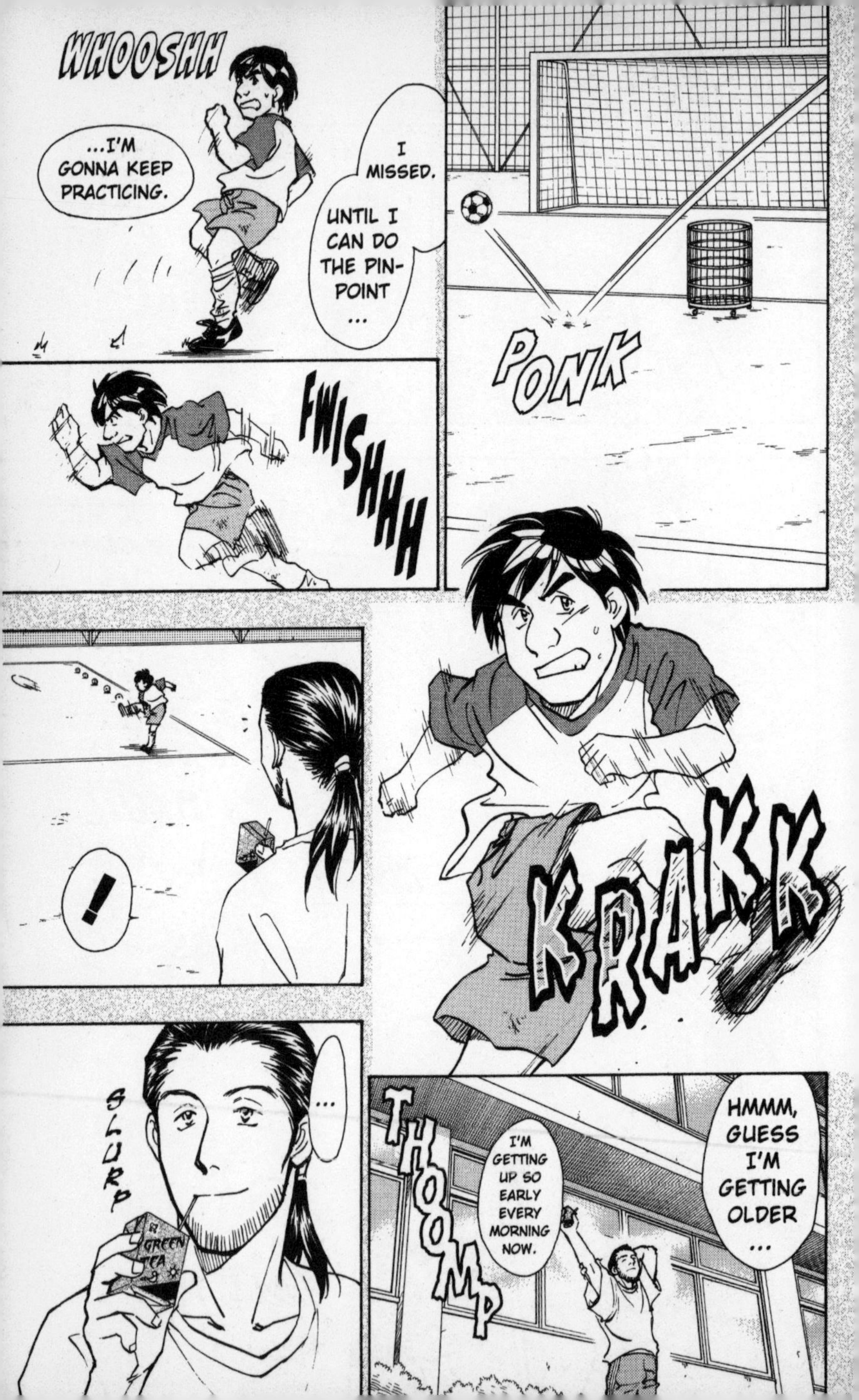
PONK
I MISSED.
UNTIL I CAN DO THE PIN-POINT ...
WHOOSHH
...I'M GONNA KEEP PRACTICING.
FWISHHH
KRAKK
!
HMMM, GUESS I'M GETTING OLDER ...
I'M GETTING UP SO EARLY EVERY MORNING NOW.
THOOMP
...
SLURP
GREEN TEA

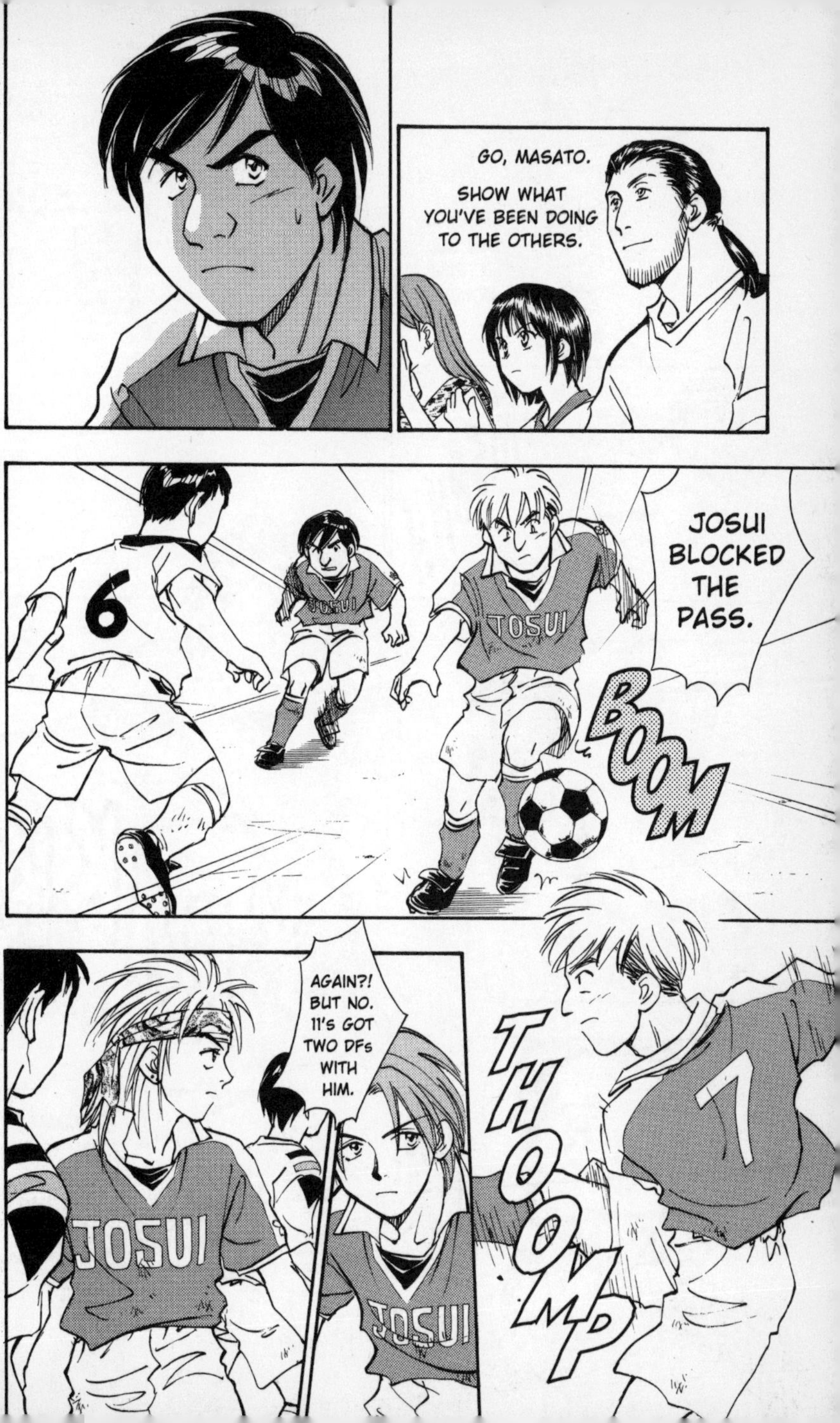
GO, MASATO.
SHOW WHAT YOU'VE BEEN DOING TO THE OTHERS.
JOSUI BLOCKED THE PASS.
6
JOSUI
TOSUI
BOOM
7
THOOOMP
AGAIN?! BUT NO. 11's GOT TWO DFs WITH HIM.
JOSUI
JOSUI

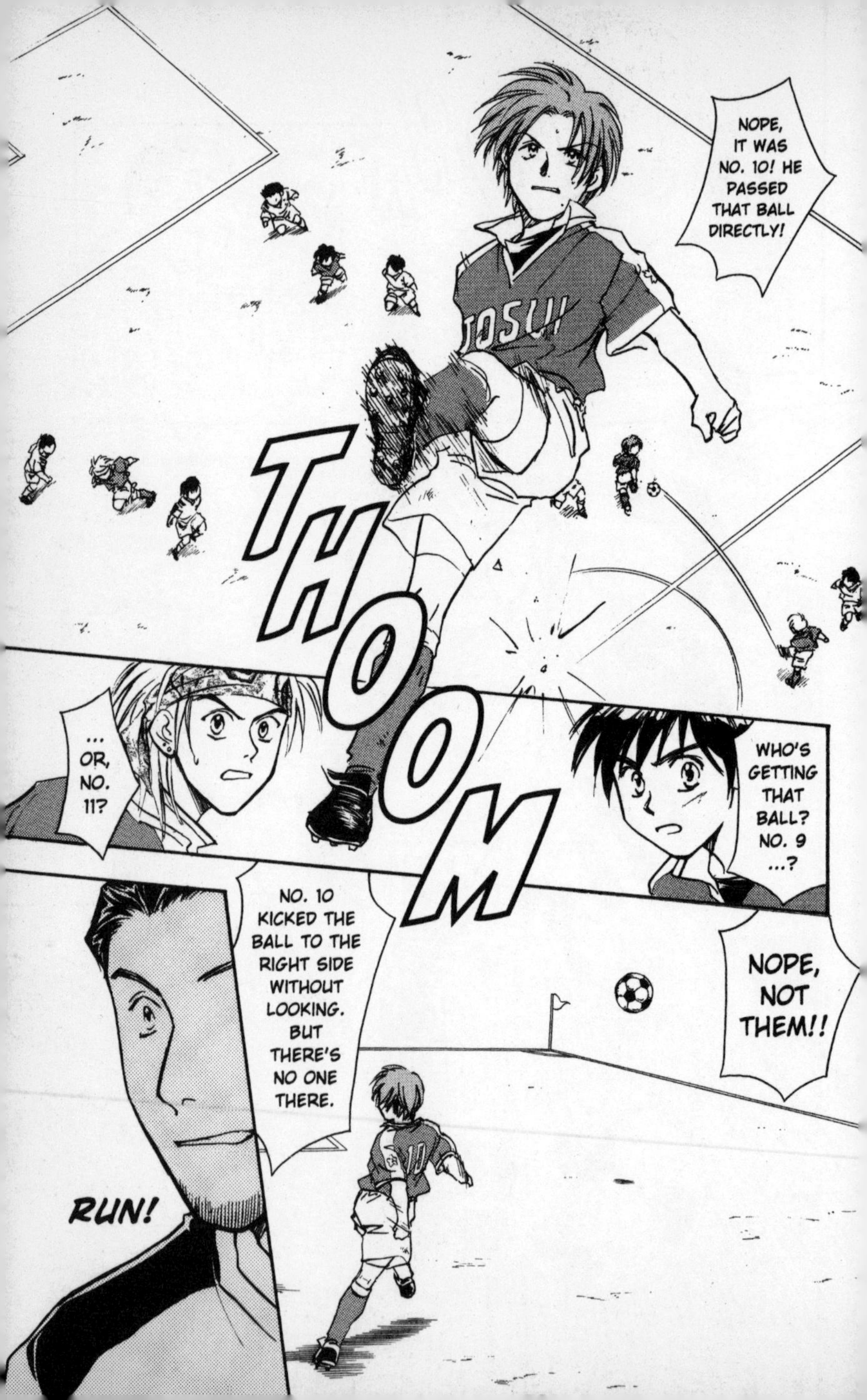
NOPE, IT WAS NO. 10! HE PASSED THAT BALL DIRECTLY!
THOOM
WHO'S GETTING THAT BALL? NO. 9 ...?
... OR, NO. 11?
NOPE, NOT THEM!!
NO. 10 KICKED THE BALL TO THE RIGHT SIDE WITHOUT LOOKING. BUT THERE'S NO ONE THERE.
RUN!

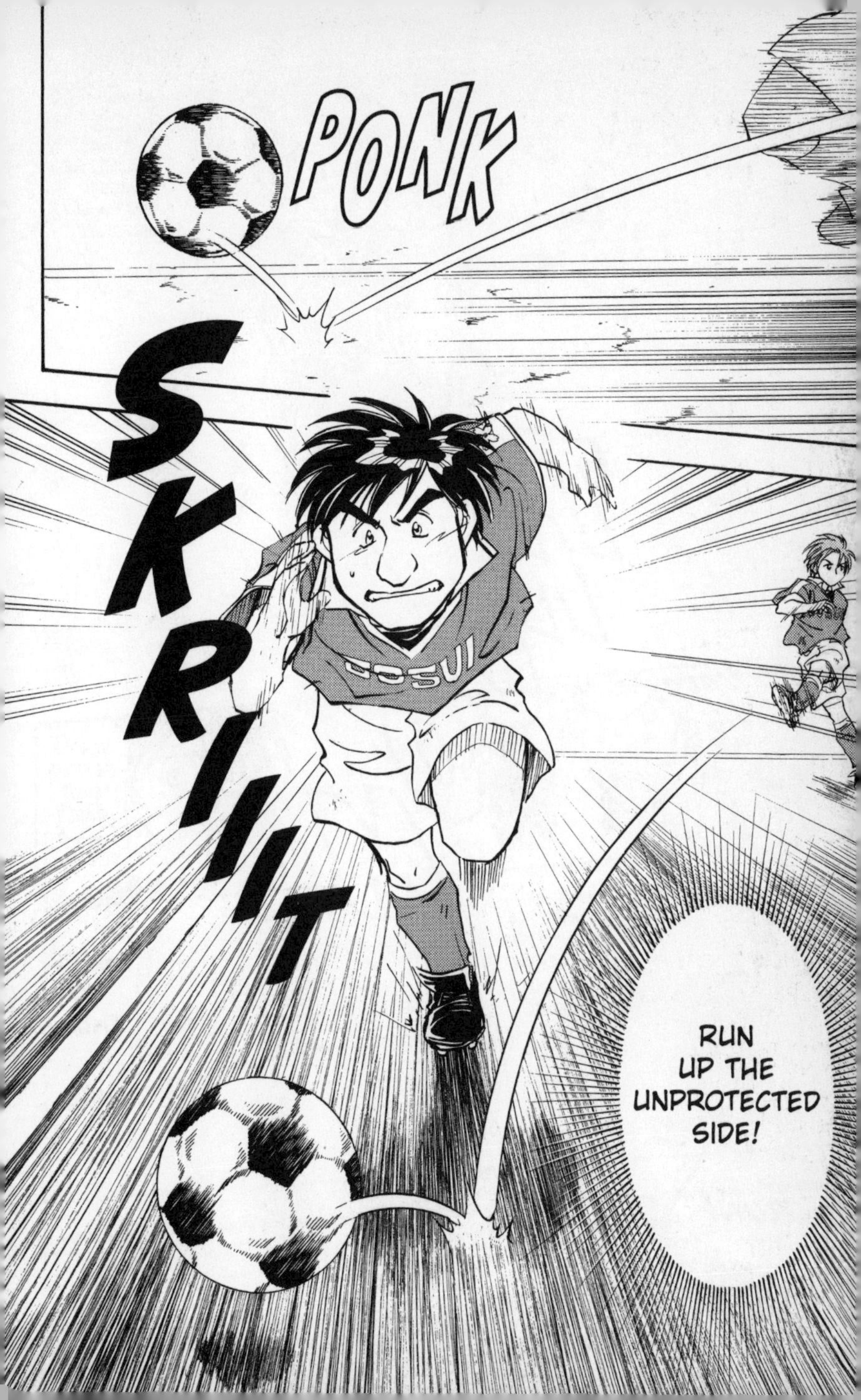
PONK
SKRIIIT
RUN UP THE UNPROTECTED SIDE!

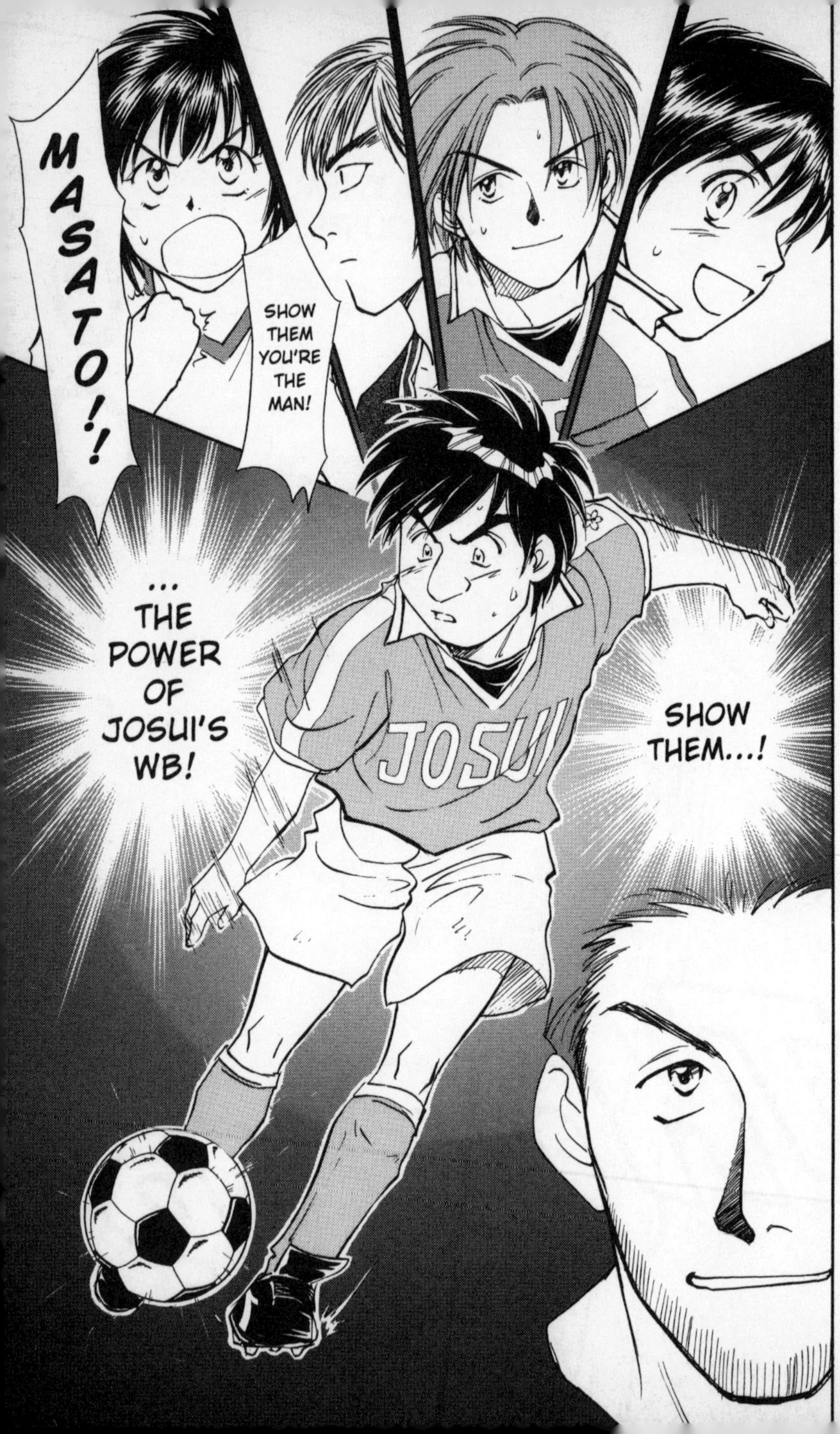
SHOW THEM YOU'RE THE MAN!
MASATO!!
SHOW THEM...!
... THE POWER OF JOSUI'S WB!
JOSUI

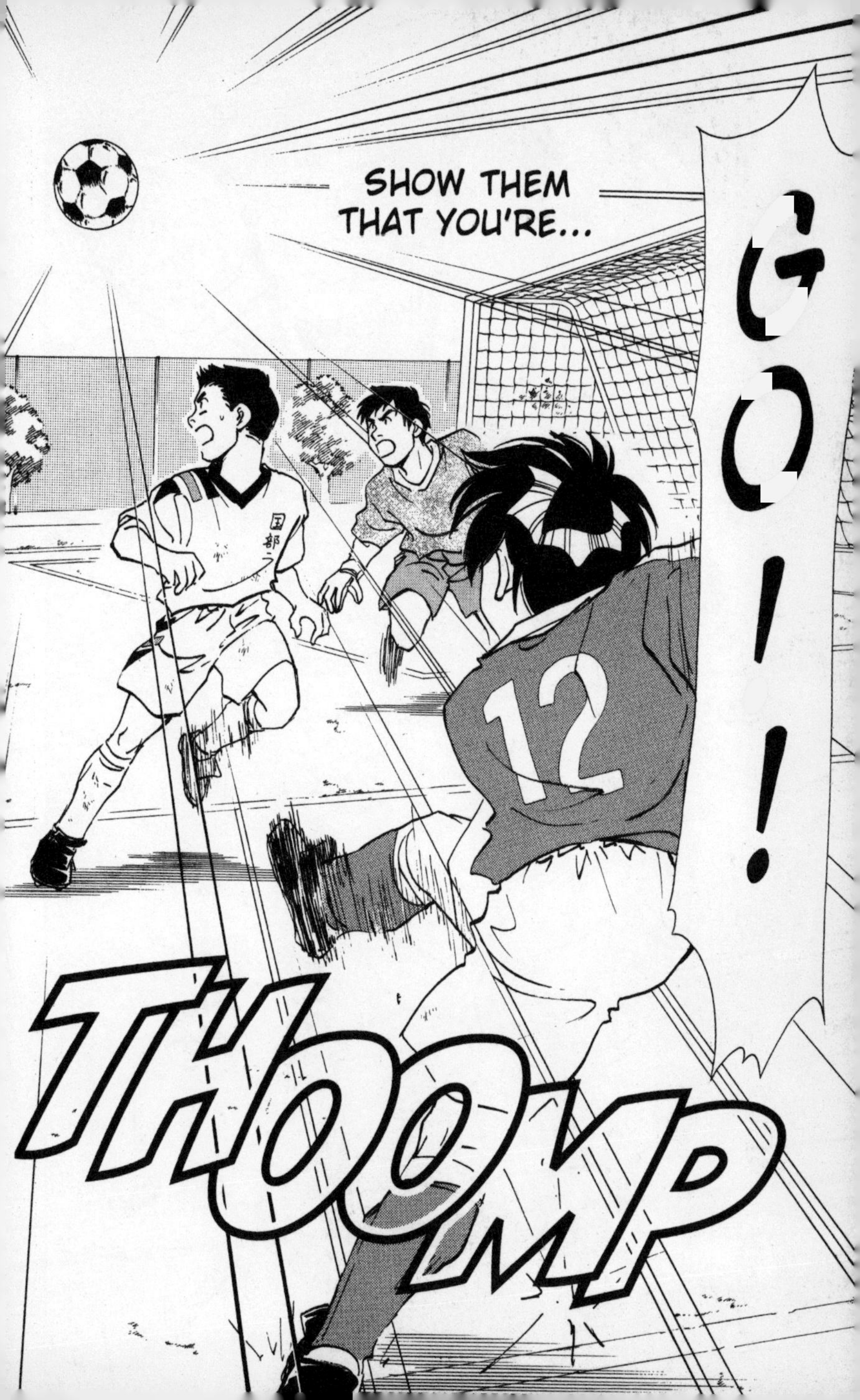
SHOW THEM THAT YOU'RE...
GO!!
THOOMP

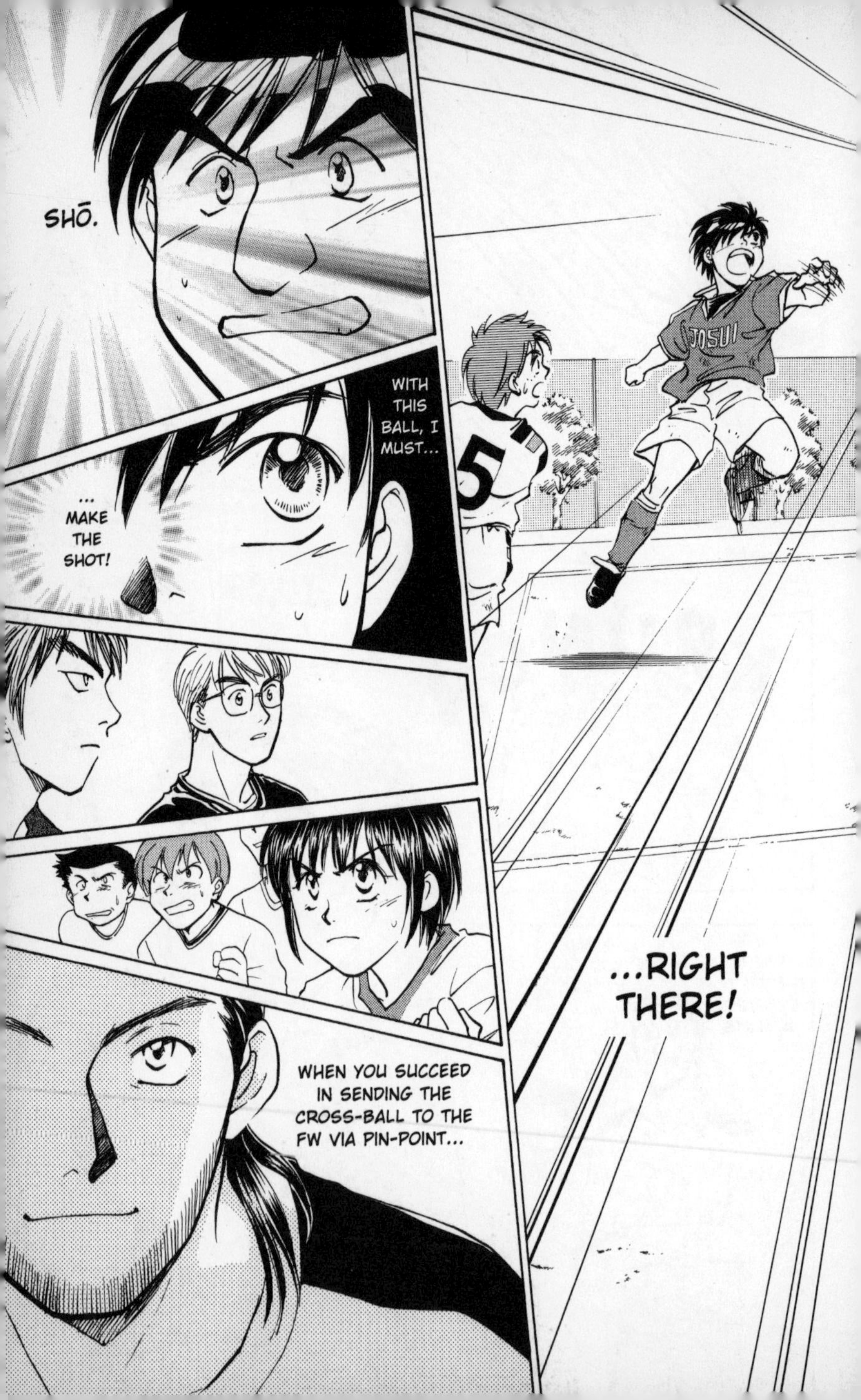
SHŌ.
WITH THIS BALL, I MUST...
...MAKE THE SHOT!
WHEN YOU SUCCEED IN SENDING THE CROSS-BALL TO THE FW VIA PIN-POINT...
JOSUI
5
...RIGHT THERE!

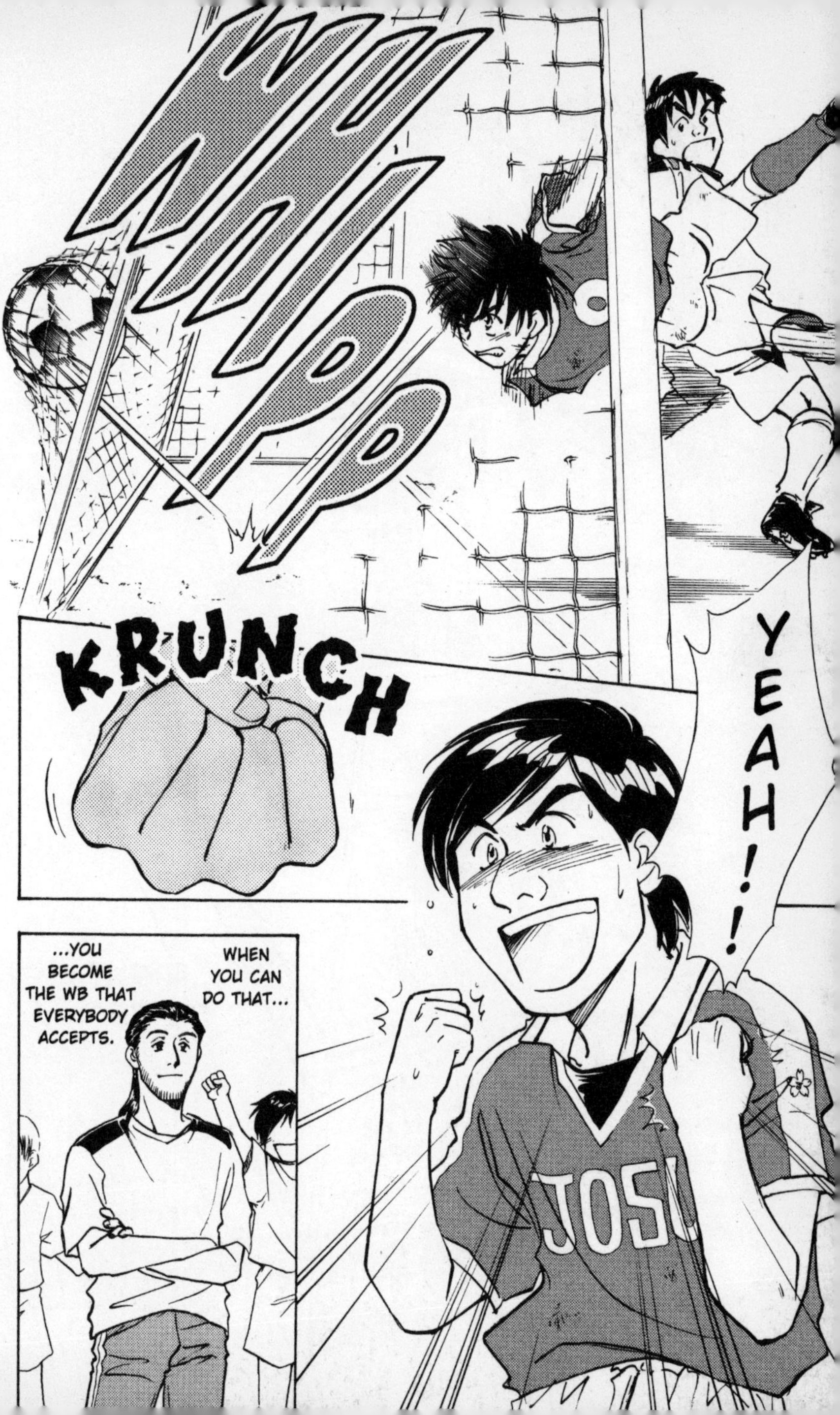
YEAH!!
KRUNCH
WHEN YOU CAN DO THAT...
...YOU BECOME THE WB THAT EVERYBODY ACCEPTS.

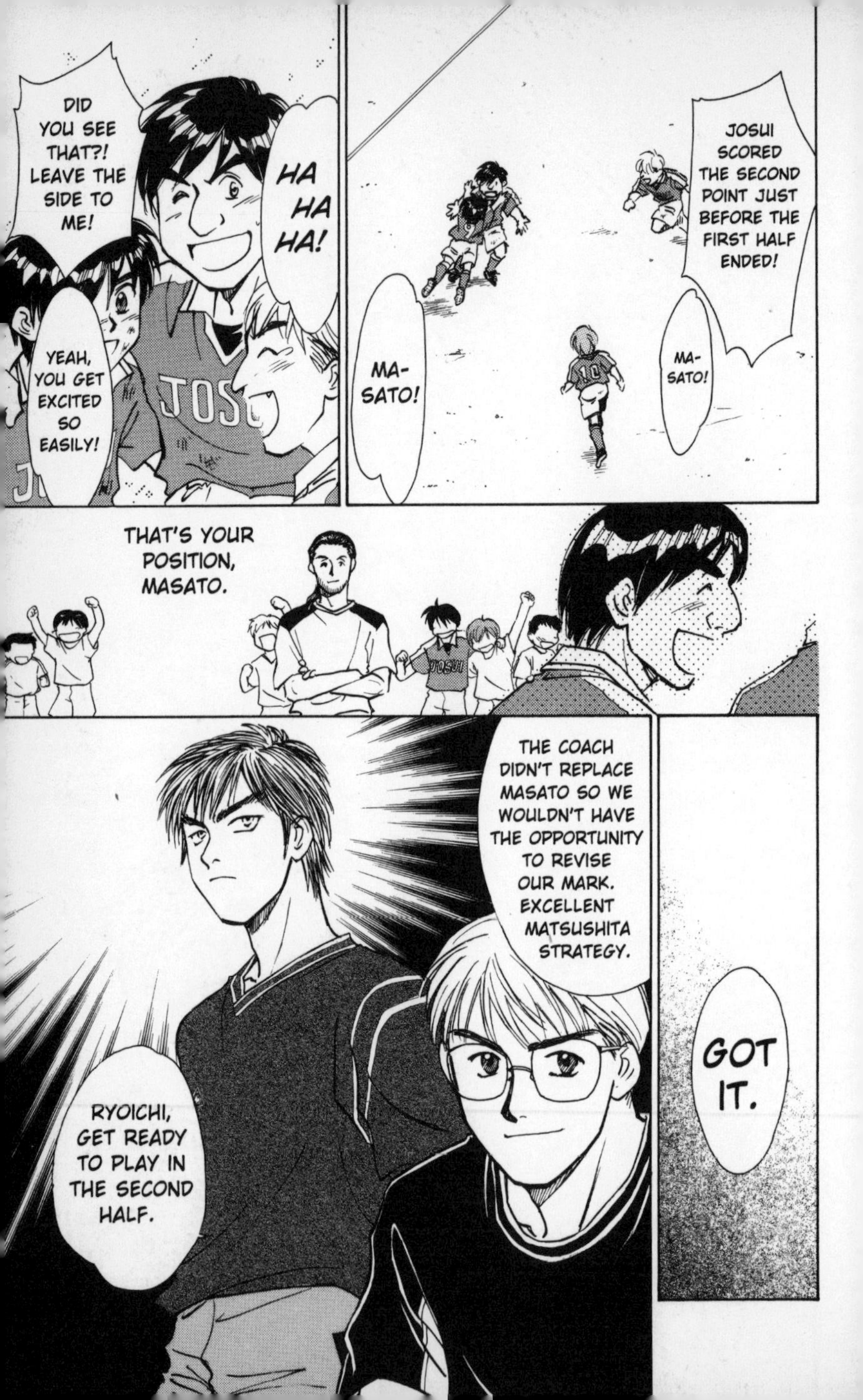
JOSUI SCORED THE SECOND POINT JUST BEFORE THE FIRST HALF ENDED!
MA-SATO!
MA-SATO!
HA HA HA!
DID YOU SEE THAT?! LEAVE THE SIDE TO ME!
YEAH, YOU GET EXCITED SO EASILY!
THAT'S YOUR POSITION, MASATO.
THE COACH DIDN'T REPLACE MASATO SO WE WOULDN'T HAVE THE OPPORTUNITY TO REVISE OUR MARK. EXCELLENT MATSUSHITA STRATEGY.
GOT IT.
RYOICHI, GET READY TO PLAY IN THE SECOND HALF.

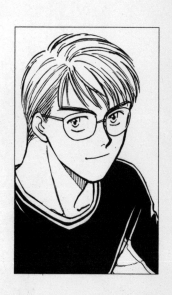

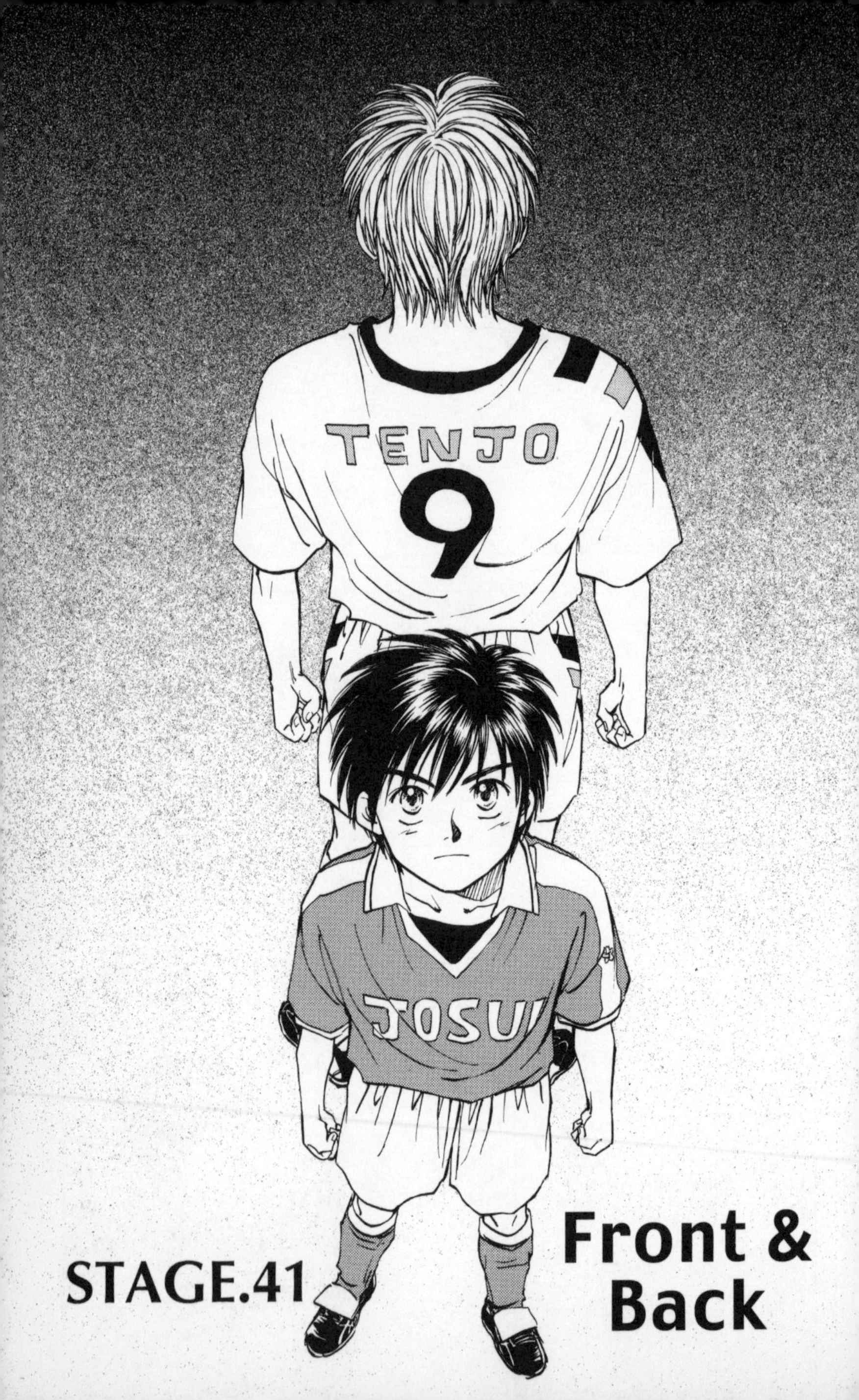

STAGE.41 Front & Back

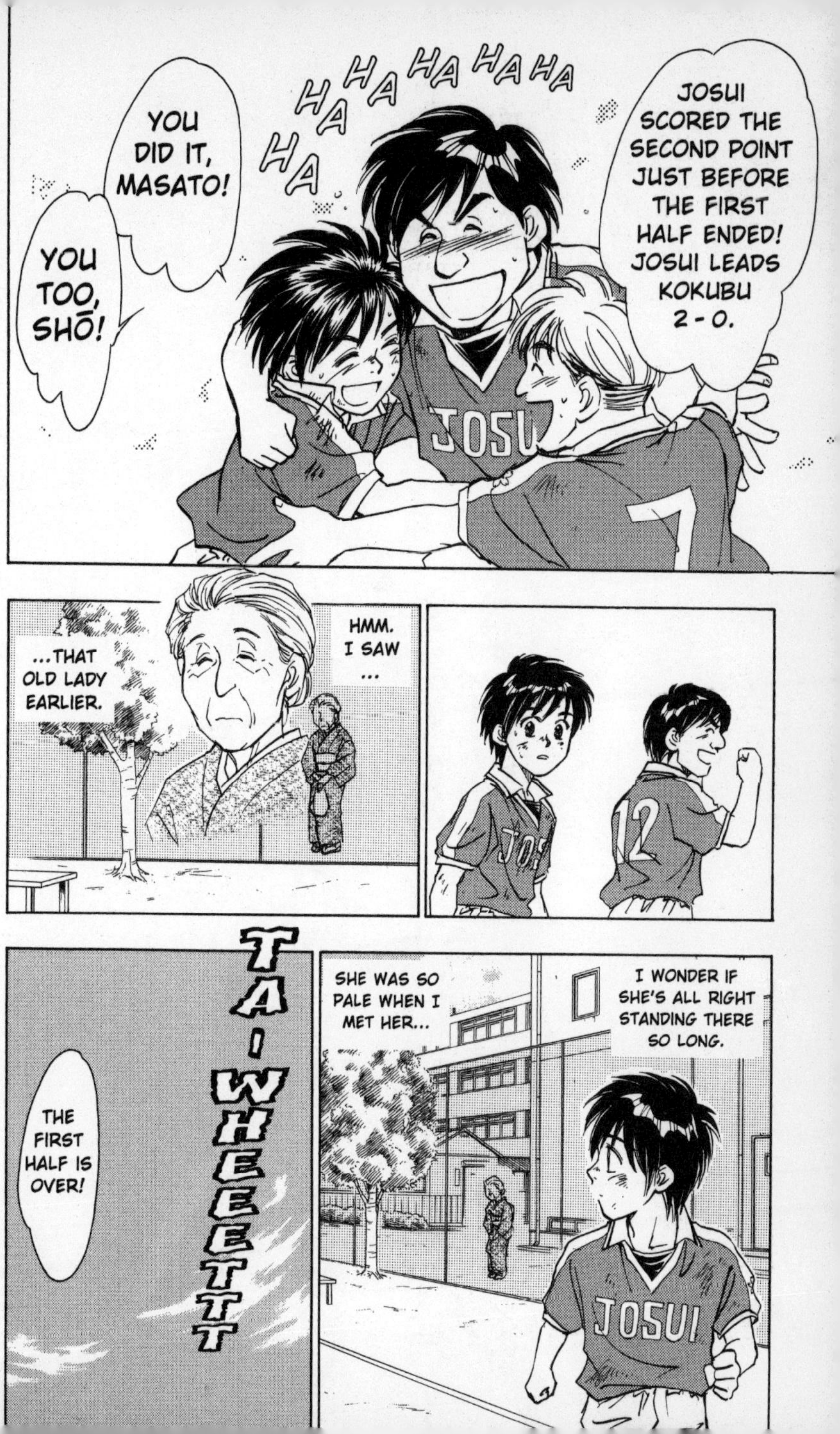
JOSUI SCORED THE SECOND POINT JUST BEFORE THE FIRST HALF ENDED! JOSUI LEADS KOKUBU 2-0.
HAHAHAHAHAHAHA
YOU DID IT, MASATO!
YOU TOO, SHŌ!
HMM. I SAW ...
...THAT OLD LADY EARLIER.
I WONDER IF SHE'S ALL RIGHT STANDING THERE SO LONG.
SHE WAS SO PALE WHEN I MET HER...
TA-WHEEETTT
THE FIRST HALF IS OVER!

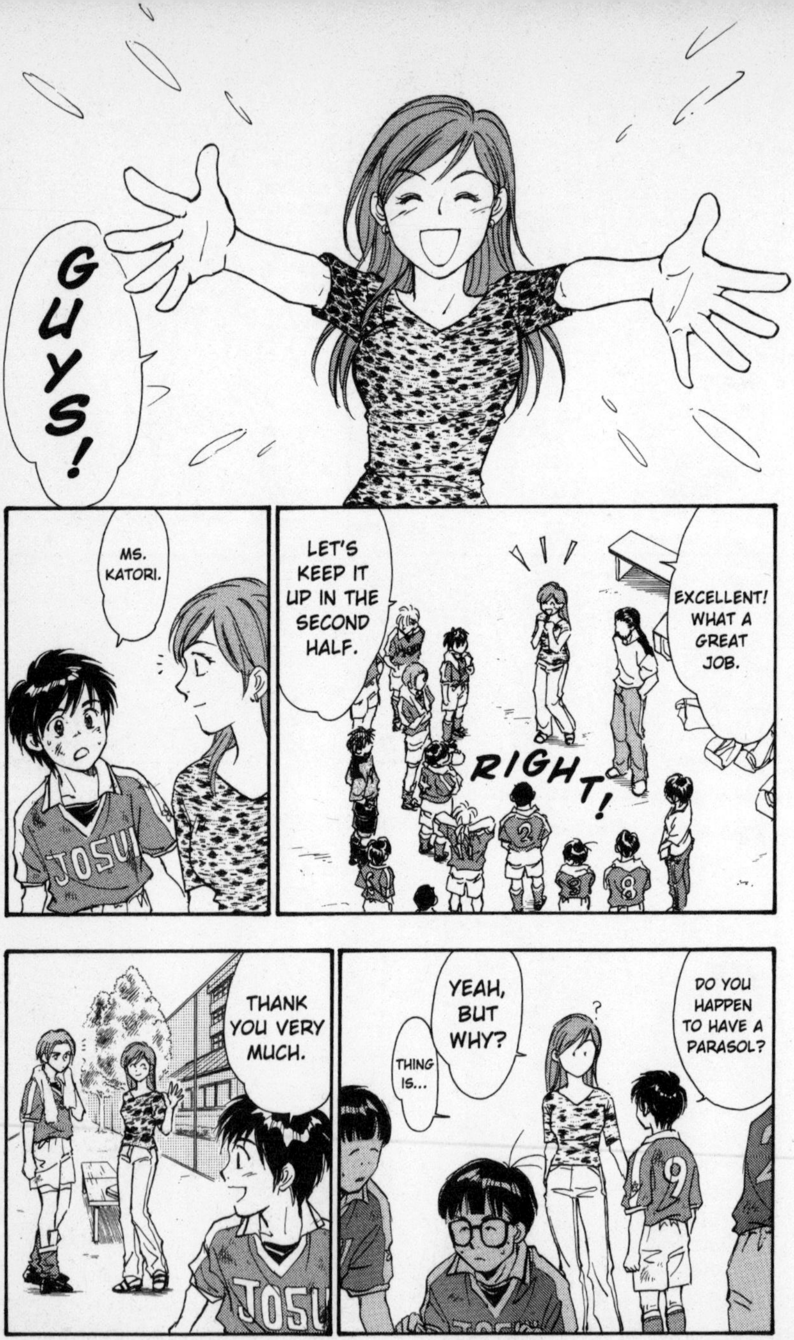
GUYS!
EXCELLENT! WHAT A GREAT JOB.
LET'S KEEP IT UP IN THE SECOND HALF.
RIGHT!
MS. KATORI.
DO YOU HAPPEN TO HAVE A PARASOL?
YEAH, BUT WHY?
THING IS...
THANK YOU VERY MUCH.

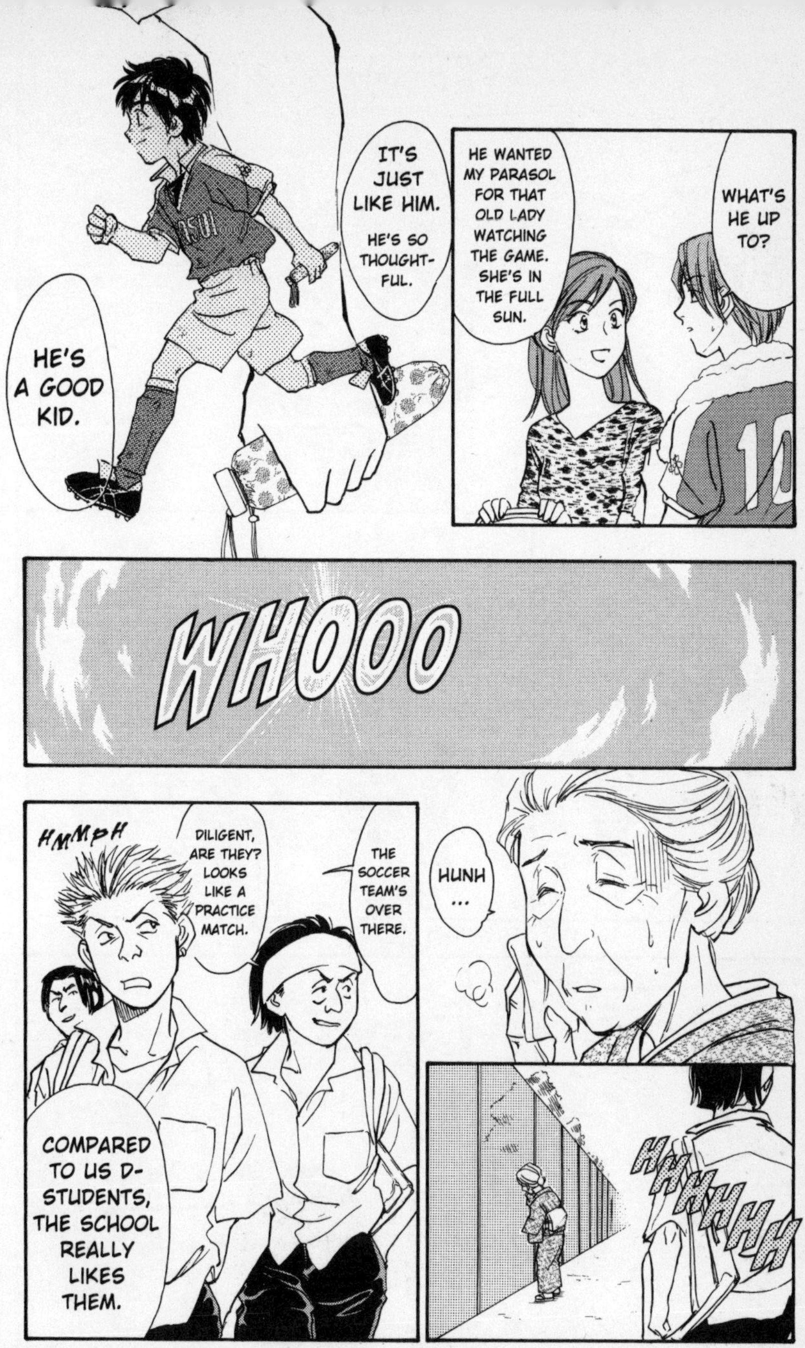
WHAT'S HE UP TO?
HE WANTED MY PARASOL FOR THAT OLD LADY WATCHING THE GAME. SHE'S IN THE FULL SUN.
IT'S JUST LIKE HIM.
HE'S SO THOUGHT-FUL.
HE'S A GOOD KID.
WHOOO
HUNH ...
HHHHHHH
THE SOCCER TEAM'S OVER THERE.
DILIGENT, ARE THEY? LOOKS LIKE A PRACTICE MATCH.
HMMPH
COMPARED TO US D-STUDENTS, THE SCHOOL REALLY LIKES THEM.

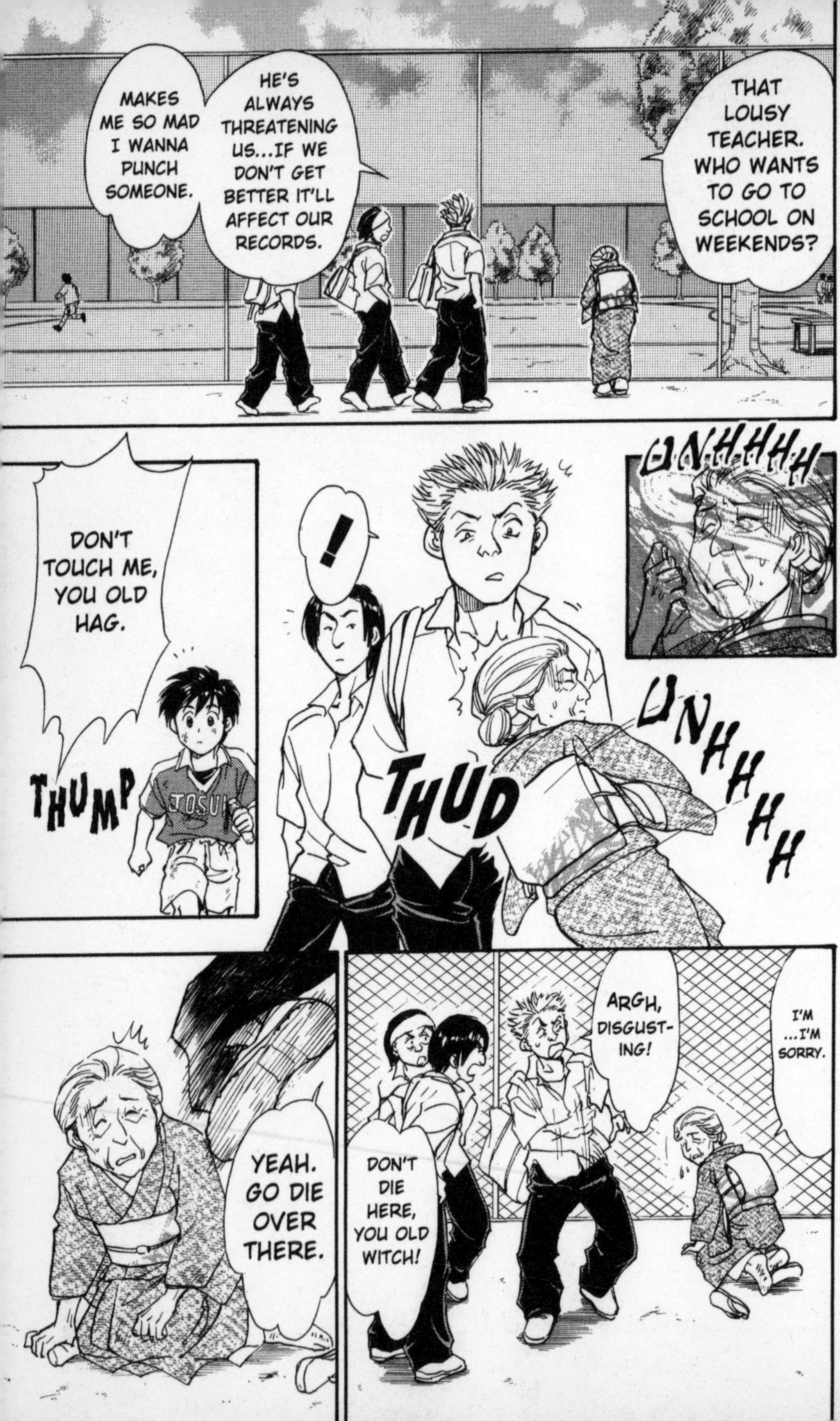
THAT LOUSY TEACHER. WHO WANTS TO GO TO SCHOOL ON WEEKENDS?
HE'S ALWAYS THREATENING US...IF WE DON'T GET BETTER IT'LL AFFECT OUR RECORDS.
MAKES ME SO MAD I WANNA PUNCH SOMEONE.
UNHHHH
!
THUD
UNHHHHH
DON'T TOUCH ME, YOU OLD HAG.
THUMP
I'M ...I'M SORRY.
ARGH, DISGUST-ING!
DON'T DIE HERE, YOU OLD WITCH!
YEAH. GO DIE OVER THERE.

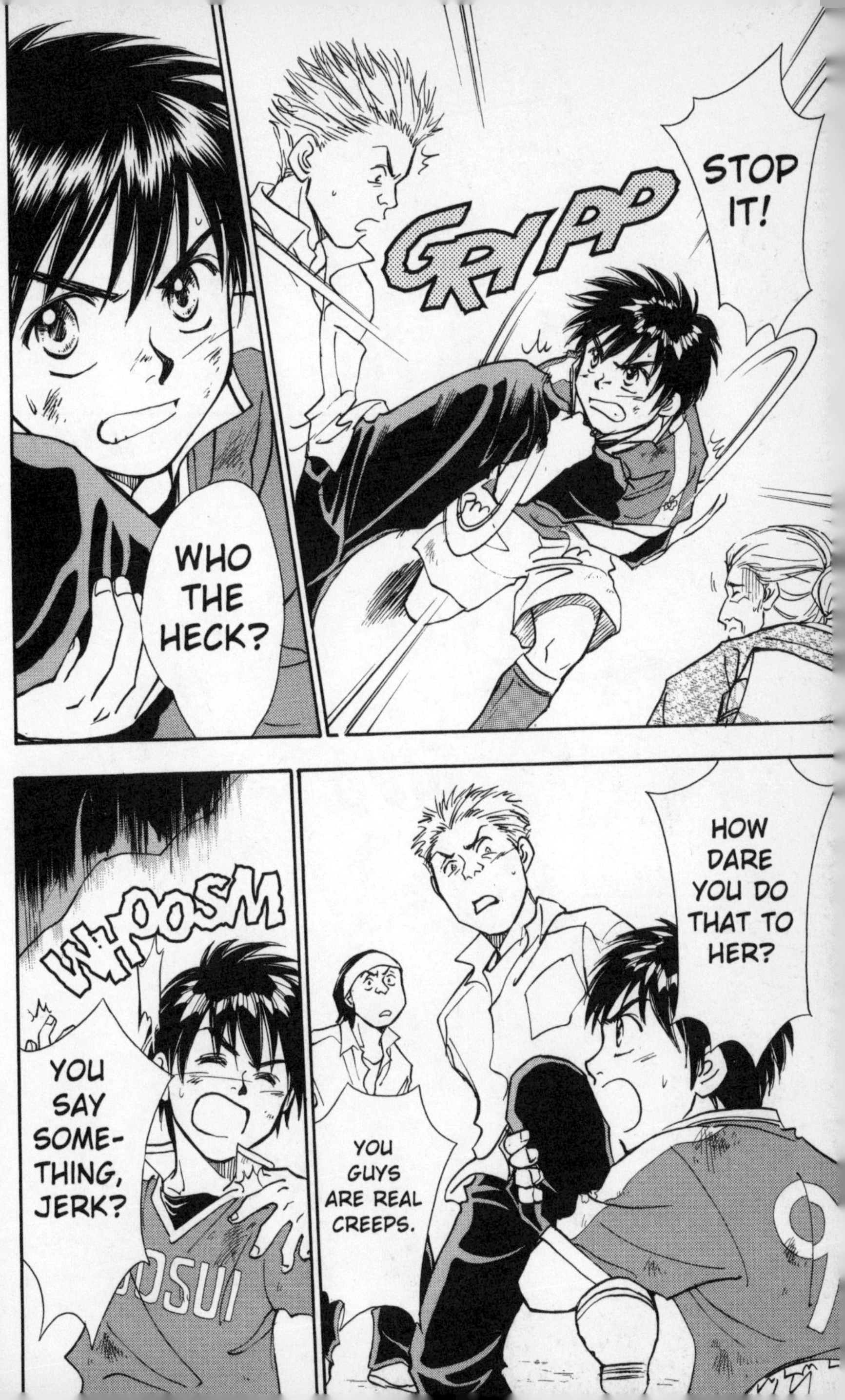
STOP IT!
GRIPP
WHO THE HECK?
HOW DARE YOU DO THAT TO HER?
YOU GUYS ARE REAL CREEPS.
WHOOSM
YOU SAY SOME-THING, JERK?

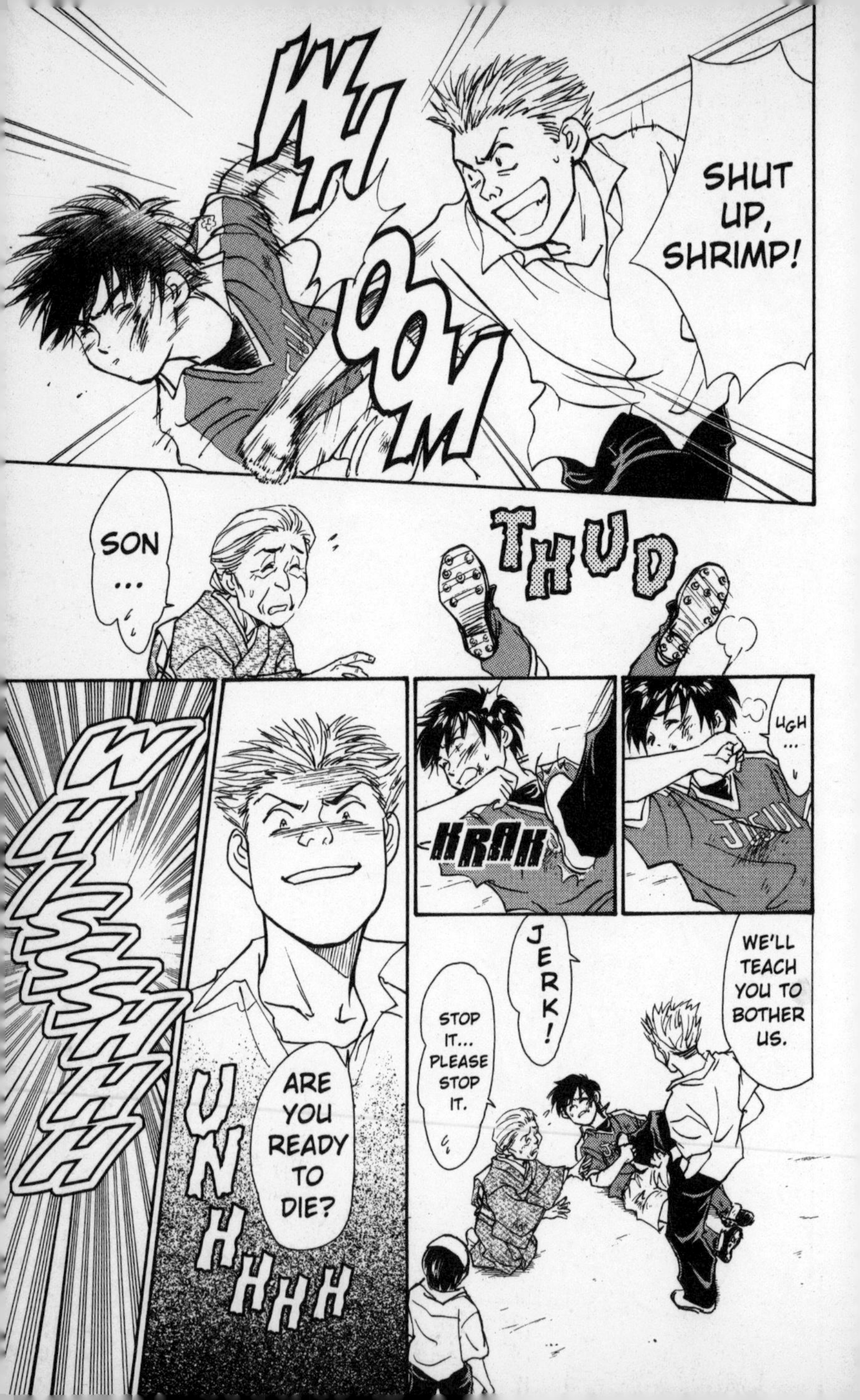
SHUT UP, SHRIMP!
WHOOM
THUD
SON ...
UGH ...
KRAK
WE'LL TEACH YOU TO BOTHER US.
JERK!
STOP IT... PLEASE STOP IT.
ARE YOU READY TO DIE?
UNHHHHH
WHISSHHHH

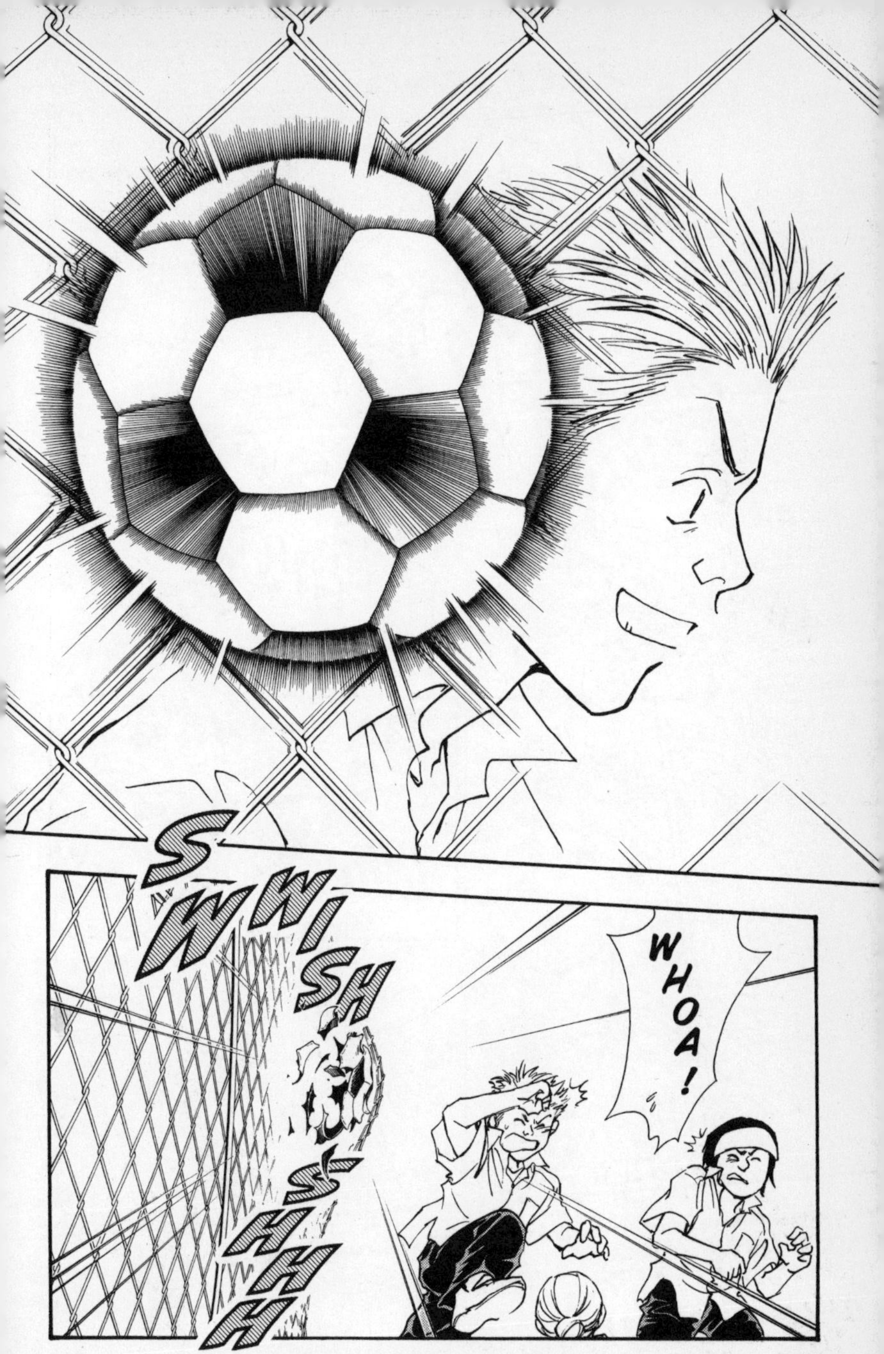
SWISH
SSHHH
WHOA!

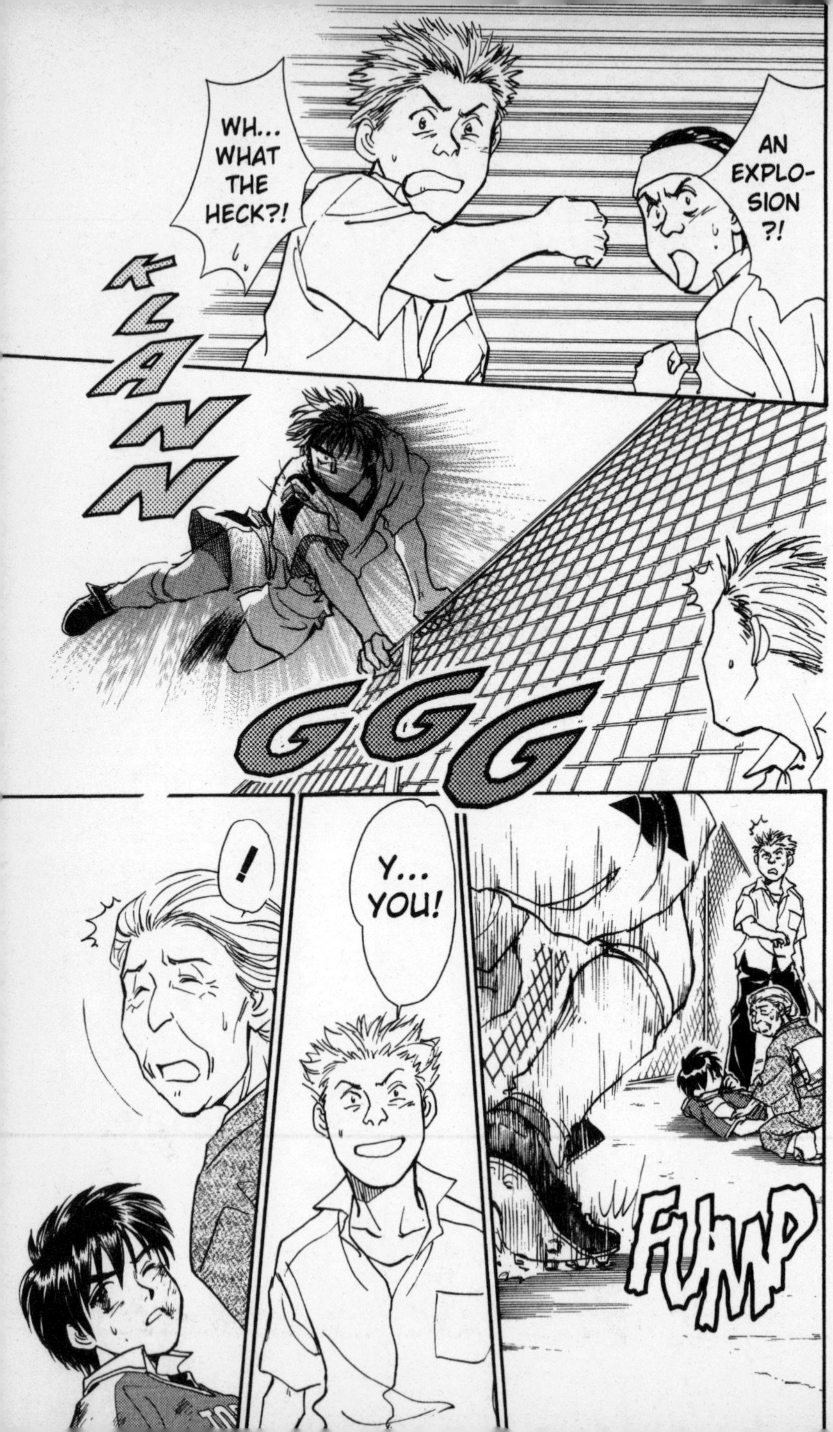
AN EXPLOSION?!
WH... WHAT THE HECK?!
KLANN
GGG
FUMP
Y... YOU!
!

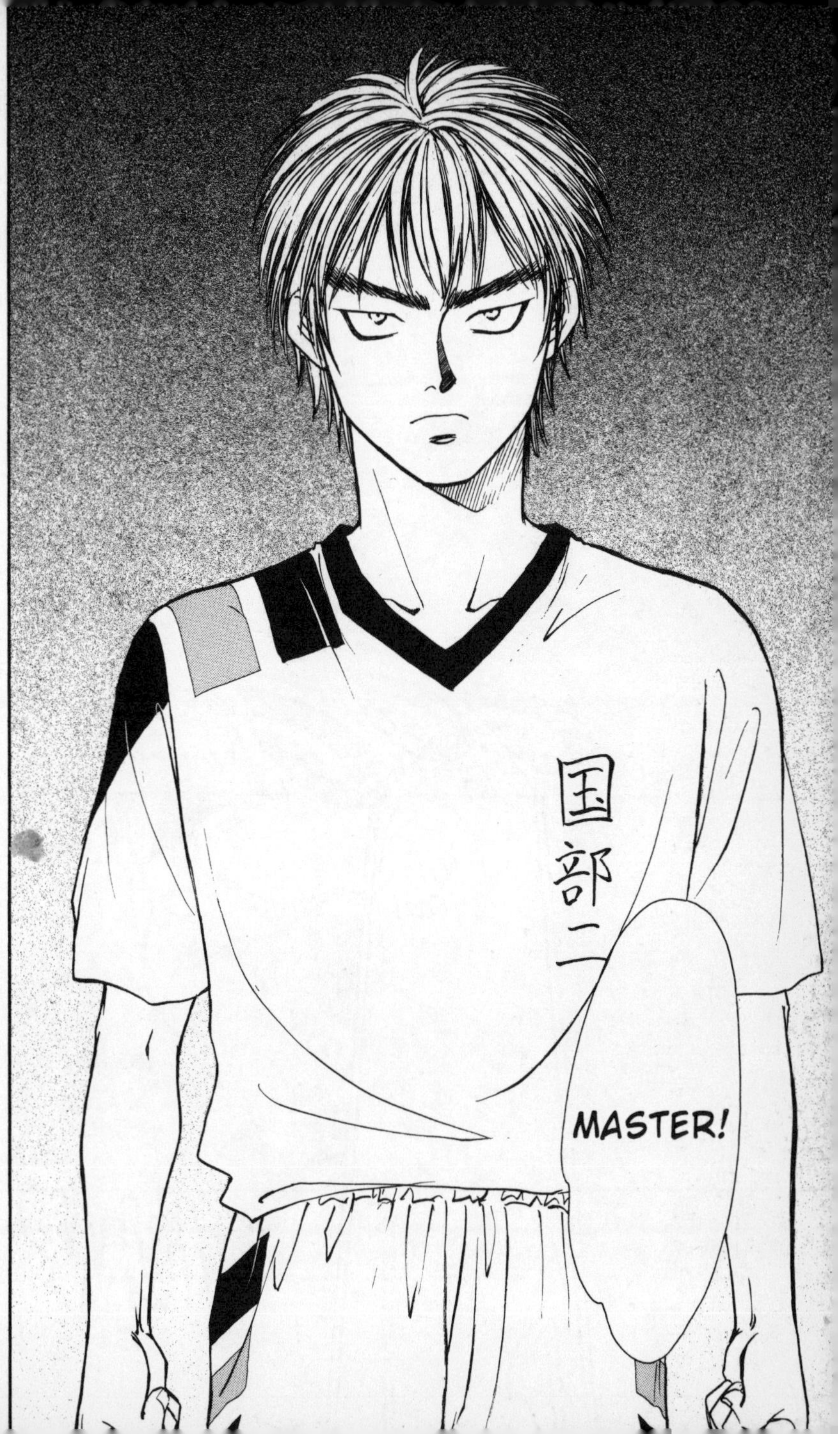
MASTER!
国部一

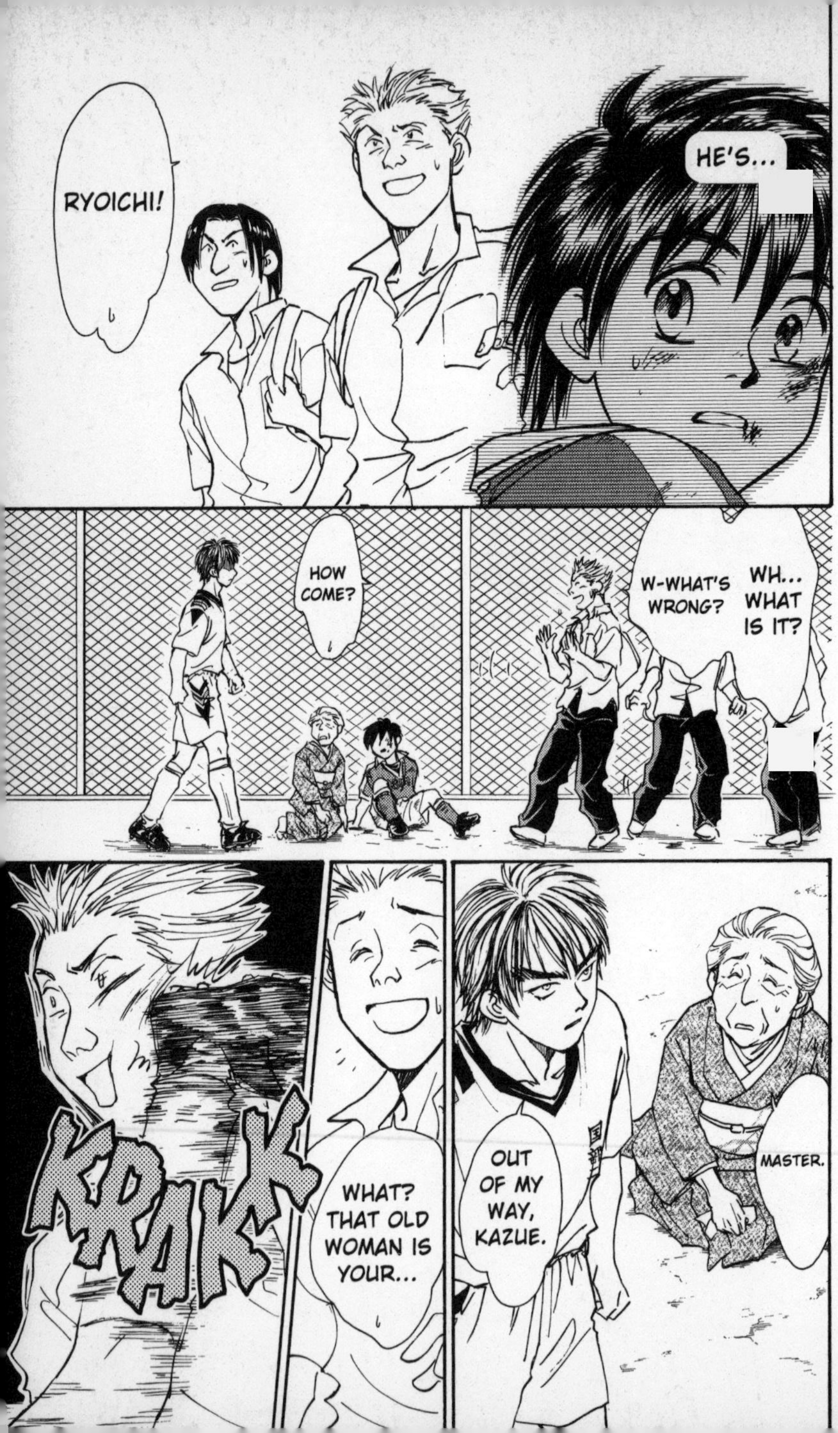
HE'S...
RYOICHI!
WH... WHAT IS IT?
W-WHAT'S WRONG?
HOW COME?
MASTER.
OUT OF MY WAY, KAZUE.
WHAT? THAT OLD WOMAN IS YOUR...
KRAK

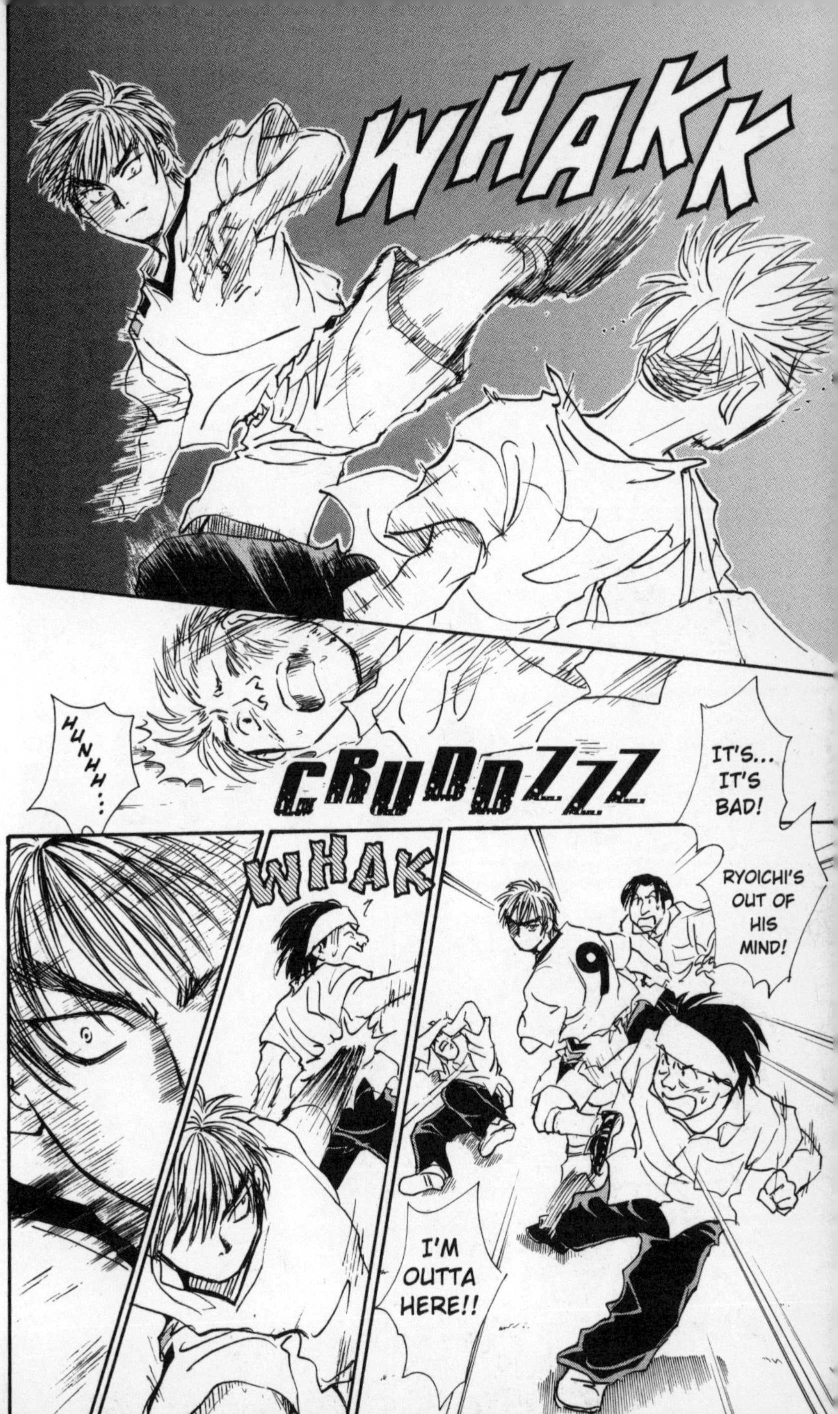

WHAKK
CRUDZZZ
HUNHH...
IT'S... IT'S BAD!
RYOICHI'S OUT OF HIS MIND!
I'M OUTTA HERE!!
WHAK

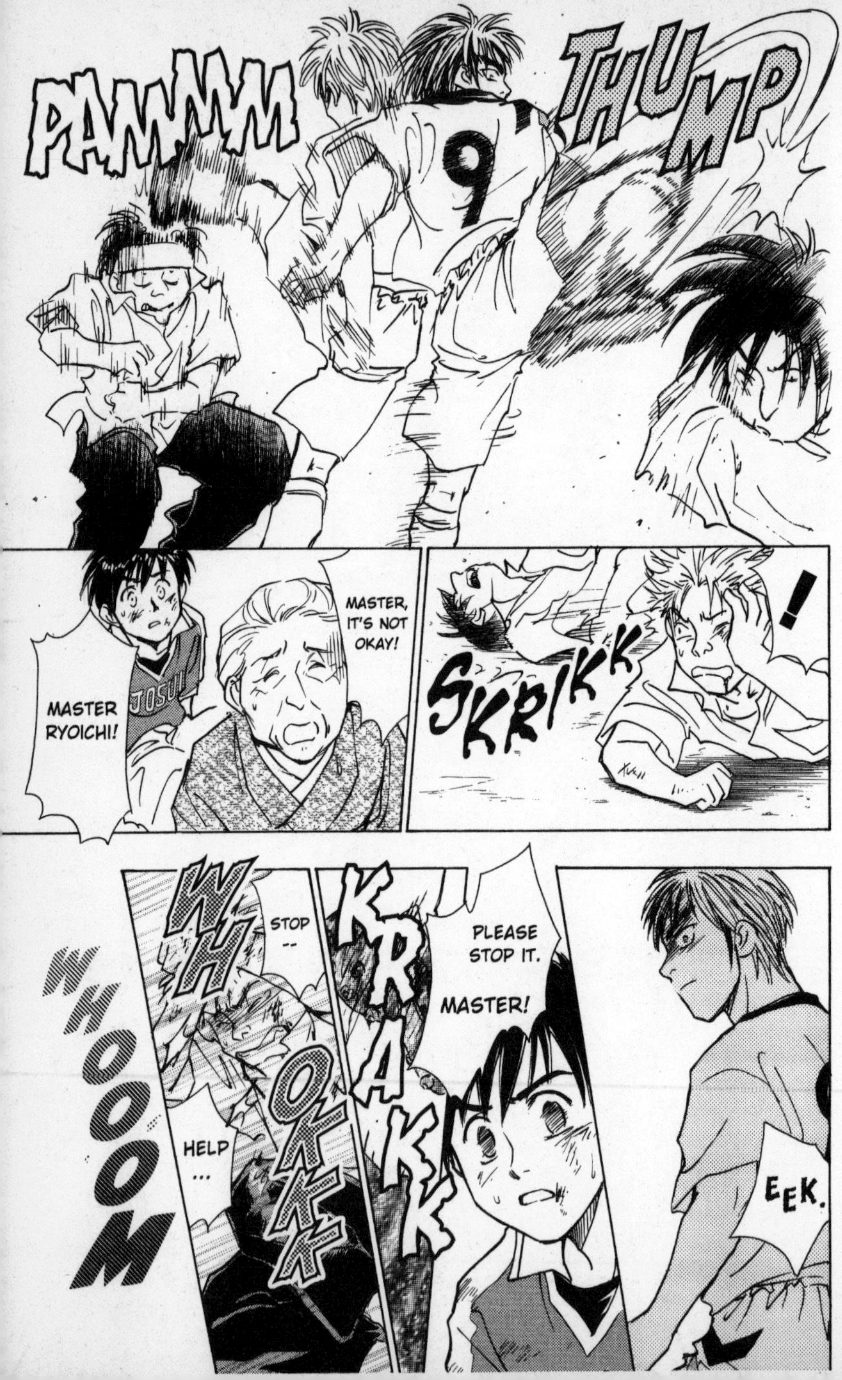
THUMP
PAMMM
!
SKRIKK
MASTER, IT'S NOT OKAY!
MASTER RYOICHI!
EEK.
PLEASE STOP IT.
MASTER!
KRAKK
STOP --
HELP ...
WHOKKK
WHOOOOM

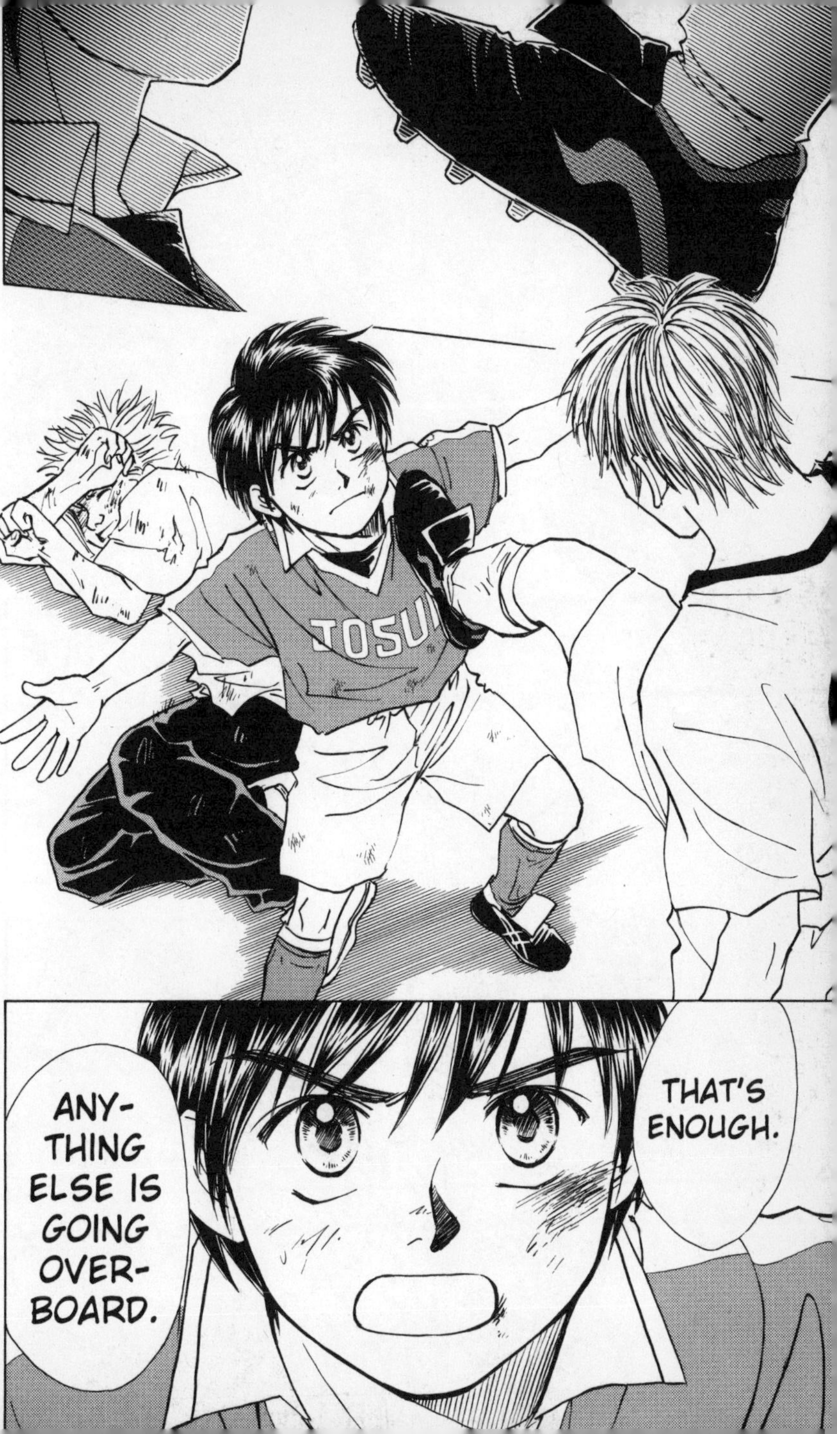
THAT'S ENOUGH.
ANY-THING ELSE IS GOING OVER-BOARD.

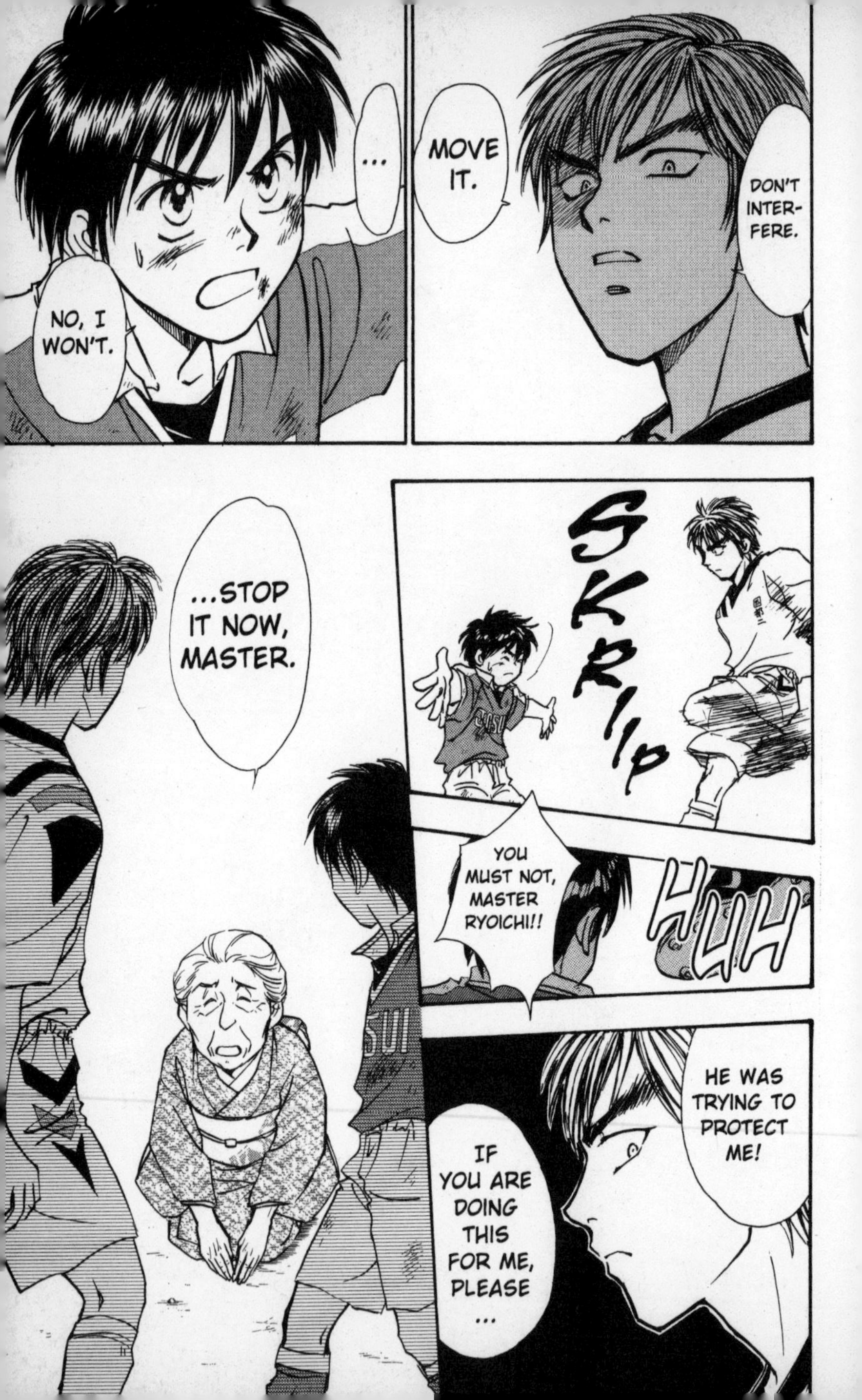
MOVE IT.
DON'T INTERFERE.
...
NO, I WON'T.
SKRIIP
YOU MUST NOT, MASTER RYOICHI!!
HUH
HE WAS TRYING TO PROTECT ME!
IF YOU ARE DOING THIS FOR ME, PLEASE ...
...STOP IT NOW, MASTER.

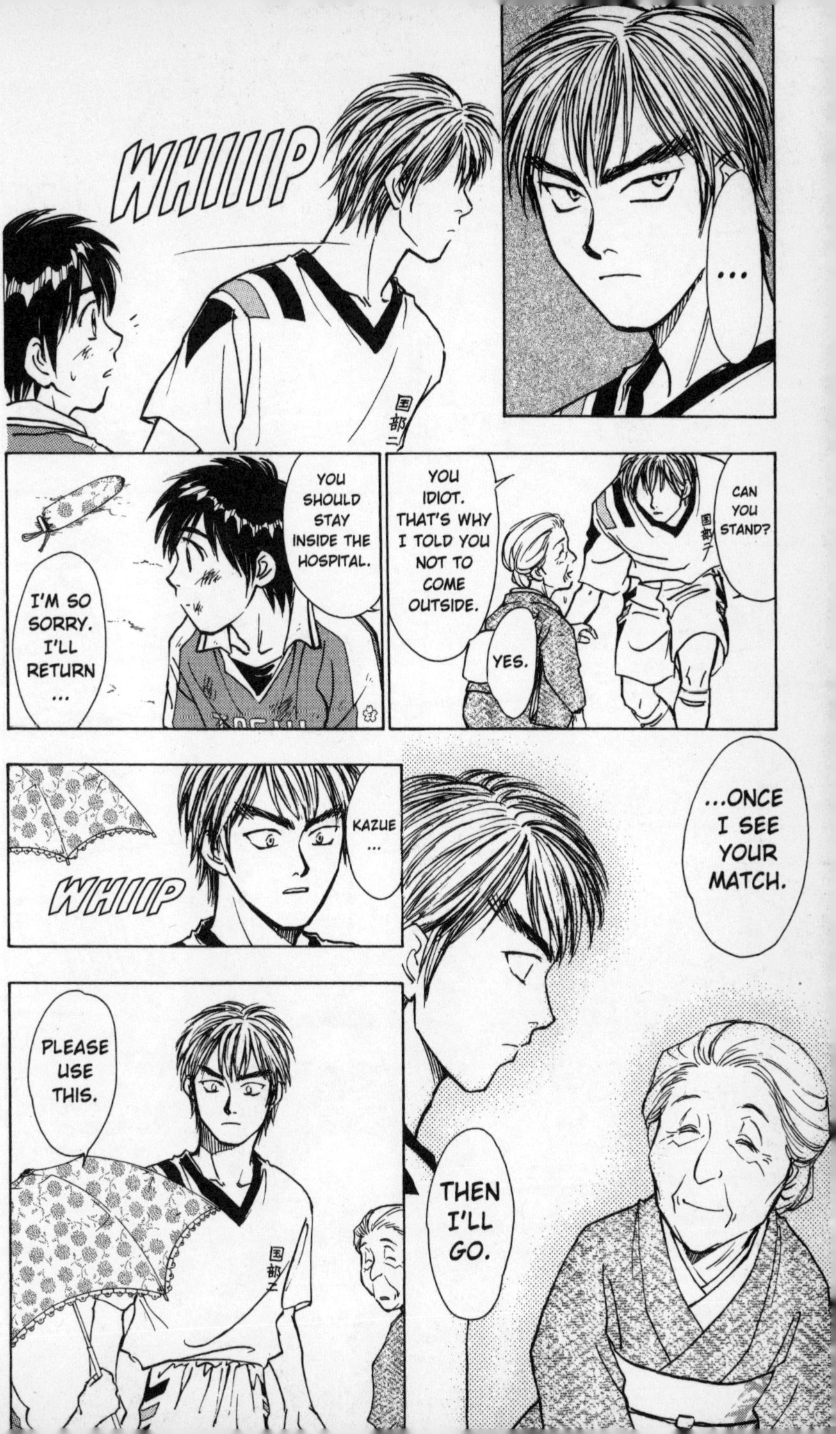
...
WHIIIP
CAN YOU STAND?
YOU IDIOT. THAT'S WHY I TOLD YOU NOT TO COME OUTSIDE.
YES.
YOU SHOULD STAY INSIDE THE HOSPITAL.
I'M SO SORRY. I'LL RETURN ...
...ONCE I SEE YOUR MATCH.
THEN I'LL GO.
KAZUE ...
WHIIP
PLEASE USE THIS.

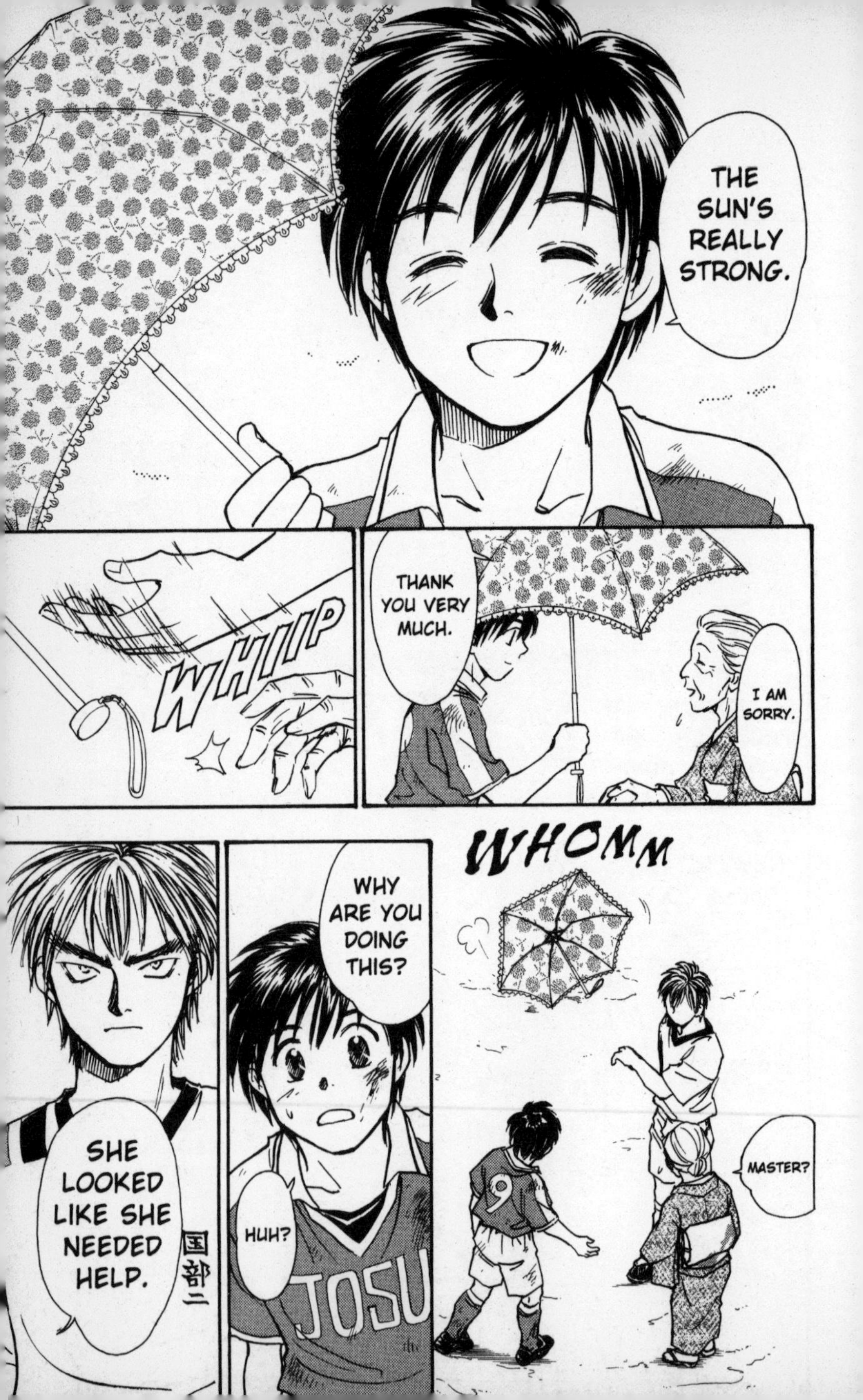
THE SUN'S REALLY STRONG.
I AM SORRY.
THANK YOU VERY MUCH.
WHIIP
WHOMM
MASTER?
WHY ARE YOU DOING THIS?
HUH?
SHE LOOKED LIKE SHE NEEDED HELP.
国部二

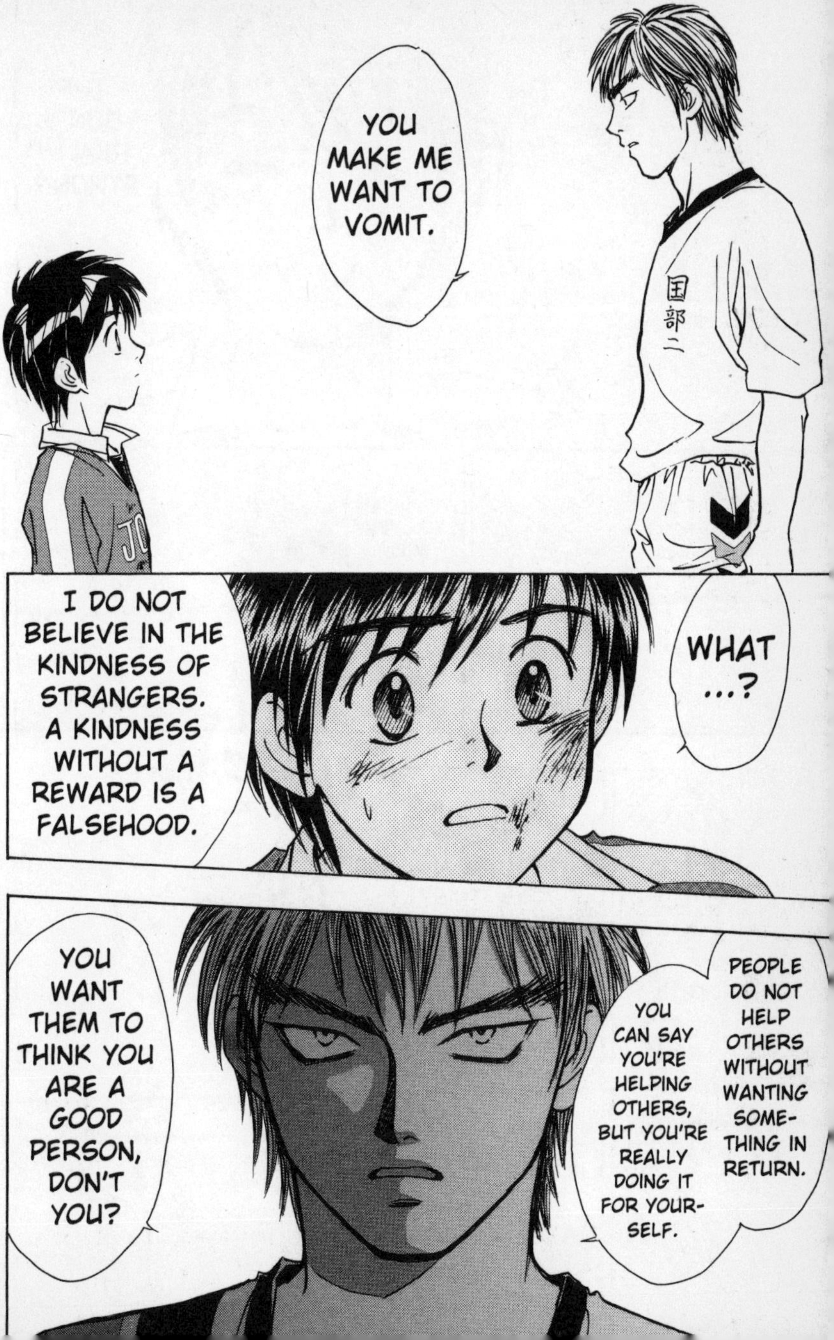
YOU MAKE ME WANT TO VOMIT.
WHAT ...?
I DO NOT BELIEVE IN THE KINDNESS OF STRANGERS. A KINDNESS WITHOUT A REWARD IS A FALSEHOOD.
PEOPLE DO NOT HELP OTHERS WITHOUT WANTING SOME-THING IN RETURN.
YOU CAN SAY YOU'RE HELPING OTHERS, BUT YOU'RE REALLY DOING IT FOR YOUR-SELF.
YOU WANT THEM TO THINK YOU ARE A GOOD PERSON, DON'T YOU?

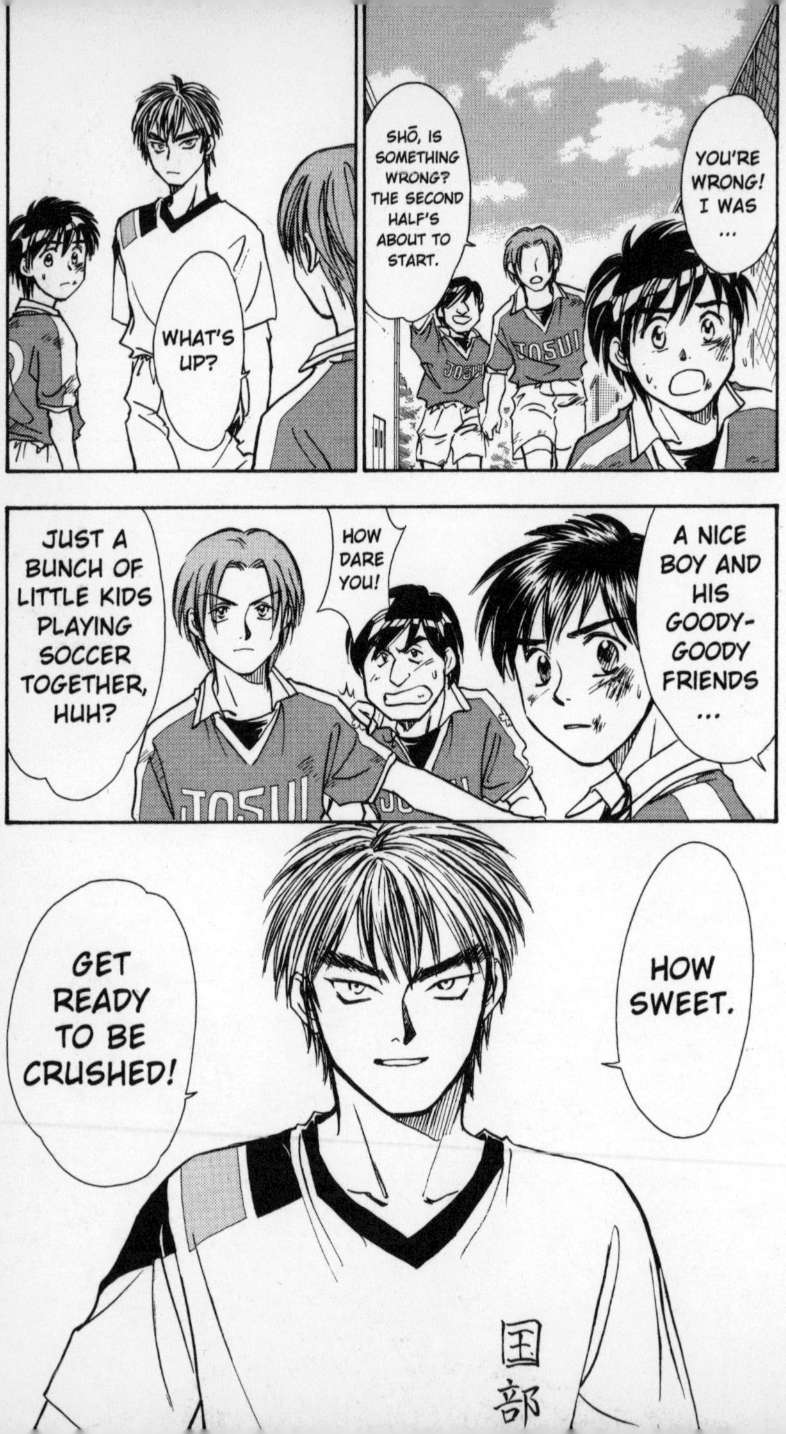
YOU'RE WRONG! I WAS ...
SHŌ, IS SOMETHING WRONG? THE SECOND HALF'S ABOUT TO START.
JOSUI
WHAT'S UP?
A NICE BOY AND HIS GOODY-GOODY FRIENDS ...
HOW DARE YOU!
JUST A BUNCH OF LITTLE KIDS PLAYING SOCCER TOGETHER, HUH?
HOW SWEET.
GET READY TO BE CRUSHED!
国部

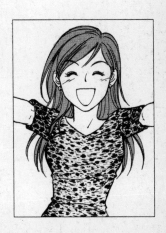

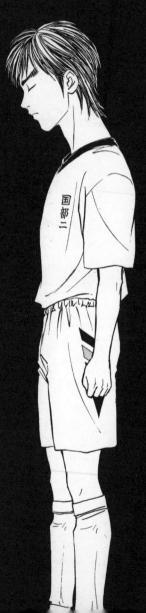

STAGE.42 Declaration of War!

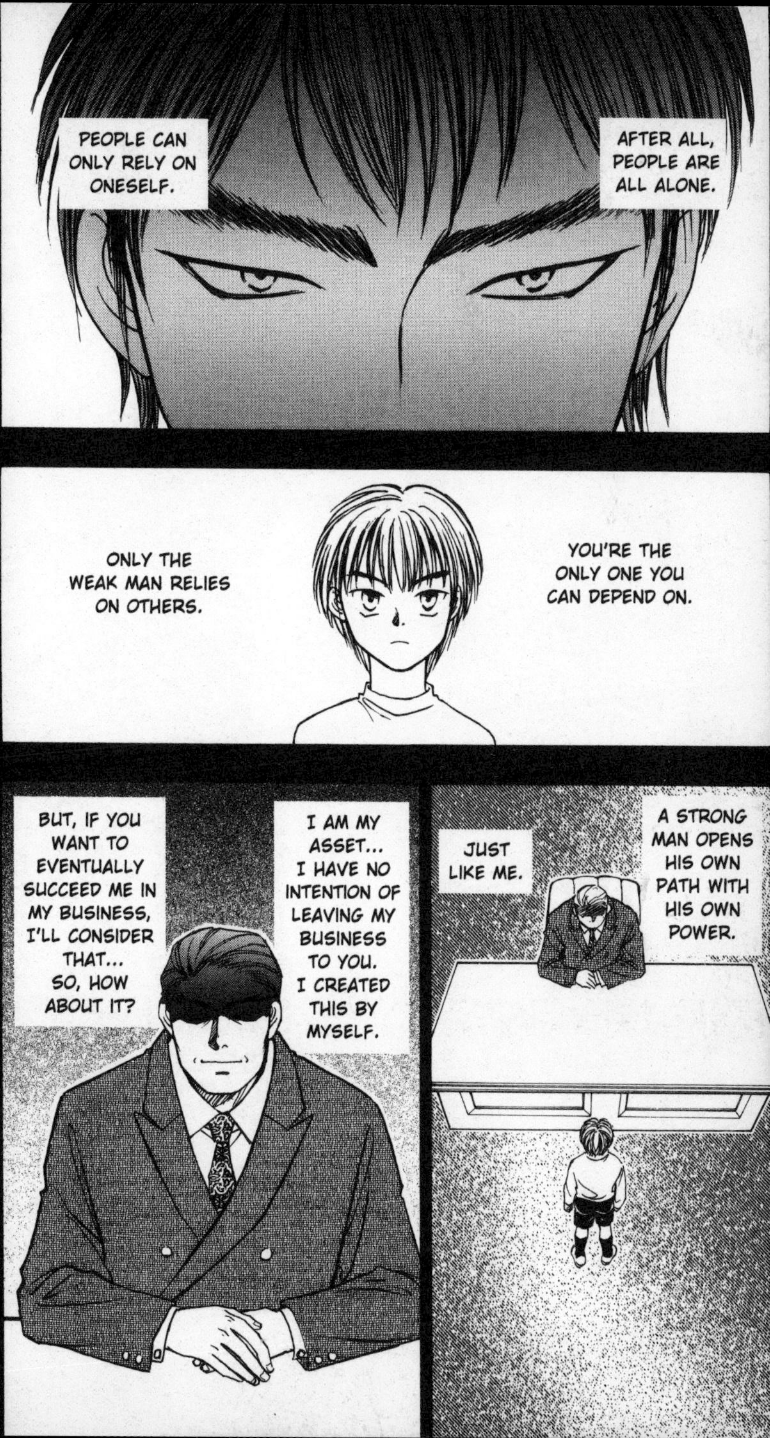
AFTER ALL, PEOPLE ARE ALL ALONE.
PEOPLE CAN ONLY RELY ON ONESELF.
YOU'RE THE ONLY ONE YOU CAN DEPEND ON.
ONLY THE WEAK MAN RELIES ON OTHERS.
A STRONG MAN OPENS HIS OWN PATH WITH HIS OWN POWER.
JUST LIKE ME.
I AM MY ASSET... I HAVE NO INTENTION OF LEAVING MY BUSINESS TO YOU. I CREATED THIS BY MYSELF.
BUT, IF YOU WANT TO EVENTUALLY SUCCEED ME IN MY BUSINESS, I'LL CONSIDER THAT... SO, HOW ABOUT IT?

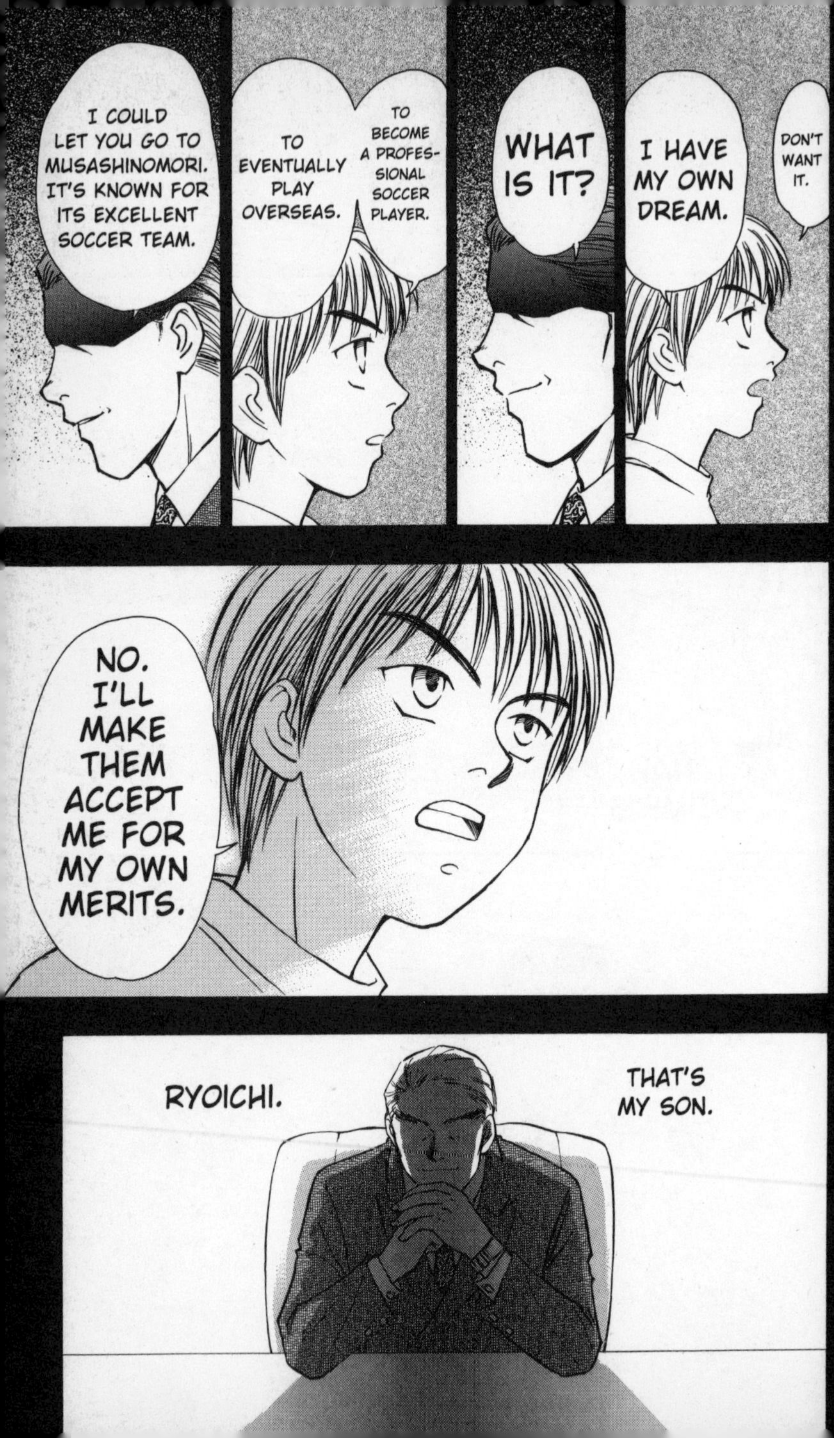
DON'T WANT IT.
I HAVE MY OWN DREAM.
WHAT IS IT?
TO BECOME A PROFES-SIONAL SOCCER PLAYER.
TO EVENTUALLY PLAY OVERSEAS.
I COULD LET YOU GO TO MUSASHINOMORI. IT'S KNOWN FOR ITS EXCELLENT SOCCER TEAM.
NO. I'LL MAKE THEM ACCEPT ME FOR MY OWN MERITS.
THAT'S MY SON.
RYOICHI.

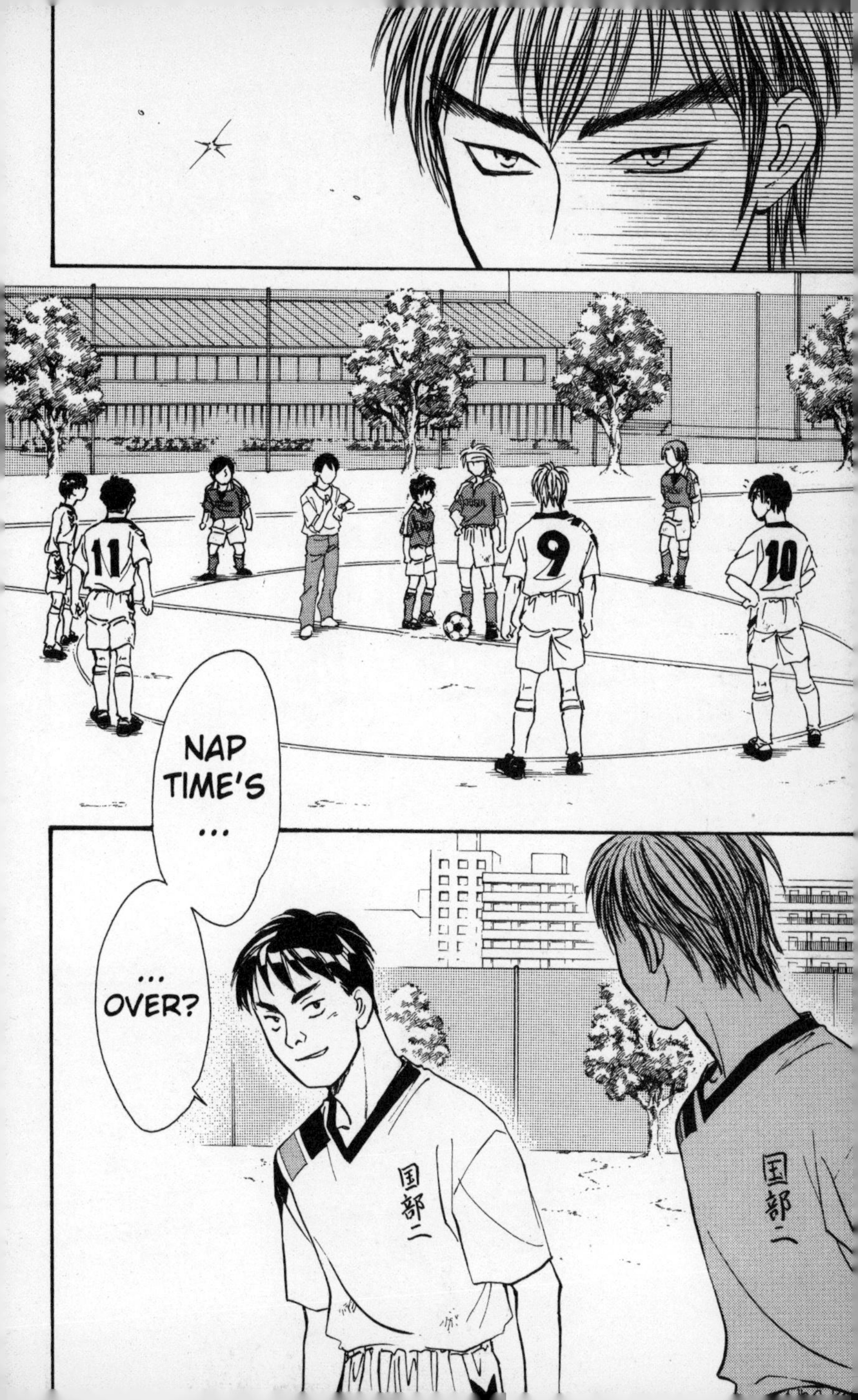
NAP TIME'S ...
... OVER?
9
10
11
国部二
国部一

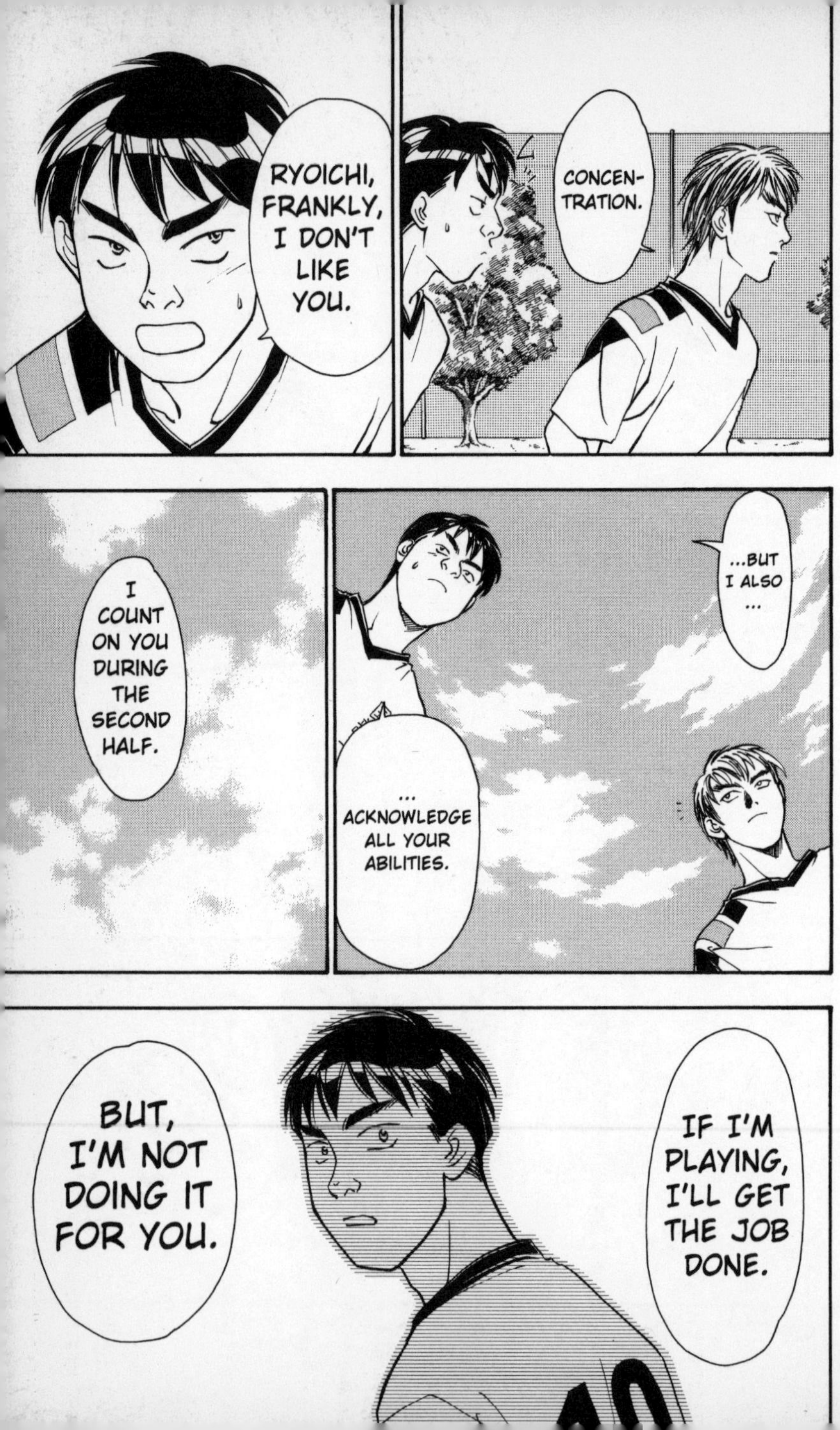
CONCEN-TRATION.
RYOICHI, FRANKLY, I DON'T LIKE YOU.
...BUT I ALSO ...
... ACKNOWLEDGE ALL YOUR ABILITIES.
I COUNT ON YOU DURING THE SECOND HALF.
IF I'M PLAYING, I'LL GET THE JOB DONE.
BUT, I'M NOT DOING IT FOR YOU.

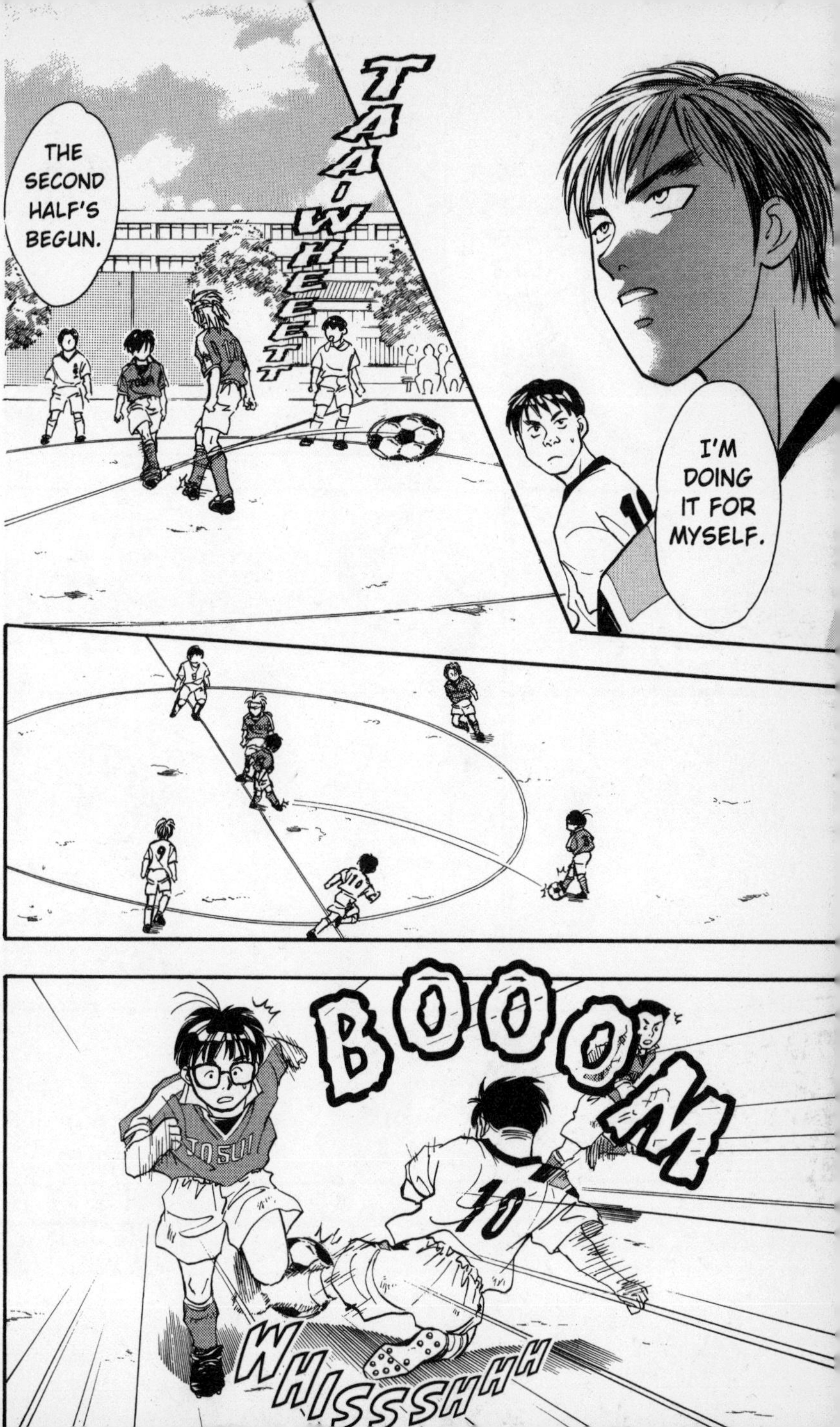
I'M DOING IT FOR MYSELF.
TAAWHEEETT
THE SECOND HALF'S BEGUN.
BOOOM
WHISSSHHH

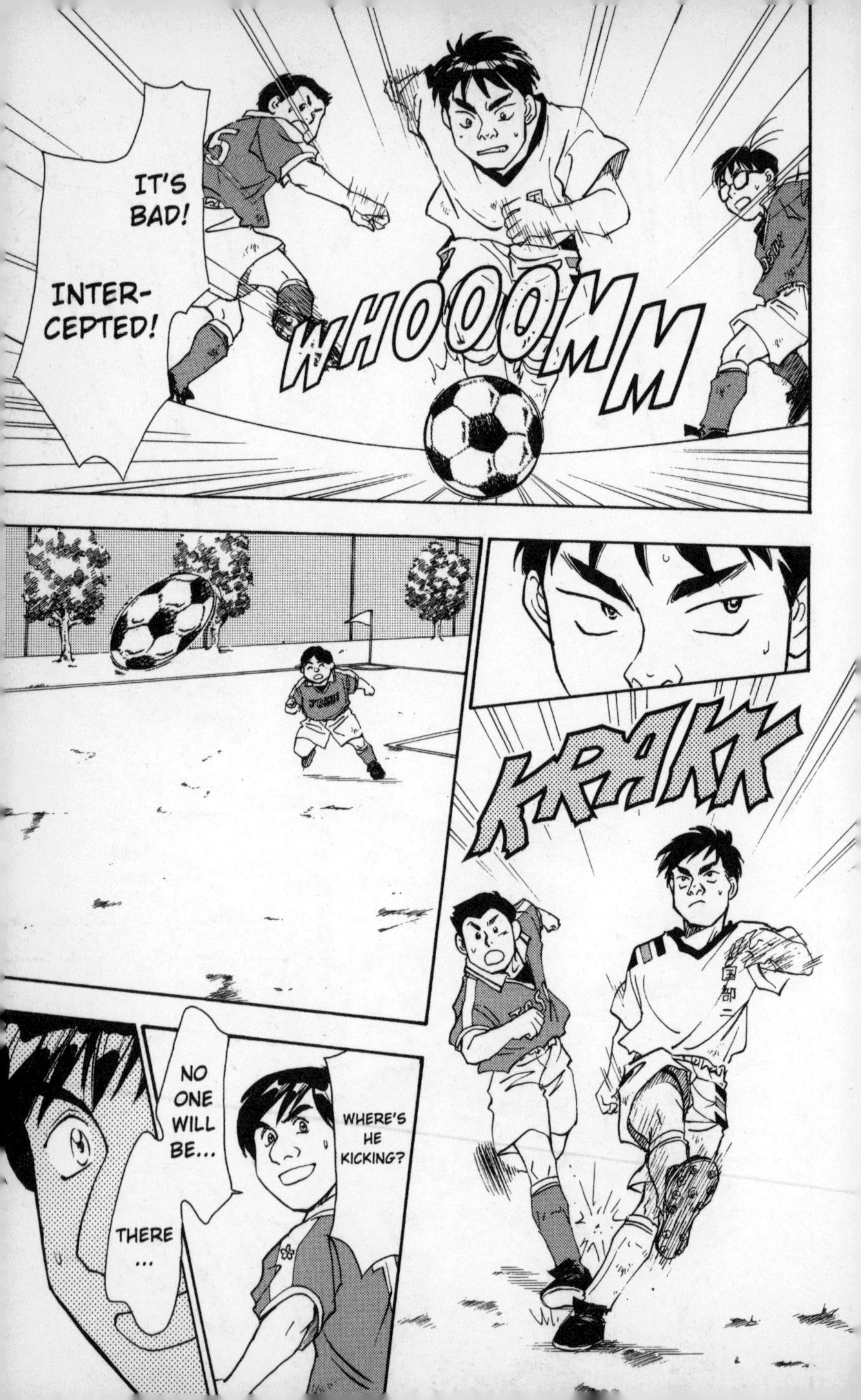
IT'S BAD! INTER-CEPTED!
WHOOOMM
KRAKK
WHERE'S HE KICKING?
NO ONE WILL BE... THERE ...

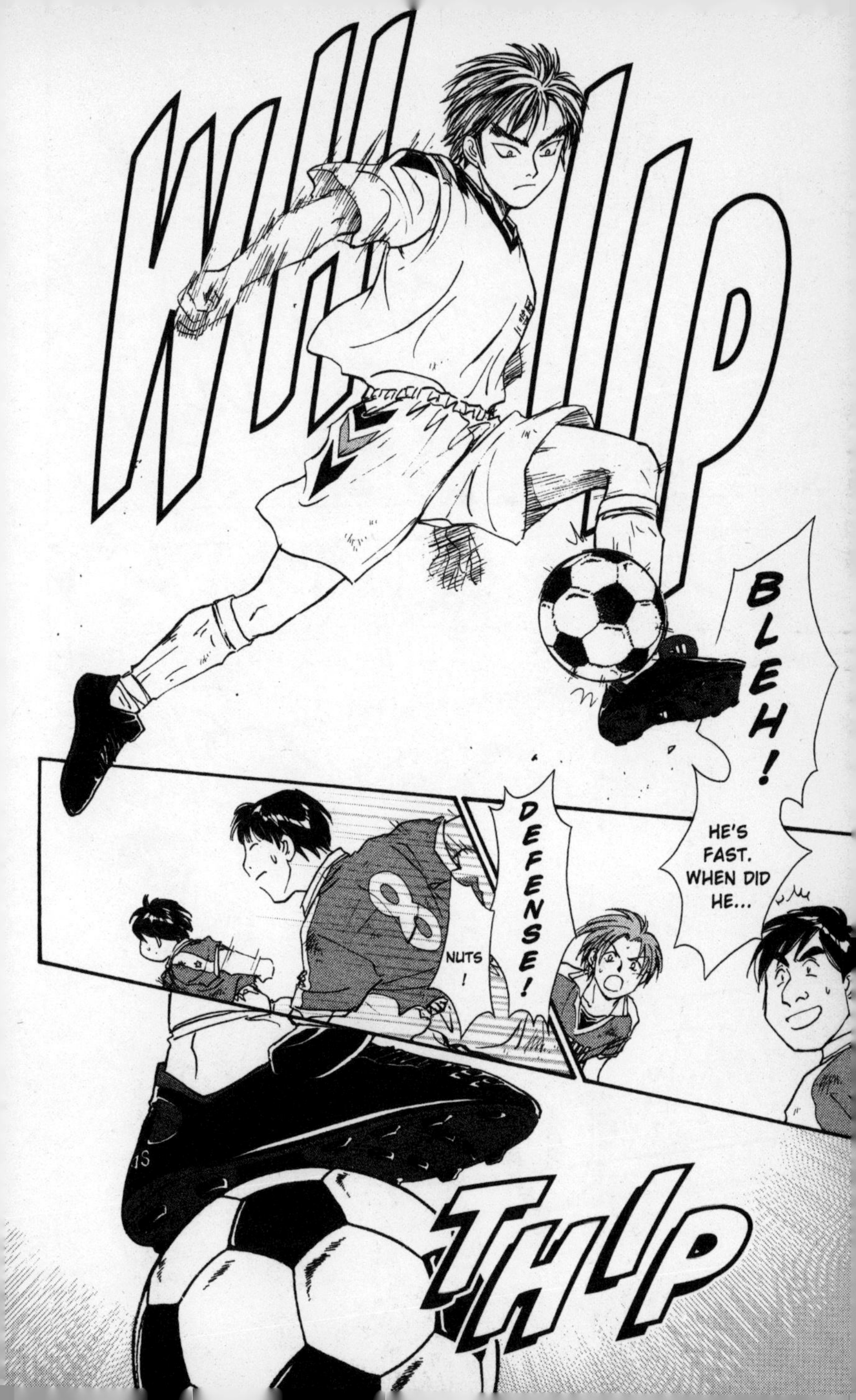
WHIP
BLEH!
HE'S FAST. WHEN DID HE...
DEFENSE!
NUTS!
THUP

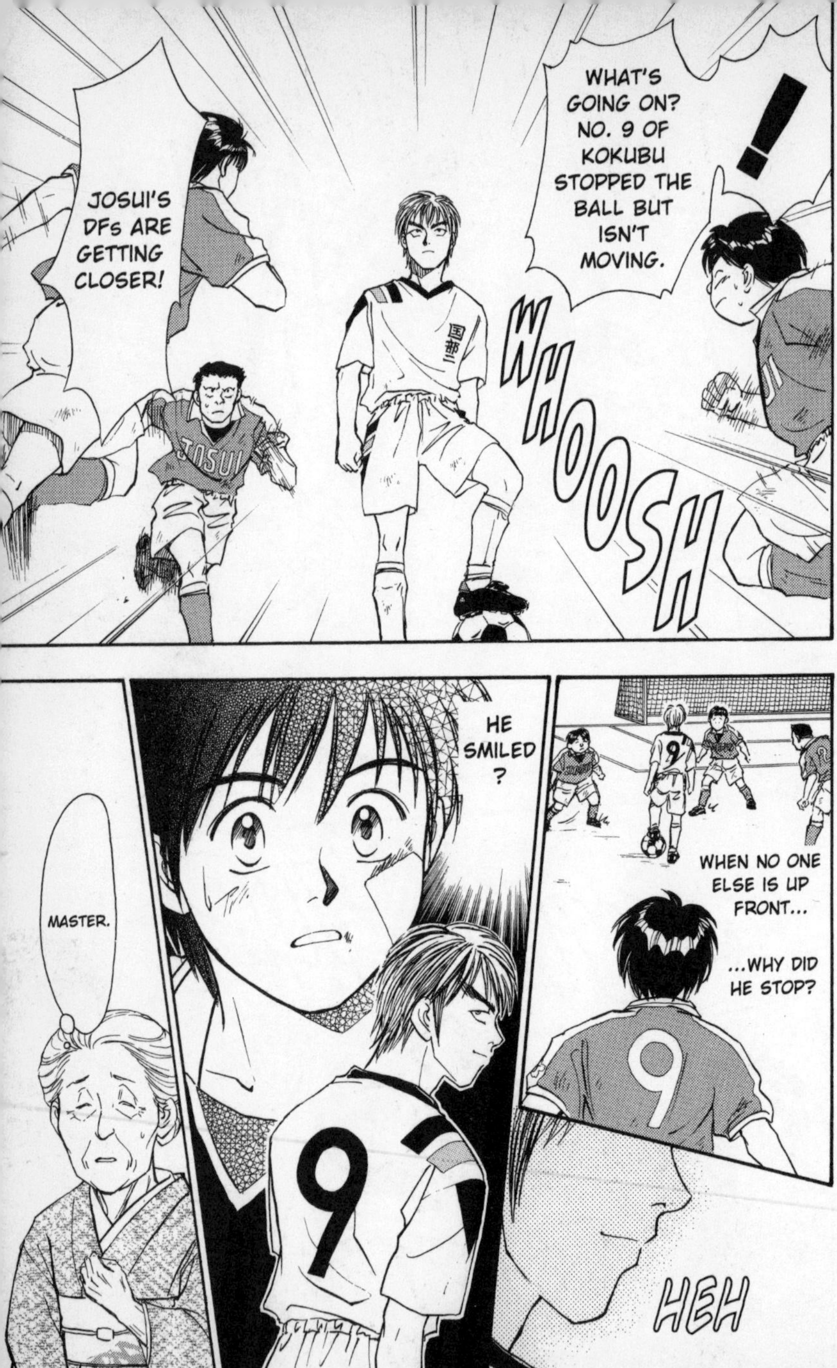
WHAT'S GOING ON? NO. 9 OF KOKUBU STOPPED THE BALL BUT ISN'T MOVING.
!
JOSUI'S DFs ARE GETTING CLOSER!
WHOOSH
WHEN NO ONE ELSE IS UP FRONT...
...WHY DID HE STOP?
HE SMILED?
HEH
MASTER.

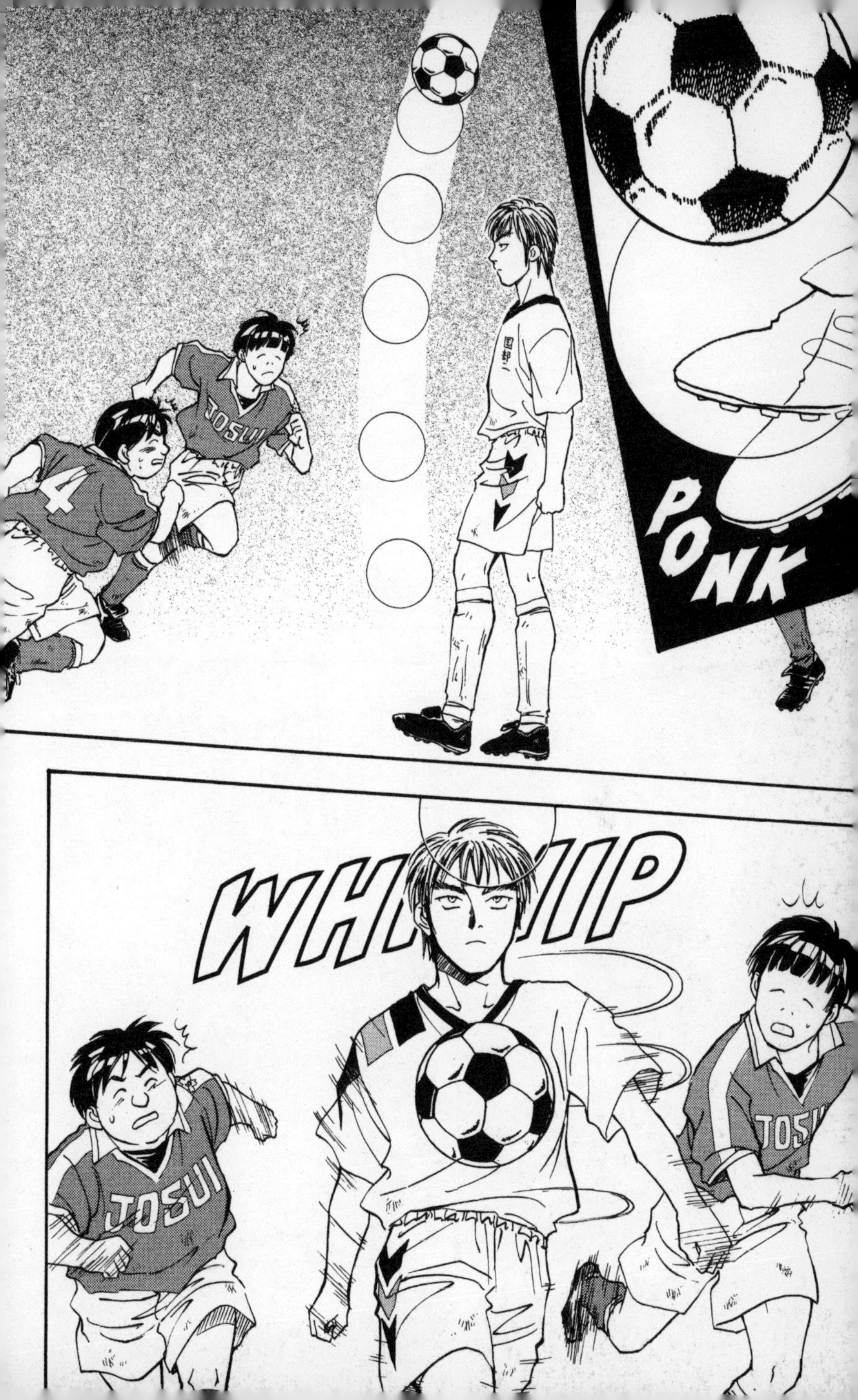
PONK
JOSUI
JOSUI
JOSUI

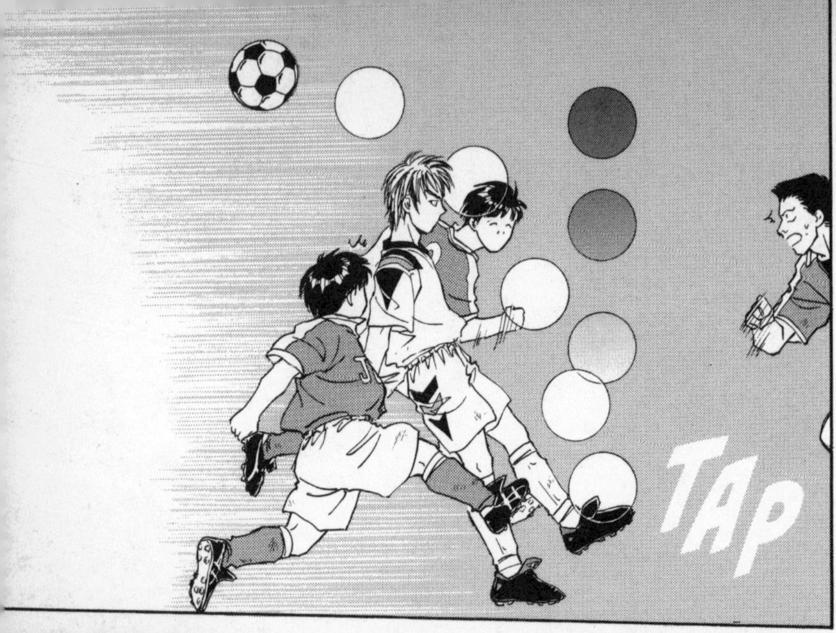
TAP
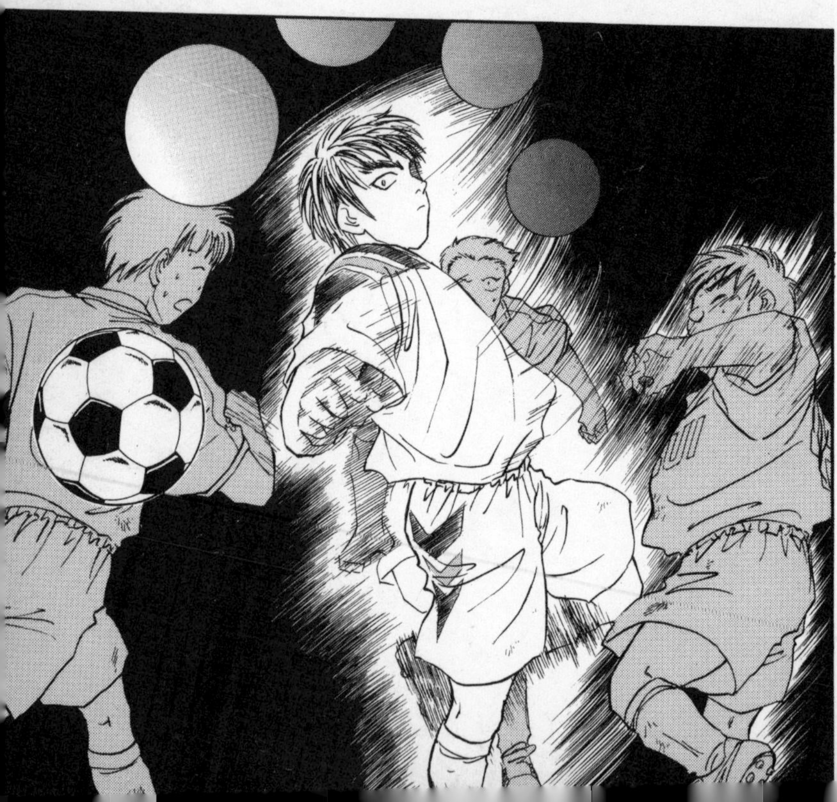

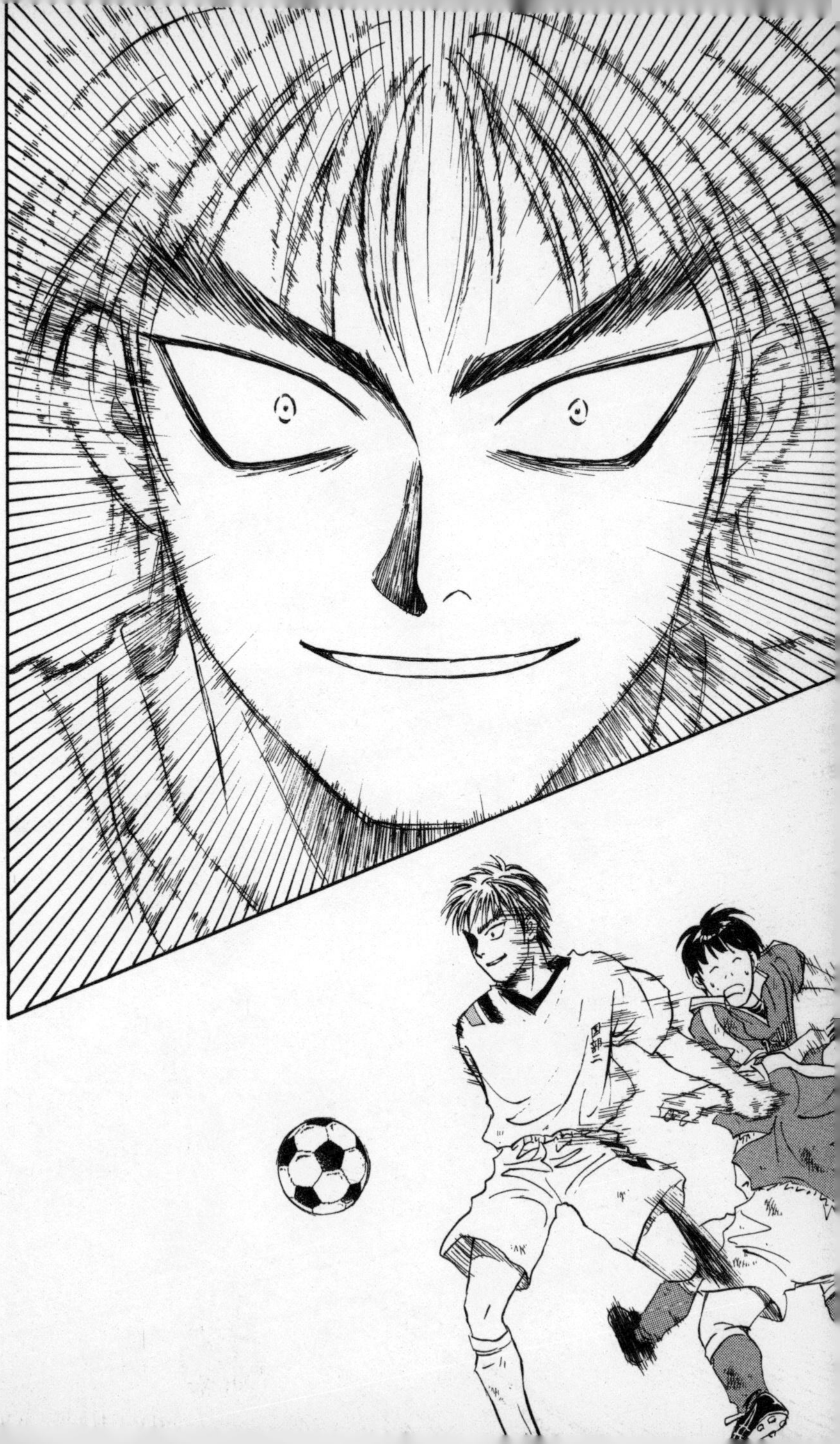

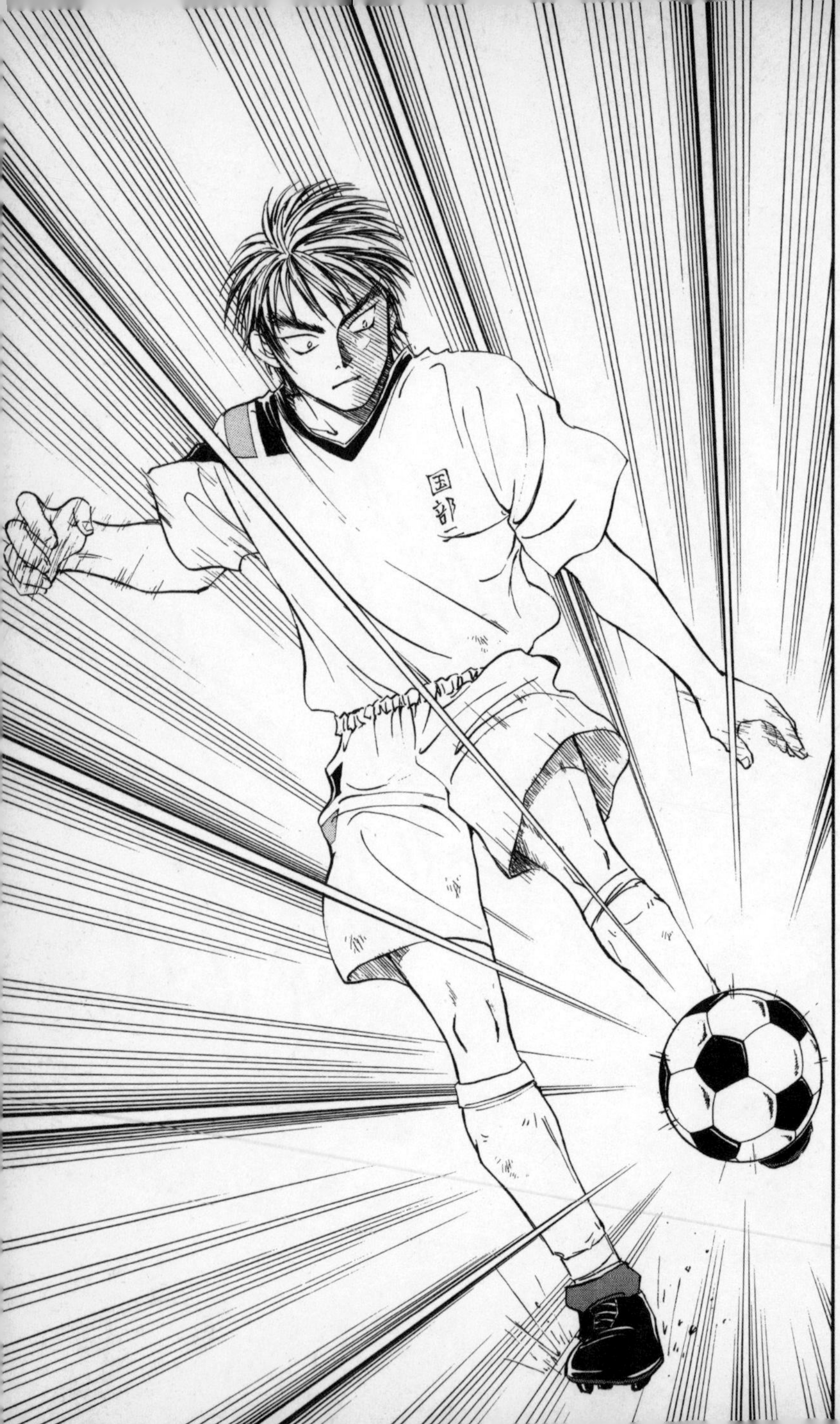
国部

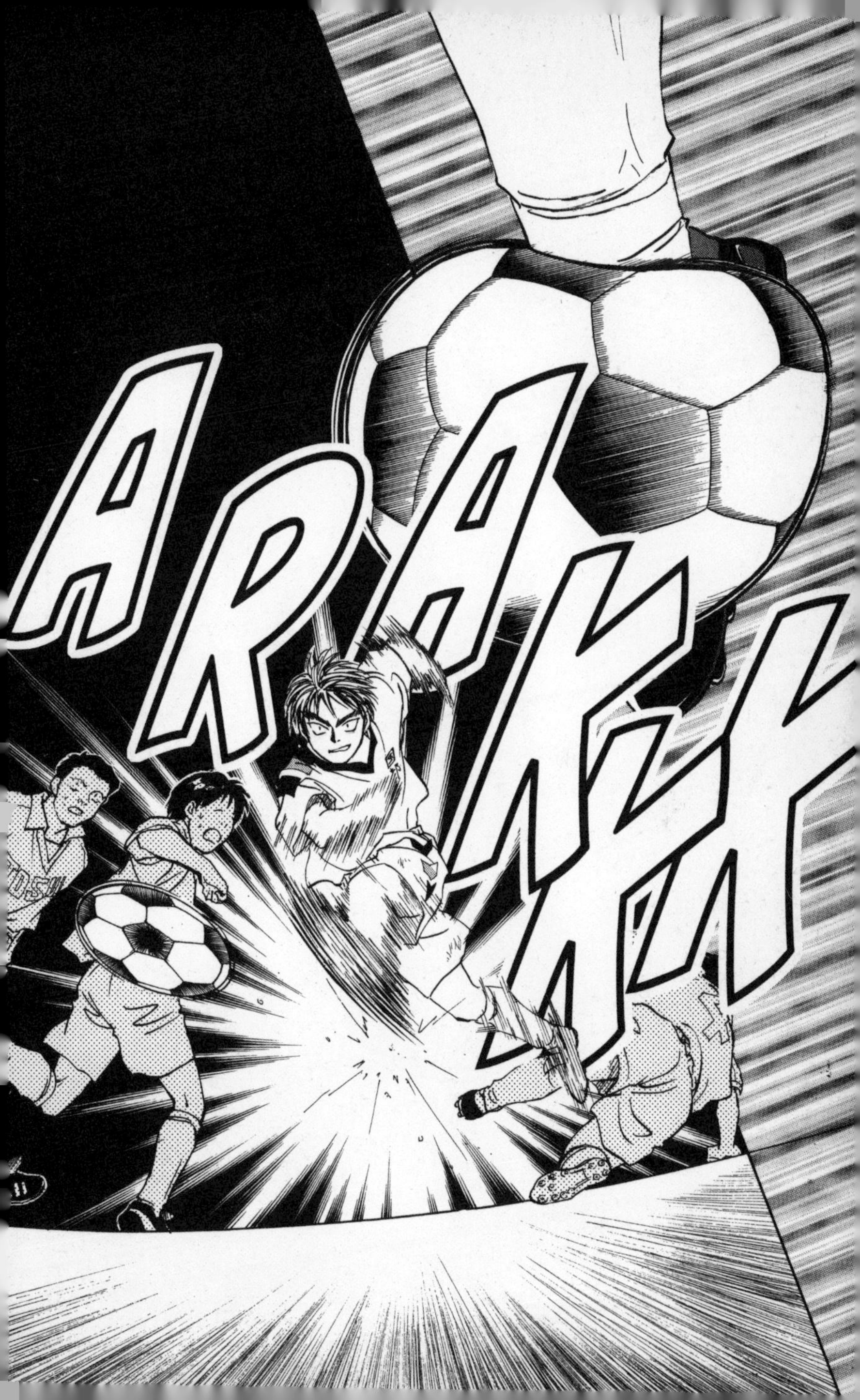

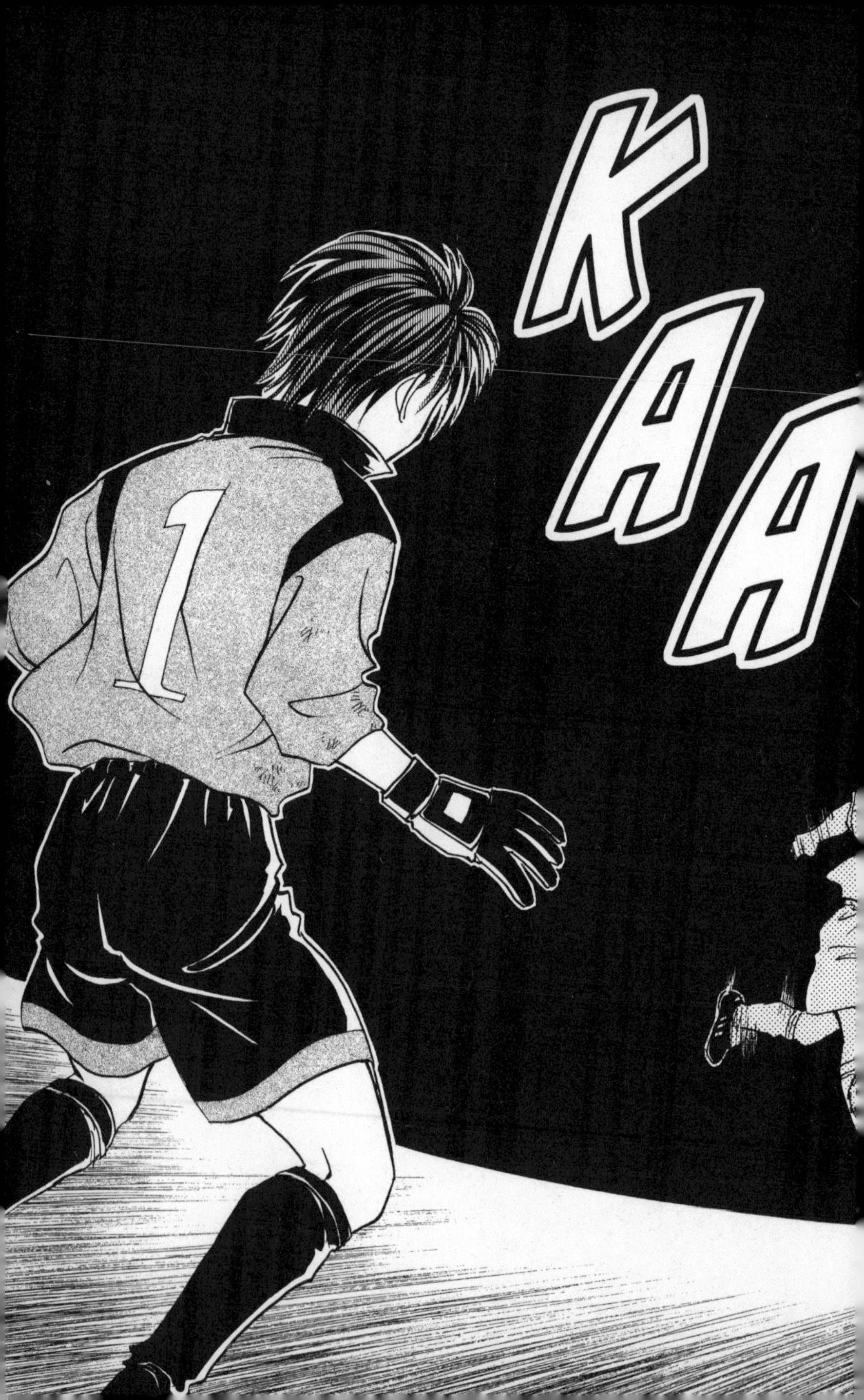
KAAA

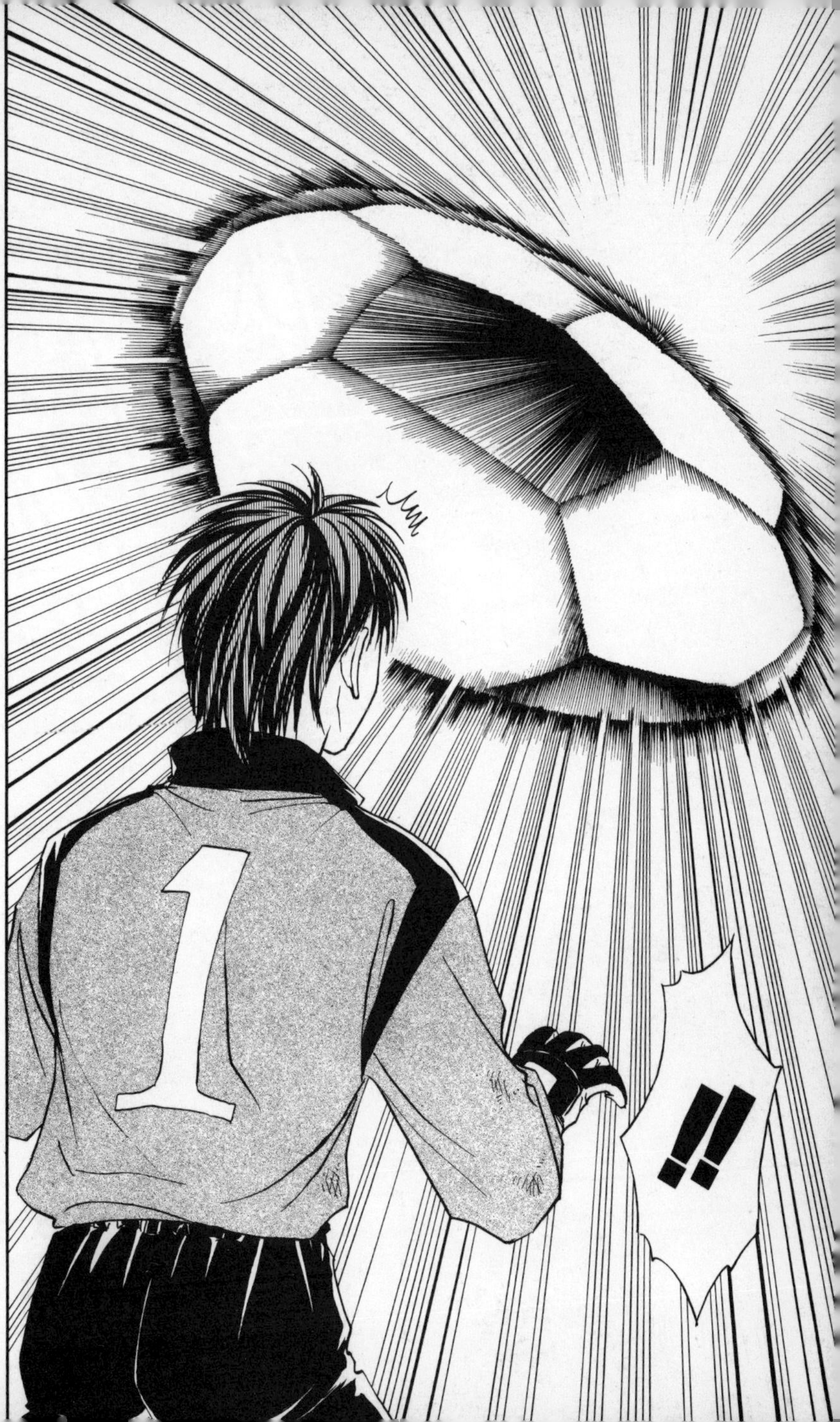
!!

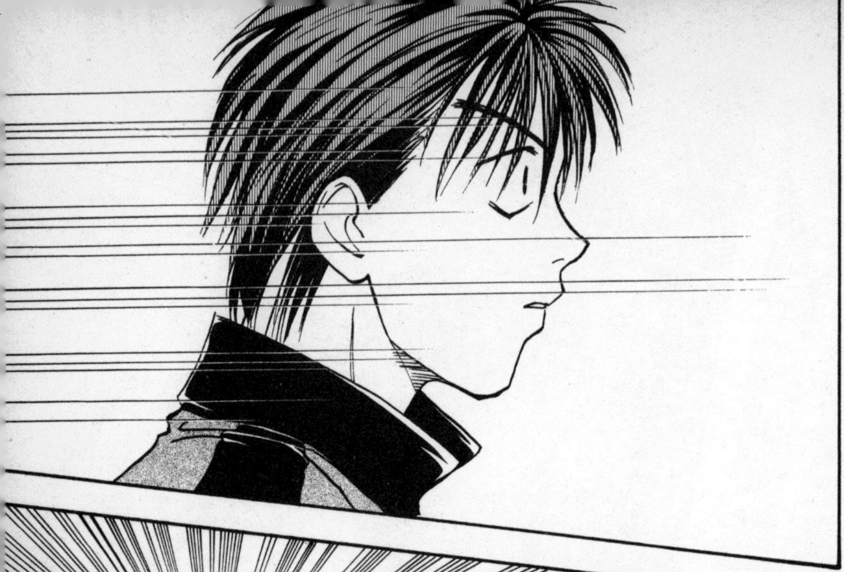

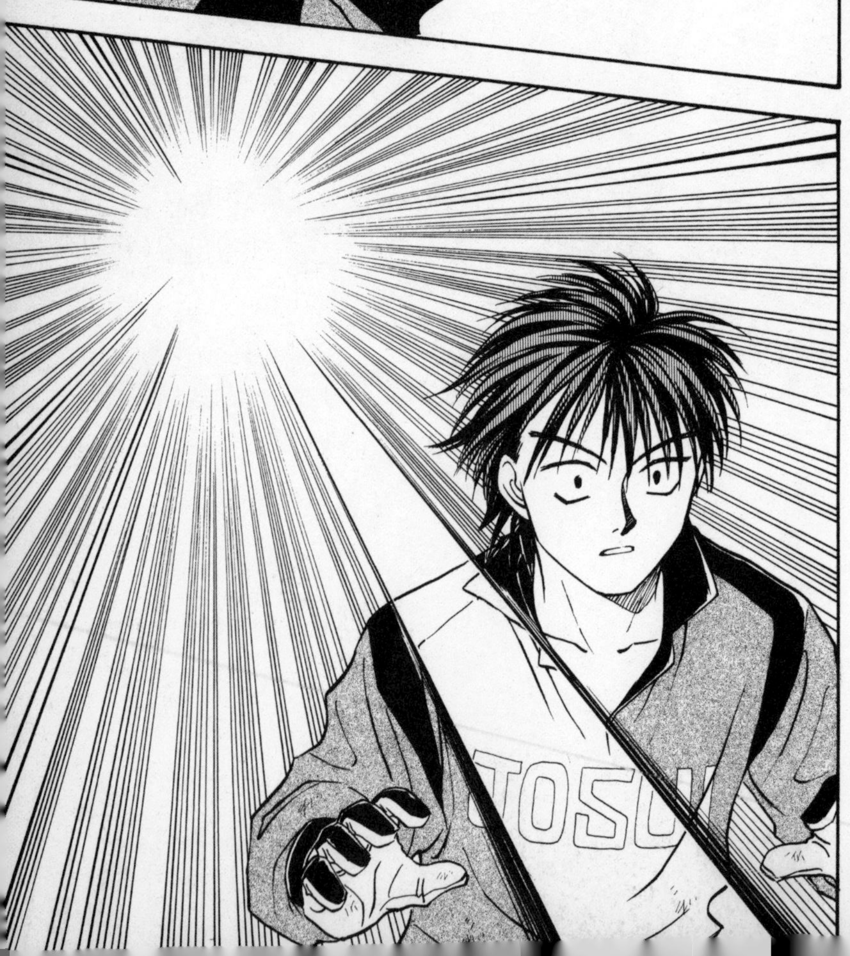
TOSU

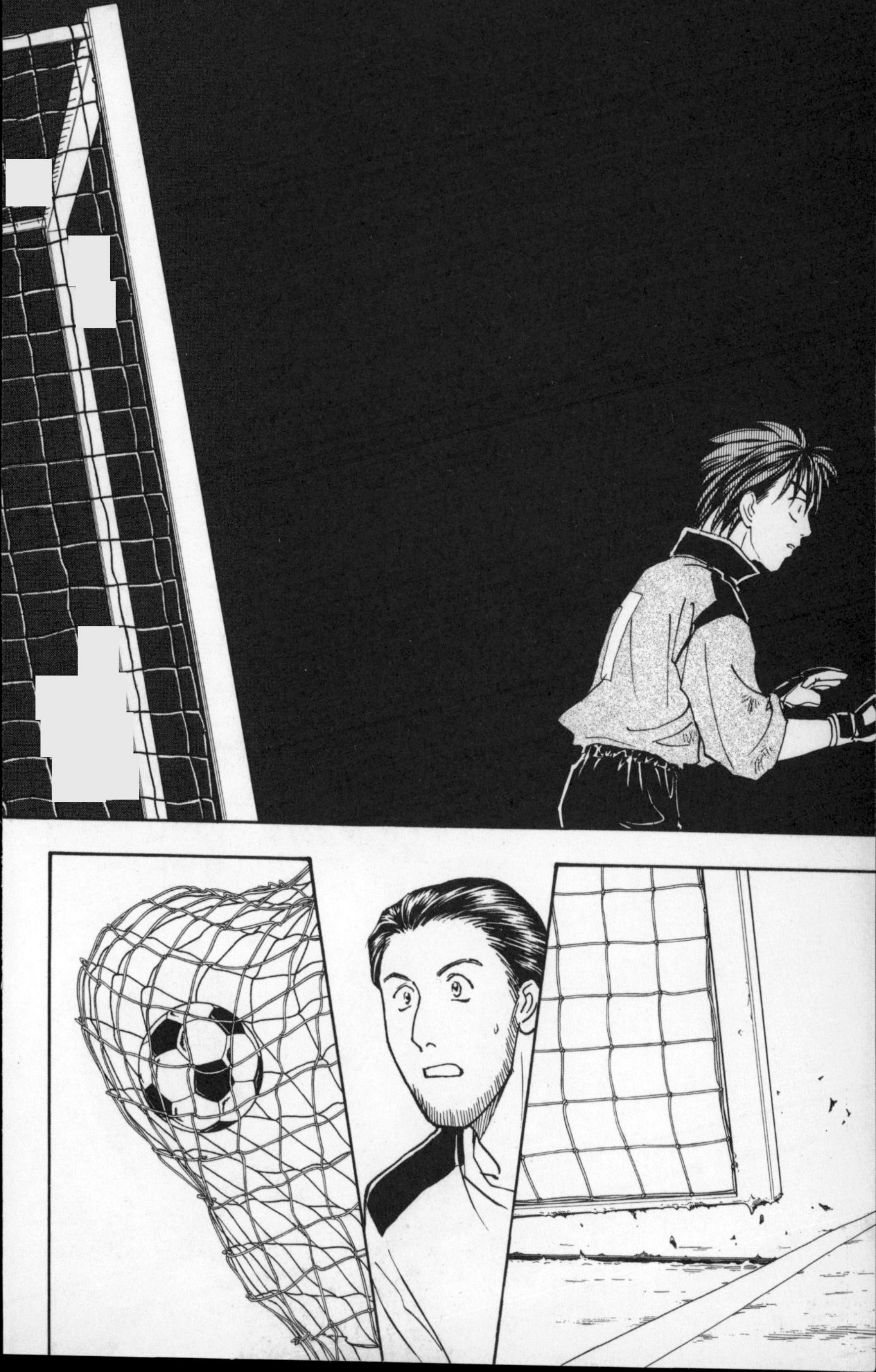

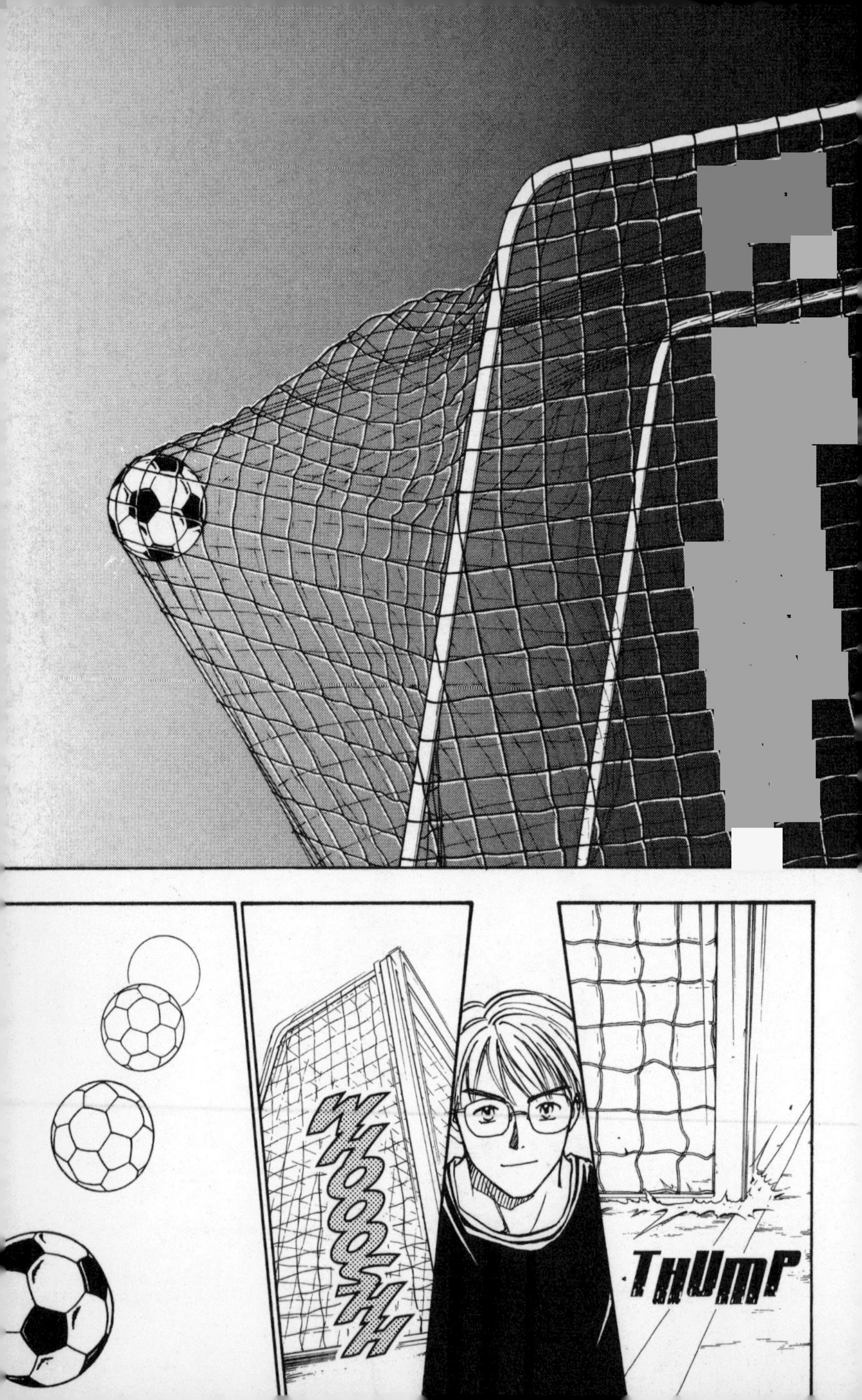
THUMP
WHOOOSHH

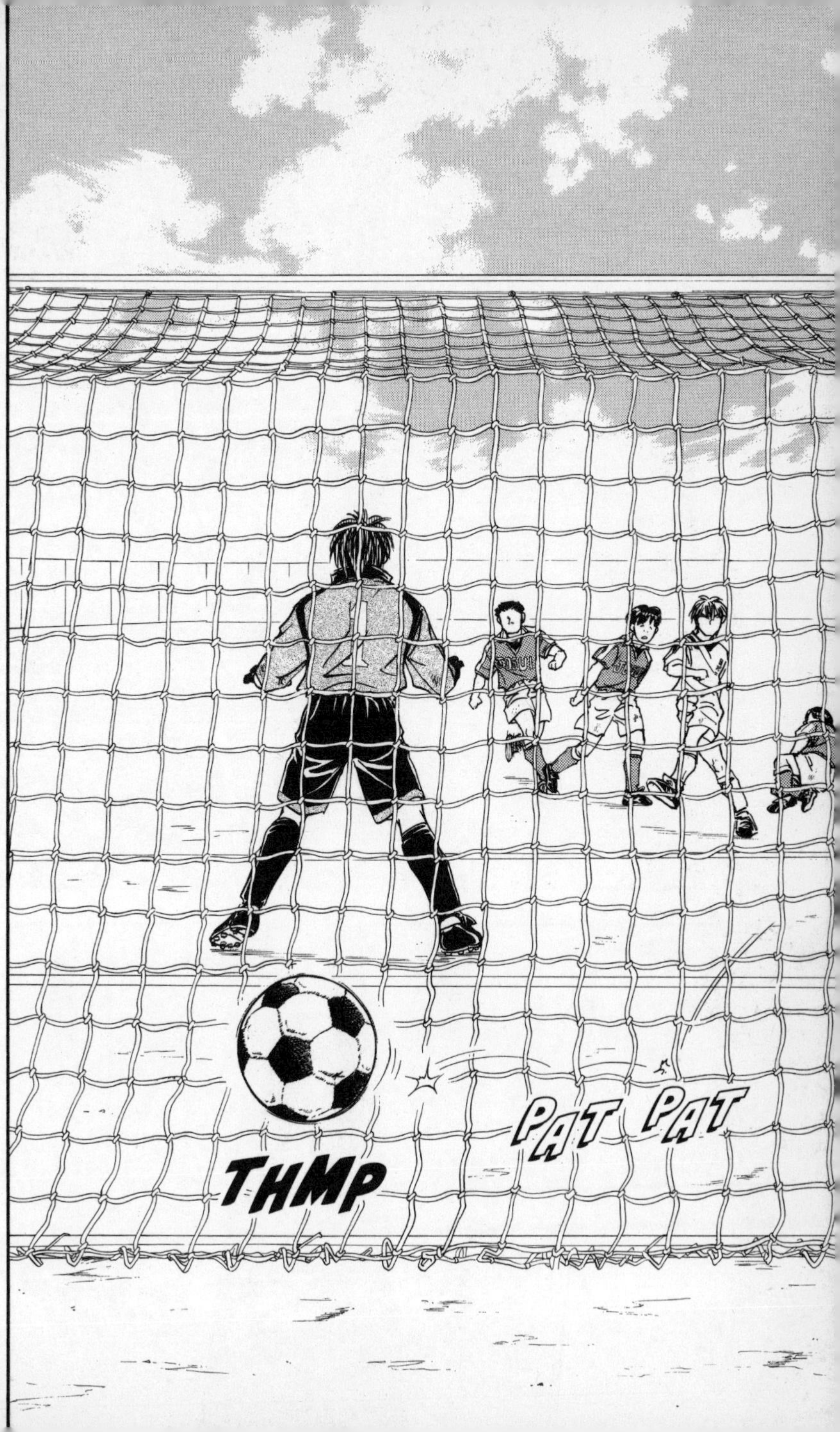
PAT PAT
THMP

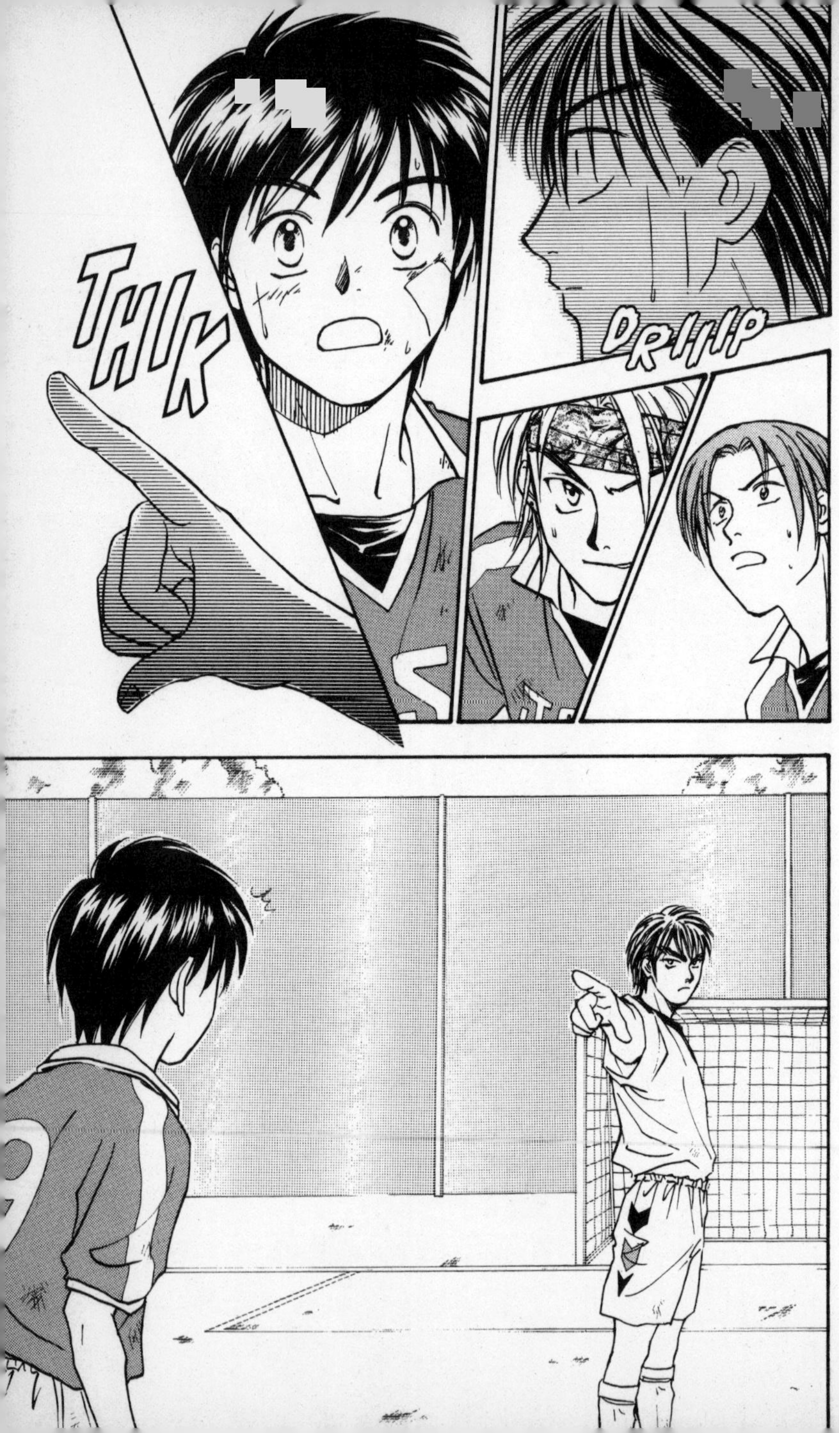
DRIIIP
THIK

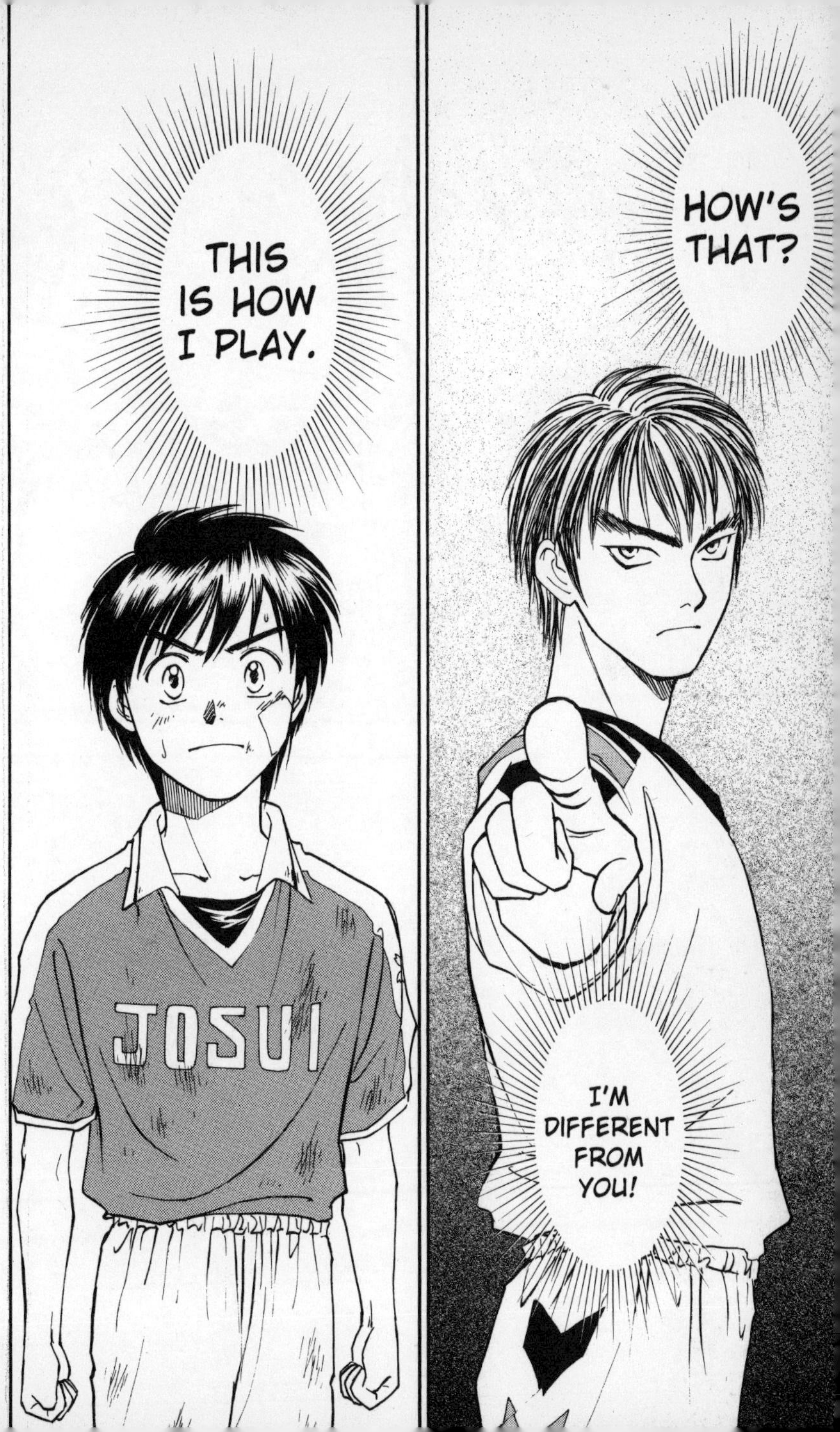
HOW'S THAT?
I'M DIFFERENT FROM YOU!
THIS IS HOW I PLAY.
JOSUI

STAGE.43

Your Soccer, My Soccer

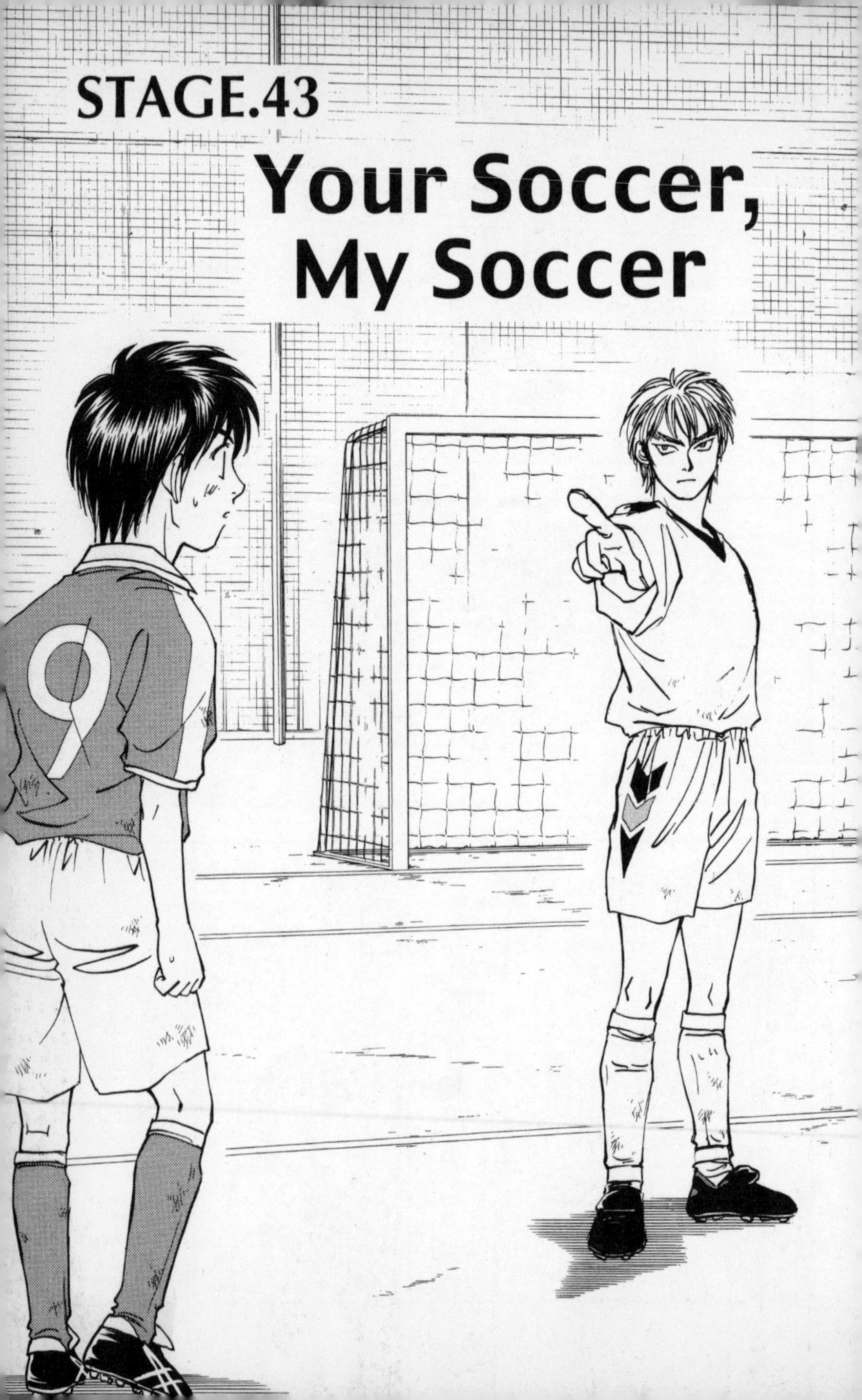

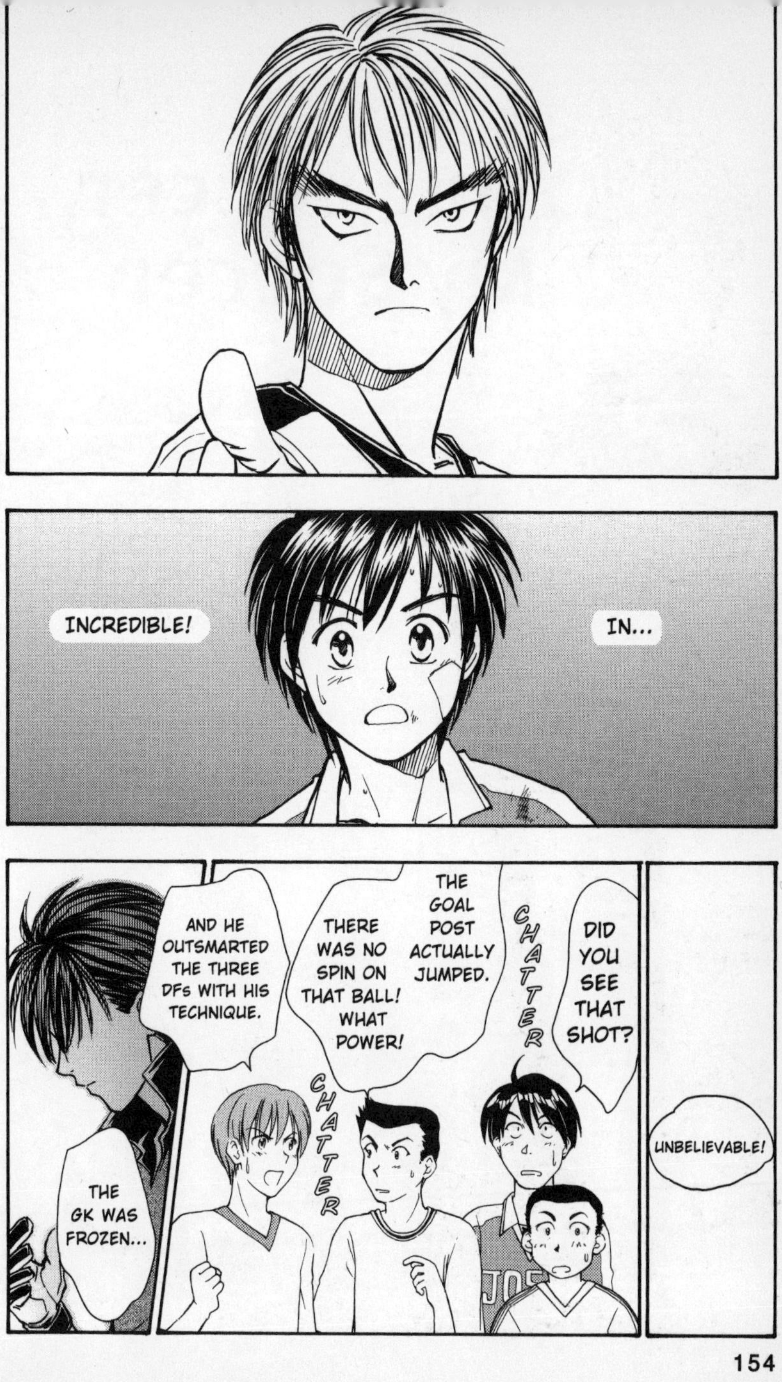
IN...
INCREDIBLE!
UNBELIEVABLE!
DID YOU SEE THAT SHOT?
CHATTER
THE GOAL POST ACTUALLY JUMPED.
THERE WAS NO SPIN ON THAT BALL! WHAT POWER!
CHATTER
AND HE OUTSMARTED THE THREE DFs WITH HIS TECHNIQUE.
THE GK WAS FROZEN...

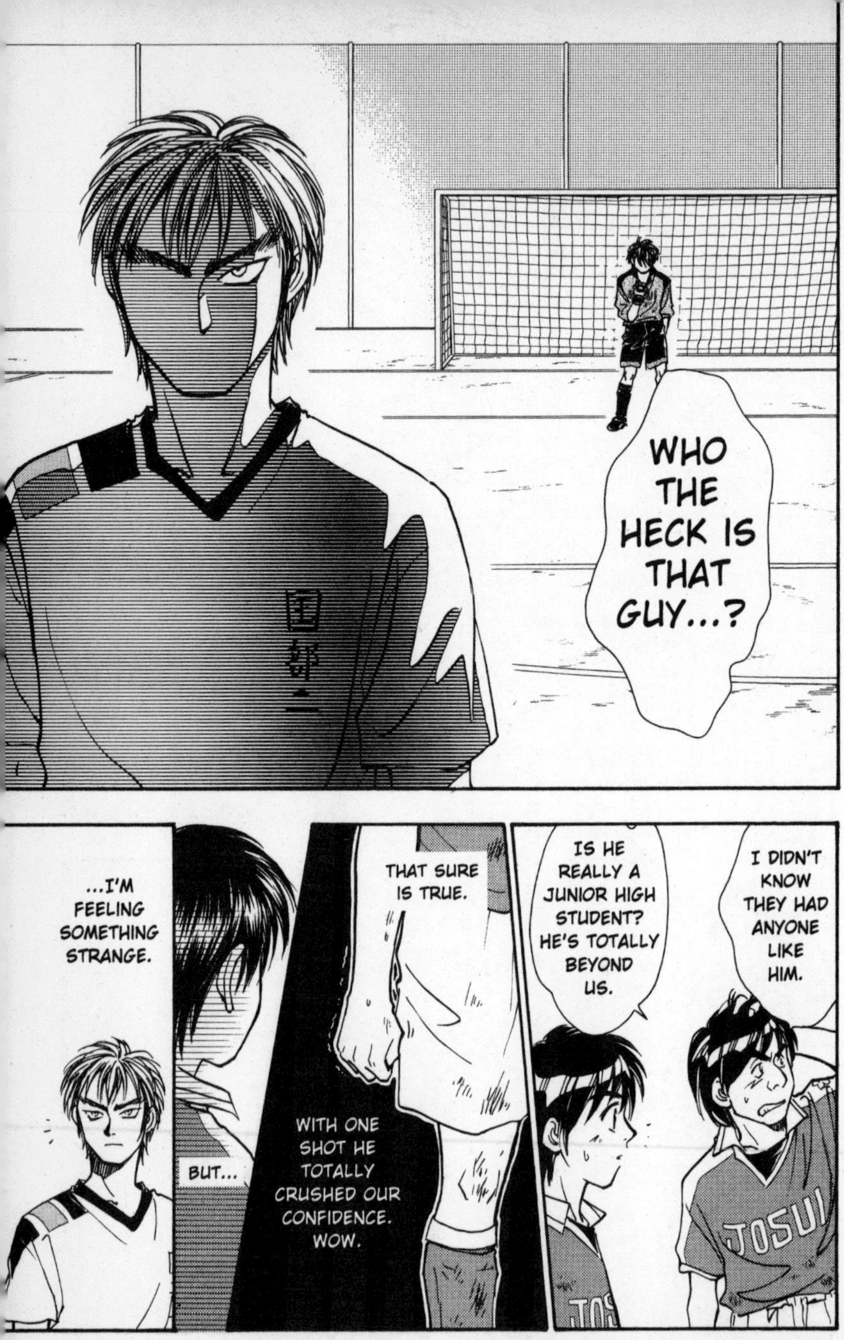
WHO THE HECK IS THAT GUY...?
I DIDN'T KNOW THEY HAD ANYONE LIKE HIM.
IS HE REALLY A JUNIOR HIGH STUDENT? HE'S TOTALLY BEYOND US.
JOSUI
THAT SURE IS TRUE.
WITH ONE SHOT HE TOTALLY CRUSHED OUR CONFIDENCE. WOW.
BUT...
...I'M FEELING SOMETHING STRANGE.

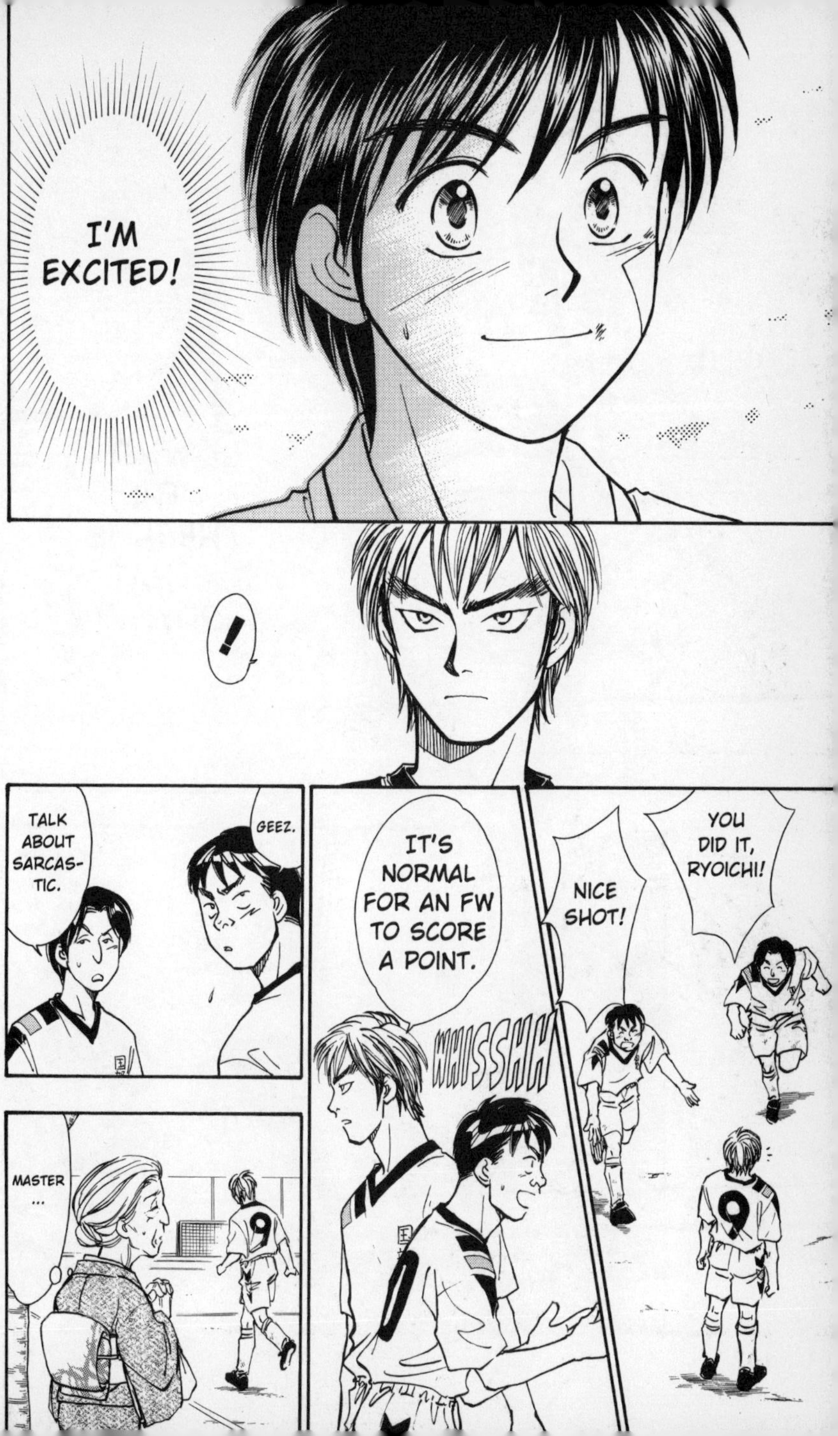
I'M EXCITED!
!
YOU DID IT, RYOICHI!
NICE SHOT!
IT'S NORMAL FOR AN FW TO SCORE A POINT.
WHISSHH
GEEZ.
TALK ABOUT SARCASTIC.
MASTER ...

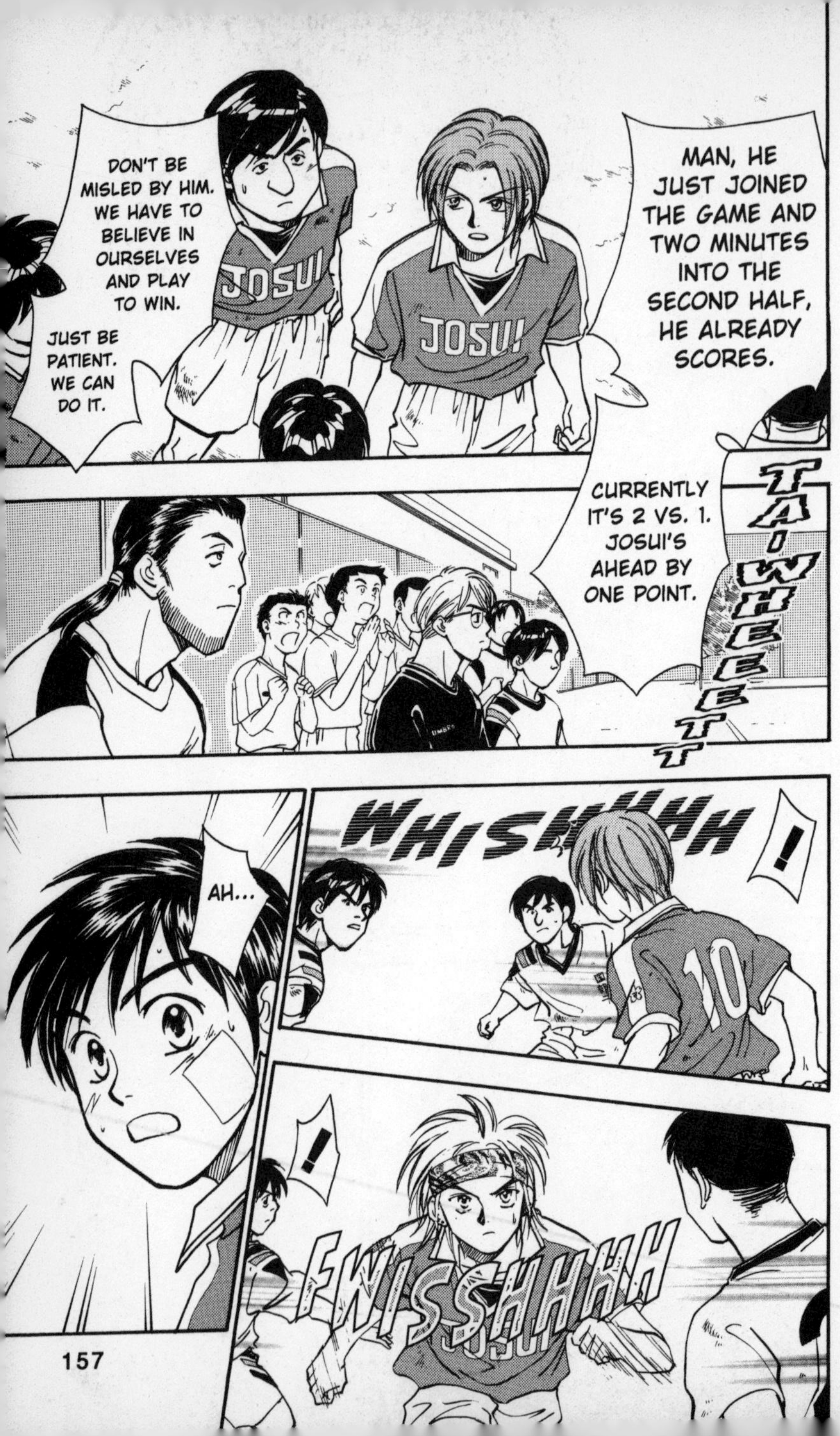

MAN, HE JUST JOINED THE GAME AND TWO MINUTES INTO THE SECOND HALF, HE ALREADY SCORES.
DON'T BE MISLED BY HIM. WE HAVE TO BELIEVE IN OURSELVES AND PLAY TO WIN.
JUST BE PATIENT. WE CAN DO IT.
CURRENTLY IT'S 2 VS. 1. JOSUI'S AHEAD BY ONE POINT.
TA-WHEEETT
WHISHHHH
!
!
FWISSHHHH
AH...

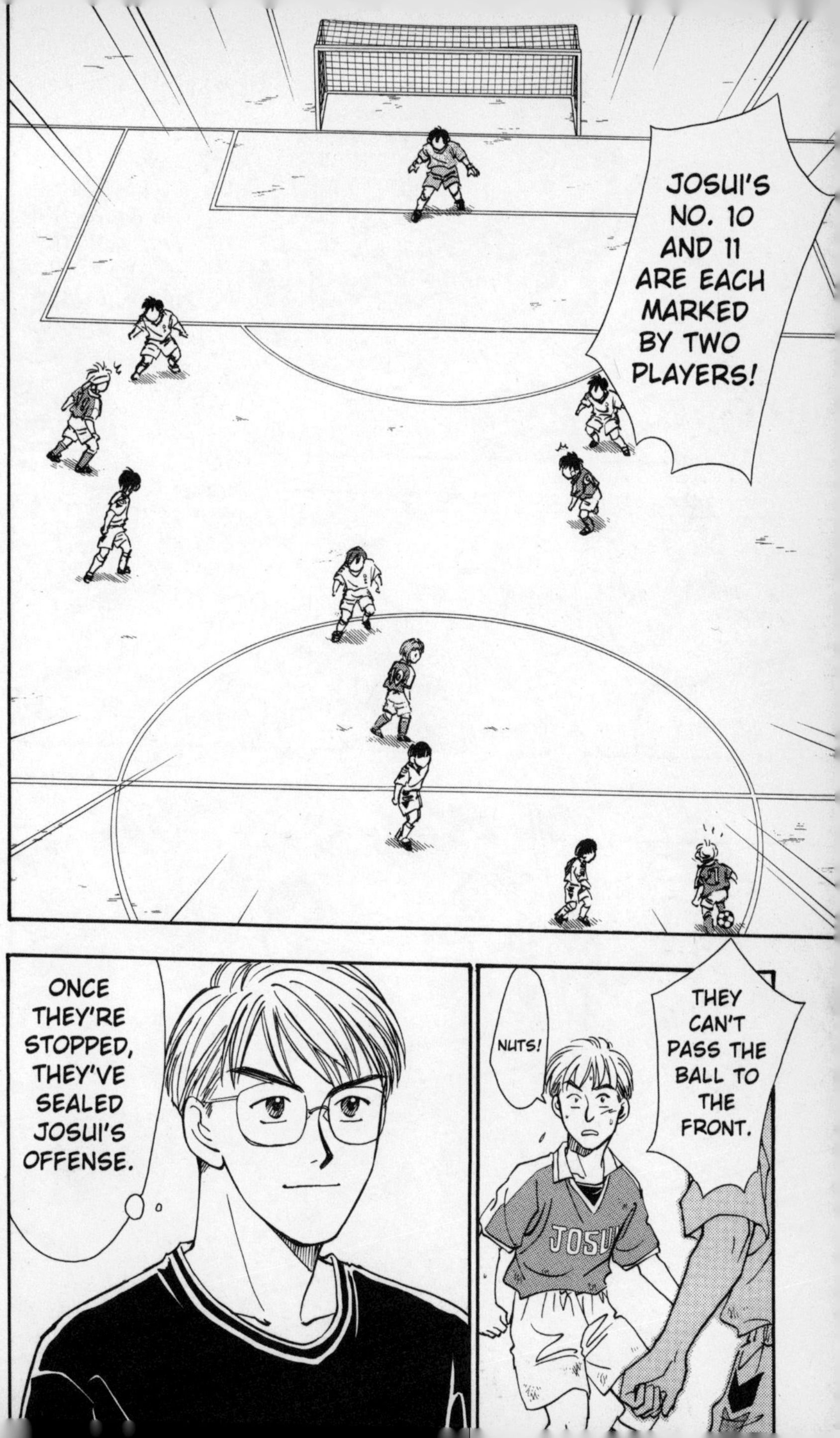
JOSUI'S NO. 10 AND 11 ARE EACH MARKED BY TWO PLAYERS!
THEY CAN'T PASS THE BALL TO THE FRONT.
NUTS!
ONCE THEY'RE STOPPED, THEY'VE SEALED JOSUI'S OFFENSE.
JOSUI

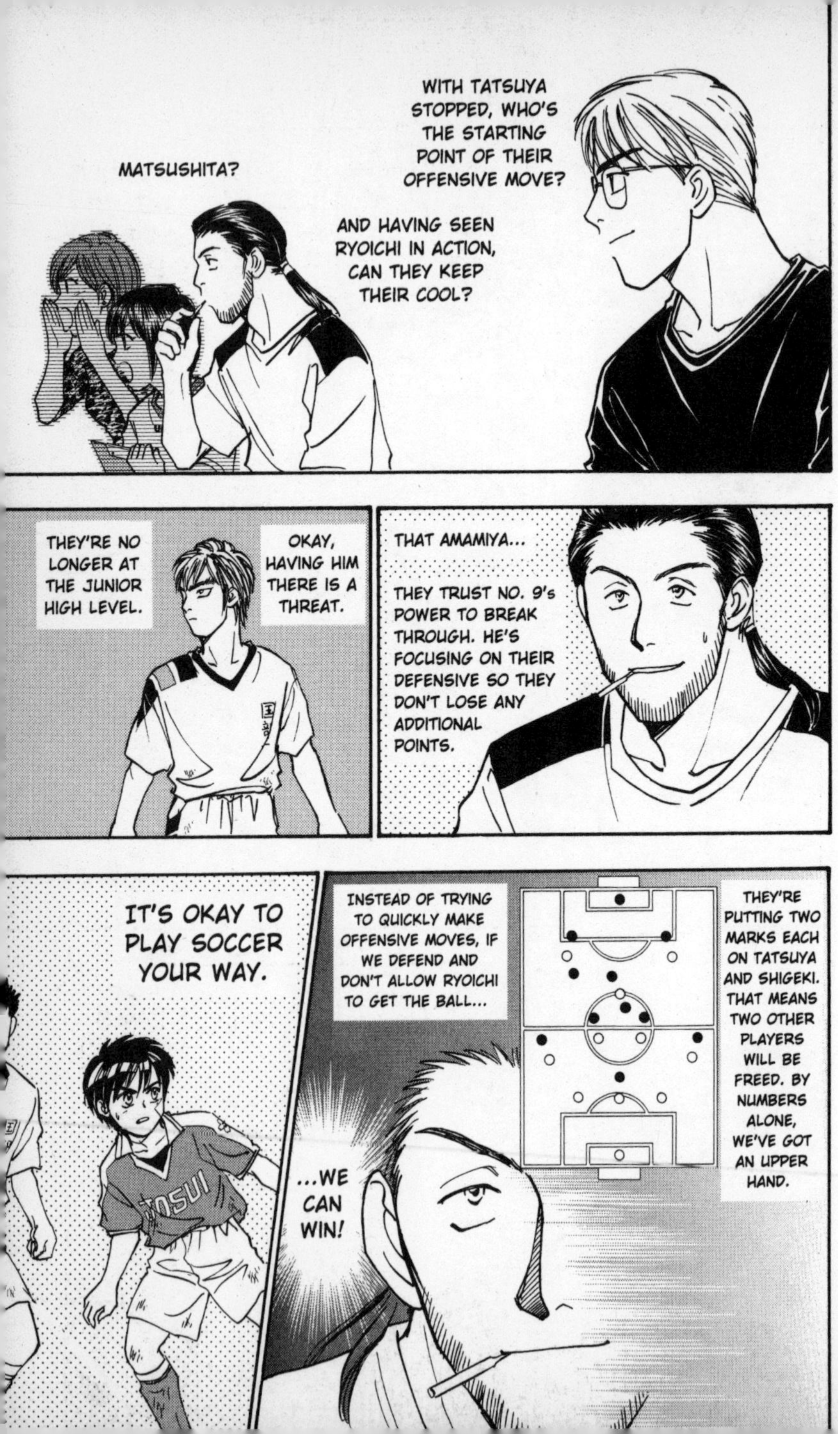
WITH TATSUYA STOPPED, WHO'S THE STARTING POINT OF THEIR OFFENSIVE MOVE?
AND HAVING SEEN RYOICHI IN ACTION, CAN THEY KEEP THEIR COOL?
MATSUSHITA?
THAT AMAMIYA...
THEY TRUST NO. 9's POWER TO BREAK THROUGH. HE'S FOCUSING ON THEIR DEFENSIVE SO THEY DON'T LOSE ANY ADDITIONAL POINTS.
OKAY, HAVING HIM THERE IS A THREAT.
THEY'RE NO LONGER AT THE JUNIOR HIGH LEVEL.
THEY'RE PUTTING TWO MARKS EACH ON TATSUYA AND SHIGEKI. THAT MEANS TWO OTHER PLAYERS WILL BE FREED. BY NUMBERS ALONE, WE'VE GOT AN UPPER HAND.
INSTEAD OF TRYING TO QUICKLY MAKE OFFENSIVE MOVES, IF WE DEFEND AND DON'T ALLOW RYOICHI TO GET THE BALL...
...WE CAN WIN!
IT'S OKAY TO PLAY SOCCER YOUR WAY.

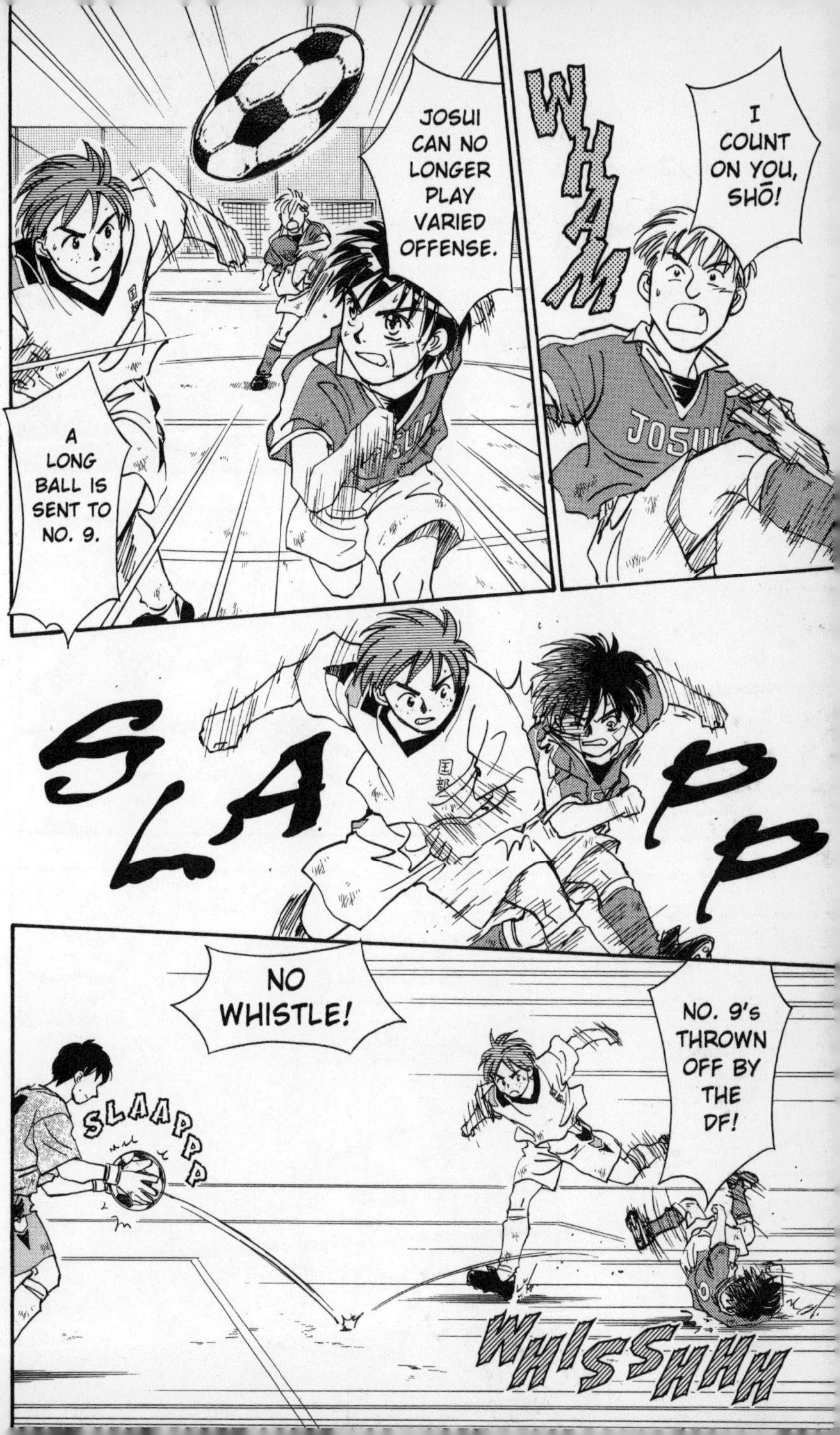
I COUNT ON YOU, SHŌ!
WHAM
JOSUI CAN NO LONGER PLAY VARIED OFFENSE.
A LONG BALL IS SENT TO NO. 9.
JOSUI
SLAPP
NO. 9's THROWN OFF BY THE DF!
NO WHISTLE!
SLAAPPP
WHISSHHH

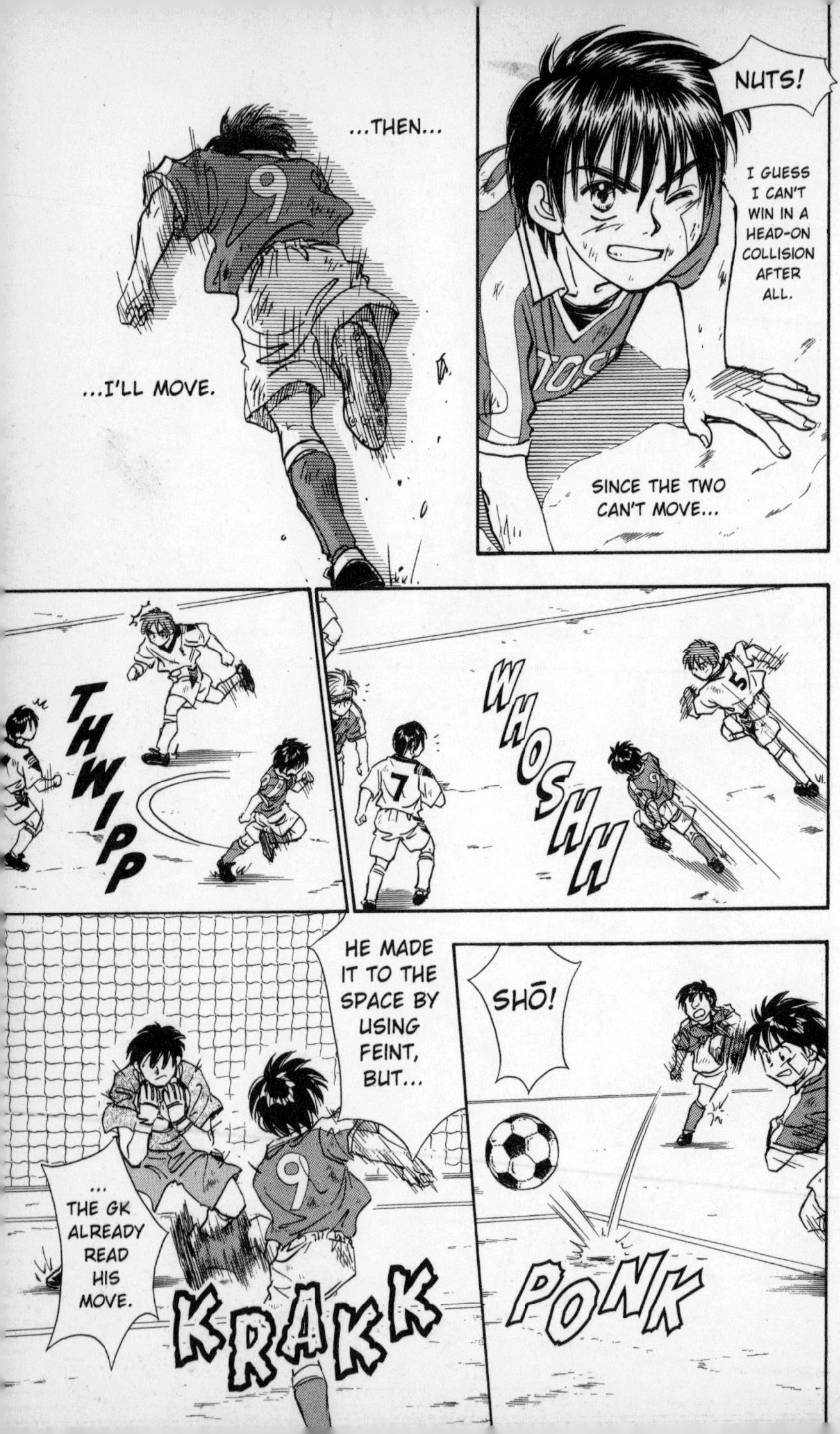
NUTS!
I GUESS I CAN'T WIN IN A HEAD-ON COLLISION AFTER ALL.
SINCE THE TWO CAN'T MOVE...
...THEN...
...I'LL MOVE.
WHOSHH
THWIPP
SHŌ!
PONK
HE MADE IT TO THE SPACE BY USING FEINT, BUT...
...THE GK ALREADY READ HIS MOVE.
KRAKK

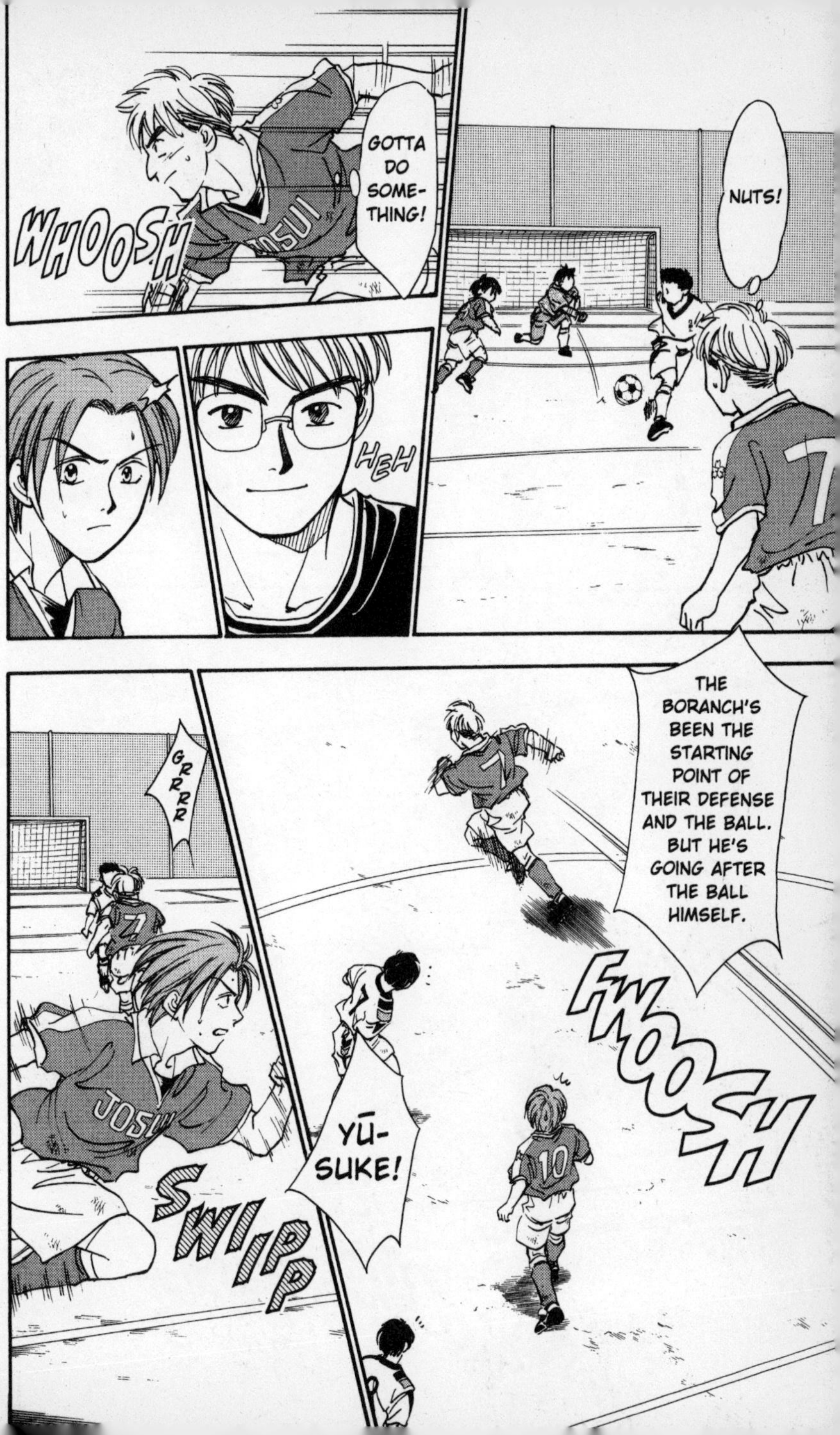
NUTS!
GOTTA DO SOME-THING!
WHOOSH
HEH
THE BORANCH'S BEEN THE STARTING POINT OF THEIR DEFENSE AND THE BALL. BUT HE'S GOING AFTER THE BALL HIMSELF.
FWOOCH
YŪ-SUKE!
GRRRR
SWIPP

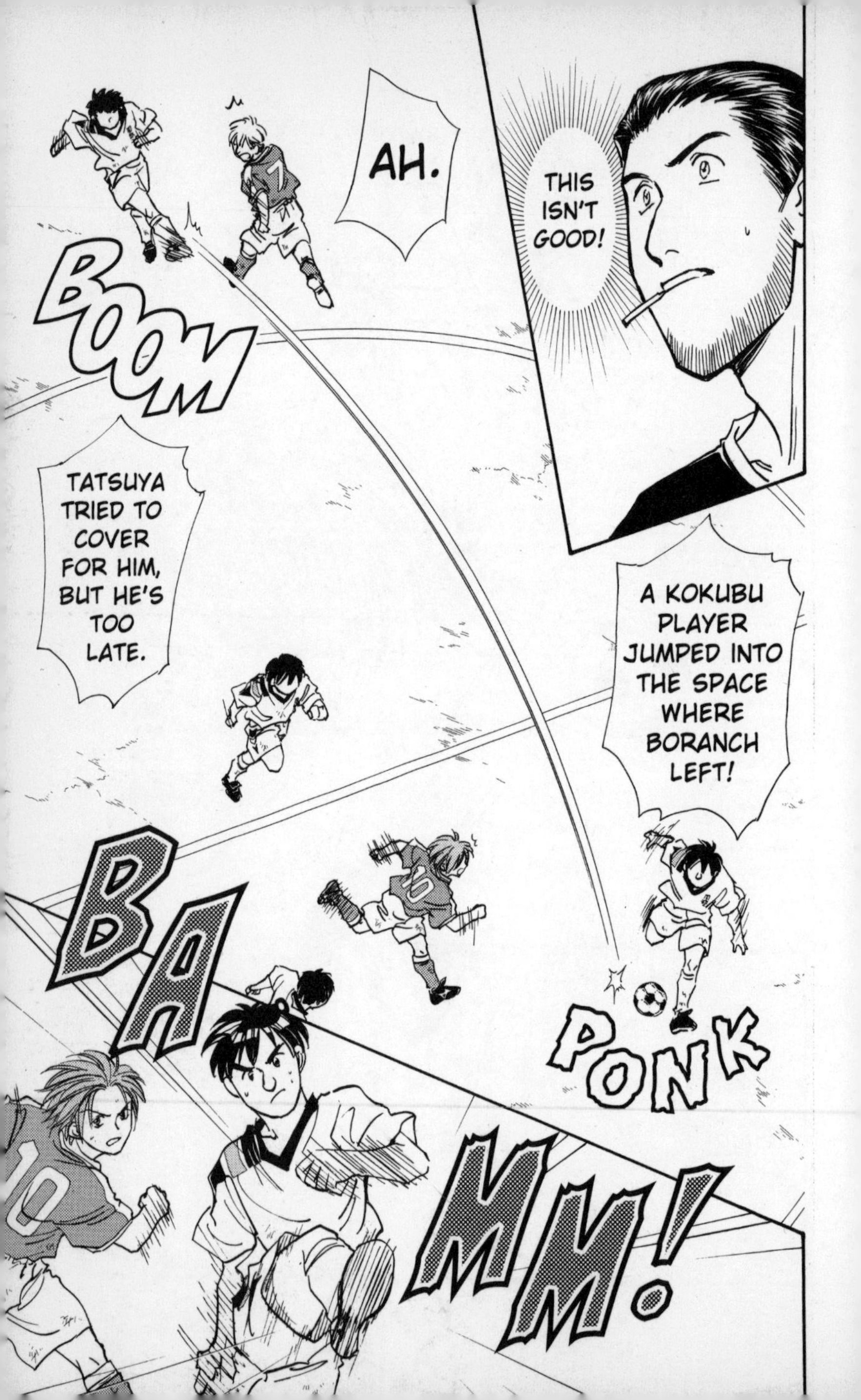
THIS ISN'T GOOD!
AH.
BOOM
A KOKUBU PLAYER JUMPED INTO THE SPACE WHERE BORANCH LEFT!
TATSUYA TRIED TO COVER FOR HIM, BUT HE'S TOO LATE.
PONK
BAMM!

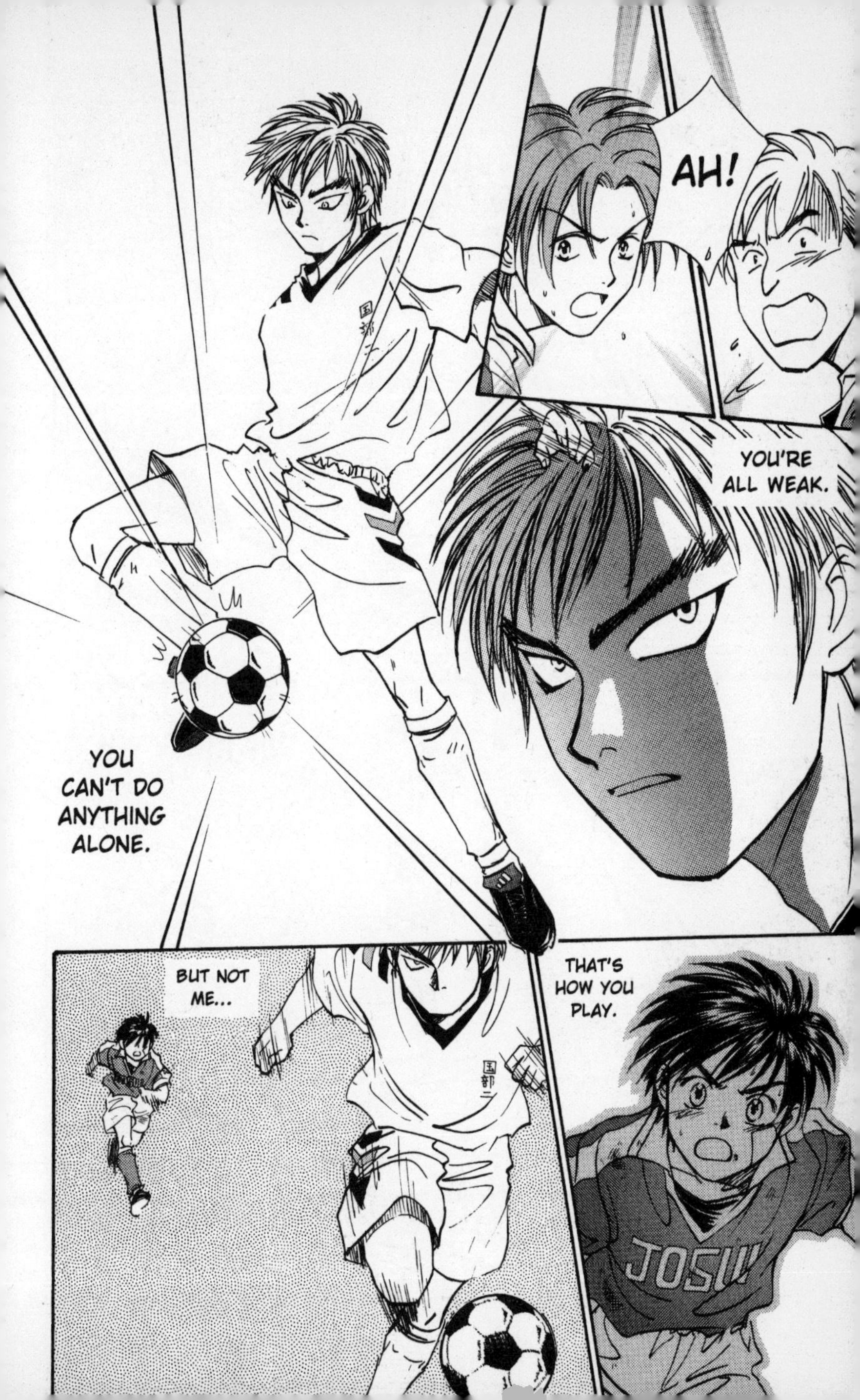
AH!
YOU'RE ALL WEAK.
YOU CAN'T DO ANYTHING ALONE.
THAT'S HOW YOU PLAY.
BUT NOT ME...

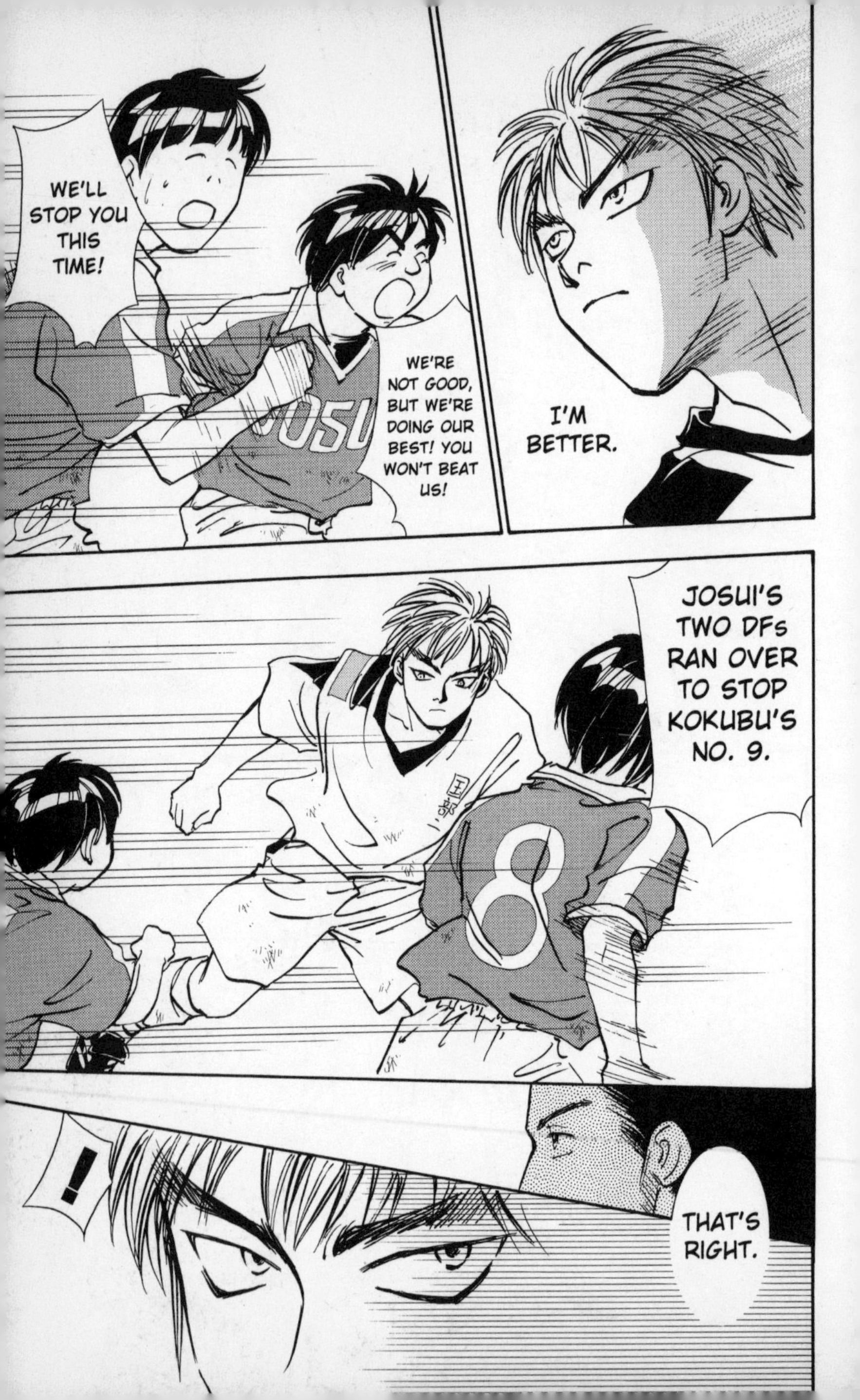
I'M BETTER.
WE'LL STOP YOU THIS TIME!
WE'RE NOT GOOD, BUT WE'RE DOING OUR BEST! YOU WON'T BEAT US!
JOSUI'S TWO DFs RAN OVER TO STOP KOKUBU'S NO. 9.
THAT'S RIGHT.
!

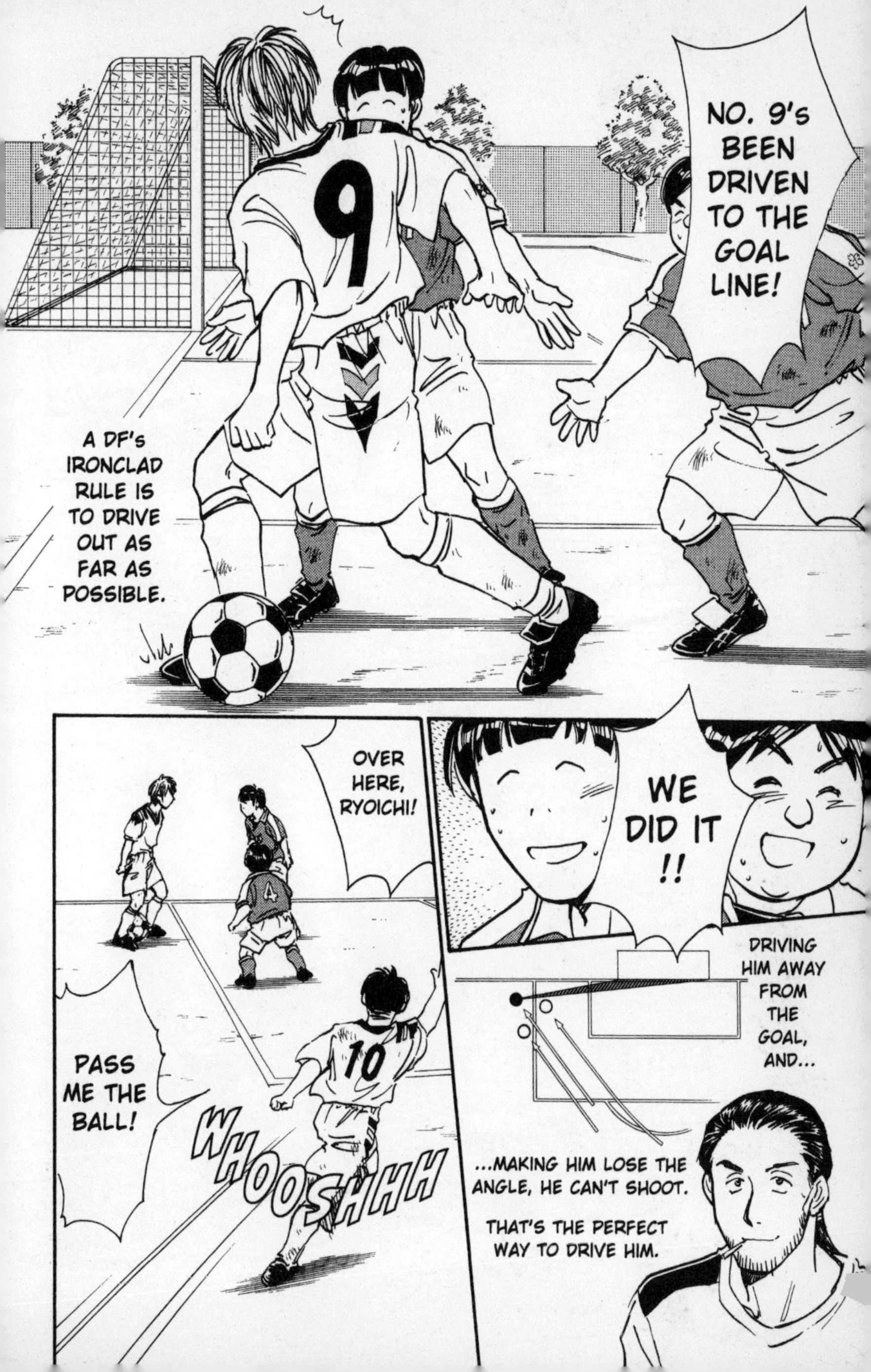
NO. 9's BEEN DRIVEN TO THE GOAL LINE!
A DF's IRONCLAD RULE IS TO DRIVE OUT AS FAR AS POSSIBLE.
WE DID IT !!
DRIVING HIM AWAY FROM THE GOAL, AND...
...MAKING HIM LOSE THE ANGLE, HE CAN'T SHOOT.
THAT'S THE PERFECT WAY TO DRIVE HIM.
OVER HERE, RYOICHI!
PASS ME THE BALL!
WHOOSHHH

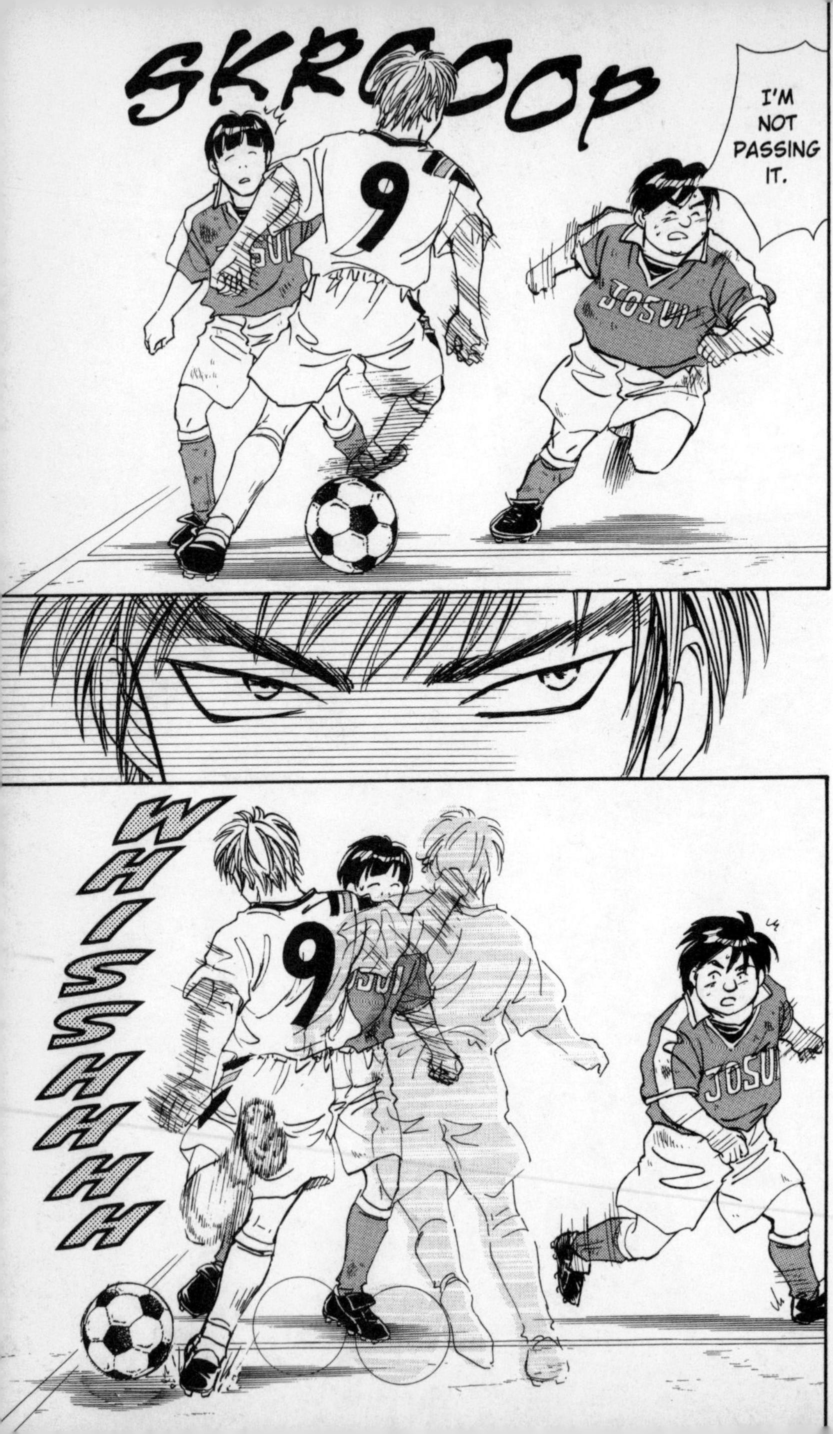
I'M NOT PASSING IT.
WHISSHHHH

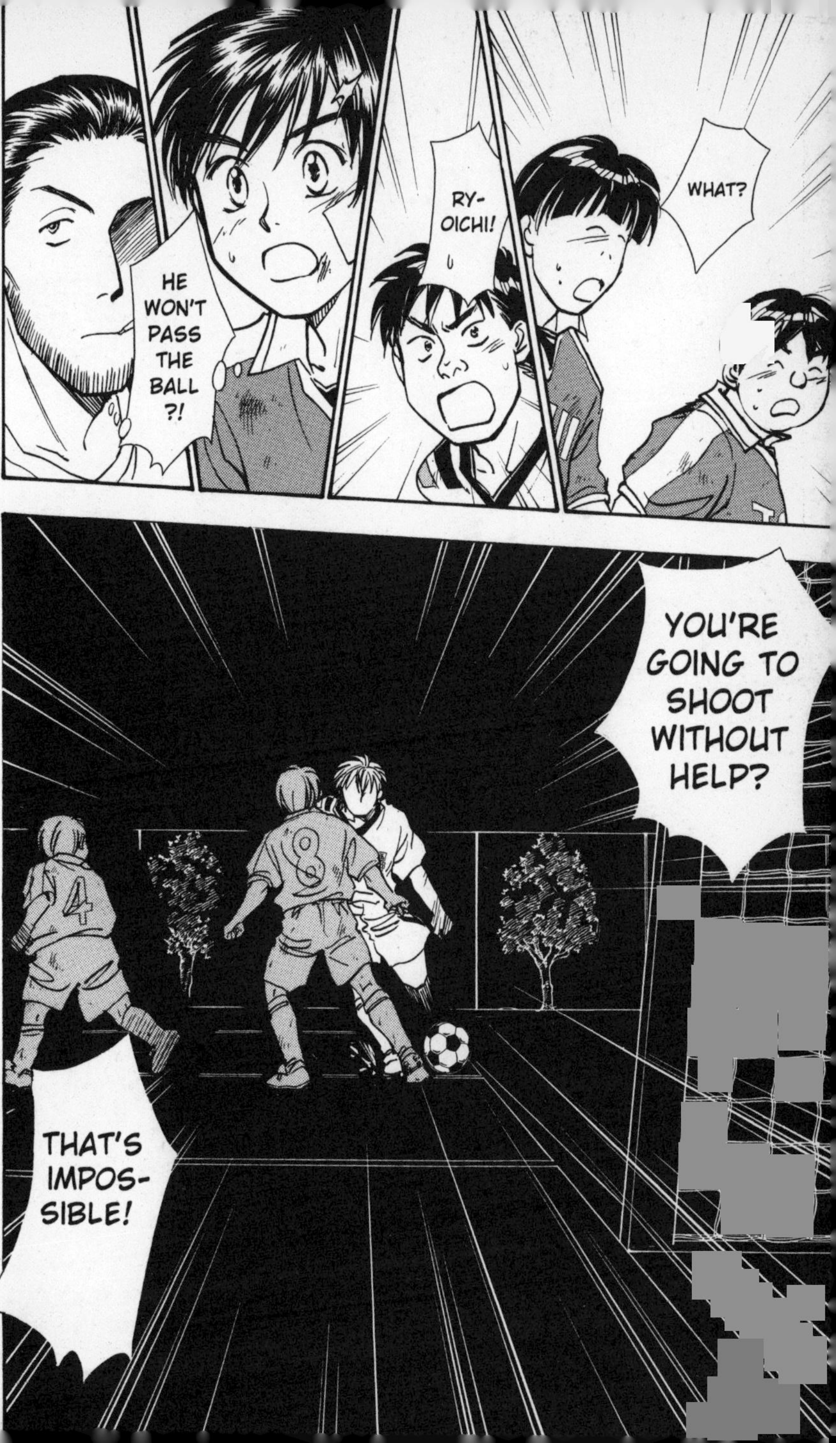
WHAT?
RY-OICHI!
HE WON'T PASS THE BALL ?!
YOU'RE GOING TO SHOOT WITHOUT HELP?
THAT'S IMPOS-SIBLE!

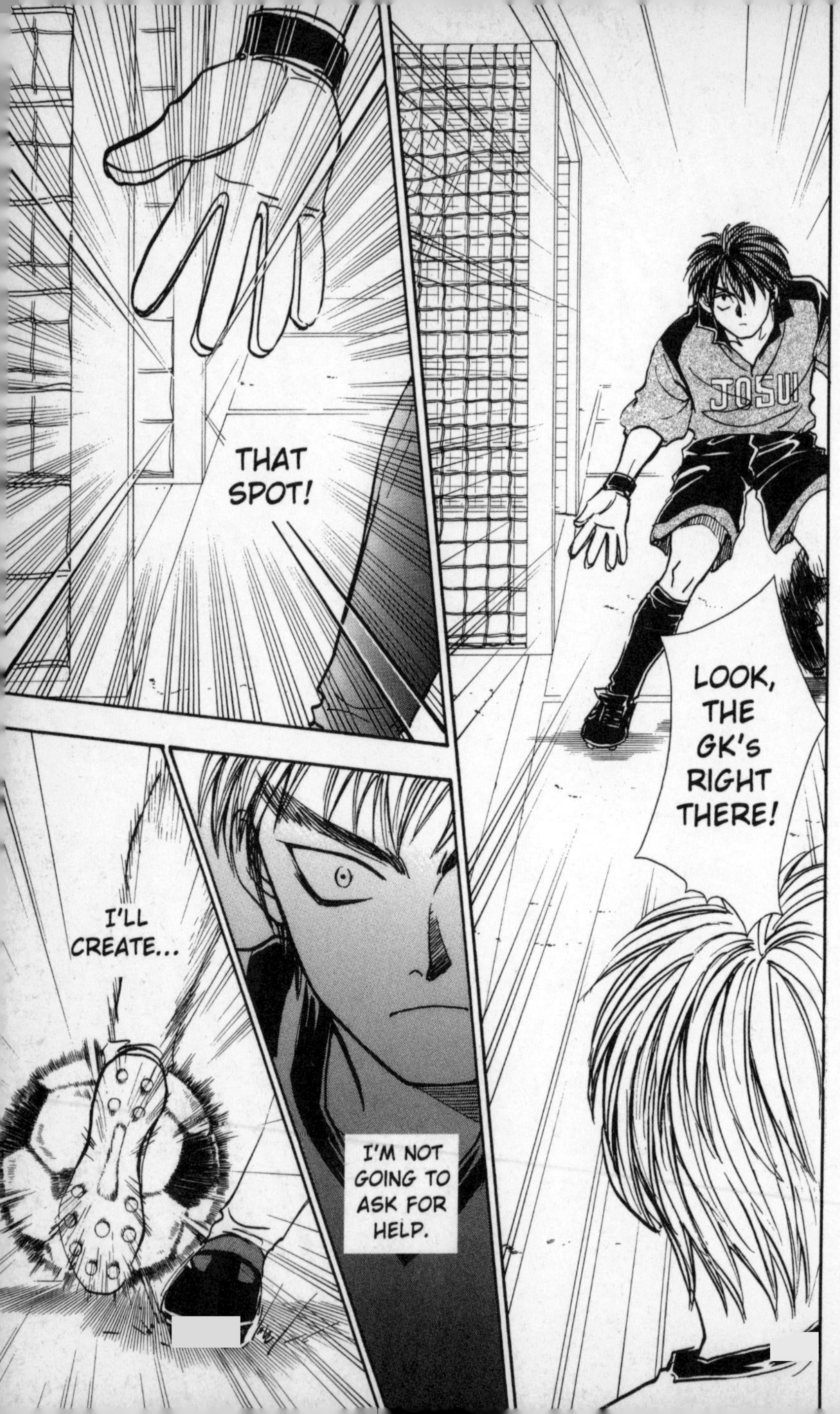
LOOK, THE GK's RIGHT THERE!
THAT SPOT!
I'M NOT GOING TO ASK FOR HELP.
I'LL CREATE...

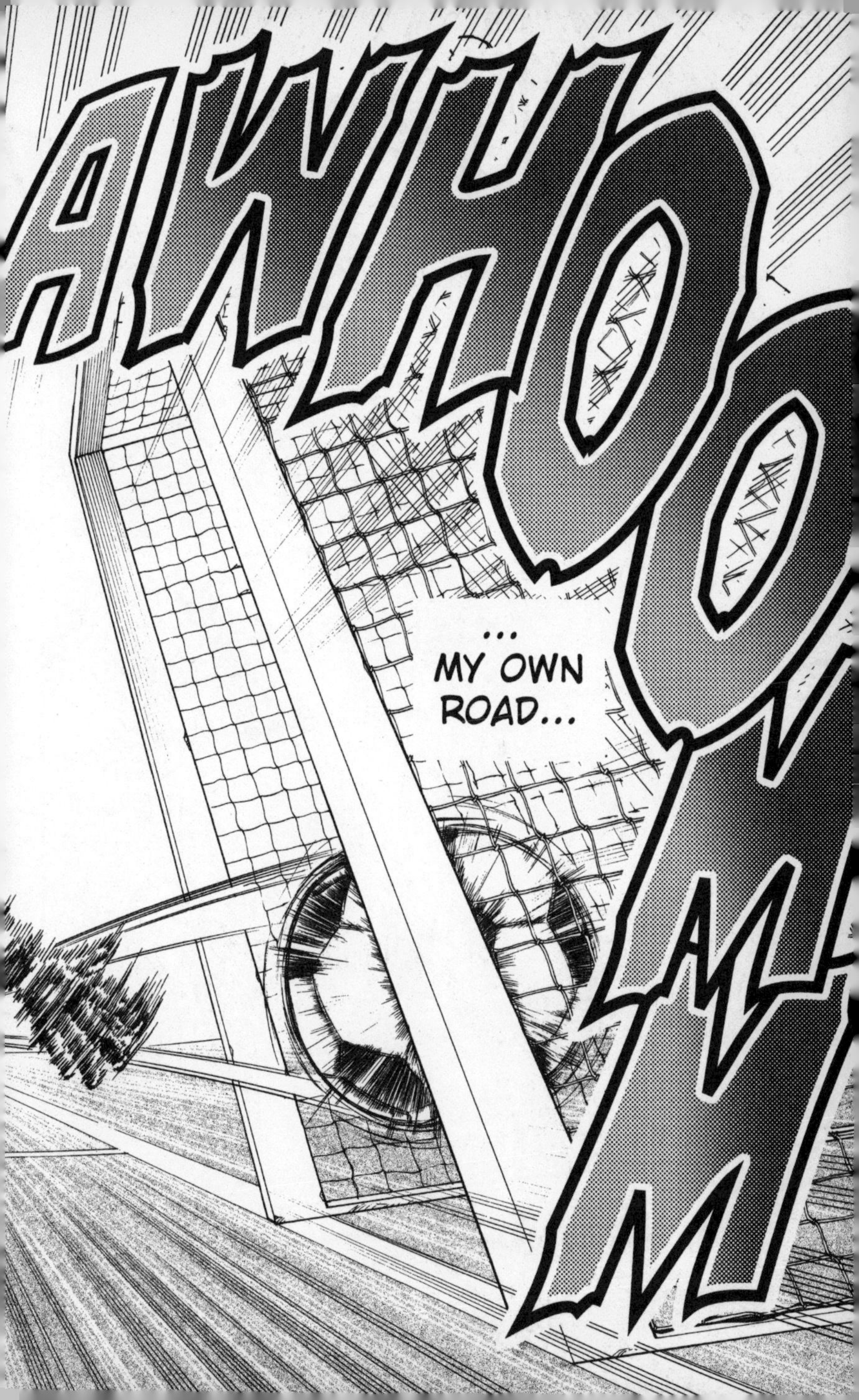
... MY OWN ROAD...

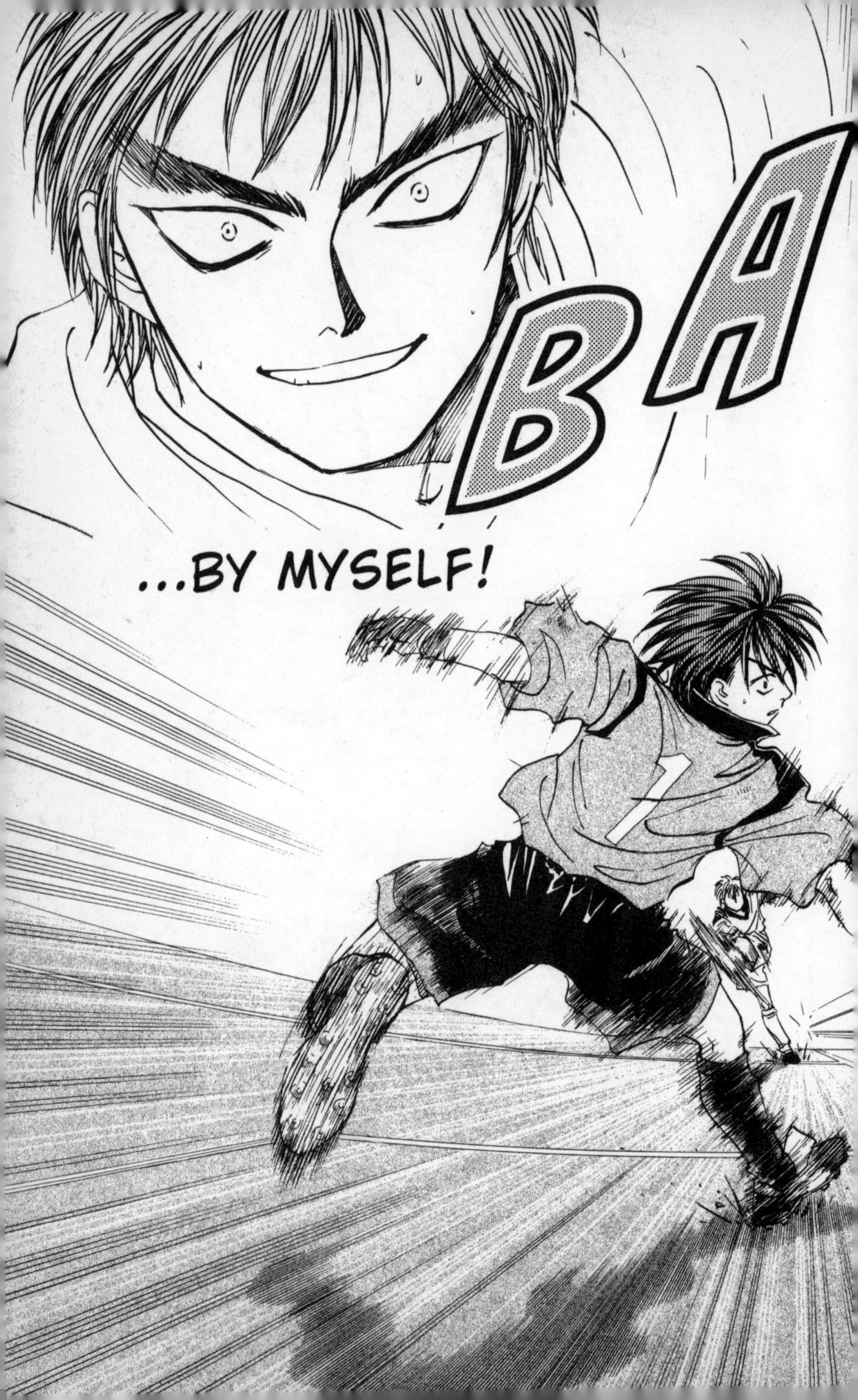
BA
...BY MYSELF!

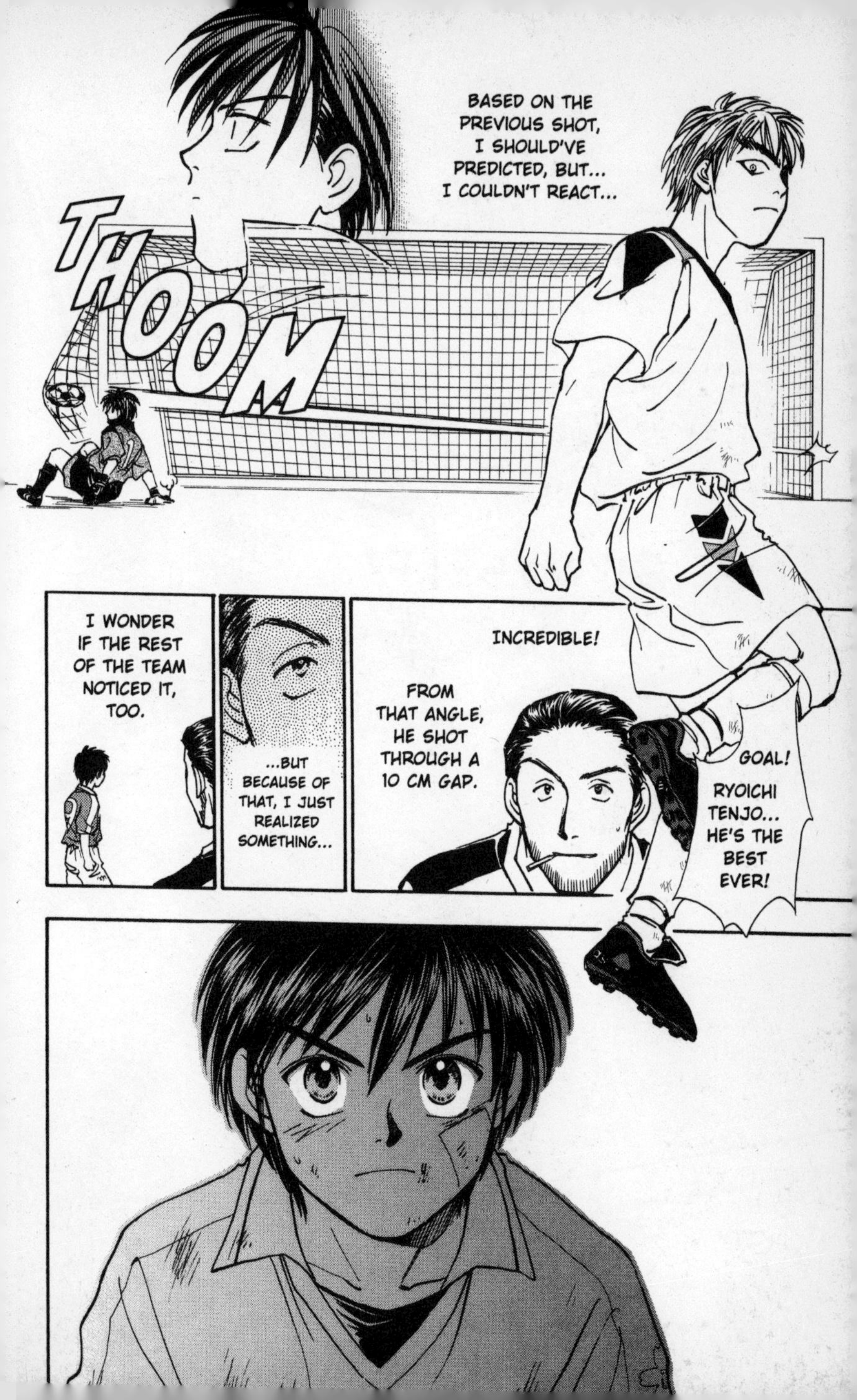
BASED ON THE PREVIOUS SHOT, I SHOULD'VE PREDICTED, BUT... I COULDN'T REACT...
THOOM
INCREDIBLE!
FROM THAT ANGLE, HE SHOT THROUGH A 10 CM GAP.
GOAL! RYOICHI TENJO... HE'S THE BEST EVER!
...BUT BECAUSE OF THAT, I JUST REALIZED SOMETHING...
I WONDER IF THE REST OF THE TEAM NOTICED IT, TOO.

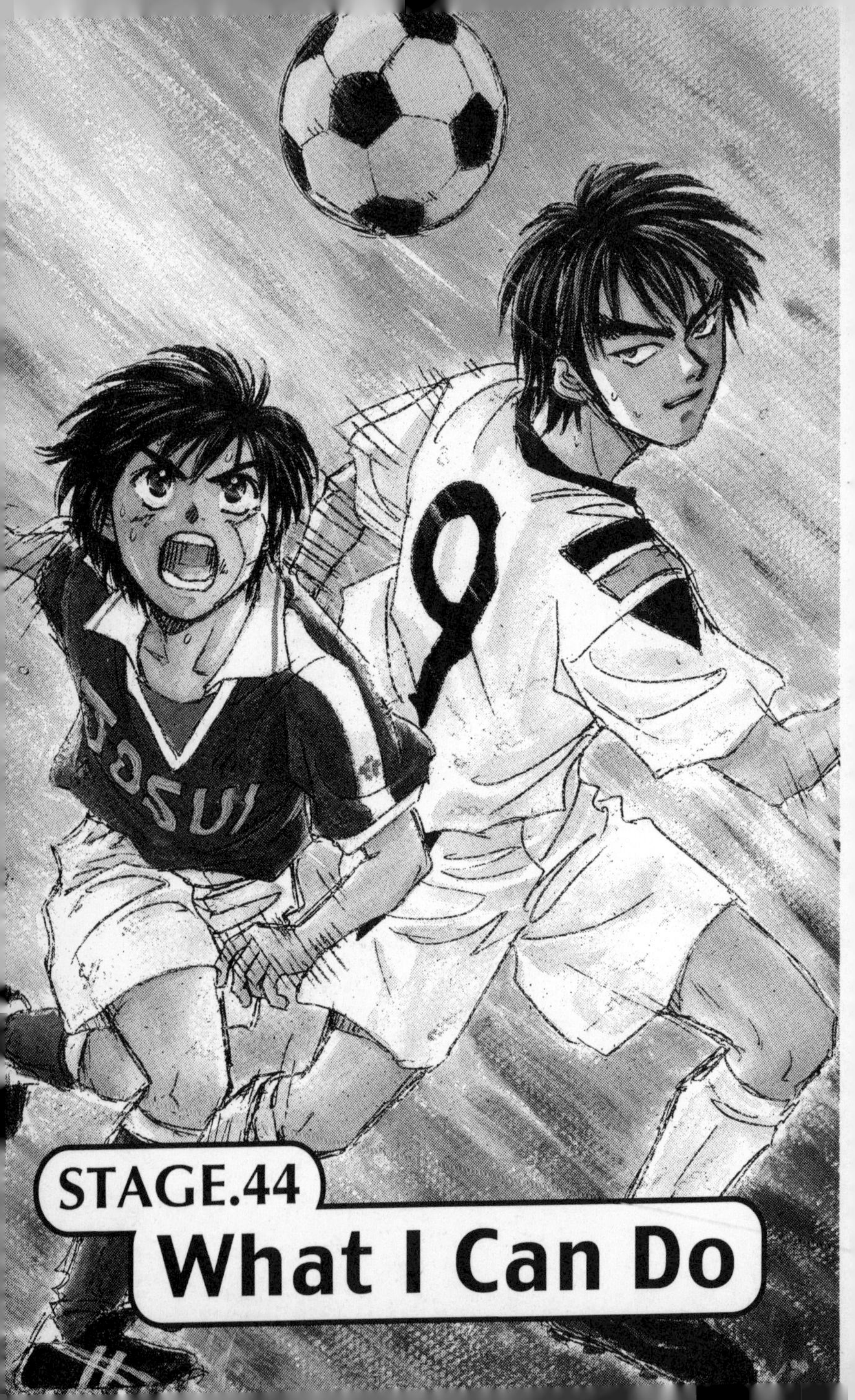
STAGE.44
What I Can Do

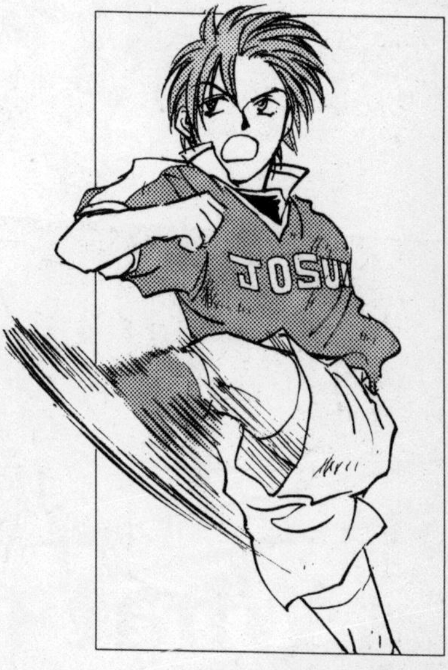
JOSU

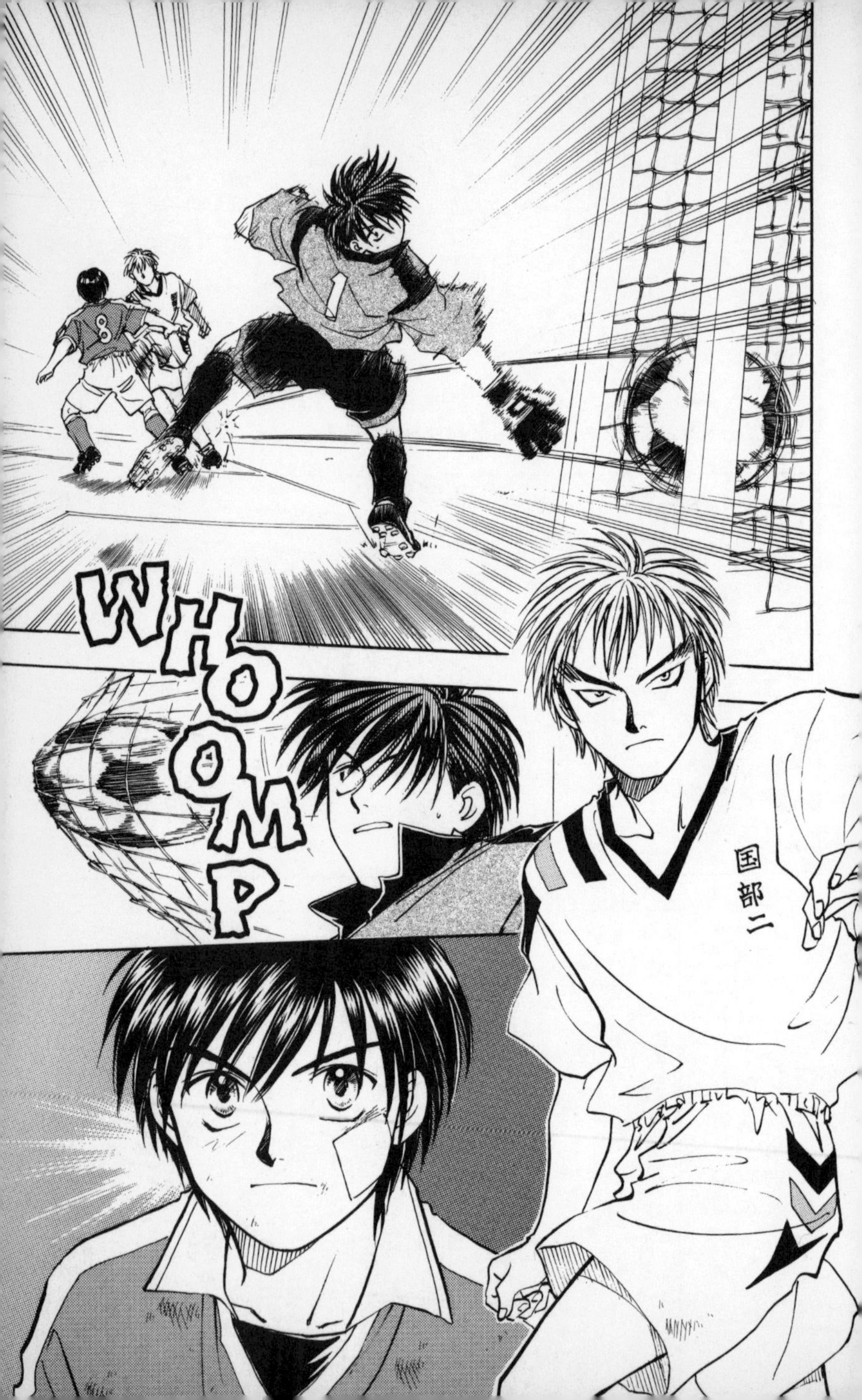
WHOOMP
国部二

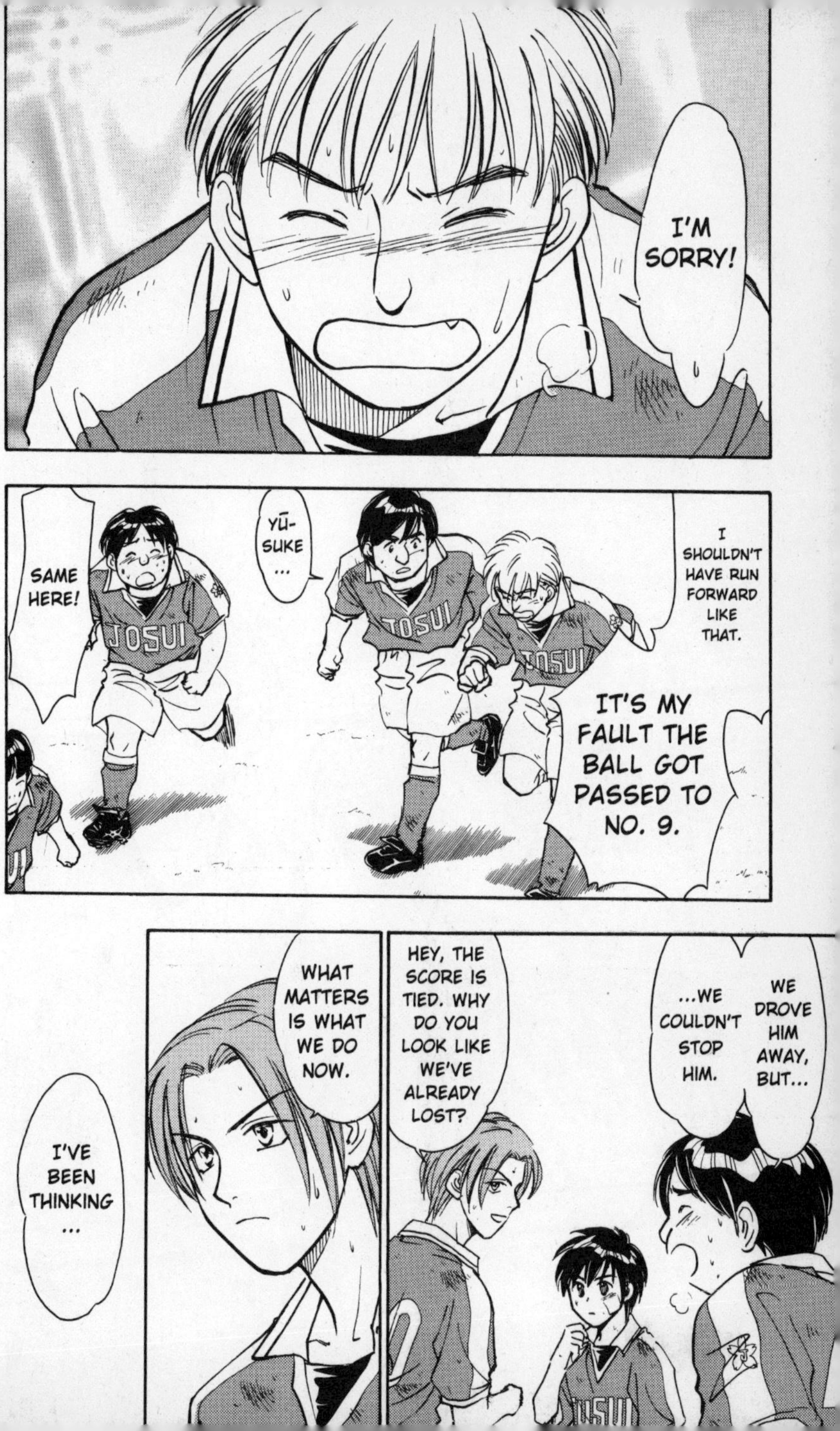
I'M SORRY!
I SHOULDN'T HAVE RUN FORWARD LIKE THAT.
IT'S MY FAULT THE BALL GOT PASSED TO NO. 9.
YŪ-SUKE...
SAME HERE!
WE DROVE HIM AWAY, BUT...
...WE COULDN'T STOP HIM.
HEY, THE SCORE IS TIED. WHY DO YOU LOOK LIKE WE'VE ALREADY LOST?
WHAT MATTERS IS WHAT WE DO NOW.
I'VE BEEN THINKING...

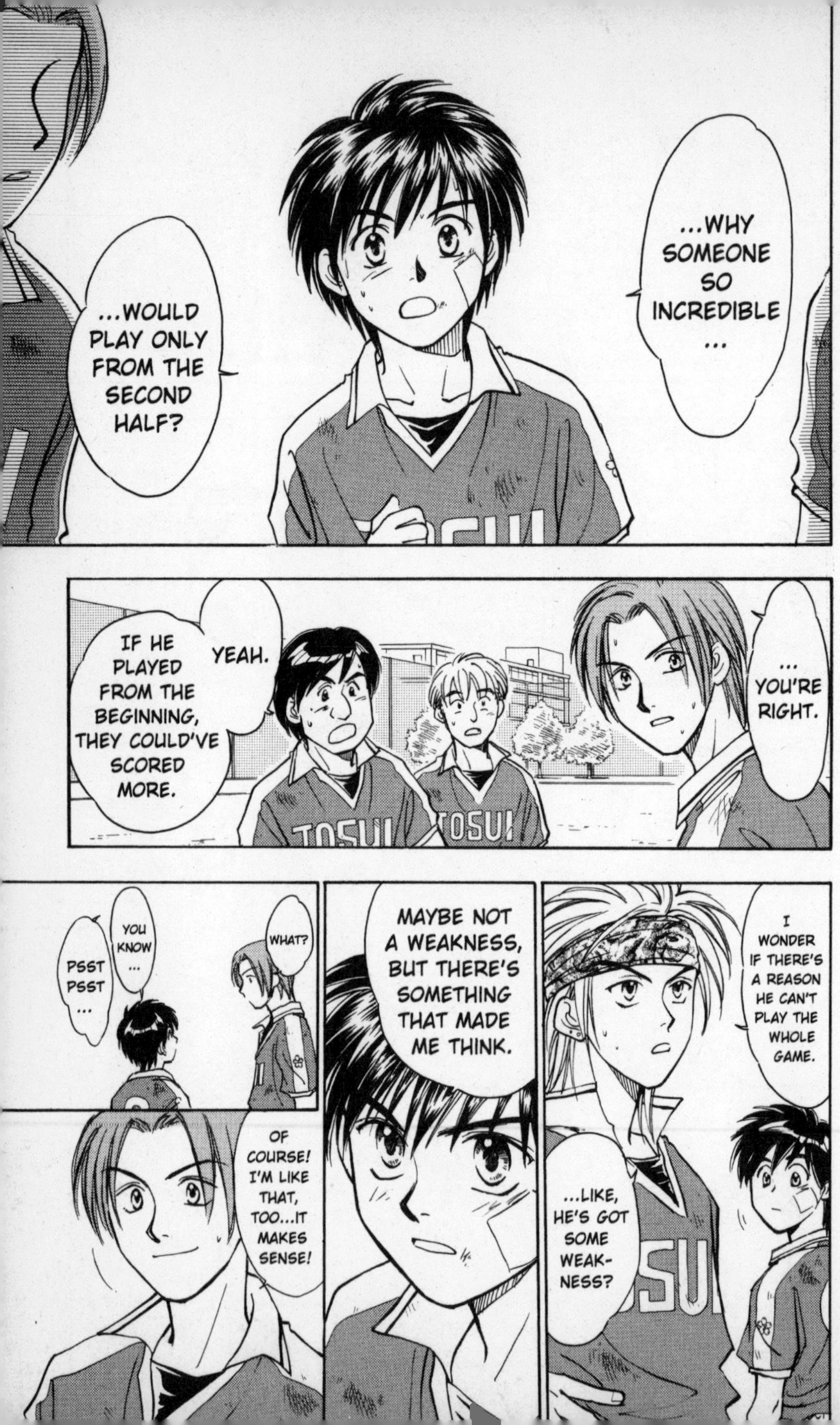
...WHY SOMEONE SO INCREDIBLE ...
...WOULD PLAY ONLY FROM THE SECOND HALF?
... YOU'RE RIGHT.
YEAH.
IF HE PLAYED FROM THE BEGINNING, THEY COULD'VE SCORED MORE.
I WONDER IF THERE'S A REASON HE CAN'T PLAY THE WHOLE GAME.
...LIKE, HE'S GOT SOME WEAK-NESS?
MAYBE NOT A WEAKNESS, BUT THERE'S SOMETHING THAT MADE ME THINK.
WHAT?
YOU KNOW ...
PSST PSST ...
OF COURSE! I'M LIKE THAT, TOO...IT MAKES SENSE!

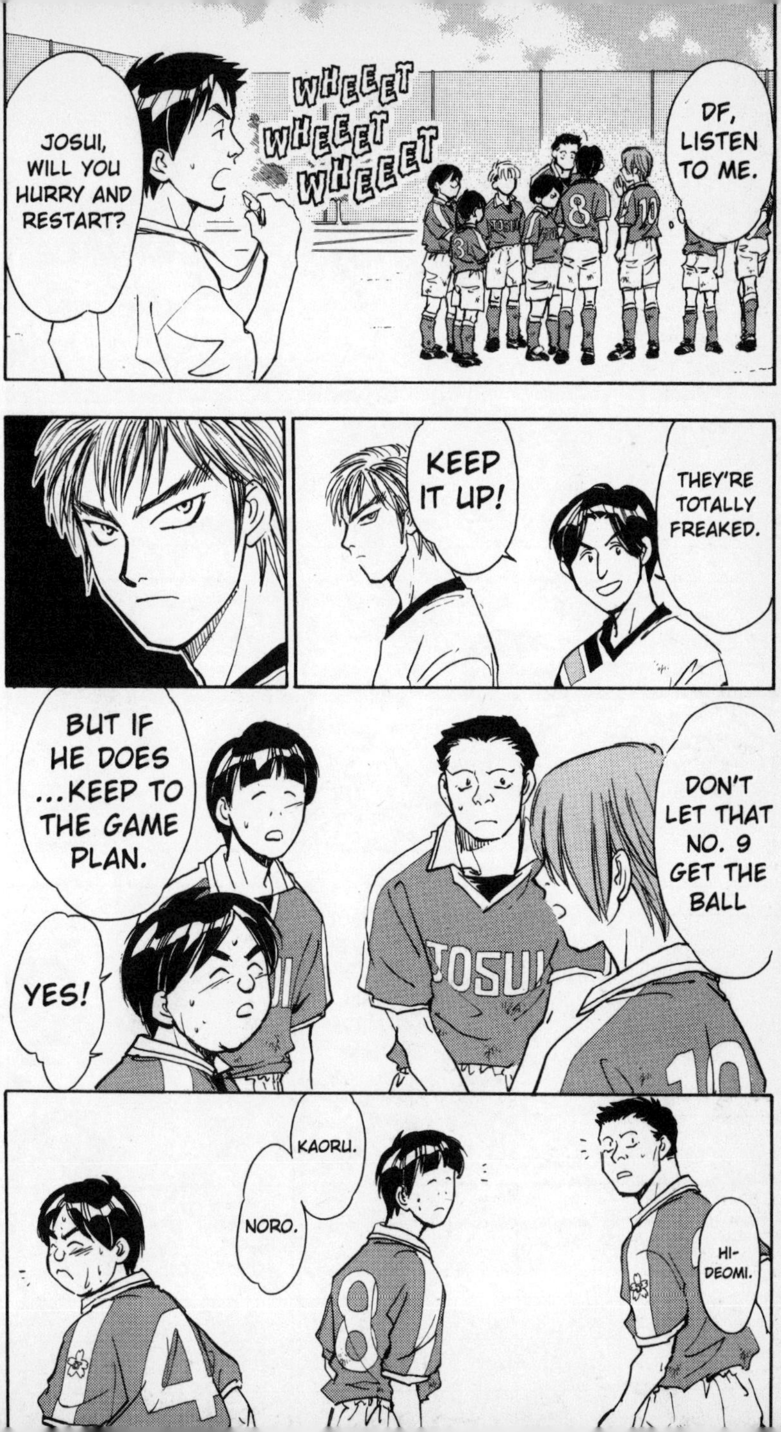
DF, LISTEN TO ME.
WHEEET WHEEET WHEEET
JOSUI, WILL YOU HURRY AND RESTART?
THEY'RE TOTALLY FREAKED.
KEEP IT UP!
DON'T LET THAT NO. 9 GET THE BALL
BUT IF HE DOES ...KEEP TO THE GAME PLAN.
YES!
HI-DEOMI.
KAORU.
NORO.

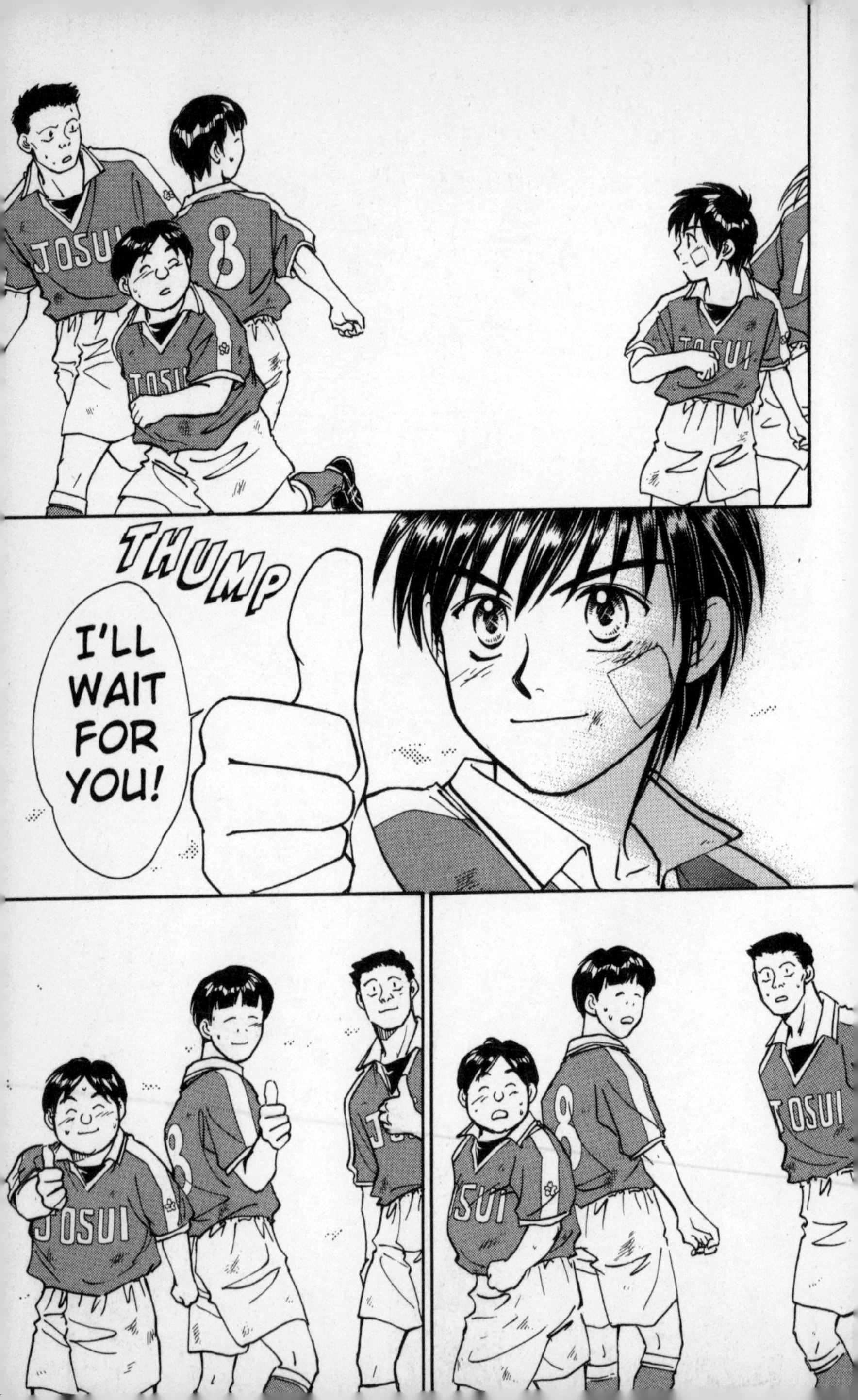
THUMP
I'LL WAIT FOR YOU!

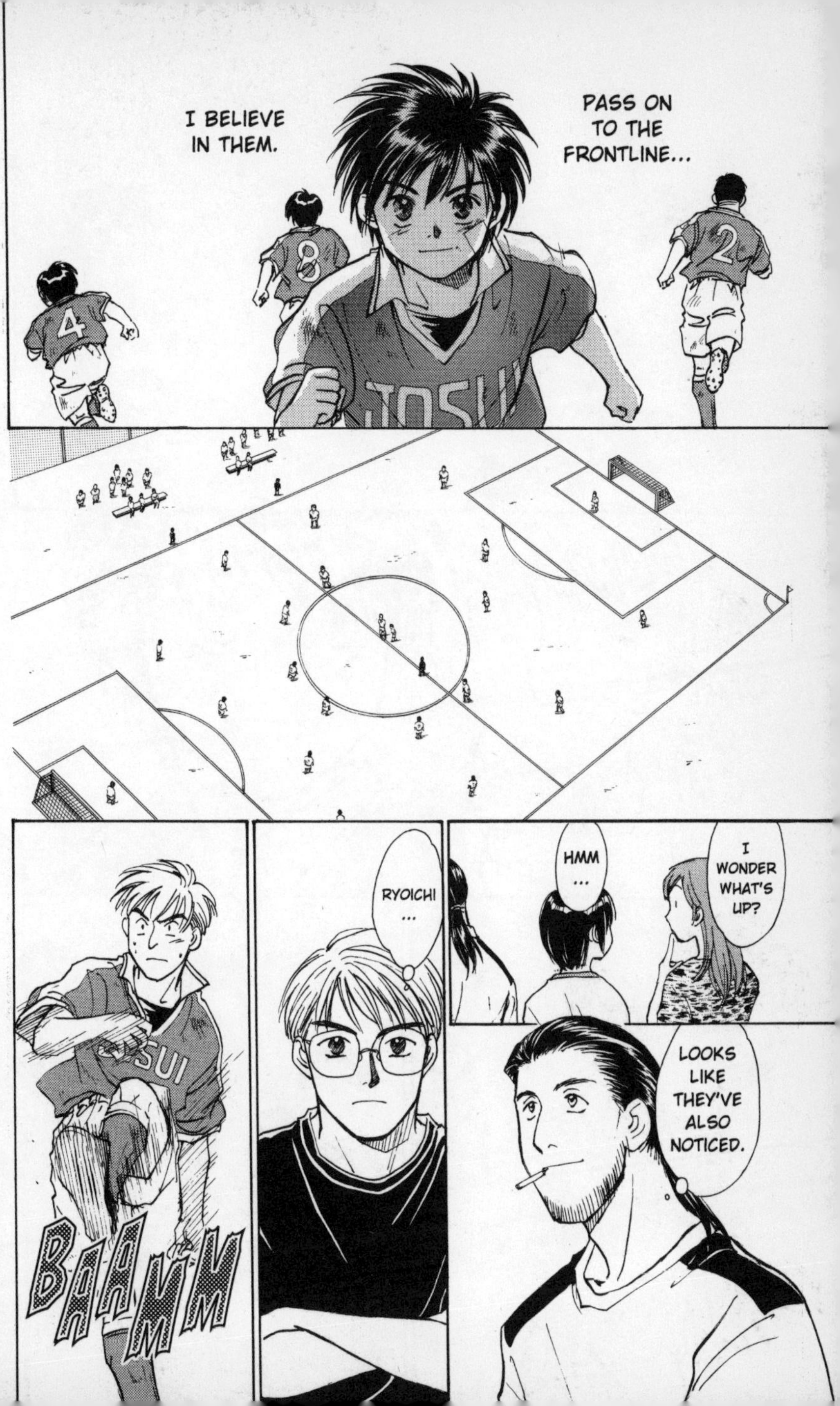
PASS ON TO THE FRONTLINE...
I BELIEVE IN THEM.
I WONDER WHAT'S UP?
HMM ...
LOOKS LIKE THEY'VE ALSO NOTICED.
RYOICHI ...
BAAMM

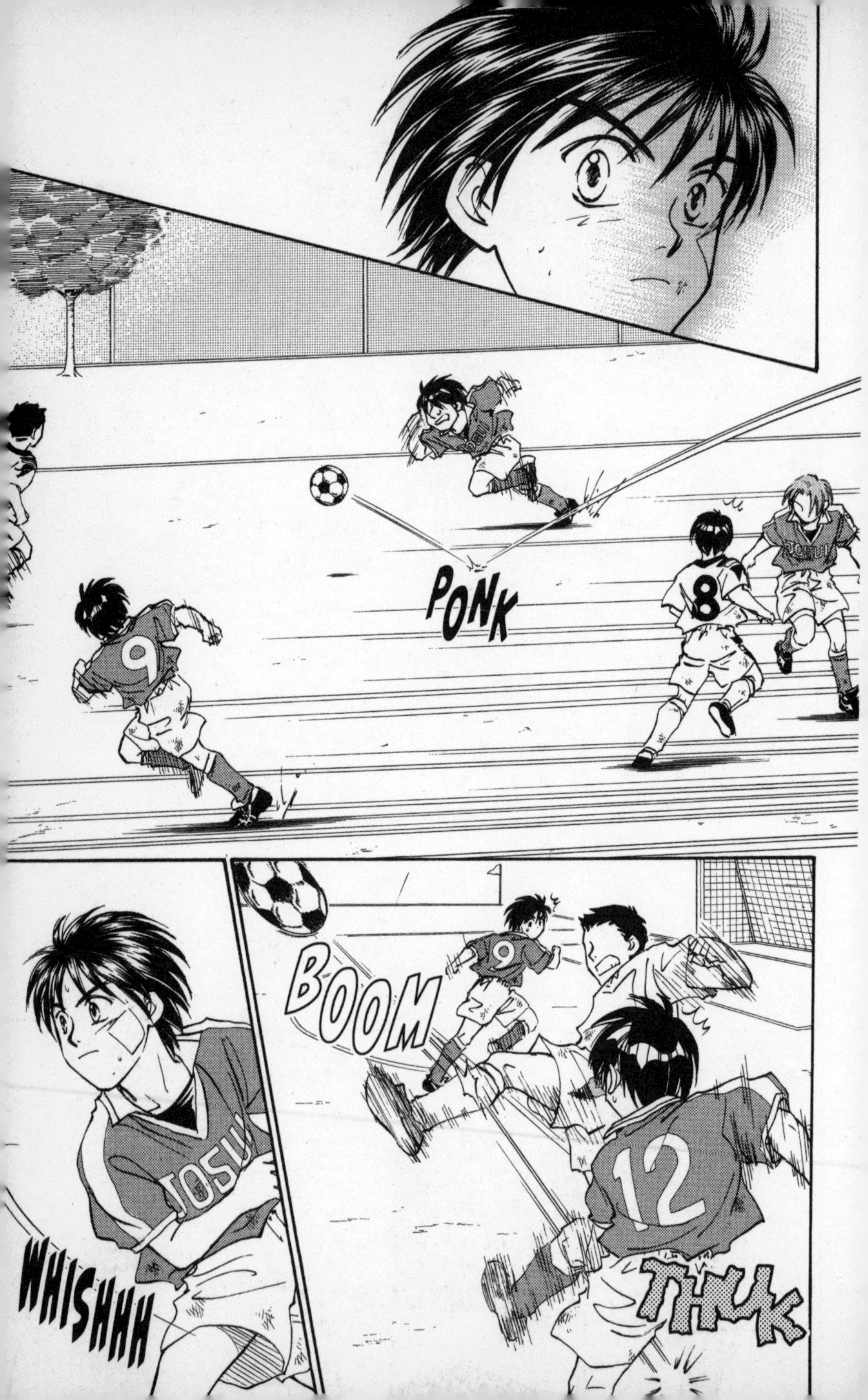
PONK
BOOM
THUK
WHISHHH

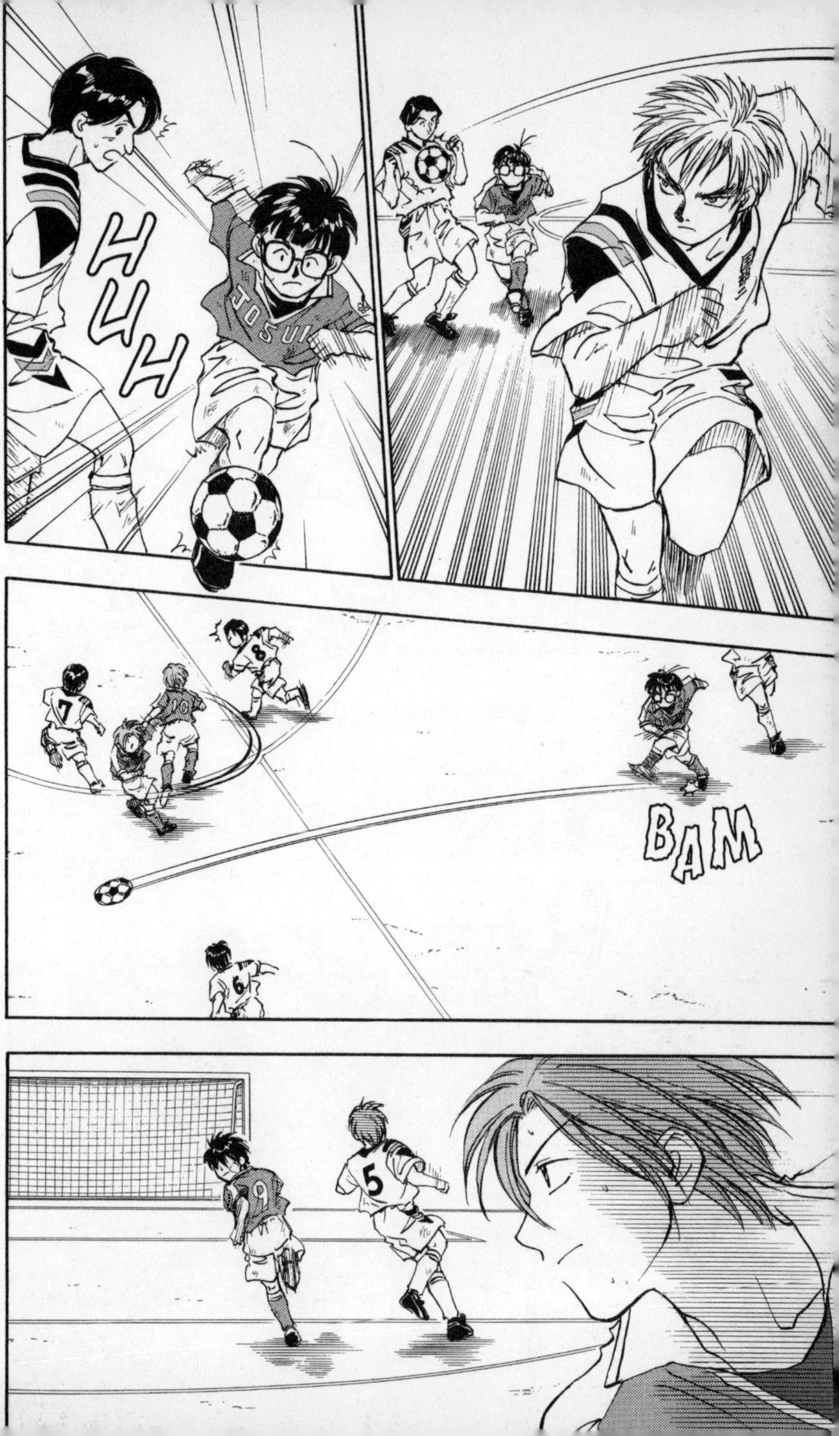
HUH
BAM

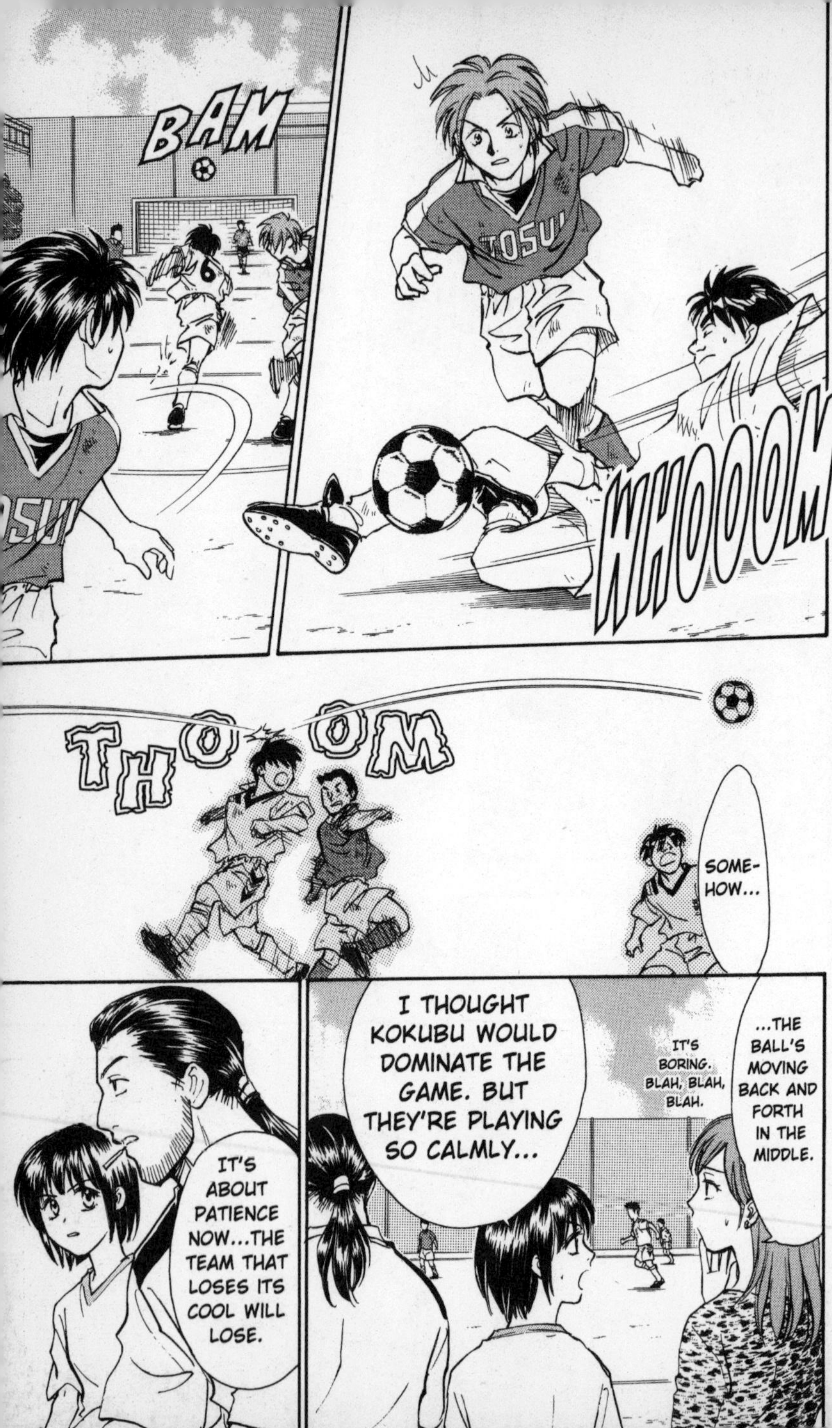
WHOOOM
BAM
THOOM
SOME-HOW...
...THE BALL'S MOVING BACK AND FORTH IN THE MIDDLE.
IT'S BORING. BLAH, BLAH, BLAH.
I THOUGHT KOKUBU WOULD DOMINATE THE GAME. BUT THEY'RE PLAYING SO CALMLY...
IT'S ABOUT PATIENCE NOW...THE TEAM THAT LOSES ITS COOL WILL LOSE.

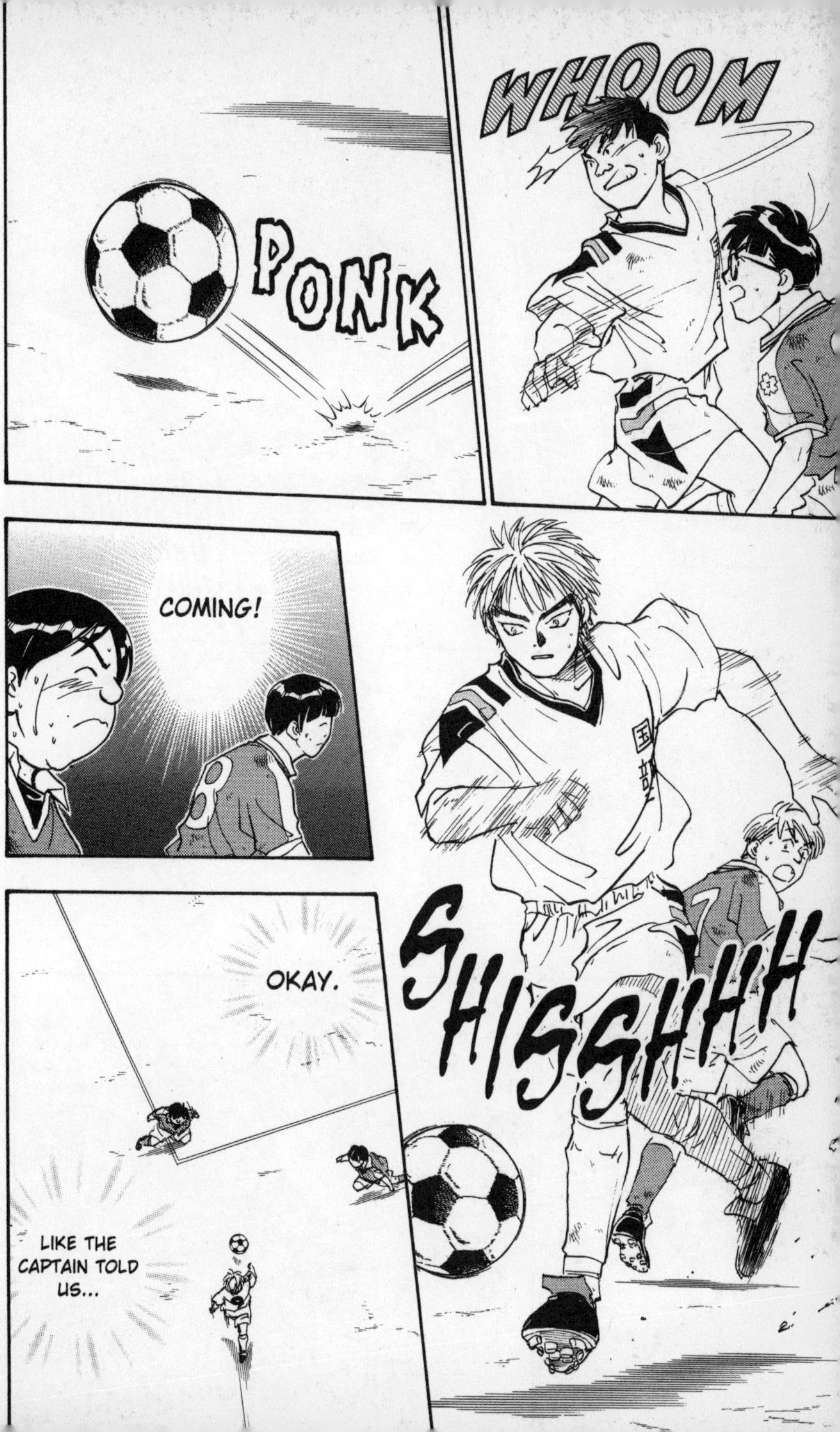
WHOOM
PONK
SHISSHHH
COMING!
OKAY.
LIKE THE CAPTAIN TOLD US...

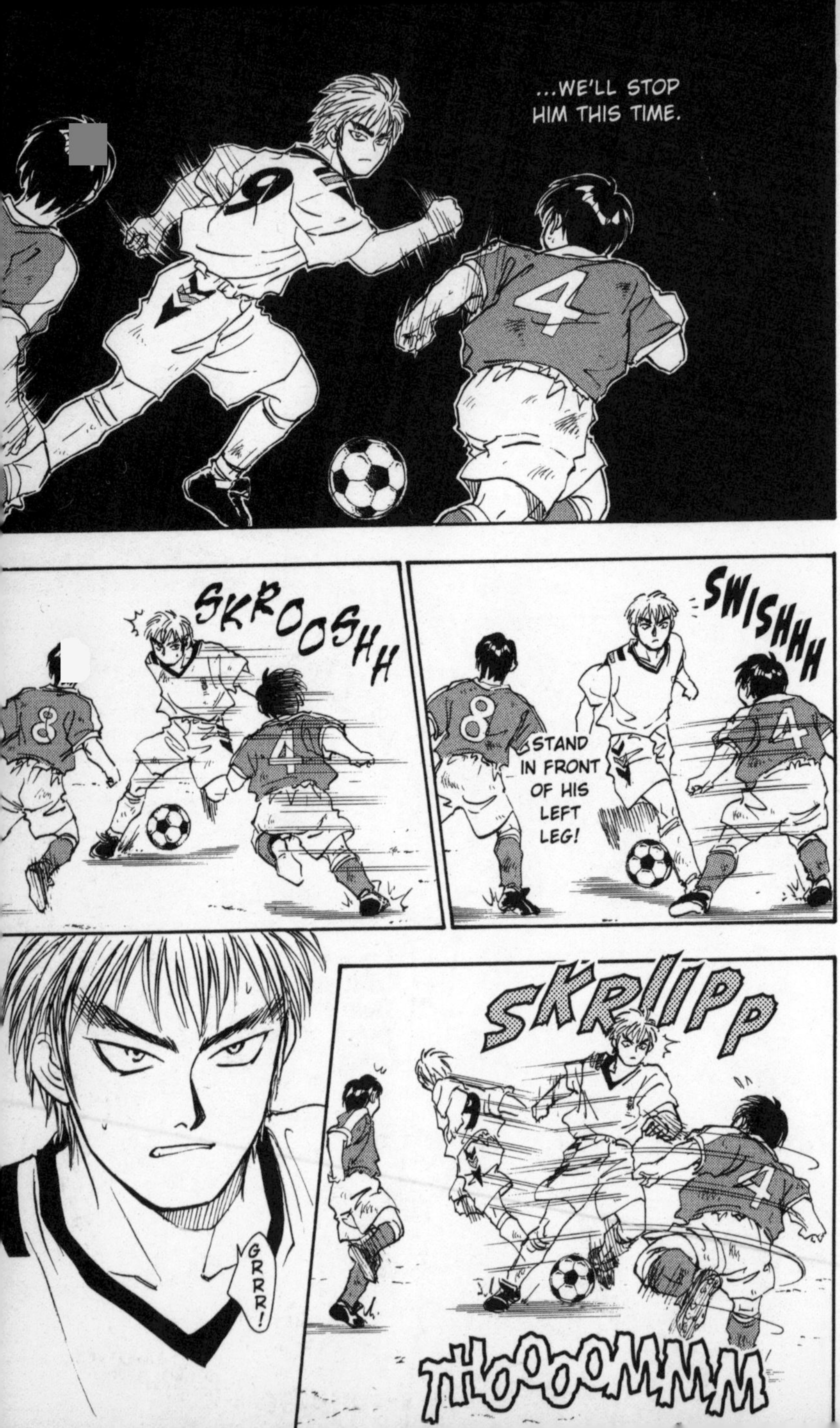
...WE'LL STOP HIM THIS TIME.
SWISHHH
STAND IN FRONT OF HIS LEFT LEG!
SKROOSHH
SKRIIPP
THOOOMMM
GRRR!

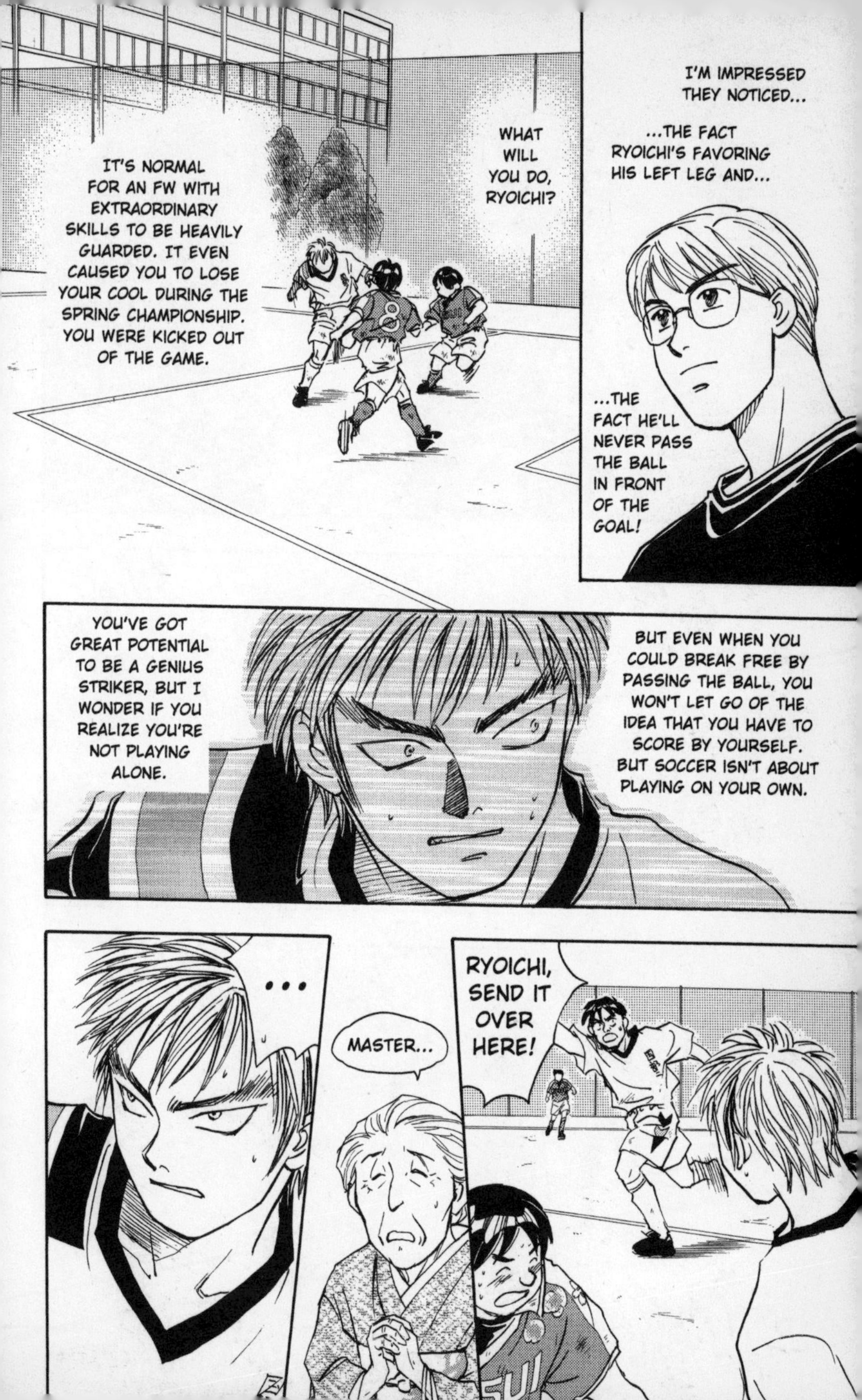
I'M IMPRESSED THEY NOTICED...
...THE FACT RYOICHI'S FAVORING HIS LEFT LEG AND...
...THE FACT HE'LL NEVER PASS THE BALL IN FRONT OF THE GOAL!
WHAT WILL YOU DO, RYOICHI?
IT'S NORMAL FOR AN FW WITH EXTRAORDINARY SKILLS TO BE HEAVILY GUARDED. IT EVEN CAUSED YOU TO LOSE YOUR COOL DURING THE SPRING CHAMPIONSHIP. YOU WERE KICKED OUT OF THE GAME.
BUT EVEN WHEN YOU COULD BREAK FREE BY PASSING THE BALL, YOU WON'T LET GO OF THE IDEA THAT YOU HAVE TO SCORE BY YOURSELF. BUT SOCCER ISN'T ABOUT PLAYING ON YOUR OWN.
YOU'VE GOT GREAT POTENTIAL TO BE A GENIUS STRIKER, BUT I WONDER IF YOU REALIZE YOU'RE NOT PLAYING ALONE.
RYOICHI, SEND IT OVER HERE!
MASTER...
...

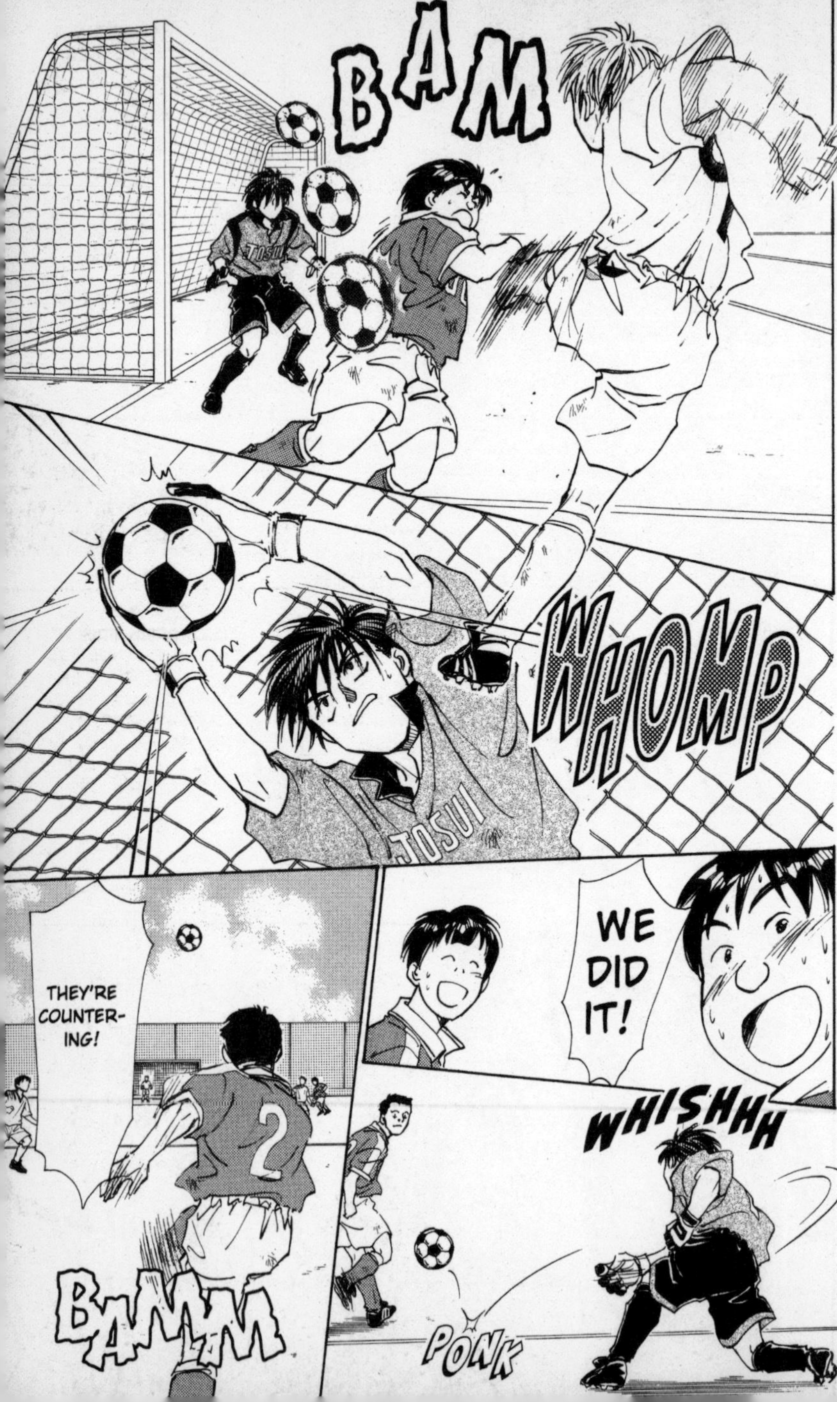
BAM
WHOMP
WE DID IT!
WHISHHH
PONK
THEY'RE COUNTER-ING!
BAMM

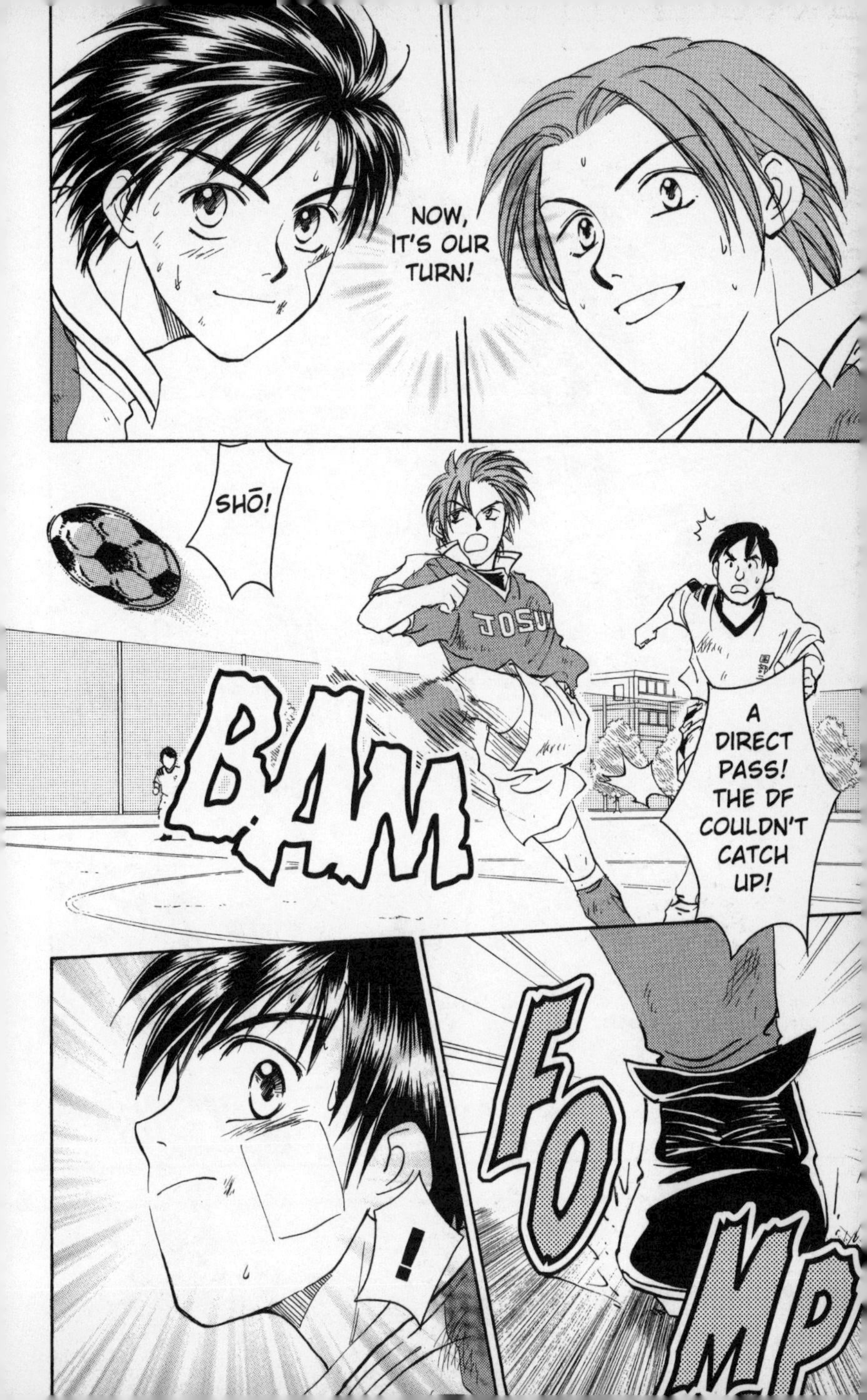
NOW, IT'S OUR TURN!
SHŌ!
BAM
A DIRECT PASS! THE DF COULDN'T CATCH UP!
FOMP
!

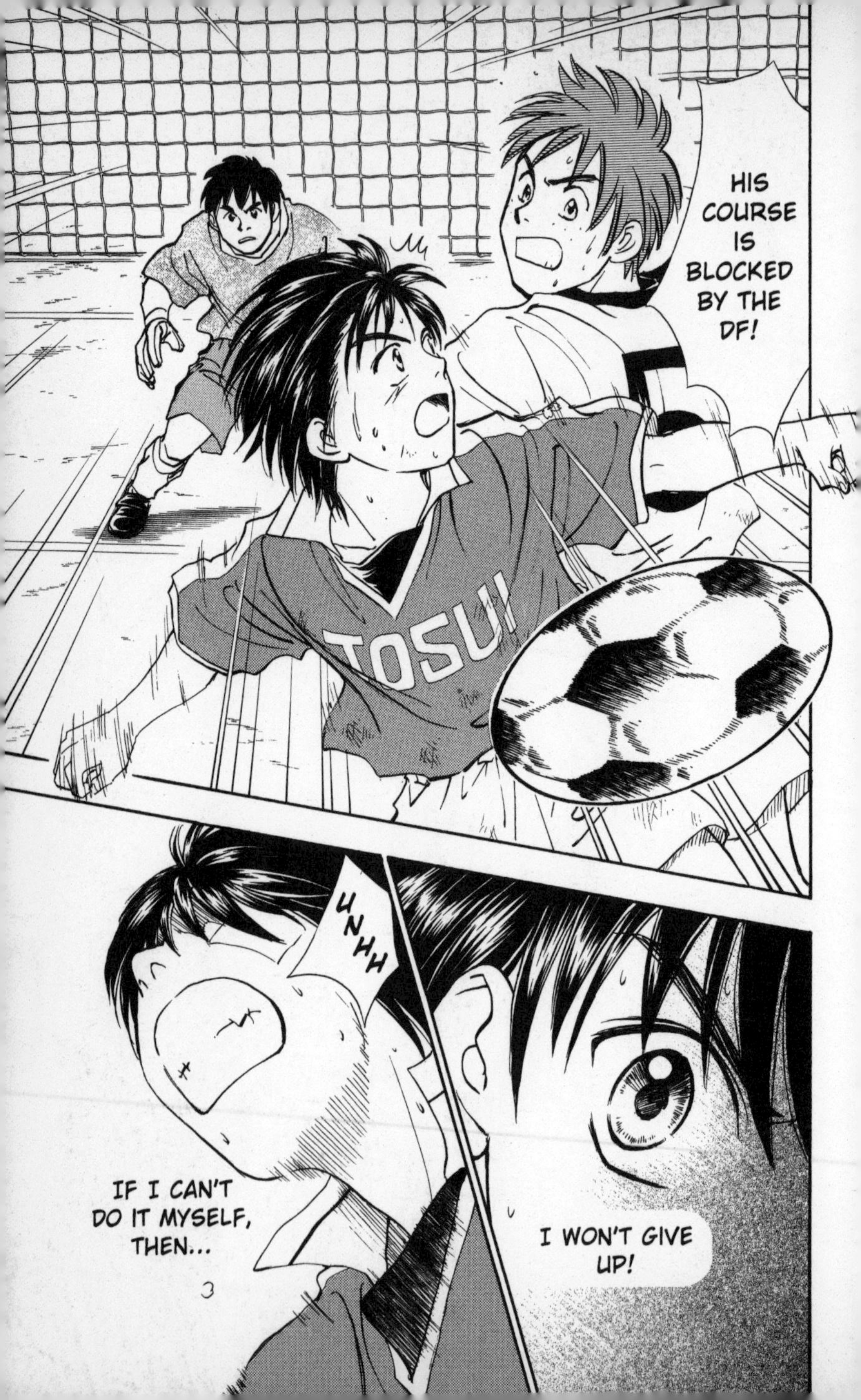
HIS COURSE IS BLOCKED BY THE DF!
I WON'T GIVE UP!
UNHH
IF I CAN'T DO IT MYSELF, THEN...

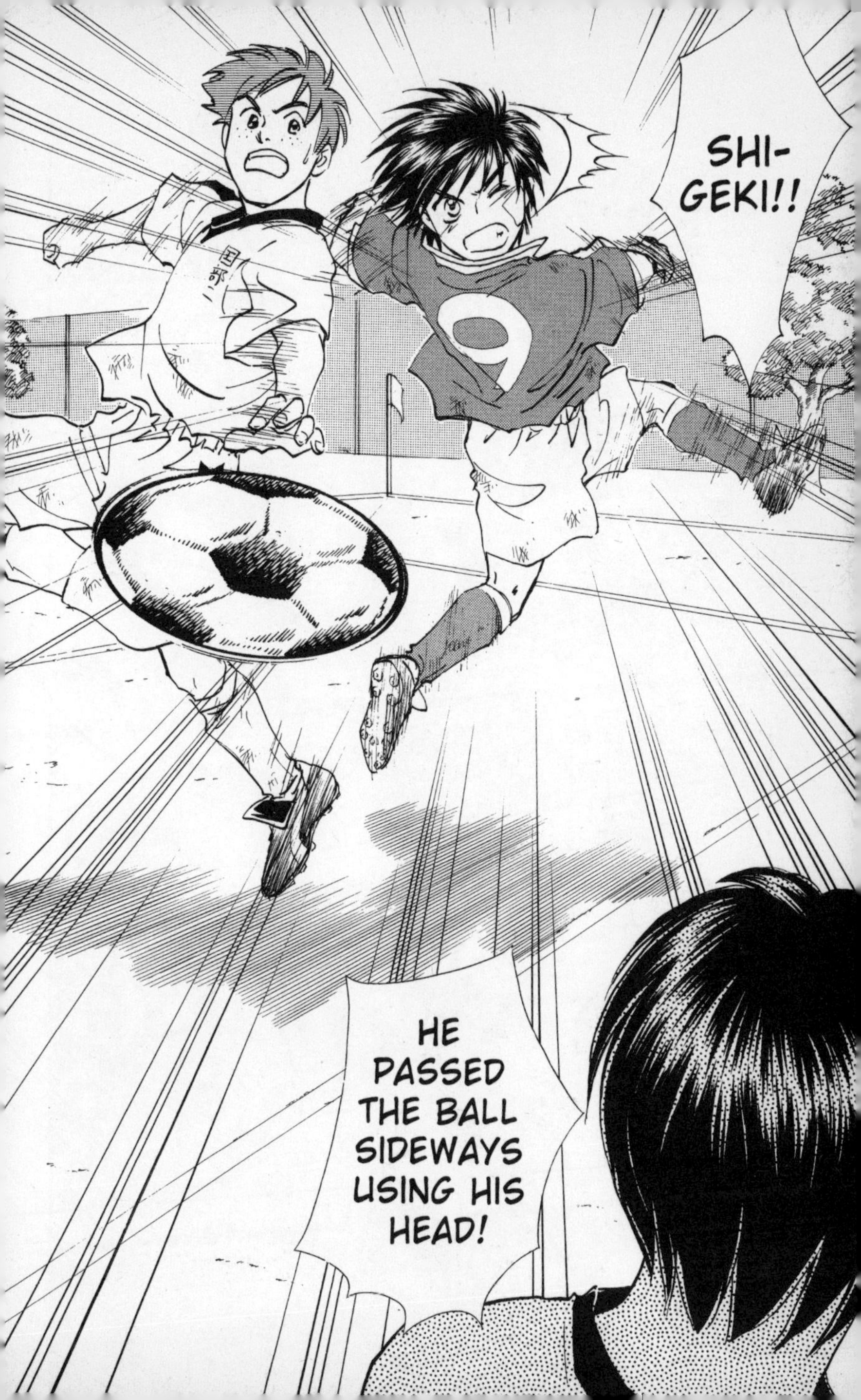
SHI-GEKI!!
HE PASSED THE BALL SIDEWAYS USING HIS HEAD!

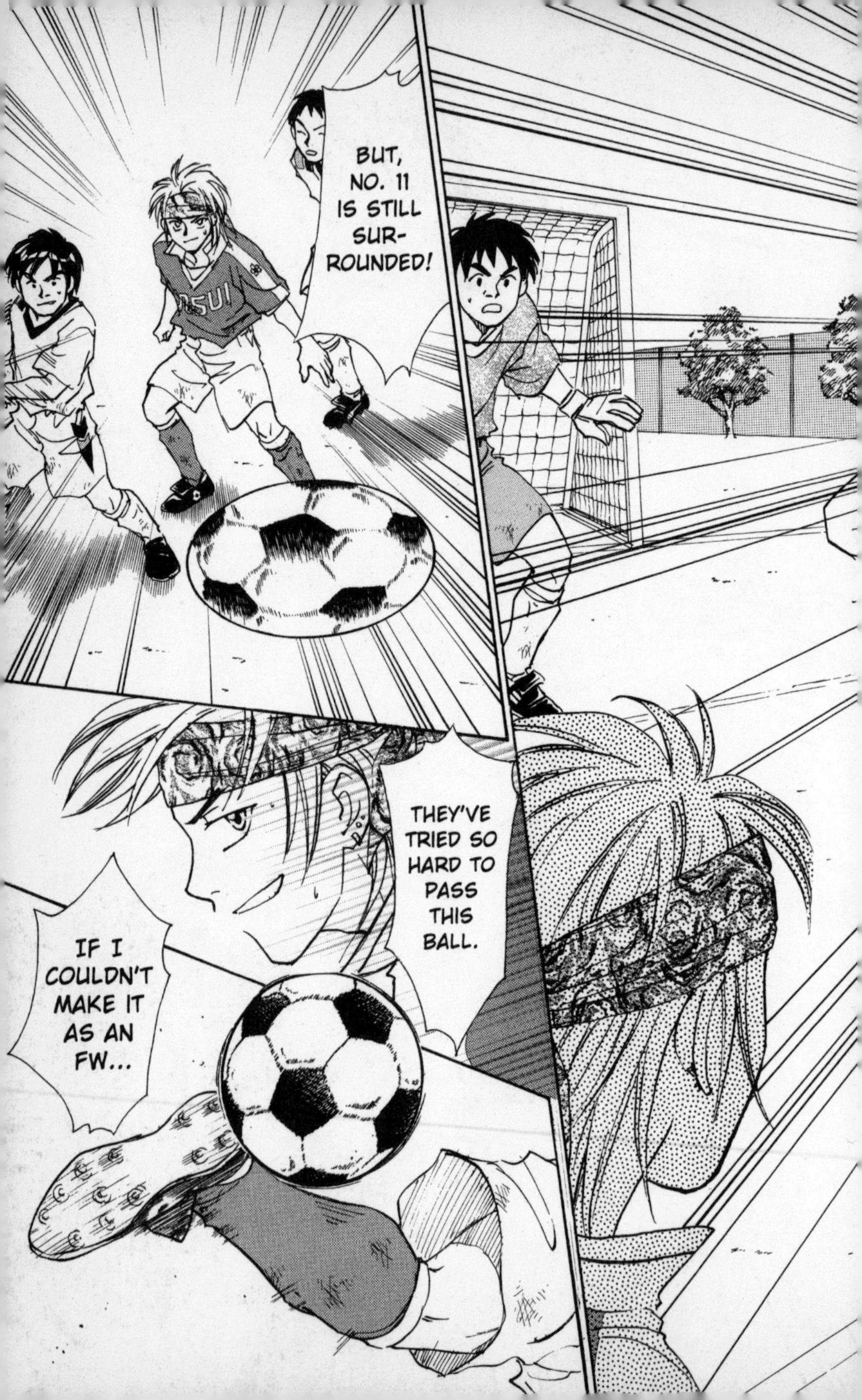
BUT, NO. 11 IS STILL SUR-ROUNDED!
THEY'VE TRIED SO HARD TO PASS THIS BALL.
IF I COULDN'T MAKE IT AS AN FW...

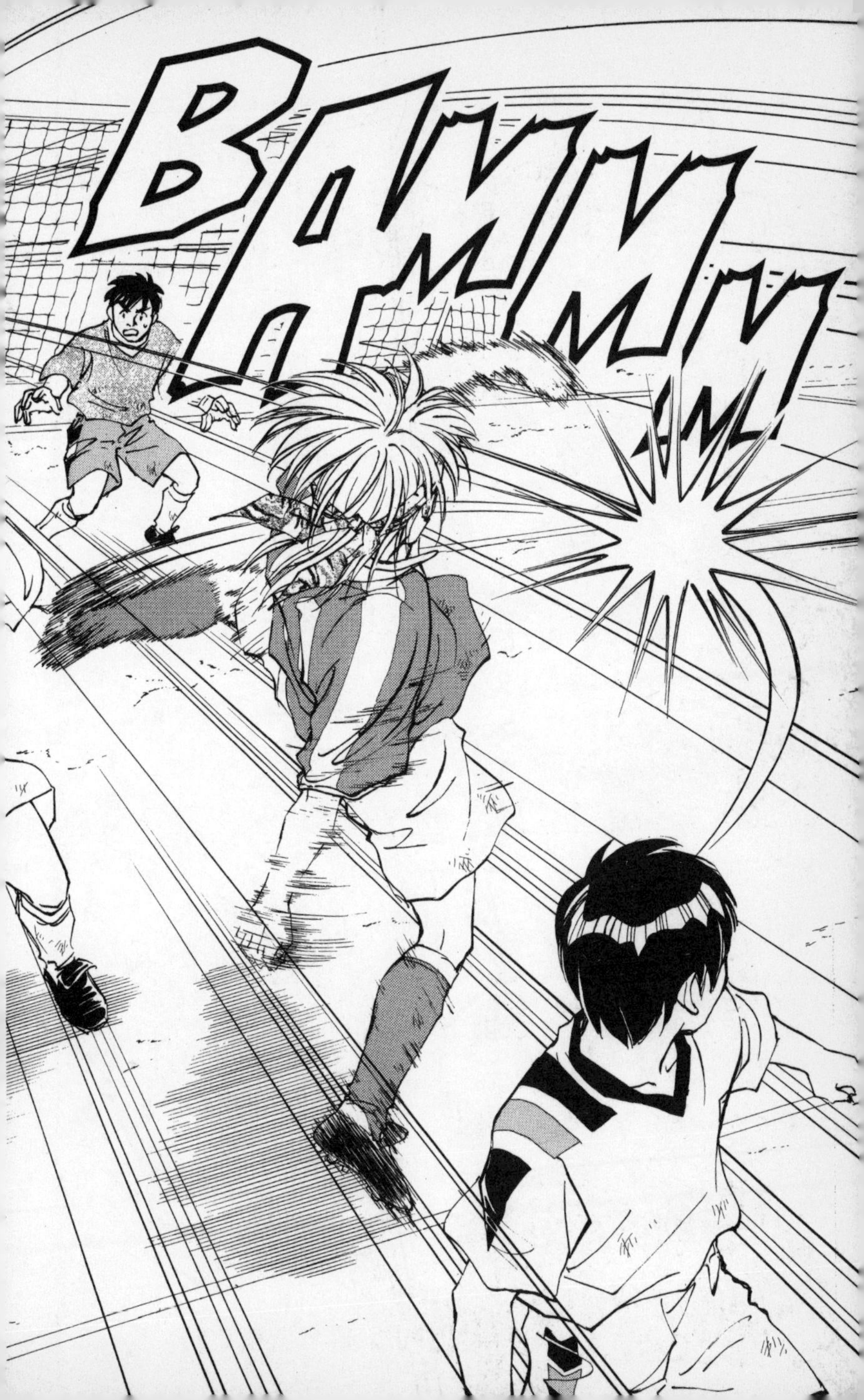
BAMMMM!

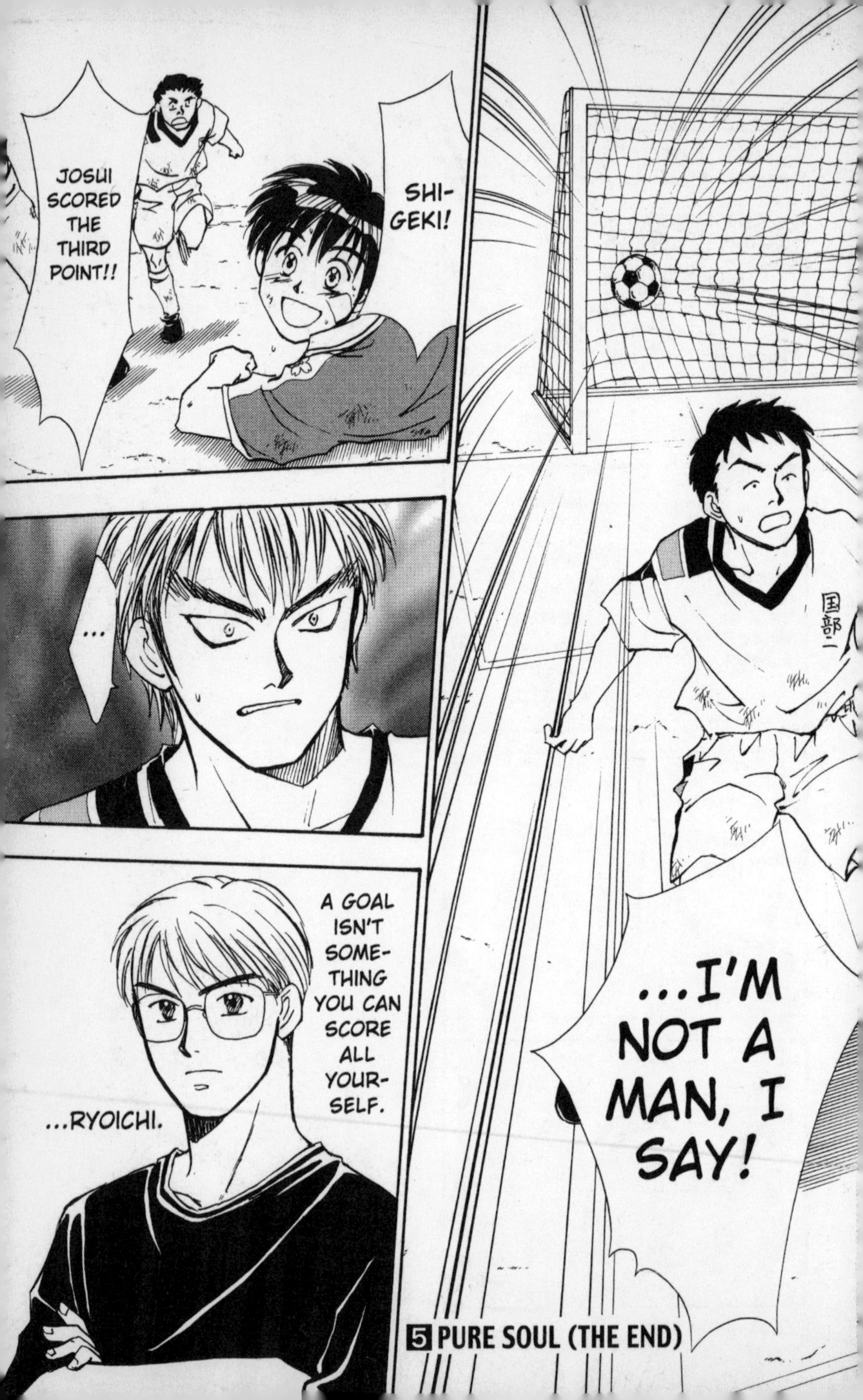
...I'M NOT A MAN, I SAY!
SHI-GEKI!
JOSUI SCORED THE THIRD POINT!!
...
A GOAL ISN'T SOMETHING YOU CAN SCORE ALL YOURSELF.
...RYOICHI.
5 PURE SOUL (THE END)

SMALL WHISTLE! THEATRE!!

MASTER...

MANGA BY **SEKI**, ASSISTANT S

Ms. Katori's Taste

ABOUT YUKI...
...WHAT ARE YOU GOING TO DO WITH HER?
WANT SOME COFFEE?
THANKS.
IF SHE CONTINUES TO STAY WITH US...
THEY'LL BE HAVING SOME ARGUMENTS.
I'M LETTING THEM HAVE A MEETING.
THEY NEED TO THINK ABOUT IT AND COME UP WITH THEIR OWN ANSWER.
I TRUST THEM.
SLURP
SUPER SWEET !!
WHAT THE HECK IS THIS?
SPLURT
?

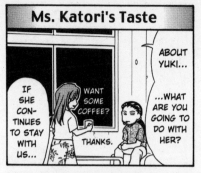

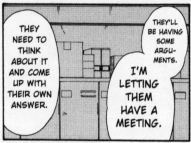

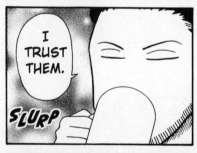

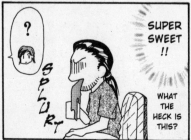

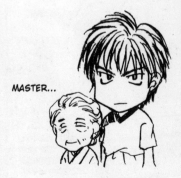

Shō–Smile

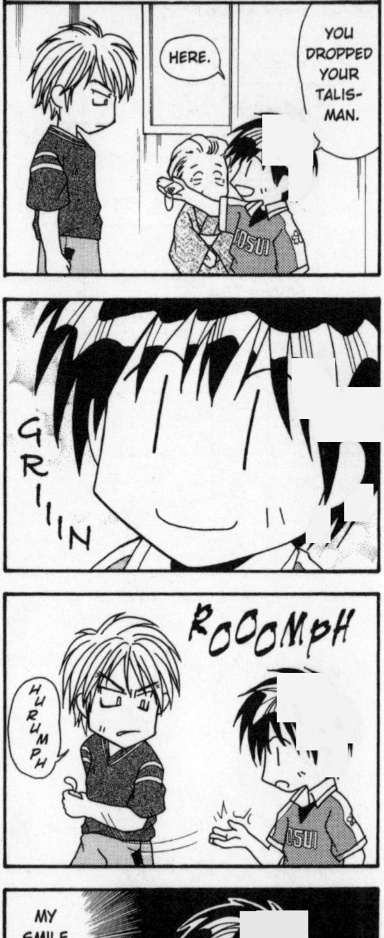
YOU DROPPED YOUR TALIS-MAN.
HERE.
GRIIIN
ROOOMPH
HURUMPH
MY SMILE DOESN'T WORK?!

Amamiya's Wish

-- Bomber Tenjo --

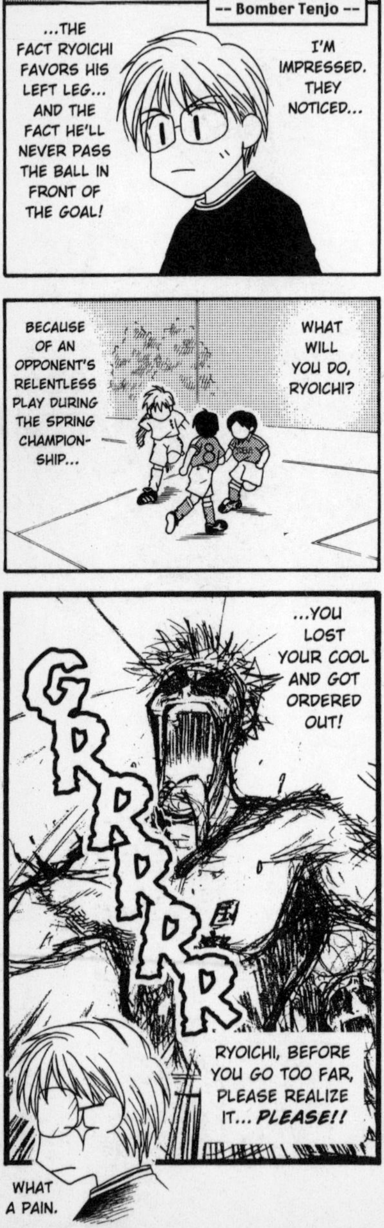
I'M IMPRESSED. THEY NOTICED...
...THE FACT RYOICHI FAVORS HIS LEFT LEG... AND THE FACT HE'LL NEVER PASS THE BALL IN FRONT OF THE GOAL!
WHAT WILL YOU DO, RYOICHI?
BECAUSE OF AN OPPONENT'S RELENTLESS PLAY DURING THE SPRING CHAMPION-SHIP...
...YOU LOST YOUR COOL AND GOT ORDERED OUT!
GRRRRR
RYOICHI, BEFORE YOU GO TOO FAR, PLEASE REALIZE IT... PLEASE!!
WHAT A PAIN.

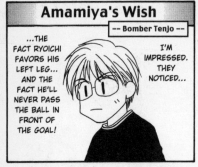

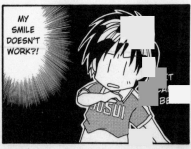

DAISUKE NOTE

EDITION WITH THE CHARACTERS WHO ADD DRAMA TO ***WHISTLE!*** AS PROTAGONIST'S ENEMY.

PERSONAL DATA	
BIRTHDAY:	NOVEMBER 11, 1984
SIZE:	180 cm 63 kg
BLOOD TYPE:	B
FAVORITE FOOD:	RICE BALL (WITH TUNA) MADE BY HIS OLD NANNY
WHAT HE DISLIKES:	DOGS
HOBBY AND SPECIAL SKILLS:	SOCCER

RYOICHI TENJO

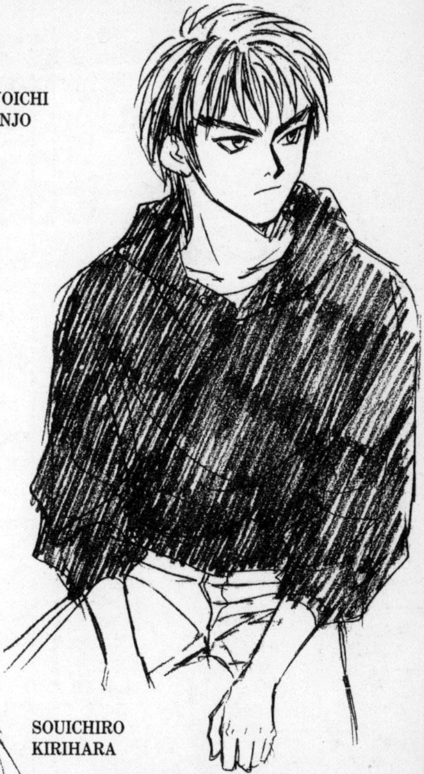

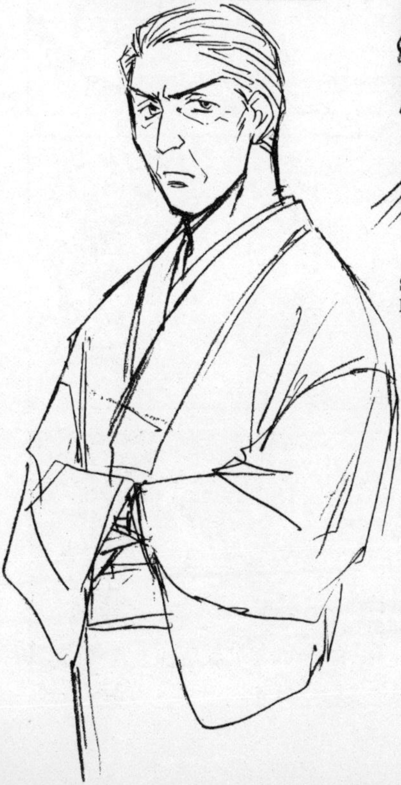

SOUICHIRO KIRIHARA

PERSONAL DATA	
BIRTHDAY:	APRIL 19th, 1955
SIZE:	194 cm 68 kg
BLOOD TYPE:	A
FAVORITE FOOD:	SOBA NOODLES
WHAT HE DISLIKES:	INSTANT CUP NOODLES
HOBBY AND SPECIAL SKILLS:	MAKING SOBA, RECITATION OF CHINESE POEMS

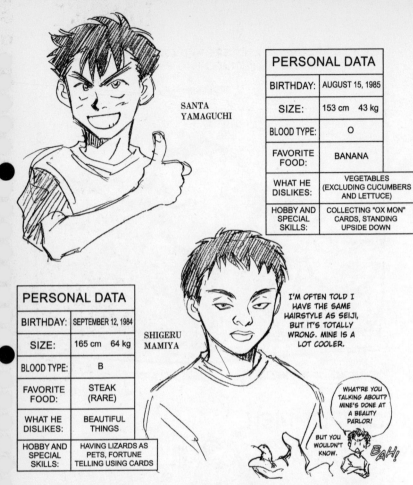

SANTA
YAMAGUCHI

PERSONAL DATA

BIRTHDAY:	AUGUST 15, 1985
SIZE:	153 cm 43 kg
BLOOD TYPE:	O
FAVORITE FOOD:	BANANA
WHAT HE DISLIKES:	VEGETABLES (EXCLUDING CUCUMBERS AND LETTUCE)
HOBBY AND SPECIAL SKILLS:	COLLECTING "OX MON" CARDS, STANDING UPSIDE DOWN

PERSONAL DATA

BIRTHDAY:	SEPTEMBER 12, 1984
SIZE:	165 cm 64 kg
BLOOD TYPE:	B
FAVORITE FOOD:	STEAK (RARE)
WHAT HE DISLIKES:	BEAUTIFUL THINGS
HOBBY AND SPECIAL SKILLS:	HAVING LIZARDS AS PETS, FORTUNE TELLING USING CARDS

SHIGERU
MAMIYA

I'M OFTEN TOLD I HAVE THE SAME HAIRSTYLE AS SEIJI, BUT IT'S TOTALLY WRONG. MINE IS A LOT COOLER.

WHAT'RE YOU TALKING ABOUT? MINE'S DONE AT A BEAUTY PARLOR!

BUT YOU WOULDN'T KNOW.

BAH!

♡ ♡ ♡ HERE'S WHO GETS VALENTINE'S CHOCOLATES!! ♡ ♡ ♡

NO. 1 TATSUYA
NO. 2 SHŌ
NO. 3 SHIGEKI

NO. 4 DAICHI
NO. 5 KATSURŌ
NO. 6 KŌ
NO. 7 SEIJI
NO. 8 SOUJŪ
NO. 9 TAKUMI HOHMUZU KYOSUKE (X-CONNECTION, 24 HOURS)

NO. 12 RYOICHI, COACH AMAMIYA, AKIRA, IMAI, SHIGERU, NORO, YUKI , ITARU & MR. KAKU (THE SINGING FLAME)

OTHER HIGUCHI SENSEI, ASSISTANT EDITOR

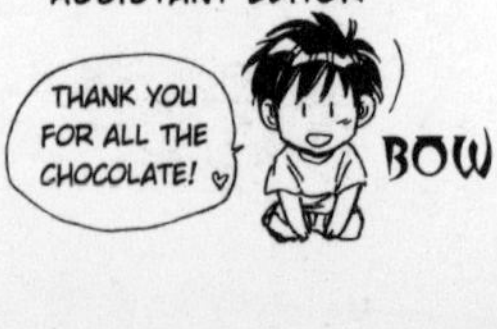

THANK YOU FOR ALL THE CHOCOLATE! ♡

BOW

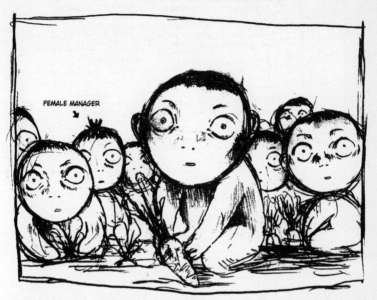

FEMALE MANAGER

CEREMONY OF APPRECIATION BY JOSUI'S "CARROT GROWER'S CLUB"

ILLUSTRATION BY MESO AIKO

CARROT DISH
THANK YOU

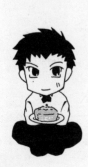

AS EXPECTED, WE RECEIVED RECIPES FOR CARROT HOTCAKES AND CARROT CAKES. WE ALSO RECEIVED VARIOUS OTHER RECIPES INCLUDING CARROT RICE AND CARROT SOUP. AMONG THEM, THERE WERE RECIPES WITH ILLUSTRATIONS, MAKING THEM EASY TO UNDERSTAND. THANK YOU FOR SENDING ALL THESE LETTERS!!

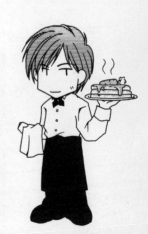

ILLUSTRATION BY ASSISTANT S

Whistle! Behind the Production

DRAFTING SCHEDULE, SORT OF...

	MIDDAY	EVENING	MIDNIGHT -- MORNING
SUNDAY	Naming and meeting, and revising the names -- the effort that's continued since Thursday. Make sure to eat lunch.	Start drafting. Continue drafting. Continue drafting no matter what. Make sure to eat.	Draft something. Suddenly, think of reading fan letters. Then, draft. Continue drafting.
MONDAY	Gather assistants. Have them make lunch. Have them put pen on the draft no matter which draft. Have them complete every one of them.	Put pen for the time being. Put pen still. No matter what, put pen. Time for dinner!	More work on putting pen. We're still putting pen. Suddenly, the naming development begins to bother me.
TUESDAY	MIDDAY	EVENING -- MORNING	
	Should I fix the spots that bother me? Another meeting, maybe. And more drafting. Perhaps lunch.	Yet again, put pen. A lot more work putting pen. Feels like having a dinner. Have a vicious battle against the extreme sleepiness.	
WEDN	Negative power amplifies. Draft is finally up. Have a meeting with Mr. In-charge. However, my soul is gone. Once dead, there's no one who'll pick up the dead body.		

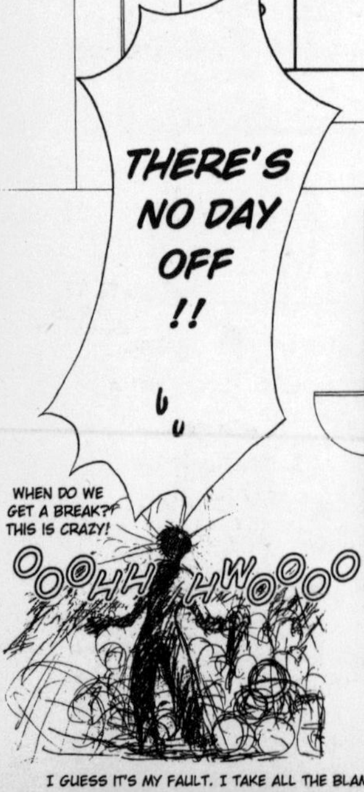

THERE'S NO DAY OFF !!
WHEN DO WE GET A BREAK?? THIS IS CRAZY!
OOOHHH HWOOOOO
I GUESS IT'S MY FAULT. I TAKE ALL THE BLAME.

KITCHEN
DINNER
DRYING RACK
REFRIGERATOR
ARE YOU WORKING? (TEL)
WIDE SHOW
COPY MACHINE
ENTRANCE WAY
LAUNDRY
CLOSET
SHOWER
FLUSH

Work Place

IF YOU SLEEP HERE, YOU'RE SUPPOSED TO GROAN...

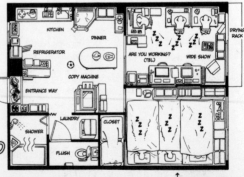

Next in Whistle!

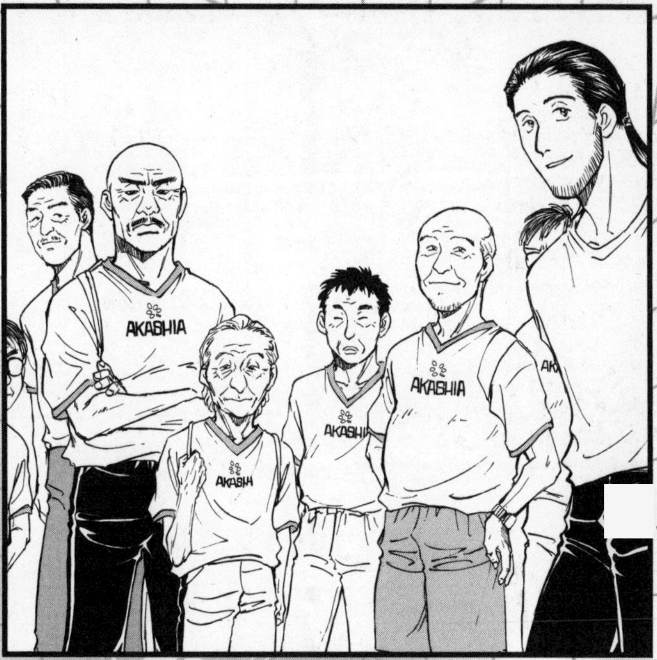
AKASHIA
AKASHIA
AKASHIA
AKASHIA

BE THERE

Whether it's Ryoichi Tenjo, the cocky one-man scoring machine, or Seiji Fujishiro, his former teammate, there's always somebody who can teach Shô a little bit more about the game he loves so much. But, believe it or not, Josui's hardworking FW was not always such a soccer nut. There was a time when he didn't know the World Cup from a sippy cup. Find out what ignited Shô's passion for soccer in the first place…and meet his grade-school mentor who encouraged him from the beginning!

Available Now!

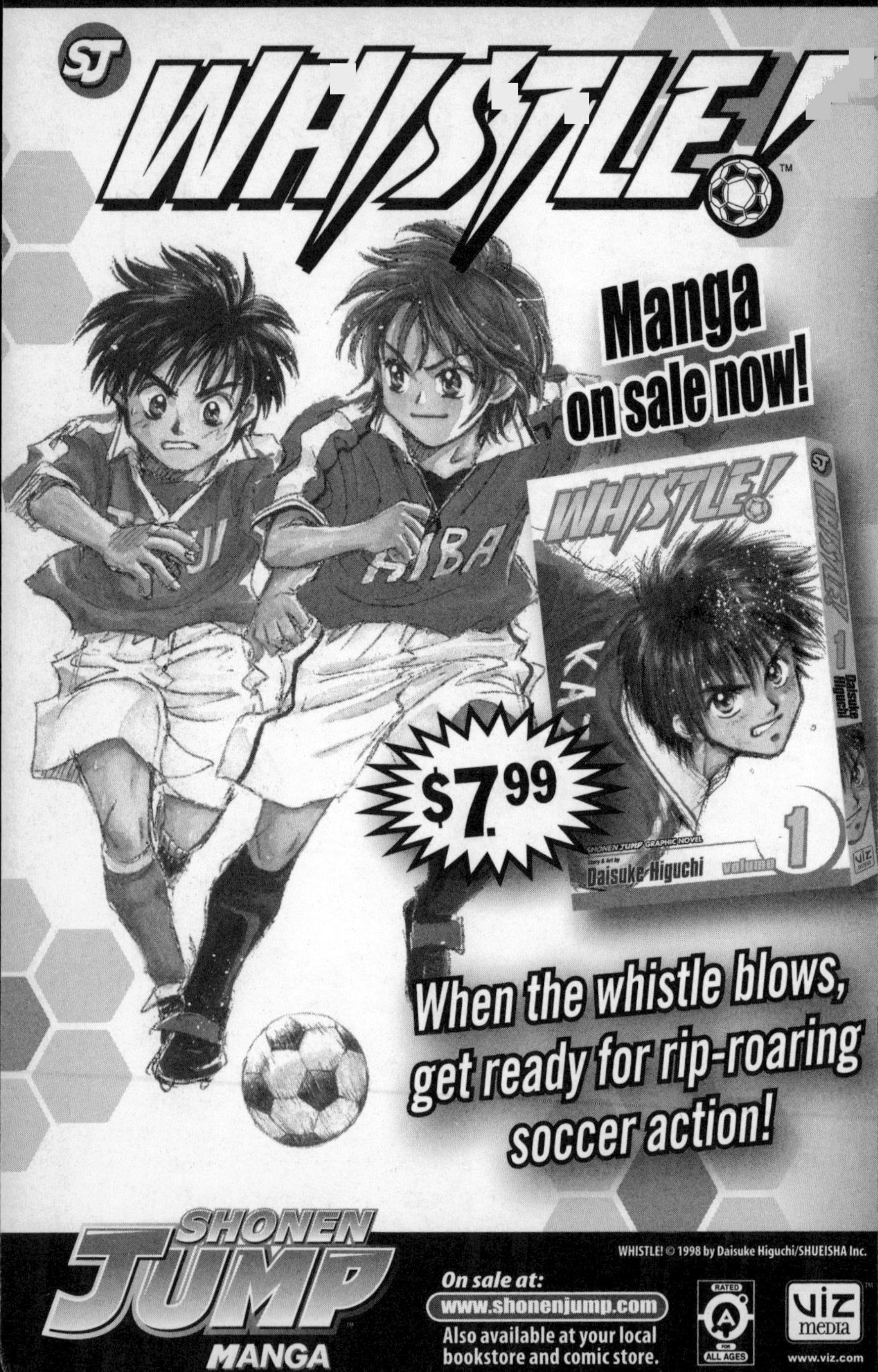
SJ
WHISTLE!™
Manga on sale now!
WHISTLE!
SJ
WHISTLE!
1
Daisuke Higuchi
SHONEN JUMP GRAPHIC NOVEL
Story & Art by
Daisuke Higuchi
volume 1
VIZ
$7.99
When the whistle blows, get ready for rip-roaring soccer action!
SHONEN JUMP MANGA
WHISTLE! © 1998 by Daisuke Higuchi/SHUEISHA Inc.
On sale at:
www.shonenjump.com
Also available at your local bookstore and comic store.
RATED A FOR ALL AGES
VIZ media
www.viz.com

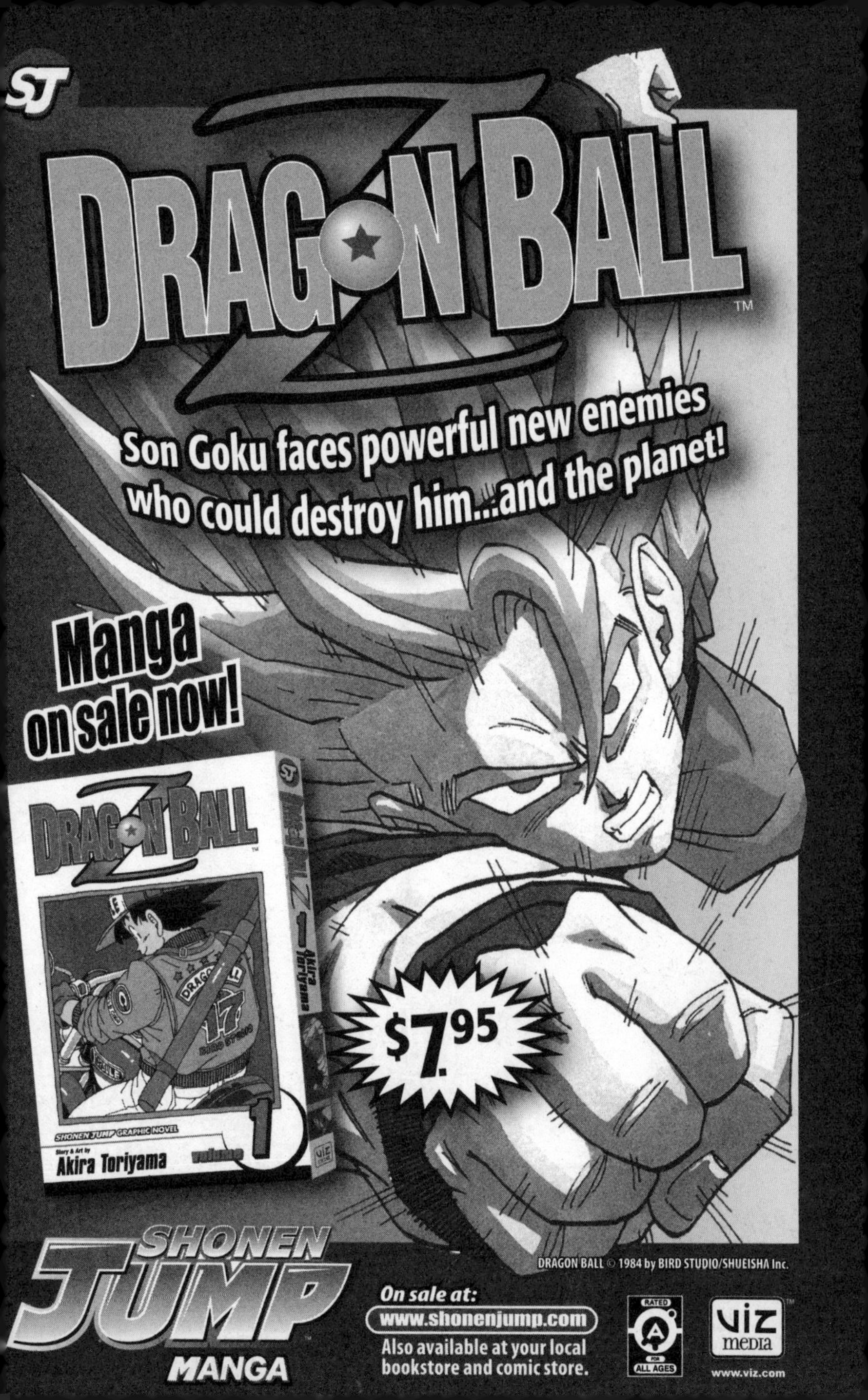
SJ
DRAGON BALL Z™
Son Goku faces powerful new enemies who could destroy him...and the planet!
Manga on sale now!
DRAGON BALL Z™
SHONEN JUMP GRAPHIC NOVEL
Story & Art by Akira Toriyama
volume 1
$7.95
DRAGON BALL © 1984 by BIRD STUDIO/SHUEISHA Inc.
SHONEN JUMP MANGA
On sale at:
www.shonenjump.com
Also available at your local bookstore and comic store.
RATED A FOR ALL AGES
viz media
www.viz.com

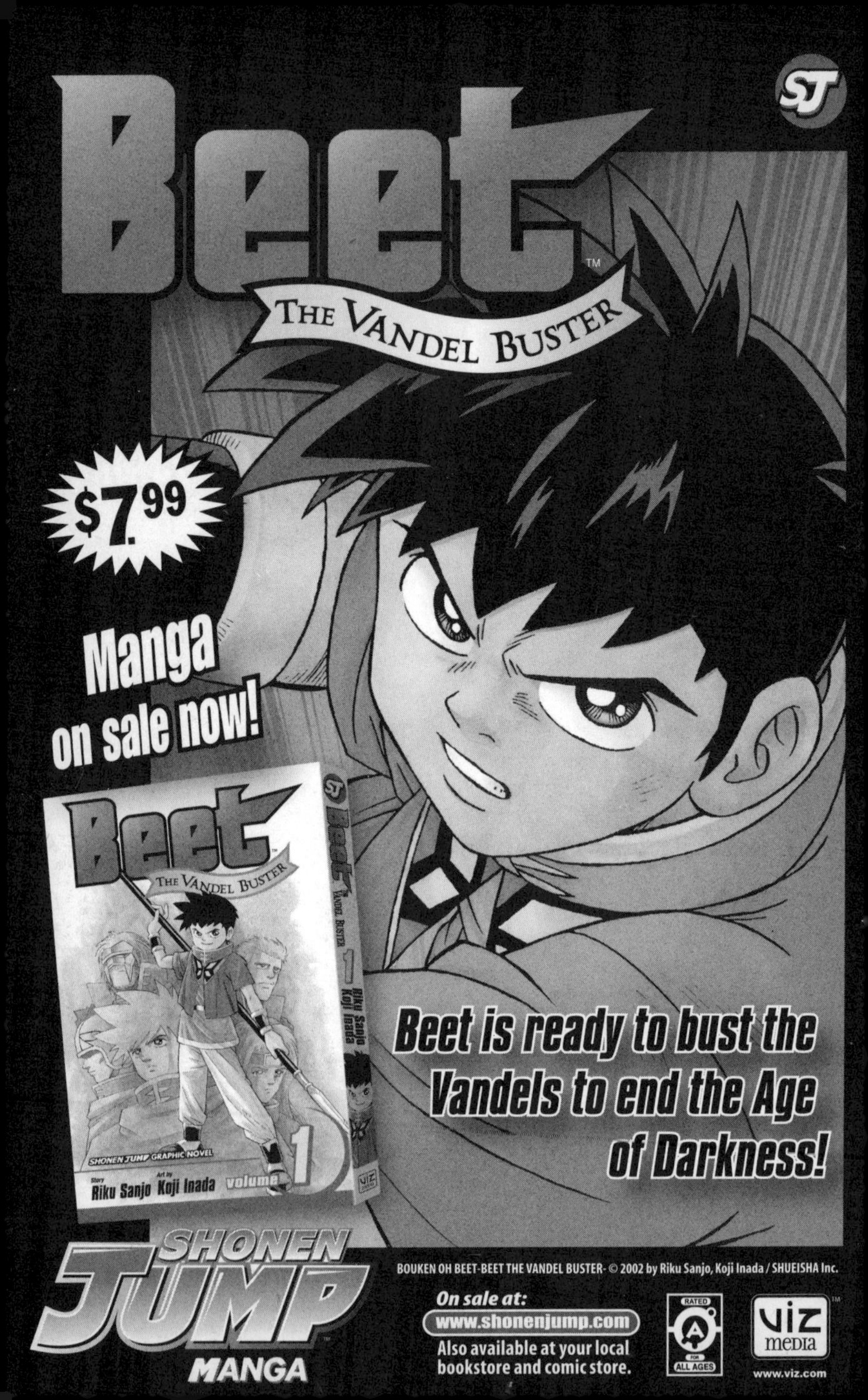
SJ
Beet™
THE VANDEL BUSTER
$7.99
Manga
on sale now!
SJ
Beet™
THE VANDEL BUSTER
SHONEN JUMP GRAPHIC NOVEL
Story Riku Sanjo
Art by Koji Inada
volume 1
Beet is ready to bust the Vandels to end the Age of Darkness!
SHONEN JUMP MANGA
BOUKEN OH BEET-BEET THE VANDEL BUSTER- © 2002 by Riku Sanjo, Koji Inada / SHUEISHA Inc.
On sale at:
www.shonenjump.com
Also available at your local bookstore and comic store.
RATED A FOR ALL AGES
VIZ media
www.viz.com

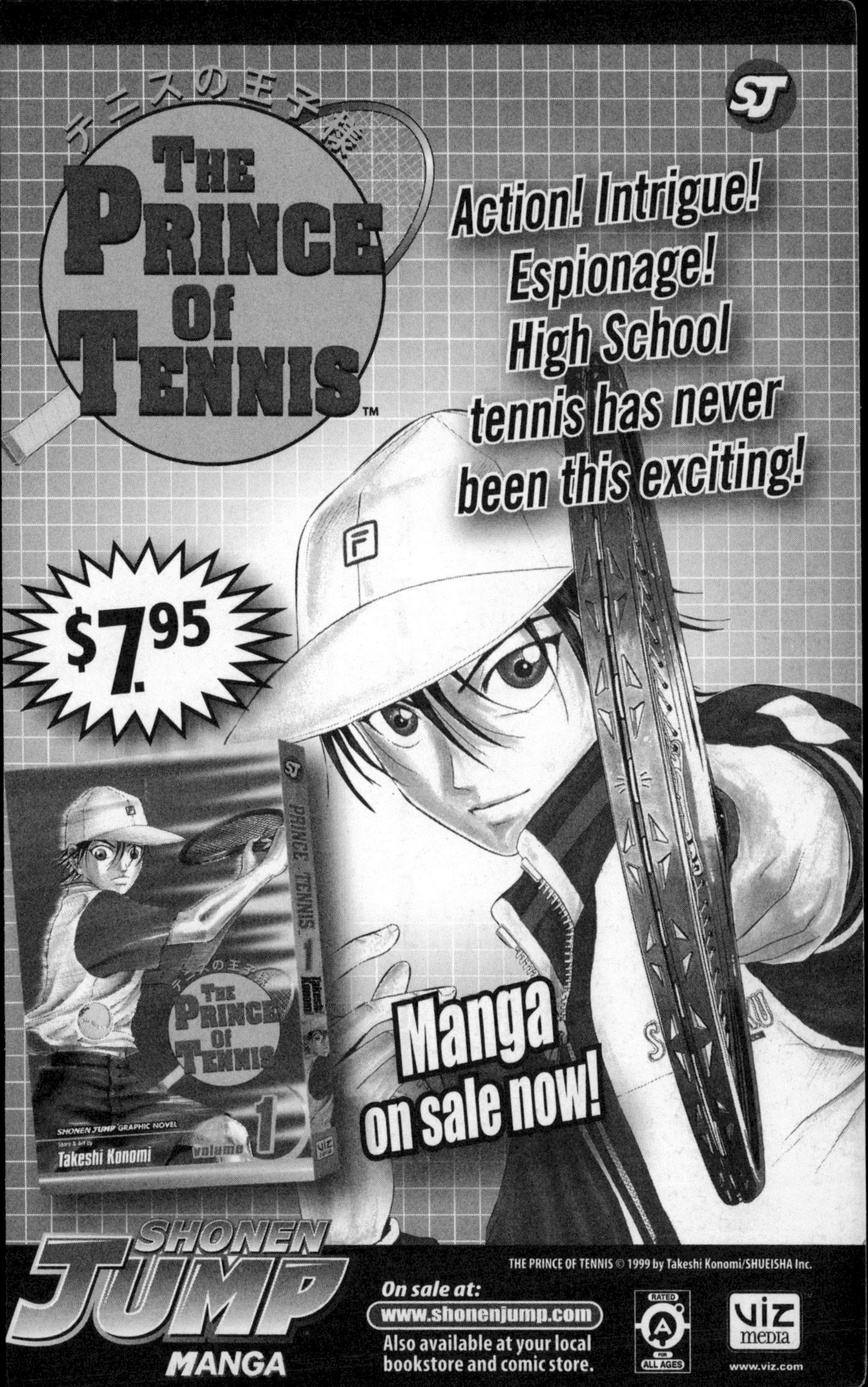
SJ
テニスの王子様
THE PRINCE OF TENNIS™
Action! Intrigue! Espionage! High School tennis has never been this exciting!
$7.95
THE PRINCE OF TENNIS
SHONEN JUMP GRAPHIC NOVEL
Takeshi Konomi
volume 1
Manga on sale now!
SHONEN JUMP MANGA
THE PRINCE OF TENNIS © 1999 by Takeshi Konomi/SHUEISHA Inc.
On sale at:
www.shonenjump.com
Also available at your local bookstore and comic store.
RATED A FOR ALL AGES
VIZ media
www.viz.com

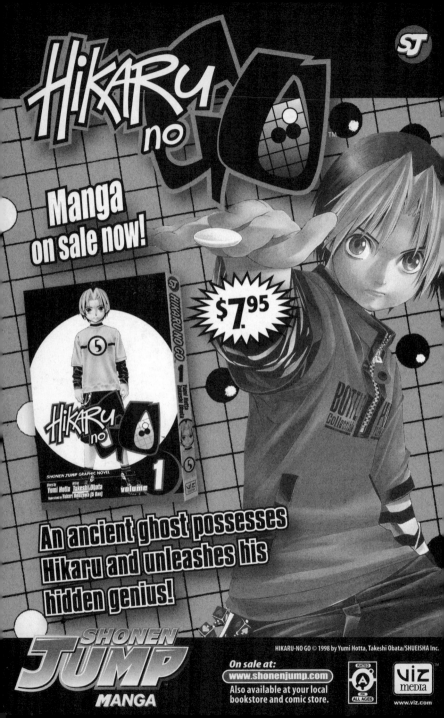

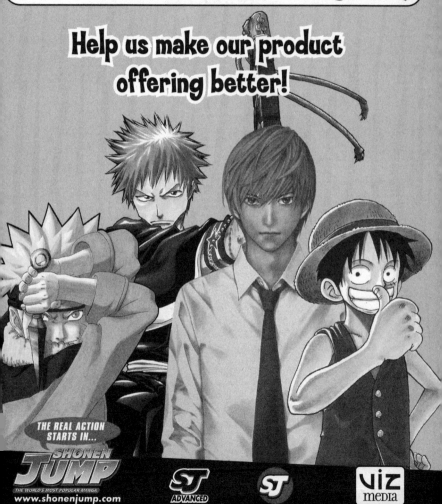

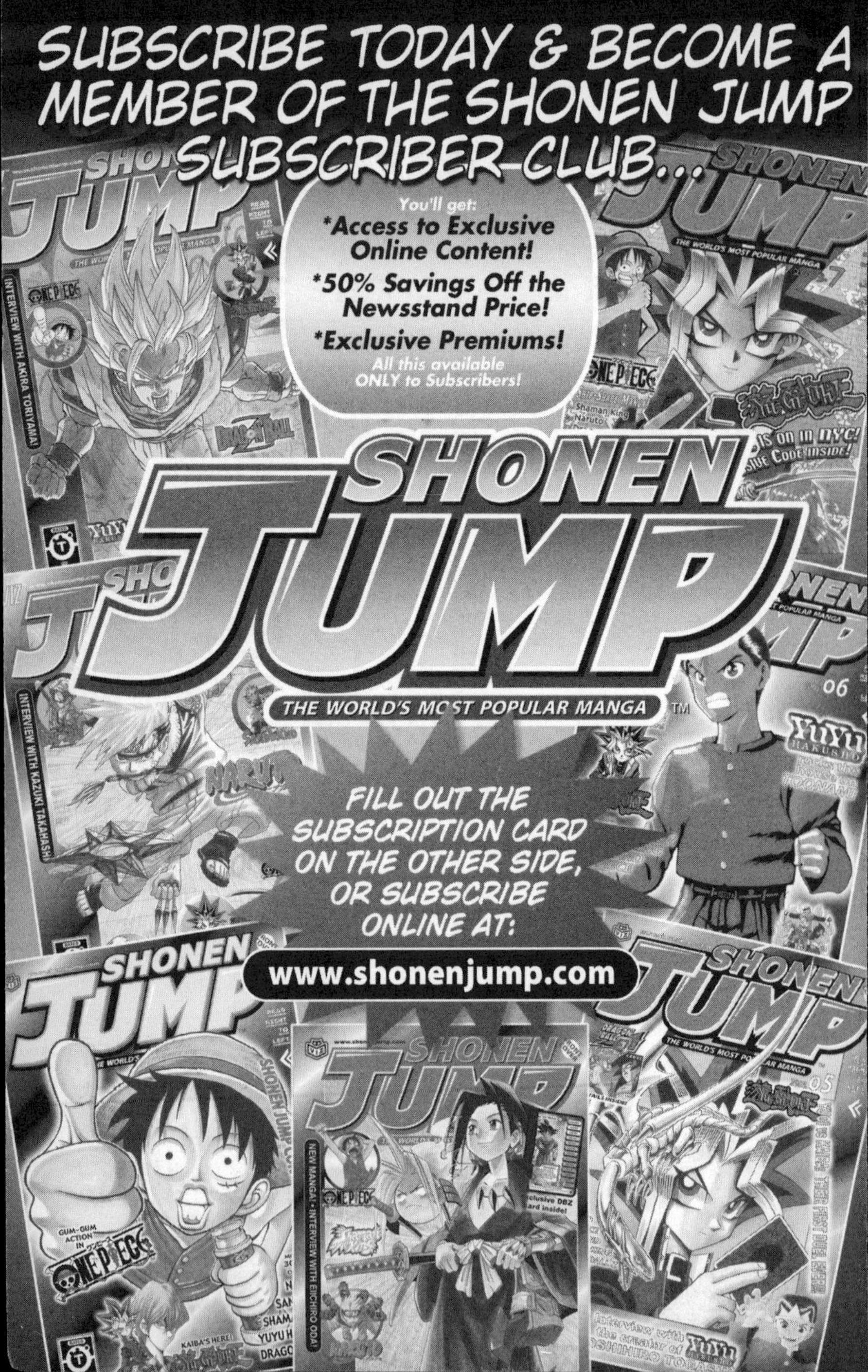
SUBSCRIBE TODAY & BECOME A MEMBER OF THE SHONEN JUMP SUBSCRIBER CLUB...
You'll get:
*Access to Exclusive Online Content!
*50% Savings Off the Newsstand Price!
*Exclusive Premiums!
All this available ONLY to Subscribers!
SHONEN JUMP
THE WORLD'S MOST POPULAR MANGA
FILL OUT THE SUBSCRIPTION CARD ON THE OTHER SIDE, OR SUBSCRIBE ONLINE AT:
www.shonenjump.com